ARC OF THE MEDICINE LINE

· TONY REES ·

ARC
OF THE
MEDICINE
LINE

MAPPING THE WORLD'S
LONGEST UNDEFENDED BORDER
ACROSS THE WESTERN PLAINS

UNIVERSITY OF NEBRASKA PRESS
Lincoln

DOUGLAS & MCINTYRE
Vancouver/Toronto

First published in Canada by Douglas & McIntyre Ltd.
2323 Quebec Street, Suite 201
Vancouver, British Columbia · Canada v5t 4s7
www.douglas-mcintyre.com

Published in the United States of America by the
University of Nebraska Press
Lincoln NE 68588-0630
www.nebraskapress.unl.edu
∞

Library and Archives Canada Cataloguing in Publication
Rees, Tony, 1948–
Arc of the medicine line : mapping the world's longest undefended border
across the western plains / Tony Rees. Includes bibliographical references and index.

ISBN 978-1-55365-278-6

1. Canada—Boundaries—United States. 2. United States—Boundaries—Canada.
3. Northwest, Canadian—History—1870-1905. I. Title.
FC186.R43 2007   971.2'02   c2007-902757-1

U.S. Library of Congress Cataloging in Publication Data
Rees, Tony, 1948–
Arc of the Medicine Line : mapping the world's longest undefended
border across the western plains / Tony Rees.
p. cm.
Includes bibliographical references and index.
ISBN-13: 978-0-8032-1791-1 (cl. : alk. paper) · ISBN-10: 0-8032-1791-9 (cl. : alk. paper)
1. Northern boundary of the United States—History—19th century. 2. High Plains (U.S.)—History—
19th century. 3. Cartography—Northern boundary of the United States—History—19th century.
4. Astronomy—Northern boundary of the United States—History—19th century. 5. Frontier and
pioneer life—High Plains (U.S.) 6. United States—Relations—Canada. 7. United States—Relations—
Great Britain. 8. Canada—Relations—United States. 9. Great Britain—Relations—United States.
10. Indians of North America—Government relations—History—19th century. I. Title.
F854.R44 2007   910'.02145—dc22   2007030035

Editing by Jonathan Dore
Jacket and text design by Jessica Sullivan
Jacket photograph © Francis G. Mayer/CORBIS
Interior photos courtesy of Glenbow Museum
Map by C. Stuart Daniel/Starshell Maps
Printed and bound in Canada by Friesens
Printed on acid-free paper that is forest friendly (100% post-consumer
recycled paper) and has been processed chlorine free.

All interior photos were taken by the Royal Engineers during the course of drawing the
49th Parallel. They are reproduced here from a set of prints housed at the Glenbow Archives in
Calgary, Alberta, Canada. The reference numbers are from the Glenbow collections.

Douglas & McIntyre gratefully acknowledges the financial support of the Canada
Council for the Arts, the British Columbia Arts Council, the Province of British Columbia
through the Book Publishing Tax Credit, and the Government of Canada through
the Book Publishing Industry Development Program (BPIDP) for its publishing activities.

For Donna

CONTENTS

———

From a high point in the cutting

about three miles from its commencement,

the mounds marking the 49th parallel on the prairie

to the eastward could be seen stretching

in a gentle but well defined curve for a distance of 15 miles,

thus giving the spectator a very graphic idea

of the size and figure of the earth.

Captain Albany Featherstonhaugh,
ROYAL ENGINEERS
Turtle Mountain, Manitoba, July, 1873.

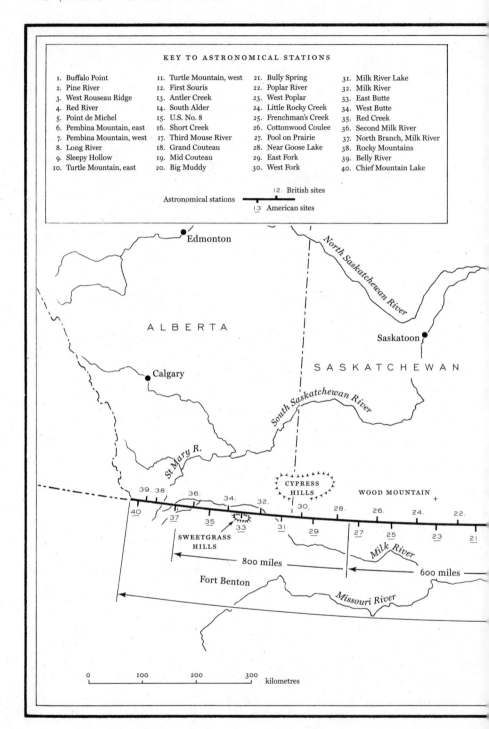

KEY TO ASTRONOMICAL STATIONS

1. Buffalo Point
2. Pine River
3. West Rouseau Ridge
4. Red River
5. Point de Michel
6. Pembina Mountain, east
7. Pembina Mountain, west
8. Long River
9. Sleepy Hollow
10. Turtle Mountain, east

11. Turtle Mountain, west
12. First Souris
13. Antler Creek
14. South Alder
15. U.S. No. 8
16. Short Creek
17. Third Mouse River
18. Grand Couteau
19. Mid Couteau
20. Big Muddy

21. Bully Spring
22. Poplar River
23. West Poplar
24. Little Rocky Creek
25. Frenchman's Creek
26. Cottonwood Coulee
27. Pool on Prairie
28. Near Goose Lake
29. East Fork
30. West Fork

31. Milk River Lake
32. Milk River
33. East Butte
34. West Butte
35. Red Creek
36. Second Milk River
37. North Branch, Milk River
38. Rocky Mountains
39. Belly River
40. Chief Mountain Lake

Astronomical stations —————— |2. British sites

|3 American sites

MAP | *xi*

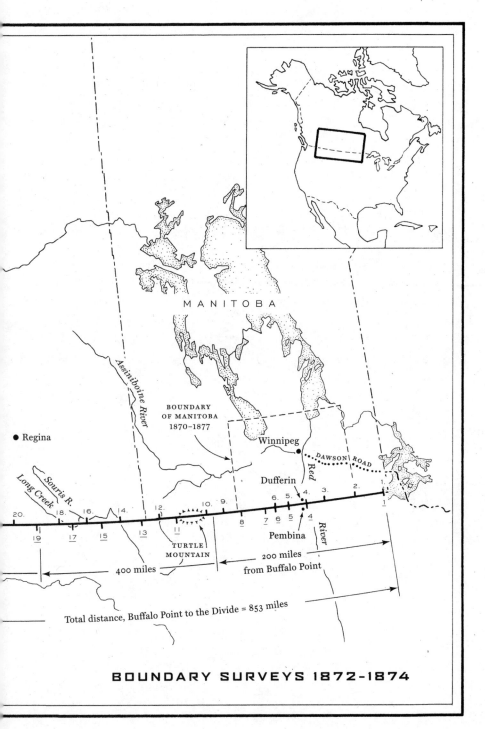

MANITOBA

BOUNDARY
OF MANITOBA
1870–1877

● Regina

Winnipeg

Assiniboine River

DAWSON ROAD

Red

Dufferin

Souris R.

Long Creek

Pembina

River

20. 18. 16. 14. 12. 10. 9. 6. 5. 4. 3. 2. 1.

8. 7. 6. 5. 4. 1.

19 17 15 13 11 TURTLE
MOUNTAIN

400 miles

200 miles
from Buffalo Point

Total distance, Buffalo Point to the Divide = 853 miles

BOUNDARY SURVEYS 1872-1874

NOTES
ON THE TEXT

T HIS STORY takes place on the high plains of western North America in the last quarter of the nineteenth century and involves not only soldiers and civilians from the United States but from Great Britain and the new nation of Canada, too, not to mention resident populations of Metis and various First Nations, both "American" and "Canadian."

In an attempt to avoid the minefield of constantly evolving contemporary nomenclature (in Canada, "Blackfoot" and "Peigan," but in the United States, "Blackfeet" and "Piegan"; "Dakota," "Lakota" or "Sioux"; "reserve" or "reservation" and so forth) I have stayed with the terminology that was in general use at the time, except for certain terms that would be patently offensive to modern sensibilities. In the cause of accuracy and honesty, however, those terms might still appear in direct quotations.

This is also a story about astronomy, topography and cartography, all measured, recorded and described in the Imperial system. Rather than introduce an endless series of parenthetical conversions to the metric system (something I find annoying and distracting in my own reading), I, too, have used the Imperial system, something that will not trouble British or American readers but may be a mystery to younger Canadians, for which I apologize.

INTRODUCTION

———

THIS PLACE DRAWS me in every time I come down into Milk River country. Buffeted back on my heels by the perpetual wind on this blazing bright afternoon at the end of summer, I am back in the Sweetgrass Hills.

In my scramble up the slick, dry grass that rises steeply from the gravel of Alberta's Highway 500, I have broken any number of laws and become, within the space of a couple of hundred yards, both illegal alien and instant expatriate. Latitude 49° North—the "Medicine Line" to the First Nations of the northern plains—is somewhere directly below me, but I'm not sure which of the innocuous barbed-wire fences marks the international boundary between Canada and the United States.

Fifteen miles to the west, the border crossing between Sweetgrass, Montana and Coutts, Alberta is the busiest anywhere between Minnesota and the West Coast, funnelling traffic from every western interstate up toward Calgary, Edmonton and the start of the Alaska Highway. Fifteen miles to the east, the customs officers at the tiny port of Aden–Whitlash work a regular nine-to-five and, on an average day, get to interview no more than a dozen people, most of them friends and neighbours. But here in these hills, between the flag-waving, uniformed regulation of the official crossing points, you have to look hard to find one of the boundary markers, a thin string of small obelisks carefully spaced about a mile apart and with no continuous barrier between them. They are the only sign of what both sides have always liked to call "the longest undefended border in the world."

Looking north from the shoulder of the Sweetgrass Hills, the full compass of Alberta's Milk River country is visible in one stunning sweep. To the northeast I can make out the low, flat-topped shimmer of the Cypress Hills. Even at a distance of better than sixty miles, they still show the black sheen of the evergreen cover for which they were named. Almost as far away to the west, the barely perceptible swell of the Milk River Ridge belies its status as a grand continental watershed, defining the old line between Rupert's Land and Louisiana, between waters flowing to Hudson Bay and those bound for the Gulf of Mexico.

Between these two low-slung atolls is 120 miles of pure space, stretching away beyond the narrow snake of the Milk River to disappear, at the eye's limit, in the haze that blurs the place where the sky begins. From here, I can read the curve of our pale ochre sphere as surely as if I were at sea.

Today the borderland below is a wide, empty sweep of wheat fields and pasture, measured by a grid of gravel roads that sees little traffic and few people who do not make their lives here. It has been much this way for more than a century now, but there was a moment that first broke the great silence shrouding this place, and that moment changed it forever.

In late July of 1874, the Sweetgrass Hills sheltered the greatest accumulation of scientists, teamsters, scouts, cooks and soldiers to be seen anywhere in this part of the world before the coming of the railways. Out on the flats below me, the men of the boundary commissions—American, British and Canadian—established an astronomical station and the last of their supply depots as they prepared to draw the Medicine Line across the final hundred miles of the nearly nine hundred between Manitoba's Lake of the Woods and the Continental Divide. In the brief weeks between the time the surveyors and the soldiers swept into the Milk River country below Wood Mountain, Saskatchewan, and the day in early August when they crossed the Milk River Ridge and dropped into the valley of the St. Mary River, they witnessed, and played a singular part in, the beginning of the end for the open west. That hot, dry summer of 1874 marked the outside world's final assault on this last frontier.

Every trace of the base camp is long gone, but from these heights it is still possible to sense how it all must have looked before the rapid-fire events of the 1870s closed this last wild place.

For nearly two centuries, the great ellipse of the Milk River country had remained a quiet eye in the swirling storm of imperial aspirations, both Native and white. Change, in the form of the horse and the gun, the explorer, the trapper and the smallpox virus, had been leaching into this land for decades. It came slowly at first, building by small increments in ways the land could absorb. When, finally and inevitably, the wider world focussed its attention on this last place, it hit the Milk River country, quite literally, with all the speed and power of a locomotive.

Within a few weeks of the surveyors' brief visit, the North-West Mounted Police would come through on their own long march, establishing their string of forts and clockwork patrols along the north side of the new line. Within two years, most of the 7th Cavalry escort that had guarded the American boundary commission surveyors through two seasons in the field would lie dead in the valley of the Little Bighorn. In less than a decade, the bison would be gone and the offspring of Scottish cattle would graze on the abandoned grasslands as the Canadian Pacific and Great Northern railways spiked their tracks toward them at breakneck speed.

Once there were only the wandering bison and the transient peoples who shadowed them in their circular migrations across the infinite shortgrass but, by the 1870s, the whole life of the vast northern plains had spun down to this one place. Were I to continue my climb to the summit of these ancient volcanic hills, I could look out on three graveyards that mark the end of the first centuries-old life of this country.

Forty miles away to the southwest, the Tiber Dam and the great bend of the Maria's River mark the place where, in 1870, the South Peigan were slaughtered into final submission. Just three years later, under the dark caps of the Cypress Hills, Little Soldier and his small band of Assiniboine met their end at the hands of Montana wolfers, a bloody catalyst that brought in the Mounties to give final shape to a new nation. And before the decade was out, away on the southeastern horizon beneath the slumped silhouettes of the Bear Paw Mountains, it remained only for Chief Joseph and his band of fugitive Nez Perce to bring it all to an end. As much a foreigner in this place as the astronomers and the cavalrymen, it was Joseph's lot to hand back the horses and the guns that had made everything possible.

The wind hisses past me through the pale brown grass and hums through the fence wire, carrying with it the great ferruginous hawks and the diminutive dryland sparrows, each equally indifferent to the Medicine Line and to the blood and the politics that bisected this huge land more than a century ago. North and south of the line, the native grasses are the same and even the rolling geometry of wheat stubble and fallow stripe does not seem to break cleanly along some carefully surveyed perforation. There is nothing here to say that this is not still one horizon-stretching singularity.

But I know how small a place this has suddenly become and I cannot shake my unease at being somewhere I should not be. In a moment, September 11, 2001 changed everything, and I look down and see those barbed-wire fences in a different light—marking what can no longer be called "the longest undefended border in the world."

PROLOGUE:

SEPTEMBER 18, 1872

IT HAD TAKEN more than two centuries of blood, bravado and barter, of grand imperial designs and even grander battles fought half a world away. But in the end, it had all come down to this one small moment.

The men who gathered on the grassy bank beside the Red River of the North on that bright, late summer day were British, American and Canadian. Together, over the next two years, they would arc a precise, pencil-thin line across nine hundred miles of forest, swamp and high plains desolation and, with it, draw the long course of empire in North America to a close. Over the following decade or so, the boundary would take on its popular name: the Medicine Line. It was probably the Sioux who first began to use the term in the late 1870s after Sitting Bull and his people crossed into Canada following the battle of the Little Bighorn. Although it was never more than a string of widely spaced markers with no continuous barrier between them, the line was said to have "strong medicine" since it seemed to have the power to stop the pursuing U.S. Cavalry in its tracks.

The members of the United States Northern Boundary Commission had been moving into camp at Fort Pembina, Dakota Territory, for more than a month. Their opposite numbers, the officers and men of the Royal Engineers, representing the British North American Boundary Commission, had only just arrived early that morning at the end of a voyage from their headquarters in Chatham, England. With their twenty tons of baggage unloaded and stacked beside an old Hudson's Bay Company trading post, the British officers set off for their first official meeting with the Americans. At some point along the course of their half-mile walk to the south (though they could not have stated with any certainty exactly where) they crossed the 49th Parallel.

Leading the march was thirty-seven-year-old Captain Donald Roderick Cameron, chief commissioner of the British and Canadian contingent. Cameron differed from his fellow officers in two significant details: his career had been made in the Royal Artillery, rather than the Royal Engineers, and his appointment to the boundary commission was based not upon his field experience as a surveyor but on his political and social connections in Ottawa.

Born in Scotland and given his military education in France, Cameron was commissioned in 1856 and spent the first part of his career in India, distinguishing himself in the Bhutan campaign of 1864–65. He left India soon after and found himself posted to the British garrison at Halifax in Nova Scotia, which had just become one of the founding provinces of Canada in 1867. It was there he met and, in 1869, married Emma Tupper, daughter of Sir Charles Tupper, the long-time Nova Scotia politician then serving under Prime Minister Sir John A. Macdonald in Canada's first national government.

While Britain seemed to view the surveying of the last gap in the boundary with the United States as unfinished business—a sort of "parting gift" to the new dominion—the Canadian government clearly saw it as an opportunity to assert its status as an independent nation. In addition to agreeing to pay half the cost of the commission, Canada asked that it might be given leave to recommend its own man for the position of chief commissioner. When the Foreign Office in

London was unable to convince either of its own preferred choices to take the appointment, Britain agreed to the Canadians' candidate, and Charles Tupper, by then president of the Privy Council, could tell his son-in-law that he had the job.

In fact, the boundary commission was Cameron's second posting to the banks of the Red River, but he could hardly have been remembering his previous visit with any great warmth. In 1869 he had been aide-de-camp to the man who was supposed to become Manitoba's first lieutenant governor, William McDougall, when the latter made an ill-fated attempt to assume his vice-regal seat during the height of Louis Riel's Red River Rebellion. Cameron himself was said to have been stopped at a Metis barricade and provided great amusement to the defenders by pacing back and forth, closely examining the situation through a monocle and demanding the removal of what they remembered him calling "that blawsted fence." It would not be surprising to discover that a somewhat aggrandized version of Cameron's "previous experience" in the Red River valley, brief and foolish as it might have been, had been one of Ottawa's selling points to secure his appointment to the boundary commission.

With a thin, full beard making his long face seem even longer, Cameron looked more Oxford don than artillery officer. Although the monocle had been replaced by a pair of wire-rimmed pince-nez, the man had retained his stiff formality. While both commissions would allow very relaxed rules for the wearing of uniforms, Cameron would rarely be seen without a full suit, collar and tie.

Accompanying Cameron were four senior officers. First among them was Chief Astronomer Samuel Anderson. Newly promoted to captain in acknowledgement of his appointment, Anderson was a young officer who had risen swiftly and surely to his position as second-in-command of the British North American Boundary Commission. Born in London in 1839, the son of a Scottish solicitor who was registrar of affidavits in the High Court of Chancery, Anderson was educated at the University of St. Andrew's and the Edinburgh Military Academy before being selected for the Royal Military Academy at Woolwich in 1857. An award-winning student, he was gazetted a lieutenant in the Royal Engineers in December 1858. Thin-lipped and prematurely thin of hair, his customary moustache and long mutton chops had already begun to fill out to a full beard, perhaps longer and more luxurious than would have been permitted on the Engineers' parade grounds. Where Cameron was distant, rigid and brittle, Anderson was relaxed and congenial, making him a popular and well-respected field officer. He could (and would) ask a great deal of the men under his command and they would rarely disappoint him.

On the Foreign Office's putative list of candidates for chief commissioner, Anderson's name would have been in third place, directly below two more senior men with whom he had already served in the field. First on that list was Royal Engineers Colonel (later General and Sir) John Summerfield Hawkins. He had been chief commissioner for the overland portion of the boundary survey of 1858–62, which had drawn the 49th Parallel from the Strait of Georgia eastward to the crest of the Continental Divide. Second choice was Captain Charles William Wilson, also of the Royal Engineers, who had served as secretary to the Pacific Boundary Commission. Anderson's first overseas posting after graduating from Woolwich had been to that same commission, where he had successfully re-surveyed a long section of the line that had previously been badly mismeasured.

After returning to Britain from the Pacific Northwest in 1862, Anderson spent two years working on the commission's reports and maps. He was then invited to join Wilson on assignment in Syria, where they were to survey and map the Holy Land on behalf of the Palestine Exploration Fund. After a year, Anderson was home again and beginning a five-year teaching stint at the School of Military Engineering in Chatham, Kent.

As it turned out, Hawkins was not interested in returning to the field, and Wilson had just been made chief of the topographical department at the War Office. Had the Canadians not pushed for their own choice, Anderson, despite his age and comparative lack of seniority, would certainly have had both Hawkins's and Wilson's support for the role of chief commissioner, given his irreplaceable experience on the Pacific survey.

Also teaching at Chatham when the call came for him to join the boundary commission was Lieutenant Albany Featherstonhaugh (he would probably have pronounced it "Fanshaw"). His appointment came with the title of assistant astronomer, and his promotion to captain that accompanied it was effective the same day as Anderson's.

Featherstonhaugh was even younger than Anderson, celebrating his thirty-second birthday en route to Canada. Another top scholar, Featherstonhaugh had also attended the Royal Military Academy and was gazetted lieutenant in the Royal Engineers in 1859, when he was still just eighteen. His first overseas assignment was to Bermuda, followed by a posting to Halifax. It was in Halifax he met Cameron, and it was Cameron who initially thought Featherstonhaugh a good candidate for the position either of chief astronomer or commission secretary.

A quiet and reserved man, Featherstonhaugh had a close-trimmed beard and short, neatly parted hair that made him seem far more bookish than brash. More than once Anderson would note his colleague's "irritable" manner, though he usually alloyed any criticism with praise for Featherstonhaugh's tireless dedication and carefully executed work with the instruments.

Lieutenants Arthur Clitheroe Ward and William James Galwey were the commission's junior officers and both were drawn from the large pool of young Royal Engineers who had spent at least a part of their careers at the Halifax garrison. Ward had been Cameron's choice for the commission's secretary, but that title does not convey the full breadth of his administrative responsibilities. Across Ward's desk in Pembina would flow the river of requisitions, reports, bills, mail and correspondence that were required to keep more than a hundred men, nearly two hundred head of livestock and a huge inventory of equipment working smoothly in the field.

Irish-born Galwey was the junior assistant astronomer and, while he was the same age as Anderson, he had not graduated from Woolwich until 1862. Descended from a long line of Irish gentry that seems to have produced mostly doctors and lawyers, Galwey was recognized as a careful and able soldier, though his star was not rising at the same rate as his fellow officers'. Anderson found him withdrawn and somewhat taciturn, a man who required more looking after than the others.

WAITING ON THE RIVERBANK to greet the newly arrived British officers were their opposite numbers from the United States Northern Boundary Commission: Chief Commissioner Archibald Campbell and his secretary, James Bangs; Chief Astronomer Francis Farquhar and assistant astronomers William Twining, James Gregory and Francis Vinton Greene.

Of all the men assembled at Pembina on both sides of the line, Campbell was by far the most senior and experienced. Born in 1813, the son of a former New York deputy secretary of state, Campbell had graduated from West Point in 1835 but resigned his commission after only a year or so of duty in Louisiana. He then applied his engineering skills to a succession of railway and canal surveys across the south and along the eastern seaboard. In 1845 he was appointed private secretary to the U.S. secretary of war, and then chief clerk in the War Department, a position he held almost continuously until 1857.

In 1857 Campbell's combination of high-level political expertise and real-world surveying experience made him the ideal choice for a potential minefield of an assignment. In June that year he arrived in Victoria (now in British Columbia but then part of a separate crown colony) as the chief commissioner of the United States Pacific Boundary Commission. All the toxic politics and political wrangling aside, that survey was, from a technical viewpoint, a chaotic nightmare of impassable mountains and inaccessible river gorges. Just keeping the two parties supplied with food and equipment was a prodigious organizational challenge. In the end, it required nearly two hundred miles of clear-cutting and took almost seven years to draw the line (as best they could) across just four hundred miles of territory. After the Pacific survey, Campbell should have found surveying the eight hundred miles of nearly horizontal high plains little more challenging than a pleasant walk.

The balance of Campbell's senior men (with the exception of James Bangs) were, as Congress had required, career officers in the Army Corps of Engineers. Despite his comparative youth, thirty-four-year-old chief astronomer Major Francis Ulric Farquhar had already enjoyed a long and diverse career. Born in southeastern Pennsylvania the son of a prominent attorney, he had spent his school holidays with the geological survey of Pennsylvania from as early as age fourteen. Leaving school at seventeen, he found employment in St. Louis working on the first surveys for the Missouri Pacific Railroad. While still working on the survey his application to West Point was accepted, and he began his studies there in July 1857. He graduated second in his class of 1861 and was immediately pressed into service with the Engineers. As an aide-de-camp to General Heintzelman, Farquhar saw action in the Union Army during the Civil War, at Bull Run and in a half-dozen other engagements. Within two years of his graduation he had risen to the rank of captain and was chief engineer for the Army Department of Virginia and North Carolina. Following the war he returned to practical field engineering, eventually finding himself superintending engineer for harbour improvements along the eastern shore of Lake Michigan. It was from this position—and with an accompanying promotion to major—that Farquhar was seconded to the boundary commission.

In Major William Johnson Twining, both the British and American parties were fortunate to have a man who possessed a wealth of first-hand knowledge about the high plains country through which they would be working. Born in Indiana in 1839, Twining was the son of a New England clergyman who had moved west and settled in as a professor of mathematics and astronomy at Wabash College.

In his photographs, Twining seems a small, thin-faced and anemic-looking man, but clearly that appearance is somewhat deceptive. He left Indiana for Yale University in 1858, but his health failed and he returned home. The following year he was unexpectedly offered a place at West Point and, believing the outdoor life of the military would be a boon to his health, he headed east to New York. Twining graduated fourth in his class of 1863, and during two years of Civil

War service he rose quickly to the rank of brevet major and chief engineer of the Army of the Ohio. Following a post-war year as assistant professor of engineering at West Point, he was appointed chief engineer for the Department of Dakota in 1867. At that time, the Dakota Territory stretched across the whole of the high plains frontier from the Red River to the Rocky Mountains and, in more than two years of intensive travel, Twining made detailed reconnaissances of the area as far west as Turtle Mountain and the great loop of the Souris River.

Twenty-six-year-old Lieutenant James Fingal Gregory, the son of a Dutch Reformed Church minister, was raised in Troy, New York, and graduated from West Point in 1865. He received his first commission in the 5th Artillery but, by mid-1866, he had transferred to the Engineers and spent most of his early career with the geodetic survey of the Great Lakes. Probably much to his surprise, that nautical experience would prove enormously valuable two years later as the commission pushed its way into the Rocky Mountains.

Second Lieutenant Francis Vinton Greene of Rhode Island was just twenty-two, having graduated at the top of his West Point class just two years before joining the boundary commission. There had never been much doubt that Greene would pursue a military career. He was directly descended from General Nathanael Greene, one of the great military leaders of the American Revolution, while his father, General George Sears Greene, had been a hero of the Union cause at Gettysburg. Although first commissioned in the 4th Artillery, Greene had transferred almost immediately to the Engineers, and the boundary commission was his first significant field assignment. Photographs of Greene show a tall, lean young man who seems always to wear a slight grin. In one *carte de visite*, probably taken in St. Paul, Minnesota, in 1874, he is proudly wearing a full-fringed beaded buckskin jacket. His boundless enthusiasm for what he clearly saw as a great adventure comes through in his letters home and his amateur watercolours, and even expresses itself in his contribution to Campbell's otherwise sober and straightforward final report to Congress. Greene's subsequent military and civilian careers would be both the longest and the most successful of any of the officers involved, on either side of the 49th Parallel.

Commission secretary James Edgar Bangs was a young District of Columbia native who was, according to a Washington newspaper, "... gifted with brilliant mental endowments and the public schools [had] marked him as one of their brightest students."[1] Still in his early twenties at the time of the survey, he had attended Columbian College (later George Washington University) on full scholarships and graduated with highest honours in possession of both a master of arts and a bachelor of laws. Rather than take up the law, however, Bangs accepted an appointment with the ninth U.S. census and, in early 1872, he was approached to take on the secretariat of the boundary commission.

THE FIRST FIELD meeting of the boundary commissions was cheerful, informal and, without a diplomat or federal politician within a thousand miles, entirely devoid of the ruffles and flourishes, proclamation readings and long-winded speeches that would doubtless have dominated such a gathering in more civilized surroundings. Anderson was especially delighted to see Campbell again. It had been thirteen years since the completion of the Pacific survey, and they clearly still shared a mutual respect and even some affection. Anderson wrote of him, "... he is an old friend... and we had no difficulty in arranging on a joint course of action."[2]

Campbell had also met Cameron before. Three months earlier, the British commissioner and Arthur Ward had travelled to Washington, D.C., to iron out the final details before the working parties began to converge on Pembina. What the tough, experienced American commissioner had first made of his counterpart is not recorded, but Cameron had never been one to engender warm feelings among his colleagues. In fact, as the work progressed over the next two years, Anderson would be called upon time and again to act as a buffer between his "old friend" and the increasingly grating presence of Cameron.

The meeting was over in only thirty minutes, but the sense of confident professionalism and practical co-operation it established would (despite Cameron's best efforts to the contrary) rarely be seriously tested over the long, difficult months to come.

· 1 ·

AUTUMN
1872

*...the distance to the boundary line was measured
off, and an oak post fixed on it, bearing on
the north side the letters G.B., and on the south side, U.S.*

REPORTS UPON THE SURVEY

OR THE BRITISH party, the walk back down the Red River would not be a chance to enjoy the warm day or stretch out the kinks from a long month of travel in generally cramped quarters. Rather, it proved to be a double-time sprint back to their camp so that Captain Cameron, who had been on station for barely twenty-four hours, could catch the departing steamer for Fort Garry—the Hudson's Bay Company fort that formed the nucleus of the city of Winnipeg, so named just two years before.

For reasons no one could fathom, Cameron had brought his wife and four-month-old baby with him from Ottawa. On arriving, they had discovered that what had been promised as "suitable accommodations" (suitable, presumably, for the wife of a chief commissioner and daughter of the president of the Privy Council) were "nothing more than one or two dirty rooms in a house already partly occupied by the Hudson's Bay Company's clerk."[1] When Anderson and the rest of his party had arrived that morning, Cameron, who had travelled ahead with his family, convinced the captain of the steamer to delay his departure for two hours while he attended the meeting with Campbell and loaded his luggage. He was taking his wife and baby to Winnipeg to stay with friends until something much better in the way of accommodations could be arranged at Pembina.

Cameron's departure left Anderson in sole charge of organizing what was to be, by any measure, an enormous undertaking. With decades of experience in measuring and marking nearly every square foot of a huge empire on which, it was famously said, the sun never set, Her Majesty's Royal Engineers did not approach any project by half measures. That they intended to make a proper job of Britain's last great enterprise on the North American continent was clear from the resources they had marshalled at Pembina.

Travelling from Britain with Anderson, Featherstonhaugh and Galwey (Arthur Ward was already in Canada making arrangements with suppliers) were forty-four non-commissioned officers and men. These included a sergeant major and quartermaster sergeant, two sergeants, four corporals, four second corporals, five lance-corporals and twenty-seven "sappers" (as the Royal Engineers call their enlisted men). Ten of the men were qualified surveyors and draughtsmen, while the rest represented the whole range of trades essential to keeping the enterprise moving forward. In addition to a baker and a tailor, there were five carpenters, six smiths, a saddler, a sawyer, two bricklayers, a wheelwright, two shoemakers and, to keep track of it all, six clerks. In addition, four of the sappers were assigned to create a detailed photographic record of the entire operation. Their training and equipment (including portable darkrooms and nearly half a ton of supplies) had been the responsibility of Captain (later Sir) William Abney, a Royal Engineers officer and one of photography's great technical pioneers.

Each of the men had brought with him the tools of his trade, and these, together with clothing for every kind of weather, rifles, pistols, bayonets and ammunition, amounted to several tons of baggage.

Simply transporting it all from the Royal Engineers' headquarters at Chatham had been a huge operation.

Even more remarkable (and an enduring testament to the efficiency of the Royal Engineers) was that the entire complement of men and all of their equipment had been assembled, trained and made ready for departure in something less than three months.

While both countries had decided to mount substantial military operations rather than deploying more understated civilian survey-ing parties, the Americans in particular were still concerned about keeping the costs as low as possible. Using military personnel—whose salaries they would be paying anyway—and existing military supply lines made the best economic sense. For the British, although lacking any sort of military infrastructure in the heart of the Canadian west, it was still worth bringing in a troop of sappers (even at a base wage of 4 shillings a day for enlisted men and 5 shillings and 6 pence a day for their NCOs). According to Anderson, "It being granted that circum-stances might arise in which working parties might be called upon to protect themselves from lawless Indians or when working in districts where the natives are at open war with a neighbouring tribe."[2]

The Royal Engineers sailed from Liverpool on August 22, 1872, aboard the steamship *Scandinavian* and arrived in Quebec City eight days later. Anderson's first close-up view of the new nation of Canada did not impress him:

> The bold, rocky promontory on which the citadel of Québec stands suddenly comes into view at a bend of the river and very naturally gave rise to the exclamation of the original French explorers, *Quel bec!* at once suggesting a name for the place. It seemed a pity that a spot so celebrated in history and which has a peculiar inter-est to British soldiers on acct. of the gallantry with which it was captured and the death of Wolfe at the moment of victory, should now be abandoned by the Imperial Government and left without a British soldier.[3]

Whether his suggested translation for the origins of the name Que-bec—"what a beak!"—is intended to be humorous (current thinking suggests the name derives from a local Native word meaning "narrowing of the river"), Anderson's sadness at the loss of the spit-and-polish precision of the British military presence seems genuine enough. Later in the same letter to his sister he wrote:

> The Citadel of Quebec is in a hopeless want of repair and the Canadian Government will not assume any of the expenses that were formerly defrayed from England. There is a small observatory where it is the custom to fire a gun at noon and when I went there at that hour, there was no one to be seen but an old man, a sort of porter, and a bugler. Shortly afterwards the Custodian of the observatory came up, and the old porter said, "You're very late today, it is past 12 and no gun fired." The other took very little notice, said it was time enough, and the bugler who joined in the remonstrating, having just looked at the Clock & found it 5 minutes past 12 was permitted to sound the bugle call "Fire" and the gun was fired, presumably with sufficient punctuality for the listless and apathetic residents of the town and the neighbouring valley.[4]

Such a cavalier attitude toward the correct time would have been especially galling to a man in Anderson's position. For the next two years, the need to keep the exact time—an essential component in surveying—across hundreds of miles of unforgiving territory would be nearly the most important thing in his life.

When their ship had docked at Quebec, Anderson noticed that Canada's new governor general, the Earl of Dufferin, had come down to greet the arriving passengers. Disembarked as soon as possible and making his introductions to the viceregal party, Anderson found himself invited to dinner that evening. He thought the new governor general "most agreeable and affable" and was impressed that he had managed to become so popular among Canadians after so short an appointment:

> From all I have heard since he seems to be very popular, and he is already known at home as a literary man, and has filled many

public offices with distinction. He has resolved to make himself personally acquainted with all the different parts of Canada, and with that view has paid visits of several weeks duration at two places in Lower Canada, entertaining the principal people and examining the neighbourhood. He only arrived in Canada three months ago.[5]

While Anderson and Featherstonhaugh enjoyed a hastily organized unofficial dinner with Lord Dufferin and his wife, the huge weight of stores was transferred from the *Scandinavian* to another steamer docked half a mile upriver. According to Anderson: "...as the waggons of the country are like the smallest and narrowest of Brewer's drays, only taking 6 or 8 boxes at a time, we had about 40 loads and the trans-shipment took nearly the whole day....:"[6]

The next morning, the party sailed up the St. Lawrence to Montreal, a journey delayed for several hours by the boarding of a steady stream of passengers and their luggage. Anderson guessed there were nearly 900 aboard when the steamer finally got underway. In Montreal, the party's baggage was once again unloaded and moved to another waiting vessel, this time more than a mile away. From Montreal they sailed upriver toward Lake Ontario and Toronto. Anderson left the ship in Kingston and took the train to Toronto to arrange for overnight accommodations and the transshipment of their stores. By 7:00 the next morning they were aboard the Northern Railway on their way north to the Lake Huron port of Collingwood, where yet another steamer awaited them. From Collingwood, it would be four days and four nights before they arrived at Duluth, Minnesota, on the morning of September 12. The crossing of Lake Superior included at least twenty-four hours of heavy weather during which the entire party suffered terrible seasickness. Anderson was able to joke only after the fact: "This was very humiliating, and on fresh water, too!"[7]

It was in Duluth that Anderson bumped into Cameron and was introduced to his wife and child for the first time. With his family being very much his first priority, Cameron was gone within an hour on the scheduled train to the Red River, leaving Anderson to arrange for a special train to take his men and equipment. After yet another shifting of the party's gear, they were taken twenty-five miles down the track to a junction where they again unloaded and reloaded everything onto a luggage train that would take them to the railhead on the Red River at Moorhead, Minnesota.

Some time before arriving in Duluth, Anderson had telegraphed the local army commander requesting permission to take his troops into the United States. The requisite permissions were quickly received, together with the offer of an American officer to accompany them and smooth out any problems. Featherstonhaugh was later to report that, "As no particular difficulties were anticipated, it was not thought necessary to accept this kind offer, as the doing so would have entailed a long journey upon the officer concerned."[8] The consideration of the British aside, the U.S. military's willingness to allow a party of some fifty foreign soldiers to move about the country unescorted speaks volumes for the degree of trust and co-operation that would be a hallmark of the entire undertaking.

From the junction, the Northern Pacific Railway carried the party and its baggage 350 miles across the state of Minnesota to the Red River at Moorhead in about eighteen hours. After 150 miles of spectacular gorges, forests and swamps, Featherstonhaugh recorded his reaction to the Engineers' first sight of the western plains:

> The first aspect of scenery over country similar to which the party were destined to work for so many miles, could not fail to be interesting, and even impressive; but as a mere landscape, the prairie, as seen from a small elevation, has few elements of beauty. The spectator appears to be in the middle of a small circle, just as is the case at sea, and the feeling which is induced is that of an oppressive monotony.[9]

The tracks over which they were riding were only a year old, and it had been barely two months since the railway had finished its bridge across the Red and begun pushing out into the unsettled expanse of the Dakota Territory.

At Moorhead, the party once again caught up with its chief commissioner and Arthur Ward. Cameron's rushing ahead was getting him nowhere, and he agreed to accompany his men on the next stage of their journey. Stepping back in time from the comparative speed and relative luxury of the Northern Pacific, the party's stores were transferred to ox-drawn wagons for the first part of their trip north down the Red River to Pembina. The luggage took up fully eighteen wagons and, once the oxen were rounded up (they had somehow been allowed to wander away en masse, and it took hours to find them), the party plodded on its way.

It was probably the first time any of the men had travelled with oxen and, while their apparently slow gait was frustrating at first, the great beasts could keep it up for hour after hour, pulling impossibly heavy loads over rough, muddy tracks. As Anderson explained, "The oxen travelled admirably and in the three days we accomplished the journey required by them, 56 miles, each day travelling long after dark, favoured by moonlight and the most delightful weather."[10] Anderson's glowing opinion of the ox would only grow stronger over the next two years. By the end of the 1874 season, as the supply lines running west from Pembina stretched out over eight hundred miles, the British commission alone would have over two hundred of the animals in the field.

The majestic pace of the oxen was not enough for Cameron and, after the first day, he acquired a lighter carriage and headed north with his family. He would arrive at Pembina barely twenty-four hours ahead of the rest of his men.

At Frog Point, an isolated steamer stop on the Dakota side of the river in present-day Traill County, the party left the wagons behind and shifted their luggage once again, this time onto the steamer *Dakota*. It was one of a number of shallow-draft sternwheelers of the Kittson Line that plied the Red River from Winnipeg to places like Frog Point. In the summer of 1872 it was the head of navigation on the river, although that honour could have moved up or down stream according to the season or the prevailing water levels. The Red was like every plains river between the Mississippi and the Great Divide—notoriously unreliable as a transportation corridor. Frozen solid in winter, it could turn into a raging flood as the snow and ice began to melt rapidly in late April or May. In a year of little rain, it could shrink back to a sandbar-choked trickle by mid-summer and never recover before the ice came again in late October. When the river was navigable, the pilot had to be constantly on his guard against half-submerged snags and sand bars that could have shifted dramatically since his last passage. While the maps gave the impression that the Red followed a fairly straight and regular north–south course, in fact it meandered wildly across its broad valley, constantly cutting a new course into its unstable banks.

For Anderson, it was an experience not to be missed:

> The navigation of this river was managed in a most wonderful manner, as it was only 45 yards wide and about 4 feet deep, in many places only 2 feet. The draught of our steamer loaded as she was only amounted to 20 inches and we frequently grounded and had to plough thro' the mud, when the vessel quavered and cracked, and bent visibly. We spent 2 days and three nights travelling down the river, a distance of about 250 miles by water, but probably not more than 100 by land, for the river winds and twists about in the most aggravating manner.[11]

Finally, after a full month of constant travel, the commission's huge supply of stores could be unloaded for the ninth and last time. In the weeks and months ahead, as the locally procured provisions, wagons and livestock poured into the base camp, the carefully crated and well-travelled tons of equipment would become no more than the tip of a huge pyramid.

But nothing in the dozens of crates, bags and boxes that came off the deck of the *Dakota* that morning was more important than the instruments that would be used in the surveying, including three great zenith telescopes, an assortment of smaller surveyor's transits and theodolites, half a dozen sextants, more than fifty compasses and eighteen carefully synchronized chronometers. Selected, checked and packed in their fitted cases by the venerable English firm of Messrs. Troughton & Simms, they were the very state of the art in mid-Victorian field science.

In their bewildering number and variety, the instruments reflected not only the nature of the science that needed to be done, and the less-than-ideal conditions under which it would be accomplished, but also the organization of the survey itself. There would be two astronomical parties and each would carry a full set of instruments, while a third set would be kept in reserve at Pembina. The three main surveying parties would also be required to operate independently of one another, and everything they could possibly require was provided for in profusion. Anything that experience had shown could be bent, broken or frozen solid could be immediately repaired from the carefully selected stock of spare parts that would travel with the parties.

To go with the instruments there were dozens of books—multiple copies of star catalogues, refraction indexes, barometric and geodetic tables, texts on magnetism, hygrometry, logarithms and trigonometry (plane and spherical)—and sheaves of official forms. Every minute observation, every daily check of the chronometers and every reckoning of latitude and longitude were to be duly recorded on one of at least thirteen different forms, of each of which they had up to five hundred pre-printed copies.

Returning to camp after the brief meeting with the Americans, Anderson was determined to get his parties into the field as soon as possible. With his own men finally "under canvas" he turned his attention to some other new arrivals:

> A party of about 20 Canadian gentlemen were handed over, for employment on the work as Surveyors, Assistant Astronomers, Clerks, &c, and the only trouble now is to put them all without delay to profitable employment. All are most willing and I have no doubt we will get on well together. I shall be taking the Field with a party in about a weeks time, and two other parties are also being organized for the field...[12]

These Canadians, while they would take no part in the overall direction of the survey, were anything but a polite, diplomatic concession to a new nation. As it had with its nomination for chief commissioner, Canada clearly intended to exercise as much influence as possible on such matters as were directly in its national interest. On a more pragmatic note, the Canadian team members would be gaining direct field experience in their new western territories. What they would learn would prove invaluable over the following decades as thousands of square miles of raw territory were mapped, surveyed and opened to settlement.

Among the Canadians (many of whom had travelled with the Royal Engineers from Toronto) were two certified land surveyors who would take full charge of two of the surveying parties. There were also four subassistant astronomers who were to be attached to the astronomical parties under Galwey and Featherstonhaugh. Although Cameron (and probably Anderson) thought these four positions were unnecessary, the Canadian government was paying for them to be there and was convinced that, in the long run, their field experience would justify the additional expense. Surprisingly, it was Cameron who, seemingly without a hint of irony, objected to the Canadian appointments on the grounds that they were clear examples of political patronage.

Although the British may have objected to the number of Ottawa's appointments to the topographical parties, they could not really complain about the quality of the men appointed. Canadians were also appointed to fill a number of senior positions in general support and administration.

Most of the Canadians were ranked as officers and, consequently, paid the same general rates as their British colleagues. The commissary, surgeon and geologist (not due to arrive until the next spring) received $2,000 per year, while the surveyors would receive $1,800. The veterinarian was paid $1,750 and the subassistant astronomers $1,500. They would also receive the standard special allowances for clothing, equipment and other expenses.

As Anderson pushed to get his parties organized and out into the field, he was moved to observe that, although they had been in camp for a fortnight before his arrival, "... the Americans up to this time have done substantially nothing."[13] While Anderson's comment is not entirely fair (just what were the Americans supposed to have done?), the United States' effort had, to that point, been very much a case of "hurry up and wait."

BY THE END of 1861, the demarcation of the 49th Parallel from the Pacific to the Continental Divide was largely complete, but the U.S. Civil War quickly put an end to any thoughts of pushing the survey beyond the Rockies and out onto the high plains. Without those five years of bloody self-slaughter, and the years of painful reconstruction that followed, the United States and Great Britain would almost certainly have run the line to its eastern terminus by the mid-1860s. That was clear in Hawkins's general instructions from the Foreign Office at the beginning of the Pacific survey. "It is possible," he was told, "that you will hereafter be required to continue the survey from that point [the Continental Divide] to the Lake of the Woods. Her Majesty's Government have made a proposal to that effect to the Government of the United States."[14]

Each side had every reason to want the whole messy business of making boundaries brought finally to an end. For Britain, the motivation to finish the work was simple. After more than two centuries as absentee owner of a vast part of the North American continent, the greatest empire builder the world had ever seen (or would likely ever see again) was taking her leave. As they like to say in current business parlance, she was off "to pursue other interests." The wealth of the Indian subcontinent and the as-yet undeveloped riches of Africa held more appeal for Britain than a huge northern outpost, the main export of which had been the long-out-of-fashion beaver pelt and the tall, straight wooden masts for a navy that was, by now, rapidly converting to iron hulls and steam power. The fast-maturing Canadian colonies could afford to look after themselves and, with the settlement of the Oregon boundary question in 1846, the United States acknowledged that its Manifest Destiny had reached its limits at the 49th Parallel. Canada would no longer need the military and diplomatic authority of Great Britain to ensure its safety.

Wanting to leave the heart of the continent with its borders clearly marked and accepted, Britain waited for the Civil War to come to an end. In the meantime, the legal process of giving Canada its independence proceeded apace. When the British North America Act was proclaimed on July 1, 1867, the new Dominion of Canada comprised only four provinces: the two former maritime colonies of New Brunswick and Nova Scotia and what had been the united colonies of Upper and Lower Canada (joined since 1841, they entered separately as the provinces of Ontario and Quebec).

Almost immediately Canada moved to take formal possession of the huge lands that lay between the Great Lakes and the Pacific Ocean. Since the early 1860s the Hudson's Bay Company had been negotiating with the British Colonial Office to end its 200 year-old "ownership" of Rupert's Land. First granted in 1670, the company's charter gave it exclusive rights to occupy and manage the North American lands drained by the rivers that flowed into Hudson Bay. It was a watershed that stretched across the continent from northern Quebec to the foothills of the Rocky Mountains. While the Company had always resisted any challenge to its lucrative monopoly on furs and trade with the Native populations, the return on its investment had declined dramatically by the middle of the nineteenth century. Where it had once vigorously opposed any attempts at settlement on its lands, it now saw that any future profits lay in cutting those lands into homestead-sized parcels and converting its fur trading posts into general stores that would stock everything the new settlers could need.

By December 1869, the deal was done. In return for £300,000 and the right to keep one-twentieth of its fertile lands for future development as it saw fit, the Hudson's Bay Company signed Rupert's Land over to the new Dominion and joined Britain on the political sidelines of North America. On July 15, 1870, Canada carved the new province of Manitoba from a corner of Rupert's Land, and brought the rest into Confederation as the North-West Territories.

West of the Continental Divide, the Hudson's Bay Company had already become a relict of history. As a consequence of the continuing fallout from the settlement of the Oregon boundary, the company had seen its fur trade fiefdoms become the crown colonies of Vancouver Island and, on the mainland, British Columbia. In 1866 the island colony was absorbed into British Columbia which, in July 1871, joined the eastern provinces in Confederation; Canada now stretched across the full width of the continent.

Many in the far west believed that British Columbia, with its own wealth of natural resources (including newly discovered gold), had nothing to gain from any association with a country whose seats of power were more than a thousand miles away across what seemed a forbidding and largely empty semi-desert. It had taken a bold (and, many said, utterly reckless) promise from Ottawa to convince the uncertain west coast colonists they should join their future with Canada's. That promise was a transcontinental railway.

The United States had finished its first transcontinental only two years before, and Canada's promise to British Columbia would prove a far more daunting enterprise. Compounding the problems presented by the lack of population, industry and the deep pools of home-grown investment capital available to the Americans, the Canadian line would be longer and pass through far more difficult terrain than had either the Union or the Central Pacific.

Reckless though it might have been, the promise had been made, and the Canadian Pacific Railway would be built. Much of the land through which it would pass between the Great Lakes and the Continental Divide was not only largely unpopulated, it was, save for the old riverine fur trade routes, unmapped and unsurveyed. In fact, considering how long the Hudson's Bay Company had been travelling the country, the cartographic state of Rupert's Land was perfectly dismal. It was so bad that it could not have been a case of simple neglect or lack of interest. In order to protect its monopoly and counter any thoughts of settlement, the company had always discouraged the production of any detailed maps of its territory, just as it had actively opposed building decent roads and, especially, bridges. The temporary structures thrown across creeks and rivers by the Royal Engineers as they made their way west along the boundary line were among the first bridges ever built in Rupert's Land. But now the company was gone, and the railway was already pushing at the edges of its old territory. Railways require surveys, and surveys require baselines. Taking the measure of the Canadian west had to begin with the baseline of the 49th Parallel, wherever that turned out to be.

For the Americans, the need to draw the line across the high plains was equally acute, though the reasons were more complex. Just like the British, they had some unfinished business that needed to be put behind them; just like the Canadians, they were facing new and pressing issues that demanded attention.

Two matters of lingering annoyance were a consequence of the Civil War. The first, a festering dispute that had arisen over an apparently benign clause in the Oregon boundary treaty of 1846 had remained unresolved as a result of the outbreak of the war. The second—known as the Alabama Claims—had grown out of the war itself.

The Oregon Treaty, which after more than twenty years of studied avoidance had finally set the westernmost boundary between the United States and Britain, had been perfectly straightforward. The line would be at 49° North from the Continental Divide to the Strait of Georgia. Since Vancouver Island, the lower third of which lay below the 49th, was to remain wholly British, the boundary had to run across to the middle of the strait and then turn south and west to bend around the island, running down "the middle of the channel." That was a precise enough description for the commissioners (one of whom was Archibald Campbell), but it was far from definitive for those residents, both American and British, who were familiar with the island-littered waters of the strait. There were, in fact, any number of possible channels, none of which was clearly wider or more obviously important than a half-dozen others. The disagreement over which nation owned which islands finally escalated into a potentially dangerous farce involving one dead pig, two senior American generals, a clutch of Royal Navy captains and the German Kaiser.

The Alabama Claims grew out of American outrage over British aid to the Confederacy during the war. A number of Confederate warships—the *Alabama* prominent among them—had been built and equipped in Britain, and they managed to cause a good deal of serious damage to Union shipping. The claims were for direct compensation from the British for the losses.

The problem was not that the United States and Britain might come to blows over two such niggling issues. Rather, it was that the continuing lack of a resolution was fuelling the fires of American public indignation and, particularly with the Alabama Claims, giving expansionist northern senators a pulpit from which they could preach for the forcible annexation of Rupert's Land as just payment for the British debt. It was likely the work of these jingoistic senators that sank President Ulysses S. Grant's resolution to authorize the creation and funding of the Northern Boundary Commission in 1870. Why bother with the expense of drawing a boundary, they argued, when they could simply turn a battle-hardened Union army north and take the whole heart of the continent for themselves?

It was not that Grant was entirely without sympathy for the annexationists. He was simply more of a political realist. By 1870 Rupert's Land was no longer a British property, and Grant might have been less sanguine had he believed that the new Canadian owners had a ghost of a chance of holding onto their new western possessions in the face of the expected swarms of American settlers. He was certainly not prepared to launch another costly war to capture an area he believed would—perhaps even before his term expired—join the United States of its own free will.

Eventually, both the "Pig War" and the Alabama Claims were settled by the Treaty of Washington in 1872. The Kaiser, who had been asked to arbitrate the Strait of Georgia dispute, picked what he thought was a likely candidate for "the channel" from the maps with which he had been provided. The disputants, by then no doubt thoroughly sick of the whole issue, did not argue with his decision. As for the Alabama Claims, an international tribunal ordered Britain to pay the United States $15.5 million for its losses. In the fervent hope that the award would be an end to the matter, Her Majesty's government simply paid the bill.

For decades the U.S. government had taken little interest in the lands that stretched across its northern tier. There was precious little to take much interest in. Out at the extreme limits of what had been France's and then Spain's Louisiana, the fur traders and, latterly, the bison hunters had gone efficiently about their business. They asked nothing more than to be left to their work, and they returned substantial profits on what small investments were made there. In the seventy years since Lewis and Clark had paddled up the Missouri in search of a way through to the Great River of the West, American interests had been focussed much farther to the south.

Pouring across the Mississippi and out into the west, American settlers and their cavalry escorts were following the emigrant trails to the Pacific coast. With the old Spanish empire a fast-fading memory and Mexico pushed back across the Rio Grande, there was impossibly fertile soil in Oregon and gold in California, both free for the taking. As the army and the contract hunters broke the power of the bison-hunting nations over the central and southern plains, cattlemen and farmers moved in to fill the vacuum. The Civil War staunched the flow for a while, but the completion of the transcontinental railway just four years after Appomattox reopened the floodgates.

But high on the northern plains there was little to draw the attention of the cowman or the homesteader. It was a land of rough grass, short on wood and even shorter on water, where the winters lasted half the year and the hold of the Sioux and the Blackfeet, while weakened, was anything but broken. Then, as the easier lands to the east, west and south were steadily taken up in the years following the Civil War, the pressure to open the northern tier began to build.

Nowhere was that pressure felt more keenly than along the two hundred miles of the Red River (called Red River of the North in the United States, to distinguish it from the Red River that forms the Texas–Oklahoma border). This northern Red River lay between the state of Minnesota and the Dakota Territory. Admitted to the Union in 1858, Minnesota could boast a population of more than 400,000 by 1870. Rich in timber to the north and fertile farmland to the south, the Lake Superior town of Duluth and St. Paul on the Mississippi made efficient ports for its booming trade with the east, while a growing maze of railroads was connecting those ports to every corner of the state.

The Northern Pacific Railway had reached the banks of the Red in 1871, on its way to realizing Lewis and Clark's goal of forging a direct trade connection between the Pacific Northwest's natural riches and the manufactured goods of the eastern seaboard. Like Lewis and Clark, the railroad initially had no real interest in the potential of what lay between the Mississippi and the riches of the west coast. The northern tier itself was nothing more than a broad, expensive annoyance over which bridges had to be built, tunnels cut and rails laid in order to reach the real objective. But the Northern Pacific owned thousands of acres of land in the Dakotas—a government gift to help defray the cost of building the line. That land, and the homesteaders' dreams it inspired, would soon become the railway's principal source of income. It was for the interests of the Northern Pacific as much for anything else that the U.S. Northern Boundary Commission was finally ordered to the banks of the Red River.

While the first attempt to fund the commission had failed in the Senate, the signing of the Treaty of Washington made it clear there would be no American annexation of Rupert's Land. So it was that, with one significant amendment, the same joint resolution was approved by Congress on March 19, 1872. The one amendment had to do with money, and it would seriously affect the commission for the duration of its work. When U.S. Chief of Engineers General A.A. Humphries made his first plan and estimate for the project in 1870, he based them on the assumption that the Commission would have to spend three seasons in the field at a total cost of something over $300,000. Writing to the secretary of war on November 23, he had stated:

> ...a properly-organized commission, with two sets of astronomical and surveying parties to expedite the work, would require, from the estimate hereunto annexed, an expenditure of about $100,000 yearly while actually engaged upon field-duties.
>
> But it is not possible to state with certainty the length of time required to trace and mark the whole line, as the progress that would be made depends upon the nature of the country to be passed over.[15]

The more detailed British estimate, drawn up by former Commissioner Hawkins, with the advice of Wilson and Anderson and based on their combined experience with the Pacific boundary, put the cost of their share of the work at a significantly higher £100,000 (equivalent to about US$545,000 at that time). This discrepancy was only widened by the 1872 amendment. Instead of authorizing the $100,000 requested for the first season's work, Congress cut the sum by half, and added a further limitation: "That engineers in the regular service of the United States shall be employed exclusively... in the performance of the duties contemplated in this act, without any additional salary."[16]

With the authorization for the survey finally in place, Archibald Campbell was appointed chief commissioner in June 1872 and ordered to organize, equip and move his party to Pembina as soon as possible. While the appointment could not have come as a complete surprise (Campbell would almost certainly have been consulted during the drawing-up of the original estimates), only a man with Campbell's experience could have had his parties assembled, equipped and ready to go to work by mid-September.

Campbell's first order of business was to arrange a meeting with his British counterpart. To that end, Donald Cameron, with his secretary Arthur Ward, rushed to Washington in July. They reached quick agreement on a wide range of operational and administrative details, and with that, Cameron was off to Ottawa to meet with Canada's surveyor general and confirm the appointments of the Canadian civilians being assigned to the survey. Ward busied himself with supply contracts and a hundred other details.

Campbell, although terribly pressed for time, had more than one significant advantage over his British colleagues: he was far closer to Pembina, and he could rely on the most senior army officials in Washington for their assistance. The secretary of war directed the chief of engineers to detail the senior officers, and then ordered the quartermaster-general to furnish the commission with all the livestock, wagons and other necessaries it might need and have them waiting at Fort Abercrombie on the Red River, just south of Moorhead. In a telling example of how tight the U.S. budgets really were, Campbell was told that, when he was finished with the mules and wagons, they were to be returned to the quartermaster at Fort Abercrombie "in good condition." At the same time, Captain A.A. Harbach and Company K of the 20th Infantry were ordered to report to Fort Pembina and prepare for escort duty.

In early July, Francis Farquhar and his fellow officers were dispatched to Saint Paul to organize their field parties. Campbell followed soon after and, having decided that everything was in readiness, he and his men took the train to Fort Abercrombie to meet their transport. On August 29, the United States Northern Boundary Commission moved out of Abercrombie and marched north to Pembina. On September 5, they set up camp just south of where they believed the 49th Parallel to be and waited for the British to arrive. It was there that Samuel Anderson and his colleagues found them on the morning of the 18th, doing "substantially nothing."

ACCORDING TO CAMPBELL, at their meeting that first morning they discussed the general plan of operations for the remainder of the 1872 season, including "the mode of surveying and marking the boundary," and agreed that "a point on the forty-ninth parallel of north latitude, close to the western bank of Red River, should be the point of the boundary first to be ascertained."[17] They would not be the first men to try to fix the precise location at which the 49th Parallel crossed the Red River, but they would be the last.

The Red River Colony was the first and only farming settlement to be permitted (albeit reluctantly) by the Hudson's Bay Company. Founded in 1812 by company director Thomas Douglas, the Fifth Earl of Selkirk, as a refuge for displaced Scottish crofters, the settlement occupied 116,000 square miles of southern Rupert's Land, running the entire length of the Red River valley from Lake Winnipeg into what is now South Dakota and stretching out to the east and west across substantial portions of present-day Minnesota and Manitoba. The heart of the colony was at the confluence of the Red and Assiniboine rivers (the site of today's city of Winnipeg), with a second administrative centre located at Pembina.

It was a measure of the company's indifference, if not outright hostility, toward the colony (it was very much Selkirk's personal project) that when, in 1818, the United States and Great Britain first formally agreed that the boundary between them should run west along the 49th Parallel from Lake of the Woods to the Continental Divide, the company raised little objection to the loss of a substantial part of its lands to the south of that line. Whatever furs there had been in the upper Red River valley had long been trapped out, and the governors had yet to develop any interest in the potential value of its farmland.

In the summer of 1823, Colonel Stephen Long of the U.S. Army's Topographical Engineers was on a government-sponsored expedition to discover the source of the Minnesota River (then known as the St. Peter's). Since he was to be in the general vicinity, he was also ordered to determine the location of the 49th Parallel where it crossed the Red River near Pembina, and to mark it clearly on the ground. His visit was perhaps anticipated by the Hudson's Bay Company. Just a month or two before, it had taken its own astronomical observations and, having determined that its trading post at Pembina was probably well south of the parallel, promptly abandoned it.

Long's astronomer, one Mr. Calhoun, spent four days at his instruments and determined that their party was camped at precisely 48° 59' 27" North latitude. A flagpole was raised and, according to a published account of the event, "In honor of the President of the United States, this place received the name of Camp Monroe." There was more ceremony to follow:

> The magnetic meridian having been ascertained to be 13° 17' 25" east, the distance to the boundary-line was measured off, and an oak post fixed on it, bearing on the north side the letters G.B., and on the south side, U.S. On the 8th of August at noon the flag was hoisted on the staff... A national salute was fired at the time, and a proclamation made by Colonel Long that, by virtue of the authority vested in him by the President of the United States, the country situated upon Red River above that point [i.e. to the south] was declared to be comprehended within the territory of the United States.[18]

A few later fixes generally confirmed the accuracy of Long's oak post and, in 1845, the Hudson's Bay Company built a new store a quarter of a mile to the north of it. But when British explorer Captain John Palliser visited in 1857, his observations suggested that the parallel was actually nearly four hundred yards to the north of Long's post, bringing the location of the Hudson's Bay store perilously close to the border yet again. Appreciating the delicacy of his position (or lacking confidence in his mathematics), Palliser didn't push the point and "accepted" the earlier markers. For the few people who lived nearby, it was all much ado about nothing. In fact, as an indication of how little anyone in the vicinity cared about the international boundary, some prankster had pulled up Long's marker years before and turned it around so that "G.B." faced south. It had since rotted into the ground without anyone ever having bothered to turn it around.

Then, in 1870, the whole business erupted once again, and this time it had the potential to create serious problems. In fact, it would prove to be the proverbial "last straw" that finally brought Cameron and Campbell and their teams of astronomers and surveyors together on the banks of the Red River.

Officially, President Grant and his army commanders were worried about increasing trouble with the Sioux and its effect on the new railway. Unofficially, they were concerned about the recent rebellious turn in Fort Garry and the Red River Colony. In early 1870, a survey was commissioned to determine the location for a new American military post at the extreme northeastern corner of the Dakota Territory. It was first thought that the post would be west of the river valley and its volatile flood plain, but the site finally selected was just a few hundred yards from the river and a long mile south of the village of Pembina. Just for the record, however, army surveyor Captain David Porter Heap was ordered to confirm the location of Long's parallel and mark it accordingly.

In May, Heap took his readings, did his calculations and made his fix—fully 4,600 feet north of Long's post. Supremely confident in his work, Heap hammered a string of stakes thirty-five miles west along his new line before he left for Fort Wadsworth, deep in the Dakota Territory.

When Heap's line once again placed the Hudson's Bay post firmly within the United States, an enthusiastic American customs inspector named John C. Stoever sprang into action. He invaded the company's post, took a detailed inventory of its contents and began to figure the duty owed. On June 23, 1870, he wrote to the secretary of the treasury in Washington to announce his coup and request further instructions. Utterly nonplussed, the treasury secretary contacted Secretary of State Hamilton Fish, who immediately sensed the gravity of the situation and called the British representative in Washington, Sir Edward Thornton, in for a meeting.

Unsure of how to react and needing time to contact his government for instructions, Thornton begged to maintain the pre-Heap status quo in the meantime. Secretary Fish spoke to President Grant and the excitable Mr. Stoever was instructed to stay away from the Hudson's Bay store pending further developments.

It was then that Secretary Fish decided the time was right to settle the boundary once and for all. While that was being organized, he suggested, the British might be well advised to send one of their own surveyors to check Heap's work. Thornton requested a copy of Heap's report and calculations (supposedly filed at St. Paul in early July 1870) but they could not be found. The Foreign Office, seeing little alternative, agreed to Fish's proposal for an international commission and President Grant forwarded his ill-fated request for a joint resolution in November of that year. Once again, it was "hurry up and wait" for the boundary commissions.

Although none of the three governments involved needed any further motivation to bring the boundary issue to a final reckoning, in October 1871 more trouble erupted at Pembina. This time it wasn't precipitated by over-zealous bureaucrats, faulty mathematics or even dead pigs. This time, it was the Irish. More specifically, it was the Fenians.

Founded in 1857 in Ireland and the United States, the semi-secret society known as the Fenian Brotherhood was fanatically committed to the cause of Irish independence. Almost from the beginning the society was divided on how best to achieve that goal. One faction wanted to invade the homeland directly, while another thought their best hope lay in an invasion of Canada. Presumably, they would capture the then-British colony and somehow trade it back in exchange for Ireland. At its peak, with half a million dollars at its disposal and a membership rumoured to comprise as many as ten thousand Irish-American Civil War veterans, the Brotherhood managed to launch several pre-emptive strikes against eastern Canada, and eventually did mount its own invasion of Ireland in 1867. When these missions failed, membership went into decline and what was left of the society conceived another cunning plan.

Under the leadership of self-styled "General" John O'Neill, they determined to attack Canada from the rear and moved west to Minnesota. Although Quebec had always been a favourite target of earlier Fenian campaigns (based on the assumption that the Catholic French-Canadian population would make common cause with the Irish), this time O'Neill probably thought the new province of Manitoba presented a fine opportunity, given the Metis uprising there that had begun in 1869. Unfortunately for General O'Neill, Riel's rebellion had collapsed by the time he arrived in Minnesota and the French-speaking Catholic Metis of Manitoba reacted to his presence in much the same way as had the French-Canadian Quebecois: they wanted nothing to do with the Fenians. Undaunted, O'Neill launched his invasion of Canada anyway.

He and his men made it as far as the unfortunate Hudson's Bay post and summarily set about looting it. Hearing of the trouble, American Captain Lloyd Wheaton and two companies of his 20th Infantry marched out of the new Fort Pembina and scattered the Fenians before them. The captain quickly had O'Neill and his men under arrest, their weapons confiscated and most of the loot returned to the Hudson's Bay Company.

But the comic opera did not end there. Sent to St. Paul and charged with conspiracy to violate the neutrality laws, O'Neill and his lawyer argued that there had not, in fact, been an invasion of Canada at all. Basing their argument on the location of Heap's parallel, they claimed they had never left the United States. Captain Wheaton, when called as a witness, was forced to admit that he really had no idea where the boundary actually was. On the strength of Wheaton's evidence (or, rather, the lack of it) and because there was obvious confusion about the location of the 49th Parallel, all charges against O'Neill were dismissed.

Wheaton might later find solace in knowing that he had commanded the only military action ever launched from Fort Pembina in what would be its twenty-five-year history. He had also successfully thwarted the last attempted invasion of Canada, by the Fenians or anyone else.

SO, AFTER DECADES of confusion, compromise, acrimony and ineptitude, Major William Johnson Twining of the Army Corps of Engineers, assistant astronomer to the United States Northern Boundary Commission, took his zenith telescope from its case on September 18, 1872, and began a careful series of observations. Soon thereafter, Captain Albany Featherstonhaugh of the Royal Engineers, assistant astronomer to Her Majesty's North American Boundary Commission, "...commenced to do the same on a meridian conveniently near to that of the American observatory tent."[19] Their independent findings would lead to the first official determination of 49° North Latitude east of the Continental Divide.

Finding one's precise latitude is, in principle, fairly straightforward, at least when compared with the centuries it took to develop a reliable and accurate method for determining longitude. At night, the angle of the north star, Polaris, above the horizon is exactly equal to the latitude of the observer. During daylight, the angle of the sun at noon varies according to the time of year, but combined with knowledge of the date, this angle can also tell the observer his or her latitude. The more accurately one can determine that angle, whether with a sextant or a carefully calibrated telescope, the more accurately the latitude can established. Tiny errors of observation in the sky can translate to major differences in position on the ground, and errors in observation can be compounded by inaccuracies in the instruments and in the printed tables (called ephimerides) used to co-ordinate the date with the sun's altitude. These small, unpredictable variations were the reason why all previous attempts to fix the position of 49° North at Pembina had disagreed with each other. But the more skilled and experienced the observer, and the better the instruments and tables, the closer the measurement will be to the truth, which is why everyone present in the two commissions that day was confident that, with the best-trained and best-equipped survey-ors ever sent to the Red River, and with each team observing inde-pendently as a check on the other, their new fix would be the most accurate yet.

When the calculations from both parties were compared, they disagreed by just thirty-two feet. In the spirit of practical co-opera-tion that would become the hallmark of their fieldwork (if not always their personal relationships), the two commissions agreed to split the difference and drove their first stake into the western plains precisely sixteen feet from either fix.

Of all previous attempts to mark the 49th Parallel at Pembina, Palliser's—which was within a hundred yards—had been by far the closest. Long's mark was three hundred yards to the south of the new, "official" 49° North, while Heap's was a huge twelve hundred yards—more than two-thirds of a mile—to the north. As it turned out, the beleaguered Hudson's Bay Company post *was* in Canada after all, but by a bare hundred yards. Unfortunately, the Canadian Customs house turned out to be more than five hundred feet inside the United States.

The parties would repeat the procedure of making joint observa-tions at each of the next three stations west of the Red River. For the two chief astronomers, those results would be more than satisfac-tory, meaning that there would be no need for the time-consuming business of regularly checking each other's work. Twining would later sum up the accuracy of their work:

> Of the forty-one astronomical stations, four were observed jointly
> by the two commissions, the difference in the determinations
> in each case being thirty-two feet, twenty-nine feet, seven feet
> and twenty-seven feet, respectively. As those were the first sta-
> tions observed, and as the general quality of the work constantly

improved, it is probable that if the others had been observed jointly, a very considerable reduction in the average discrepancies would have been found.[20]

It is easy to imagine the men looking up from that first small wooden marker and off toward the west. Over the course of the next twenty-four months, that was where they would be repeating their small ceremony countless times across the eight hundred trackless miles that lay between the Red River and the crest of the Continental Divide. The commissioners and their senior officers, however, were almost certainly not staring off across the plains. Rather, their thoughts were turning first to the east and the one hundred miles of birch forest, river and swamp that stretched back from the Red River to Lake of the Woods. The work on the eastern line had to be completed first, and it would, in nearly every way, prove a much sterner test than anything they would face out on the high plains.

On yet another in the unbroken succession of warm, brilliant days, as the astronomical and survey parties checked and packed their equipment for the field, their attention was drawn to skein after skein of wild geese, winging their way south down the valley, "screaming over the camps… at a great elevation."[21] Within hours, the geese were followed by a violent blizzard that raged for a full forty-eight hours. It was September 22, the first official day of fall, and a reminder of how dangerously unpredictable the weather could be at 49° North.

With his characteristic understatement, Albany Featherstonhaugh thought the blizzard "sufficiently unpleasant," but managed to find some good news as well: "The storm… was taken by the local people as a presage of a late winter, and this proved to be the case."[22]

· 2 ·

THE NORTHWEST
ANGLE

We searched the woods, and we searched the weeds,
we wallowed about in the swamp till the
very mention of the North West Point made one irritable.
. SAMUEL ANDERSON

I T IS AGREED that a line drawn from the most north-west point of the Lake of the Woods along the 49th parallel of north latitude—or, if the said point shall not be in the 49th parallel of north latitude, then, that a line drawn from the said point due north or south, as the case may be, until the said line shall intersect the said parallel of north latitude, and from the point of such intersection due west along and with the said parallel—shall be the line of demarcation between the territories of His Britannic Majesty and those of the United States, and that the said line shall form the southern boundary of the said territories of His Britannic Majesty; and the northern boundary of the territories of the United States from the Lake of the Woods to the Stony Mountains.

Thus spake Article 11 of the London Convention of 1818, corollary to Article VII of the 1814 Treaty of Ghent, which confirmed the terms of the Convention of 1806, which clarified the Treaty of Paris of 1783, and so on and so on, back to the very beginnings of British Rupert's Land and French Louisiana.

The London Convention was true to its diplomatic pedigree—straightforward yet pompous, definitive yet vague—but at least its grasp of geography was slightly more refined than that exhibited some thirty-five years earlier in the Treaty of Paris (a document that an early commentator had termed an exercise in "manifest geographical ignorance").

In that treaty (the main point of which was Britain's formal acceptance of American independence), the boundary had been defined as running from the northwesternmost point of Lake of the Woods, west to the source (or sources) of the Mississippi and thence south down the middle of the river. If the Americans were going to insist on anything in their endgame negotiations with the British, it was that the future of the Mississippi was to be entirely a matter between themselves and the Spanish (who then owned everything west of the river). It was also obvious from the wording of the treaty that no one sitting around the table in Paris in 1783 had anything but the vaguest idea of where either the northwesternmost point of Lake of the Woods or the source of the Mississippi actually were.

What had become obvious to everyone in the years between the Paris treaty and the London convention was that the source of the Mississippi was anything but west of Lake of the Woods. As we now know (and as they were beginning to suspect as early as 1800), the Mississippi is born in Minnesota's Lake Itasca, more than 150 miles directly south of Lake of the Woods.

One can only speculate about which scrap of geographical whimsy inspired the drafters of the Treaty of Paris to settle on the *northwesternmost* point of Lake of the Woods, or why that point was accepted without question in every subsequent treaty. It was enough that it had been selected, and even when subsequent explorations revealed the patent absurdity of the position, no American politician or diplomat was willing to consider changing it. So it was then, on the last day of September 1872, that the men of the United States Northern Boundary Commission set out from Fort Pembina to find the north-westernmost point of Lake of the Woods. They were followed a day later by the British, travelling by separate convoy.

Although they were engaged in a common undertaking and, where possible, camped beside each other, the American and British parties rarely travelled as one. Each was fully equipped and drew on its own main store of supplies. Even when they were at work on determining a single critical point (such as their first fix on the bank of the Red River or the coming work at Lake of the Woods), they invariably worked independently and then compared notes. While this duplication of effort may have seemed wasteful and unnecessarily cumbersome during the short season of 1872, the soundness of the plan would prove itself in the following years as the work moved out onto the high plains.

In order to reach Lake of the Woods, the astronomical parties first travelled sixty-five miles north to Winnipeg. The road from Pembina to Winnipeg was a nightmare of deep, muddy ruts that constantly stuck the heavily loaded British wagons fast and broke down the horses that were trying to pull them. Anderson was forced to replace two of the horses in Winnipeg and to hire two additional wagons to lighten the loads on the other five. He also decided to rest the other horses for an extra day before pushing on.

If the trail to Winnipeg was bad, the 130 miles of the Dawson Route, which connected the fort with Lake of the Woods, were appalling. They were deeply rutted and swampy at the best of times, and the churning of the American wagons and their six-mule hitches a day ahead had only made it worse. One morning, the British camp awoke in a thick, damp fog to find a sleeping sentry had let the horses wander. It took two hours to round up all but two of them. That meant leaving a wagon behind while its teamsters hunted up the missing animals. They had only wandered four or five miles away before they were found, but it was three days before the wagon caught up with the rest of the train. Anderson described the trip to his sister Janet:

It was 6 days journey from Fort Garry to Lake of the Woods, but our horses came along well and we made the journey in 5 days so that to the great astonishment of the American party we reached our destination on the same day as they did. The last day's journey, 30 miles in all, was through a most desolate swamp, a bottomless bog over which it is dangerous to walk as a man sinks into it to his waist. The road was supported on the branches and stems of trees and on each side there was the brown marshy water with grass and reeds growing in it.[1]

What Anderson had just traversed was the western leg of what was then Canada's only overland route between the Great Lakes and Manitoba. And what he had experienced was by far the most pleasant part of the road. The infamous Dawson Route—so named for Simon J. Dawson who, as a result of his earlier explorations in the country, was commissioned by the federal government in 1868 to build the thing—was a 480-mile nightmare that, it was said, no traveller would ever willingly attempt more than once. The only reason anyone would brave the journey was cost. It was considerably cheaper than the combined steamer-railroad journey across the Great Lakes and through Minnesota that the British Boundary Commission had taken. Anyone who had the money avoided the Dawson Route like the plague.

Steamers would carry passengers across Lake Superior from eastern Canada to the docks at Prince Arthur's Landing (where the city of Thunder Bay now stands). From there they would travel by wagon on a torturous corduroy road to the first in a succession of more than a dozen lakes and rivers. Baggage would be thrown from the wagons and jammed onto a small, usually overloaded and dangerously undermaintained steamboat or tug. At the far end of the lake, baggage and passengers would again take to wagons for another bone-rattling ride along a collapsing corduroy road, followed by another lake crossing, another wagon ride and so on for up to two weeks. Passengers were supposed to have been provided with regular meals and overnight accommodation, but the shacks they were to sleep in were foul and often open to the elements. Many passengers claimed the only meals they had were the fish they managed to catch themselves. On top of it all, the steamer captains and wagon drivers were legendary for the abuse they heaped on their customers. Passengers maintained that they had been forced to load and unload freight, chop firewood for the boilers, pump bilges and, where there were no wagons or a section of the road had fallen apart, to walk for miles through mosquito-infested swamps hauling their belongings with them. Any complaints or refusals to work were met with torrents of foul language and threats to abandon the passengers where they stood.

The Dawson was built over the old North West Company fur trade route and, while it had served well enough for freight canoes and strong paddlers, it could never have been sufficiently developed to carry large numbers of paying passengers. While the road and the steamers were dreadfully expensive to maintain, the federal government made matters worse by paying a large subsidy to the management company to keep the passenger fares low, irrespective of the number of passengers carried. The company quickly realized that the fewer the passengers, the higher their profits, and ran its business accordingly.

The opening of the Northern Pacific Railway's route from Duluth to Moorhead guaranteed that the Dawson Route would never prosper, and a few years later, after years of subsidy and endless complaints from the stream of filthy, half-starved survivors who staggered into the Winnipeg member of parliament's office, the government had finally had enough. While it never gave up on its insistence that there must be an all-Canadian route to the west, it simply recognized that paddlewheelers and corduroy roads were a thing of the past. The future lay with the railways.

Anderson and Farquhar set up their camps near where the Dawson Route steamer from Fort Frances and Rainy River dumped its passengers out onto the wagon road to Winnipeg (Anderson remarked that he had seen precious little traffic). At Pembina they had determined the location of the 49th Parallel from scratch. Here they would simply have to locate a marker that had been placed at the northwesternmost corner of the lake in 1826 by a previous joint commission and then run their line south to where the parallel intersected the shore of the lake.

To establish the southern terminus of the line, assistant astronomers Galwey and Twining were sent down to Buffalo Point:

> ... half the party were detached under Mr. Galwey to ascertain the position of the 49th Parallel at the West shore of the Lake of the Woods. They started in an 8 oared boat with 18 days provisions, in company with a United States party similarly equipped. After 3 days water journey down the Lake with the usual hair-breadth escapes from squalls and sunken rocks they reached their destination.[2]

In the same long letter in which Anderson described his journey from Winnipeg, he pushed his tongue firmly into his cheek and summed up the parties' situation at Lake of the Woods:

> [We] established our camp on a little point raised a few feet above the water, but on all sides there was swamp. And this was the site of the commencement of our labours, for the wise people who made the Treaty in 1818 decided that the Boundary was to be run from the North West point of the Lake of the Woods, up to which point a joint Commission in 1826 had surveyed... and reported that the... closing spot of their labours was in a swamp and could not be marked. They erected a monument one mile distant from this uninviting spot in a certain stated direction, and on the nearest firm ground. So all we had to do was start from this old monument of 1826 and proceed with our Boundary. But the monument was no where to be found.[3]

Anderson probably wasn't surprised. Neither would he have been surprised to learn that the story of the marker at the northwest corner of Lake of the Woods was a good deal more complicated than he knew.

In fact, it was not the "Treaty of 1818"—the London Convention—that had led to the survey of the lake. Rather, it was the joint commission established following the Treaty of Ghent in 1814 (the treaty that officially ended the War of 1812). That commission was charged with continuing to try to clear up the still-unresolved eastern seaboard boundary issues that had arisen from the Treaty of Paris and to address the difficult problem of the boundary between Lake Superior and Lake of the Woods.

The line west from Lake Superior was proving particularly intractable. Both American and Canadian fur companies still had an interest in what had been their traditional trapping grounds, even if, by the 1820s, their interest had begun to shift away from trapping and toward more general trade with the Native populations and the new settlers. Railways were years away, access to navigable waterways was still of paramount importance, and the fur companies retained considerable political clout in London and Washington.

Claims and counterclaims were thrown onto the joint commission's table, with the Americans trying to move the line as far to the north as possible, and the Hudson's Bay Company—at that time still actively trying to expand its empire—working equally hard to push it south. Both sides asserted historic rights and made pronouncements about the shape and size of the watersheds they claimed to control. These were almost entirely self-serving, and the joint commission kept a string of explorers and surveyors busy trying to find out just what the land really looked like. It was as an employee of the joint commission that the Canadian west's greatest cartographer, and arguably its greatest explorer, would make his final contribution.

In his thirty years with the Hudson's Bay and North West Companies, David Thompson had seen and mapped more of the western continent than any other man. Coming out of "retirement" at more than fifty years of age, he headed back into the west to begin an extensive survey of the country beyond Lake Superior. It was Thompson who paddled up the western shore of Lake of the Woods in 1824, taking astronomical fixes and marking his progress with a series of stakes and small cairns. It was one of these fixes that became one of several candidates for the northwesternmost point.

Anyone who looks at even a crude road atlas map of Lake of the Woods will quickly grasp that it really isn't a single body of water at all. Toward the north, it is riddled with narrow necks of water leading into large bays that could be taken either for extensions of the main lake or for separate bodies of water, each entitled to its own name. So complex is the geography of Lake of the Woods that its convoluted shoreline is said to be 65,000 miles long.

The Americans were pushing to extend the definition of what constituted Lake of the Woods, and thus wanted the northwest point established at Rat Portage (near present-day Kenora, Ontario). The Hudson's Bay Company quickly showed the British commissioners that such a point would effectively hand the Americans control over the mouth of the Winnipeg River. Further, when a line from Rat Portage was extended south to the 49th Parallel, it would force any traffic moving across the lake between Rainy River and the Red River Colony to travel through the United States and be subject to whatever regulations and tariffs the Americans chose to impose.

To counter the American claim, the British commissioners sent yet another surveyor to Lake of the Woods in 1825. Dr. Johann Ludwig Tiarks, a German with an impeccable reputation for accuracy, easily found Thompson's cairn and, from it, calculated a northwest point that would become the official British candidate. It was probably Tiarks who built the wooden crib and oak post reference marker that Anderson and Farquhar were now having so much trouble locating.

In the end, the Americans gave up on their claim for Rat Portage and grudgingly accepted Thompson and Tiarks's mark—none of which made it any easier to find forty-seven years later. Anderson wrote to his sister:

> We searched the woods, and we searched the weeds, we wallowed about in the swamp till the very mention of the North West Point made one irritable. The Americans searched, the Indians searched and tho' our observations indicated with precision

where the monument ought to be, just on the edge of a little point appearing above the marsh, it could not be found.[4]

Everyone had a theory. The locals said the lake level was much higher than usual and the monument was probably under water. Others suggested it had no doubt been burned in one of the regular forest fires, and still others were convinced it had simply rotted away.

Finally, help arrived in the person of one James McKay, a mixed-blood member of the Manitoba Legislature and manager of the Dawson Route. He located an old Ojibway chief and brought him to the site:

> At last an old Indian appeared who professed to know where the monument was and he took us to a spot among the willows in the marsh... and here under 2 feet of water were some hewn logs all charred buried in the ground and with difficulty they were got out. They enclosed a form of crib about 6 feet square. It was not very agreeable walking about up to ones knees in water, temperature only just above freezing, and examining the site of the old monument by treading. All this was neither very satisfactory nor conclusive, but the spot was close to where our observations put the monument. The old logs were brought into camp to be photographed.[5]

So it was that every opinion was proved correct: those parts of the monument which had not rotted away *had* been burned in a forest fire, and then buried underwater. While Anderson might have expressed some reservations to his sister, neither he nor Farquhar was prepared to spend so much as another hour looking for a more likely candidate.

Chief commissioners Campbell and Cameron arrived the next day from Winnipeg, and the two chief astronomers were pleased to present them with a *fait accompli*. Or so they thought.

Campbell looked at the evidence and, like his chief astronomer, he was willing to accept the reference monument, use it to find the actual point and get on with the survey. Cameron, however, much to everyone's considerable annoyance, was not so inclined.

Cameron's reticence grew from the fact that the monument was described as being on the nearest piece of solid ground to the actual mark. This, he was convinced, referred to a granite promontory standing at some distance from the alleged Tiarks monument. Anderson had noticed the rock, too, and had already studied it carefully for evidence, finding none. But Cameron insisted on yet another search of the area. He was not simply being obstinate: he had been anticipating trouble with the northwest point almost from the day of his appointment.

Cameron's original instructions from the Foreign Office had been clear: the commission's job was to make a "scientific ascertainment of a fixed geographical line" and that line was to be "a question of fact not depending upon opinion or argument." In other words, they were to draw the line exactly as they found it, and any problems would be sorted out later at a higher level. However, behind the blunt clarity of the Foreign Office's dictate lay a different, more subtle agenda, and Cameron had been made aware of it. In withholding his acceptance of the reference monument, Cameron was looking for some way to seize the Northwest Angle.

As everyone on both sides had known since the Thompson and Tiarks surveys, any line drawn south from any acceptable northwest point would pass through the Northwest Angle, a broad, roughly semicircular piece of land that pushed out into the main body of the lake from the western shore. The Angle would then become part of the state of Minnesota, though completely separated from the rest of the state by the southeastern corner of Manitoba and the waters of Buffalo Bay. It would also bring the United States border to within just a few yards of the Dawson Route ferry dock.

The suggestion that the Northwest Angle should, if possible, be "preserved" for Canada came from the former commissioner of the Pacific boundary survey, John Hawkins, and he knew what he was talking about. His work on the Pacific coast survey had created just such an anomaly at a place called Point Roberts, and years of subsequent pleading at "higher levels" had failed to remedy it.

Archibald Campbell, too, knew the story of the Pacific anomaly. He had been there with Hawkins when it was created. As the 49th Parallel was drawn out across Boundary Bay toward the middle of the Strait of Georgia, it cut through Point Roberts, a peninsula dipping south below the line, about two miles above its tip, and made the tiny landfall a part of the United States. For years, the British, and later the Canadians, had been pleading to correct what was obviously an absurd situation, but the United States had refused to give Point Roberts up. Campbell had always been opposed to the return of Point Roberts and neither was he prepared to recommend giving up the Northwest Angle.

In his final report to Congress, Campbell referred to the Angle as "this small but much-coveted and important piece of territory."[6] In that same report, however, chief astronomer Farquhar described it somewhat differently:

> ... amounting in all to about one hundred and fifty square mile, much the greater part is covered with a deep bog, on which a few scattering tamaracks struggle for existence. In some localities, where the ground is high, deciduous trees predominate, but, as a general rule, the forests are composed of coniferous trees of small size and little value.[7]

In the end, the granite promontory having been searched in vain once more, Cameron could see that there was no way he was going to be able to move the northwest point far enough to avoid cutting off the Northwest Angle and agreed to let the work on the line continue. His prevarications, though, had so annoyed Campbell that their relationship was permanently damaged.

Not so for Anderson and Farquhar (both of whom had sided with Campbell in the dispute).

> Col. Farquhar... is very genial and amusing. We are in perfect accord with regard to the work. One night when the knotty question of the identification of the monument was before the Commissioners, he was heard to start up in his sleep, and exclaim "Any

fool could tell *that* was a monument!" One of his own officers who occupied the same tent heard it and tells the story with great gusto.[8]

On October 25, as Anderson set his crews to work drawing the line south to Buffalo Point, both chief commissioners left for Winnipeg (Cameron, presumably, to write to the Foreign Office about the Angle) and everyone was happy to see them go. A week or so later, Anderson was regaled by a visiting express driver on the reputation Captain Cameron was developing among the people of Winnipeg, and he was clearly tired of hearing about it. "It is very unpleasant," he wrote to his mother, "to be the recipient of the complaints from all the residents of this country of his rudeness to them."[9]

It would be easy to dismiss Cameron as an objectionable snob whose only contribution to the boundary survey was to slow its progress and provide a focus for Anderson's sarcasm, but that would not be entirely fair. In many ways, he was in a no-win situation. He was not a trained surveyor or astronomer and, perhaps worst of all, he was not a Royal Engineer. His appointment had been political patronage and everyone knew it. Further, his short temper and condescending manner did not endear him to anyone.

Cameron's biggest problem, however, may have arisen from the fact that he really didn't have anything to do. Anderson was proving himself more than capable of running the entire show and, but for Canada's insistence on having a say in the appointment, he would most likely have been made chief commissioner. Anderson and Cameron's attitude toward each other was obviously coloured by their mutual awareness of this fact. Also, no problems had arisen of a type or seriousness that might have required Cameron's political clout or connections to resolve. He certainly seemed not to have learned from the example of his American counterpart.

Campbell was twenty years older and well past the point of feeling he had anything to prove. Having satisfied himself that the survey was in good hands and proceeding according to schedule, he was content to remain in the background, helping his secretary manage the wealth of administrative details and venturing into the field only when he was called upon to do so. Campbell's equanimity might also have stemmed from something else he knew: that he would not be spending the winter on the bleak, frozen floor of the Red River valley. The Americans would soon be leaving the field. It was the first significant impact of the congressional parsimony that had cut the funding for the American commission in half.

Campbell had already been complaining about the situation to Secretary of State Hamilton Fish. Appealing as much to American pride as anything else, he described at some length the large number of British regular soldiers in the other side's parties, the higher quality of their instruments, their having taken on the bulk of the first season's work and several other comparisons in which his commission came off second-best. It was not that he expected to see his allocation for 1872 increased. Rather he was trying to shame Congress into putting more money into the next two years' work. Such shaming might work on Secretary Fish; it had already worked on Campbell. Anderson was convinced that the Americans, for fear of being seen as not pulling their own weight, had already undertaken more fieldwork that season than they had intended.

Before he left for the winter, Campbell also managed to ensure that his relationship with Cameron was not going to improve. While in Pembina, he received news that the last outstanding piece of business from his work on the Pacific survey had finally been settled. On hearing that the Kaiser had selected the American choice for the boundary through the straits of Georgia and Juan de Fuca, Campbell took the opportunity to express his delight a little too openly for Cameron's taste, a fact that Cameron was quick to include in yet another dispatch to the Foreign Office.

With the other senior officers engaged in the hunt for the northwest marker or setting up the astronomical station at Buffalo Point, Lieutenant Greene was ordered to take a party of twenty-five men and begin work on the line east from the Red River. Leaving camp on October 2, he began tracing tangents from the river toward what he had been told would be a British party coming west toward him.

Tangent lines were used to find the boundary between the astronomical stations. Once the exact location of 49° North was established along the longitudinal axis, an east–west line would be run at exactly 90° to the axis toward the next station. However, since lines of longitude converge toward each pole, only at the equator would such an east–west line follow the line of latitude exactly. The farther north or south of the equator one draws an east–west line, the more it will angle away from—or "form a tangent" with—the true latitude. At 49° North, the tangent line deviates significantly to the south (by exactly how much depends on local conditions). From the tangent line, therefore, the actual line of latitude would be regained by running another, short line—known as an "offset"—north to the parallel, thus keeping the line running true along the latitude between the astronomically fixed points.

By November 6 Greene had reached the Roseau River, thirty-three miles from Pembina, and when Farquhar sent a message ordering him to return to base, he had still seen no sign of the British. The British party, under Featherstonhaugh, were having a much rougher time of it and were well short of reaching the Roseau when Greene was ordered back.

At the Northwest Angle, concern was growing for the two parties that had been dispatched south to Buffalo Point. When they were three days overdue, Anderson and Farquhar set off in a relief boat with eight men and a good store of provisions, tents and blankets. Galwey's boat was spotted only ten miles out ("coming along gaily" said Anderson), but the Americans, reported Galwey, were at least a day behind, though all in fine shape. Anderson and Farquhar returned to camp but three more days passed and the American boat was still not in. A party of Indians finally arrived by canoe with a letter from Twining to say that they had been beached and pinned down by a steady wind and would come along as soon as they could. It had taken them three days to row down to Buffalo Point, but it would take more than a week to row back.

By the time Twining finally came in, Farquhar had already left for Pembina, taking his party with him and leaving instructions for his assistant astronomer to do the same as soon as possible. That left Anderson alone with his cutting crew at the Northwest Angle. He summed up his work this way:

> I should like the old Plenipotentiaries who decided this Boundary Line by Treaty in 1818 to be resuscitated for a short time in order to come and live at this spot. They would probably have then decided to fix it in some other locality, instead of a swamp.[10]

By early November, the Americans were almost ready to retreat. As predicted by the locals, the equinoctial blizzard of September 22 had led to more than a month of beautiful Indian summer, but the cold nights and even colder rain of the past week had the American parties anxious to pull out before the real winter began. This time they would not be going upriver by steamer. Instead they faced a long, slow journey to take their horse- and mule-drawn wagons back to Fort Abercrombie, where they could be returned (with luck, still "in good condition") to the quartermaster. Not wanting to risk their instruments, those that were not in need of repair were left at Fort Pembina, ready for next year's work. From Abercrombie, the officers would take the railway to St. Paul (where the enlisted men would be reassigned and the non-military staff paid off) and then continue on to their winter quarters at the Corps of Engineers' hydrographic facilities in Detroit, home base for both Farquhar and Gregory. It would be seven months before they would be back to Pembina and the 49th Parallel.

Still at Lake of the Woods, Anderson's party was clear-cutting a thirty-foot-wide swath through the trees along the sixteen-mile line that defined the border between Manitoba and the Northwest Angle. Progress was made through a messy combination of rough, guesstimate surveying and slashing through dense bush. Running a line due north–south, a simple compass bearing would tell them the alignment their cut must follow, even when the forest prevented them from seeing the next astronomically fixed point they were aiming for. As for the line's east–west position, the survey crews were skilled enough to know that the exact boundary line would lie somewhere within the thirty-foot strip of clear-cut. Leaving temporary posts or stone cairns to indicate their best guess as to where that might be, they pushed on, determined to finish the work before the winter came on. At some time in the future, another survey crew would arrive to check their measurements—the task made simpler by the completed clear-cut, which allowed sightings to be taken some distance along the line of sight of the boundary. They would also install a regular series of permanent, cast-iron pillars to replace the temporary posts and cairns.

Having hired a dozen of the local Natives to work under the direction of four of his men, Anderson observed them with a mix of admiration, disdain and humour:

> The Natives of the Lake of the Woods are most independent, and little inclined or physically able for continuous hard work. It became necessary to humour them a little to prevent them abandoning a work that necessitated their being knee-deep in mud all day. The great talker of the party, who is well known throughout the country, began by a great flourish, and very soon disabled himself with his own axe, and eventually settled down as the cook of the party. He was famous for the extraordinary load of miscellaneous baggage that he would collect into one bundle and carry on his back, with the portage straps across his forehead, and jump from log to log when shifting camp down the cutting.[11]

Anderson's observations on the limited capacity of the Natives for "continuous hard work" reflect a feeling that was common among the Engineers. Cutting sight lines was a tedious, back-breaking business of chopping trees and dragging deadfall off into the bush. The local loggers and Anderson's sappers were used to such work, but the local Natives were not. According to Featherstonhaugh:

> They [the Native axemen] would commence in the morning sometimes with great vigour, but would soon stop, light a fire, and sit round it smoking; then when, after much trouble, the non-commissioned officer or sapper in charge had got them to work

again, they would suddenly break off and proceed gravely to Captain Anderson's tent, perhaps some two or three miles off, where they would ask for more pay or food. After a fortnight, only half-a-dozen of these men were able to continue at work, the others breaking down through want of stamina. They were all miserably clad, and the working in the icy water of the still unfrozen swamps was very severe upon them...[12]

Over the balance of the winter work, Anderson, Featherstonhaugh and Galwey would increasingly use their own men for the cutting while employing the Natives to do what they did better than anyone else. As Anderson's description of his camp cook suggests, they could carry extremely heavy and unwieldy loads over long distances and rough country in appalling weather. It was the kind of work their families had been doing for decades when the fur companies were still active in the area. With horses and wagons of little use in thick bush or deep winter snow, and the rivers frozen for six months of the year, it was Native bearers who had kept the supply lines open between the trading centres and the isolated outposts.

An additional problem with hiring the Native labour also presented itself:

The Indians would only work on the condition that I would take care of their wives and families during their absence. Twelve or fourteen families accordingly arrived and set up their lodges close to the Observatory Camp, and an occasional issue to them of a little flour and bacon was equally divided among their number, and used with surprising economy. After living almost entirely on moose-meat and a few roots, they have an indescribable craving for flour.[13]

Anderson considered "200 lbs. of flour and a little tea and sugar" a small price to pay for keeping his cutters out on the line.

Every member of the commissions who encountered the Native population east of the Red River, whether around the observatory stations or out in the bush, was struck by the grinding poverty in which they lived. The land they occupied seemed devoid of any real natural advantages. Big game—moose and deer—was almost non-existent, and even the hundreds of creeks and small lakes could not seem to provide enough fish to keep the thinly scattered bands sufficiently well fed. The land had been rich enough in furs to draw the attention of both American and Canadian trapping companies, but it was also the first area to be trapped out, and the companies had quickly moved on to the north and west. The country had never been heavily populated, and what small security the fur trade brought had evaporated years before. The Natives were left to scratch what life they could from a rough no man's land between the prosperous farms of the Red River valley and the booming lumber operations of the Great Lakes basin.

Winter came as a mixed blessing to the surveying and cutting parties. While it brought snowstorms and plunging temperatures, it killed off the constant plague of mosquitoes and blackflies. It also froze the swamps, making travel not just easier but, in several places, possible at all. It was clear to everyone that work on the line between Lake of the Woods and the Red River could never have been accomplished in the summer.

When the swamps froze along the Northwest Angle line, the progress of the work picked up as the men and their supplies—all of which had to be hauled in an endless stream down from the main base— could move across land that just days earlier would have sucked them down to their waists in frigid muck. By the time the cutting was finished, Buffalo Bay had frozen and Anderson chanced the ten-mile walk over its ice to the point where his south line met the 49th Parallel—a point six miles out into the bay from Galwey and Twining's astronomical station on the shore. Again taking their measurements independently, the two parties' fixes had been only twenty-nine feet apart, three feet better than their first try at Pembina. At the intersection of the lines, Anderson took a sounding through a hole cut in the ice and determined that the water was thirty feet deep. That he was willing to walk that far on early season ice to take a largely inconsequential measurement is a sign of just how thorough a job he intended to make of drawing the boundary.

The end of the cutting was an occasion for great excitement among the Natives as they "...ran forward with wild joy, shouting, and enjoying the frequent falls that they met with in rushing thoughtlessly over the ice, till they arrived at the beach-line."[14] Anderson celebrated by raising an "imposing flagstaff" and, presumably, holding some sort of short ceremony. Like the rest of the party, the beauty of the land was not something he wanted to experience any longer than he had to, and he immediately turned his party north.

The men's jubilation was short-lived. Just as they started their march, they hit a snowstorm:

> [It] came up with great fury, and, with a temperature below zero, everyone was compelled to cover his face; and retreat to the sheltered cutting in the woods was almost cut off by the severity of the storm. The true direction in which the men had to travel was only ensured by ranging the men in line, and prolonging the line of travel by looking back on those in [the] rear, who were not allowed to move till the foremost ones were placed in line.[15]

With most of the equipment already on its way back to Pembina, there was not much left to be done at the Northwest Angle, and Anderson headed for Winnipeg immediately, leaving his men to pack up the last of the stores and follow the next day.

Even over a comparatively well-established trail like the Dawson, winter travel was a hazardous business. Anderson and his driver made thirty miles the first day through a foot of snow before stopping for the night at an "emigrants' station" (one of a string of small stopping places maintained along the road). There, their landlord was "a solitary Scotchman" named Robert Scott. He was, according to Anderson, "a man of education, had quite a Library of Standard Books at his bedside, and... was employing his spare time in writing a grammar of the Indian language."[16] While they slept under their heap of blankets and bison robes, the temperature outside plummeted. When they set out at 4:00 AM, the thermometer showed –30° F, and it barely rose at all during the day.

Unable to count on, nor particularly desiring, Cameron's assistance, Anderson—back in Winnipeg two days later—was anxious to
push on to Pembina and prepare the parties for their winter work on
the line between the Red River and Lake of the Woods. Although he
was met by a note from Cameron ordering him to come on to Pembina immediately, he was forced to remain in Winnipeg to begin a
series of calculations that were critical to the accurate demarcation
of the boundary. Along with Cameron's directive, there was a telegraph message from Chicago.

The telegraph line itself had only recently been extended to Winnipeg, courtesy of an American company that had built the line up
from Minnesota. By telegraph, Anderson could synchronize his chronometers with the observatory at Greenwich, a crucial first step in
establishing the exact longitude at Pembina and, by extension, for
any place along the whole length of the boundary line. Chicago had
been selected as the intermediary between Pembina and Greenwich,
since it was the nearest major centre on the telegraph line that could
provide an accurate time signal and for which a precise longitude was
already well established.

Waiting in Chicago was Mr. Lindsay A. Russell, no less than the
deputy surveyor-general of Canada, who had been sent all the way
to Chicago for the sole purpose of transmitting the time-checks. The
arrangements for the time-checks had been made by Cameron before
he left Ottawa but no one seemed to know how long Russell had been
sitting by his key waiting for someone to come back from Lake of the
Woods to Winnipeg. Anderson himself seemed surprised by Russell's
message, and was clearly unaware of Cameron's plan. The chief commissioner may have intended to make the connection with Chicago
soon after his arrival in Pembina, in which case Russell could well
have been waiting since mid-September. One suspects Anderson
only agreed to start the checks that evening (rather than a few days
later from the headquarters at Pembina) out of sympathy for Russell,
whose near-frantic message suggested he was losing patience.

The synchronization would be straightforward enough, but the
distances involved (there were nine hundred miles of telegraph wire

between Chicago and Winnipeg) and the fact that there were some forty substations on the same line were bound to complicate the process. Anderson tells the story with a kind of detached amusement:

> So, at 6 p.m. we began. He had a Chronometer Clock at his end, and I had a Chronometer Clock at my end. Every 10 seconds by his Clock he was to send me a signal and I was to do the same. This strange performance excited the curiosity of the telegraph clerks at the intermediate stations, all of whom were warned not to interfere except at one or two stations where it was necessary to interpose auxiliary instruments to enable us to work thro' the whole distance simultaneously. Strange messages then flew between Fort Garry and Chicago. The young lady operator at St. Cloud [Minnesota] 500 miles away, first interfered and my Assistant with prompt and commendable zeal telegraphed "Miss So & So, please leave your instrument alone." Then one of the unfortunates who was in charge of one of the auxiliary instruments along the line sends to us "My instrument ain't worth a cent." Then comes a message from Chicago Observatory "Please make haste we are perishing with cold here."[17]

Eventually, the job was finished and the two men exchanged some more pleasantries about the weather before arranging to contact each other again in three days' time.

Anderson's morning stage ride to Pembina was uneventful. The eight passengers, including four women, were bundled in at four in the morning and, with stops for breakfast and lunch, found themselves at the Hudson's Bay post by 6:30 in the evening—sixty-five miles in just over twelve hours.

Anderson found the hurriedly erected tents of September gone, replaced by an impressive new headquarters. It had even been given a new name, Dufferin, in honour of Canada's new governor general. The wood-framed, clapboard-covered buildings, designed by commission secretary Arthur Ward, were of sufficient size to keep all the men and livestock through at least two winters and to provide an efficient base of operations when the supply lines began to stretch out across the plains the following spring.

The new post was dominated by the two-storey main building. On the ground floor were offices, a dining room and a kitchen, while large-windowed quarters were provided upstairs for twelve officers. Beside the main building were a barracks and mess for up to eighty rank and file, both military and civilian. Ranged nearby were a cook-house, workshops, three storehouses with 5,000 square feet of floor space, a bakery capable of producing 200 loaves in a single batch, and stabling that would eventually grow to house 180 animals. There were 18 buildings in all. Standing at a discrete distance from the main post was a small cottage, built especially for the Camerons and christened "Emmadale." For Anderson, "the whole establishment [had] quite an imposing appearance... prettily situated on a little plateau immediately overlooking the Red River." By the time construction was finished in mid-November, the post, built mostly with materials and labour brought up from Minnesota, had cost a small fortune. The final bill, as presented by contractor William Davis at the end of the month, was £6,558 12s 8d.

As November gave way to December, Anderson, "most comfortably established" in his new home, finished a long letter to Janet:

> We have very little snow, hardly enough for the sleighs, and they say we shall have a mild winter. The therm. here has only been down to 25 below zero and we are quite sheltered from the wind. With 3 or 4 exceptions, the whole party now numbering 110 are in good health, and personally I never felt better.[18]

·❸·

WINTER WORK
1872–73

---

*At night the trees, under the influence of the
frost, crack with surprising loudness, the effect being like
that of pistol shots heard at a little distance.*

ALBANY FEATHERSTONHAUGH

A S DECEMBER deepened toward the shortest day, work at Dufferin settled into the steady routine of caring for the horses and keeping the fires stoked and the larders full. And those larders, according to the charmingly named Lovelace F. Hewgill, a member of Colonel A.G. Forrest's advance survey party, were anything but austere:

> A canteen was… established with the very best of liquors brought
> direct from England, free of duty, for the use of the staff and men,
> and where everything could be bought at the moderate charge of
> five cents a glass. Many luxuries were to be had, such as Crosse &
> Blackwell's potted meats and pickles, anchovies, etc., etc. Every-
> thing was sold at a price to pay running expenses, and what small

profit was made went to improve our library, etc. Our food was of the very best, and the amount more than could be used, even when we were many miles away from semi-civilization. Such was the good management of our commissariate that a complaint in regard to the provisions was seldom, if ever, heard, and this may in great measure account for the very successful termination of the work, as it is a well known fact that a hard day's work is soon forgotten over a good dinner, and none are so apt to forget it as an Anglo-Saxon.[1]

A not-insubstantial file in the commission's papers challenges Hewgill's assertion that complaints about the food were almost non-existent. In fact Thomas Burgess, the doctor, was delegated several times to approach Cameron with demands from the men, mostly involving the lack of fresh meat in their diet, or the miserly allowances. Still, over the full life of the commission, there was never any sustained feeling that men were not getting enough to eat.

The Red River had been closed to navigation since November 12, and from the beginning of December mail runs between Winnipeg and Pembina had been suspended due to the outbreak of a highly contagious equine influenza that had infected much of the country's horse population.

If the officers and men could not read their letters from home, they could avail themselves of an impressive library. Knowing that the commission would be spending at least two long northern winters holed up in its headquarters, and that summer storms out along the line could easily trap the survey parties in their tents for days at a time, the creation of the library had been ordered during the final planning meetings at the Foreign Office in July 1872:

Featherstonhaugh has been entrusted the selection, purchase and packing of a field library—this should contain, besides books for officers and men, a supply of stationery for general use and such indoor games as may be suitable for camp and winter quarters. Weights of packages should be kept down to 100 pounds so that they may be adapted for carriage on pack animals, in dog sleighs or on men's backs.[2]

Featherstonhaugh's purchases (made through Her Majesty's Stationery Office and various London booksellers) came to well over one hundred volumes. According to his scribbled lists, the books ran the gamut from the serious devotions of seventeenth-century divine Jeremy Taylor's *Holy Living and Dying* and poet John Keble's *The Christian Year* (three copies) to the historical fiction of Charles Lever's *Charles O'Malley: The Irish Dragoon* and James Fenimore Cooper's timeless *Last of the Mohicans*. Joining four volumes of fiction by Benjamin Disraeli were a like number from Charlotte Brontë and a full twelve volumes of Anthony Trollope. Surprisingly, Charles Dickens merited only two titles—*Dombey and Son* and *Barnaby Rudge*—fewer even than the now largely forgotten Charles Reade, whose six-volume contribution to the library included such penny-dreadful titles as *Love Me Little, Love Me Long* and *It is Never Too Late to Mend*.

Non-fiction was well represented by a rich mix of general and military history—including a two-volume edition of Thomas Macaulay's *The History of England,* E.S. Creasy's *The Fifteen Decisive Battles of the World* and William Napier's six-volume history of the Peninsular War—and travel chronicles featuring Francis Galton's *The Art of Travel* and Edward Whymper's *Travel and Adventure in the Territory of Alaska*. A good selection of natural history was marked in particular by Charles Lyell's groundbreaking *Elements of Geology* and Gilbert White's charming *Natural History and Antiquities of Selborne*.

It is clear from Featherstonhaugh's list that he also attempted to acquire titles that would be of direct practical use to the officers and men. Although Viscount Milton and Walter Cheadle's 1865 chronicle *The North-West Passage by Land* might have been of marginal relevance, there can be no questioning his purchase of two copies of John Palliser's seminal report on his travels across western Canada (1857–60), nor of Irvine's account of Wolseley's Red River expedition of 1870 and its companion Journal of Operations and correspondence. Featherstonhaugh may also have attempted to acquire a copy of Sandford Fleming's early feasibility study for a Canadian transcontinental railway.

It is curious that there is no reference in Featherstonhaugh's notes to what was surely one of the most important and relevant contemporary chronicles: William Francis Butler's *The Great Lone Land: A Narrative of Travel and Adventure in the North-West of America.* The explanation may simply be that the volume, published in London in 1872, had not yet made its appearance in the bookstores when Featherstonhaugh was out on his July shopping spree. Nevertheless, comments from at least one member of the commission make it clear that there were copies of the book being read out in the camps along the line in the summer of 1873. In fact, the famous author himself had actually stopped by the commission's Pembina headquarters just a few days after they had been established.

Butler had first come to Red River in 1870 as a self-appointed spy for Colonel Garnet Wolseley during the Red River Rebellion. Reaching the river through the United States and then heading north to Riel's stronghold, he had slipped past the barricades (something Chief Commissioner Cameron had failed to accomplish the previous year) and reached Fort Garry, even managing to conduct a lengthy interview with Riel himself. Escaping to the east via the old fur trade route to Lake of the Woods, Butler had met up with Wolseley and his troops, delivered his report and returned to Fort Garry with them.

Bored by life at the settlement after the collapse of the rebellion, Butler was preparing to return to Europe when he was approached by Manitoba Lieutenant Governor Adams Archibald to undertake another intelligence operation. This time he would be travelling west, taking stock of the situation in the North-West Territories and reporting on the extent of the whiskey trade, the condition of the Native populations and any other matters that might be of interest to Manitoba's fledgling government. His enthusiasm for the chance to see more of the country would not let him wait for the spring and, in mid-October 1870, Butler and a single Metis guide left Fort Garry and embarked on a 4,000-mile trip across western Canada.

They travelled up the North Saskatchewan River to Fort Carleton and Fort Edmonton, reaching as far as Rocky Mountain House before retracing their steps. While one of Butler's recommendations called for the formation of the North West Mounted Police, it was his book that truly secured his reputation. *The Great Lone Land* immediately caught the public fancy both in eastern Canada and in Britain, becoming a best seller. Now he was back at the Red River in search of another adventure. This time he intended to travel alone across the west, over the Continental Divide into British Columbia and then home by way of California and the new American transcontinental railroad. He was to publish an account of this trip in a second volume, *The Wild North Land,* in late 1873.

ANDERSON HAD re-established telegraph contact with Russell in Chicago, and for nearly a week they sent a steady stream of their "strange messages" back and forth. Their "conversations," which involved the near-simultaneous exchange of time-checks and astronomical observations, had to take place at night:

> We set up our observatory close to the little house where the telegraph wires were led, and while one of my brother officers (Galwey) took observations on the stars to find what o'clock it was, we sent our signals to Chicago coinciding with the ticks of our clock. At the same moment our correspondent at Chicago, like a physician at the side of his patient watch in hand, felt our pulsations and counted the beats.[3]

What Anderson, Galwey and Russell were up to was establishing the exact longitude at the Pembina astronomical station. In order to determine the longitude of any point on Earth, four things are needed. The first is a fixed point where the exact, universally accepted time is known. Since the mid-eighteenth century, that point, for British mariners and soldiers, had been at the Royal Observatory in Greenwich, England (in 1885 it became accepted as a global standard). The time kept there is known as Greenwich Mean Time (GMT) and the north–south line of longitude that passes through the observatory (and continues around the globe) is called the Prime Meridian. Longitude at the Prime Meridian is expressed as 0 degrees, 0 minutes, 0 seconds (0° 0′ 0″).

The second requirement is for a timepiece—a specialized, super-accurate watch called a chronometer—that is perfectly synchronized with GMT, but located at the point for which the longitude is to be determined. Ensuring that the chronometers were exactly set to GMT was the purpose of the series of coordinated telegraph signals. The third requirement is a specialized almanac that records the precise time any of a number of stars will cross the Prime Meridian on their nightly circle of the heavens. And the fourth requirement is an instrument—such as a sextant or octant—for determining the "local" time (the time, according to the sun, where the observation is being made).

An observer at the unknown point would, through a series of careful observations, determine the local time at which a certain star crossed his local "meridian" (the north–south line running through where he is standing) on any given date. He would then compare it with the time given in the almanac for that star's crossing of the Prime Meridian on the same date. The difference in time between the two events would give the observer his longitude, expressed in degrees, minutes and seconds east or west of Greenwich, each hour of difference in time equalling 15° of longitude. To correct for errors, the observations will be repeated a number of times, and the final figure will usually be an average of all the observations.

A week of observations and exchanges gave Anderson and Galwey their answer. The astronomical station at Dufferin was 97° 13′ 51.5″ west of Greenwich. Based on the quality of their instruments and the tiny delaying effect of the telegraph line, they were confident that their fix was correct to within two seconds of arc—about 130 feet. In terms of east–west measurement, that was more than accurate enough to serve as the standard for all the observations they would subsequently take.

Before leaving England the previous August, the commission's chronometers—some eighteen in all—would have been carefully set to Greenwich time, and the morning winding of the clocks was a critical ritual, to be performed without fail, since letting them run down would compromise their accuracy. Even as Galwey lay wracked by seasickness during the Atlantic crossing, he had regularly hauled himself out of his berth just long enough to wind his charges. When Galwey finally collapsed, the task was passed to Featherstonhaugh, though he was almost as sick, and he wound them one by one from his bunk as they were carefully handed in to him by a steward. In the end, Anderson himself inherited the task, not willing to delegate it to anyone but a senior officer. To ensure the best possible accuracy before the surveying began in earnest, however, they had to be rechecked against Greenwich time—hence the long series of telegraph exchanges.

Before abandoning the field for the relative comforts of Detroit, the Americans had agreed that the British should continue work on the line between Lake of the Woods and Red River. The Americans would be billed for the cost of the work over what should have been "their" sections (the two commissions had agreed to split the work into twenty-mile segments, which would be done alternately by each party), and they had reserved the right to check the accuracy of the survey when they returned in the spring. To that end, Featherstonhaugh and his party had been out in the field continuously since late October.

The country along the line between the Red River and Lake of the Woods is marked by three significant physical features: the ridge of the Red River valley, the Roseau River and more than fifty miles of trackless swamp. From the banks of the Red to the valley ridge, the land rises only 170 feet in sixteen miles. East from the ridge, it is almost table-top flat, gaining no more than a foot for every one of the eighty miles to Lake of the Woods, and thus forming a platform on which water mostly pools rather than drains. Hundreds of small, nameless streams run into this great swamp from every direction, but only one significant river drains it. The Roseau River crosses the swamp from east to west in a shallow, sluggish arc before swinging northwest across the boundary to run into the Red thirteen miles downstream from Pembina.

Featherstonhaugh's party had headed east toward Lake Roseau. This lake—in effect no more than a three-mile-long widening of the river about sixty miles east of Pembina—was to be the site of one of two astronomical stations—places whose exact latitude and longitude had been established by astronomical observation—that would be required between Buffalo Point and the Red.

They ran into trouble almost immediately. Tired of digging their wagons out of the muck into which they were constantly sinking to the axles, Featherstonhaugh abandoned the line and, with the help of a local scout, led his men southwest for nearly twenty-five miles before turning back up toward the lake. Through it all, he was constantly reminded of the value of oxen:

> Considerable advantage was derived in getting through the soft parts of the journey from the presence of a pair of oxen amongst the teams. These animals, though apt to be looked upon as encumbrances when they are in the company of horses because they travel slowly, and can only do 15 miles a day, will take a load through bogs in which the latter are quite helpless.[4]

Lake Roseau had been chosen not only because the maps showed it to be on the boundary, but also because there was supposed to be some firm ground around its margin. In the end, neither supposition proved accurate. Not only was the lake a good six miles south of the line, it was surrounded completely by wide beds of thick reeds. (This should not have come as a surprise. In French, *roseau* means "reed.") Pushing northwest, the party finally found some solid ground in the form of a gravel ridge on the banks of the Pine River, a small watercourse that flowed south into the lake. On October 27, the instruments were set up and what would be four days of observations for latitude were begun.

It was immediately clear to everyone in the party that rather than fearing the onset of cold weather, they should have been praying fervently for its arrival. As long as the ground remained unfrozen there was no way the work of cutting tangent lines could be accomplished without endangering the health of the entire company:

These muskegs are four or five feet deep in many places; they have on the surface a skin of sod which scarcely supports the weight of a man, and when it is pierced, the muddy water rises in the hole nearly to the top. A person breaking through goes down to his middle, and has some trouble in getting out again. This, with the thermometer at zero, or but a little above it, could not fail to be a serious thing...[5]

Featherstonhaugh's estimate of the depth of the muskeg was conservative. Twining wrote elsewhere that a series of probes with a sounding pole had regularly recorded depths of up to fourteen feet before striking the hard clay pan.

Even long after the temperatures had plunged, work in the swamps remained dangerous. An early snow had pressed down the heavy grasses, effectively insulating the watery ground below and preventing it from freezing. To avoid the open ground, Featherstonhaugh put off drawing his tangent lines east toward Lake of the Woods and concentrated his efforts in the sheltering timber to the west.

After four-and-a-half miles of slashing brush and felling trees, the party emerged from the timber and out onto the open ground of the great Roseau swamp. By then, the thermometer had stuck at −20° F or lower and the cold had penetrated the ground deeply enough to make for safe, relatively easy work on the surface. But every advantage had a corresponding disadvantage. In the woods, the work was hard, but the trees provided shelter. Out in the swamp, the work was easier but there was no protection from the wind and, at those extreme temperatures, the slightest breeze would cut through the men's winter gear as if it were nothing more than a light shirt.

From his fireside at the main house in Dufferin, Anderson had been watching the temperatures fall. He had not seen or heard much from Featherstonhaugh since the beginning of October. He wrote, "I began to feel a little anxious for the working parties who were still in the field and who bravely held their ground. I accordingly decided to visit them all at their work and ascertain whether there was any imperative necessity for recalling them into winter quarters for a time and suspending outdoor operations."[6]

His concerns were not simply for Featherstonhaugh's party. There was, in fact, a great deal of activity all along the line. In addition to the astronomical business of fixing 49° North and drawing the tangents, the boundary commissions were also committed to producing detailed topographical surveys of the land, showing its contours and water features, extending between three and six miles to the north and south of the line all the way from Lake of the Woods to the Rocky Mountains. The British agreement to do the Americans' share of the winter work did not include the topographical survey south of the 49th Parallel, but there were still three topographical survey parties working along the Canadian side of the line.

The topographical work was far more important to Canada than it was to Britain and, accordingly, two of the three "standing" survey parties were under the direction of Canadian surveyors. The tangent lines east from Pointe d'Orme were being run by a thirty-year-old surveyor from Kingston, Ontario, named Alexander Lord Russell. A.L. Russell already had substantial experience in the west. Like Cameron, he had been caught up in the Red River Rebellion and subsequently found work as an assistant leveller on the railway surveys west of the Great Lakes. He had not arrived at Pembina with the rest of the appointees. By the time the chief commissioners met on the banks of the Red River, Russell had already made his way overland from Lake Superior and spent more than two weeks examining the land around Lake of the Woods in anticipation of the difficult work to come there.

A second party, under Colonel A.G. Forrest, a seasoned surveyor with a militia commission and command experience, had been pushing west from the astronomical station at Buffalo Point. Drawing their supplies from the stores left for them at the Northwest Angle, Forrest and his men had been out of touch for the longest time. The third survey party, led by Royal Engineers Sergeant R.E. Kay, was probably working alongside Featherstonhaugh, but no one at Dufferin could be sure.

The topographical survey would give Canada its first detailed and reliable picture of the nature of the lands along its southern border. Previous expeditions had provided broad, general outlines or, in more than one case, simple speculation based on very little direct evidence. With their transits and chains, compasses, measuring tapes and levels, the topographic parties would draw detailed maps of the size and course of creeks and rivers, the heights and contours of the hills and the steepness of the valley walls. They were also to keep detailed meteorological records and, in conjunction with the commission's naturalist, to note the general form of the flora and fauna and take special notice of any particular geological formations.

On the morning of December 19, with the temperature hovering at −32° F, Anderson and Chief Commissary Lawrence Herchmer, together with three sled-runner wagons and their drivers, six horses, an axeman and Anderson's servant, set out for Pointe d'Orme. They reached Galwey (back on the line after his break in Dufferin) and his party at noon on their second day out, but not before they had spent a decidedly strange night in the frozen muskeg. Anderson related the story to his sister:

> I must have dozed a little for on opening my eyes...I saw a restless figure standing at the fire, without cap or great coat, shivering and muttering "Its cold, so cold, those poor animals will be froze this night." I mixed all this up in my dream at first, and pictured the horses and this melancholy creature frozen stiff and solid where they stood. As the muttering continued I awoke and sat up, and asked the man whom I recognized as one of the drivers why he did not roll himself in his blankets and go to sleep, instead of standing there without a great coat and shivering. The melancholy man, who I have since discovered is very odd and eccentric said he could not get warm and could not sleep. So I got up and insisted on his rolling himself in my warm buffalo robes. This awoke my companion who also got up, so we piled all his buffalo robes over the melancholy man... I lit a match to read the thermometer, which stood at 43 below zero, and at the same time that I blistered one finger by touching the metal of the thermometer case... another blister was caused by inadvertently letting the match burn down

into my fingers. The sensation of burning from the cold metal and the burning match, and the blister that resulted was the same in both cases. The difference of temperature represented by these little incidents would have been interesting to note.[7]

Although it was not yet midnight, with the all the commotion and impromptu science experiments the camp was generally awake, and Anderson, after checking the horses—"all well clad with two blankets and a buffalo robe"—decided that they might as well take advantage of the brilliant moonlight and push on. It was at this point that the "melancholy man" made his reappearance: "... nearly stifled by the abundance of buffalo robes piled over him, and like a seal having dived is obliged to come to the surface to breathe, thrust his head out of bed... for a similar purpose and cheerfully volunteered the information that he was quite warm."[8]

With the horses pulling their heavy loads at a stately three miles per hour across the open marshes, the party arrived at Pointe d'Orme at noon to find everyone in good spirits and reasonably good health. Anderson, in consultation with Galwey (though not with Featherstonhaugh, who was still seven miles further east), quickly determined that there seemed no reason to take the parties back to Dufferin. Turning to Herchmer, they hatched a plan to ensure that the survey and tangent work would not be interrupted. Log cabins would be constructed at Pointe d'Orme and at Pine River (with stables added at Pointe d'Orme), each of which would be kept supplied with two months' provisions and under the care of a watchman. According to Anderson's calculations, the plan would mean that at no time would any working party be more than 20 miles away from one of the depots, and the teams bringing the supplies out from Dufferin could easily carry back any sick or injured men.

Anderson's planning was beginning to rely heavily on the crucially important organizational skills of the chief commissary, and in this he would never be disappointed. Thirty-two-year-old Lawrence Herchmer was a prosperous, well-connected farmer from Kingston, Ontario. While he had been born in England, he was descended from Hessian mercenaries who had first come to North America in the mid-eighteenth century to fight for Britain against the French. He was educated first in Britain and then at Toronto's Trinity College. He returned to Britain to attend the Royal Military Academy at Woolwich and, at the age of only 17, took an ensign's commission in the 46th Regiment of Foot, seeing service in India and Ireland. On the death of his father in 1862 Herchmer sold his commission and returned to Kingston to run the family farm, marrying in 1866. Contemporary photographs show a tall, barrel-chested man in a broad-brimmed hat, clearly used to being in charge and exuding a confidence that perhaps bordered on arrogance. Following his appointment to the boundary commission, his wife, Mary, no shrinking violet herself, joined him at Dufferin and provided invaluable service as companion and helpmate to the easily overwhelmed Emma Cameron.

The next morning Anderson walked the seven miles to see Featherstonhaugh:

> All his party looked hardened and weather beaten. The men were clothed in skin suits, but Captain F. and his two companions (two Canadian assistants) [probably William King and William Ashe] were in rags and all wanted their hair cut. Two of his horses had died probably from hard work and exposure, and I found one horse very weak and unable to work... Capt. F. was in wonderfully good spirits and as he had already arranged to shift his camp the next day to the same place where I was encamped he walked back with me in the course of the afternoon and slept in my tent that night.[9]

Featherstonhaugh, though he had no previous experience of working under such extreme conditions, was clearly enjoying himself. He had been out on the line for nearly three months but obviously had no intention of seeking the comforts of Dufferin. A word from him and Anderson would almost certainly have ordered the parties in—at least until the new depots could be built and stocked and the spell of extreme cold had broken—but he was determined to finish his work. Featherstonhaugh was considered curt and rather humourless by some of his colleagues, but his reports reflect a man who, while strongly focussed on the work at hand, was nevertheless acutely aware of the new world that surrounded him. In mid-October a display of the northern lights above Lake Roseau moved him beyond the purely scientific:

> ... besides the usual bows and streamers, an arch of light about two degrees wide was formed passing through the zenith from east to west. A constant wave or pulsation of luminosity advanced from the eastern end of this arch and travelled slowly by successive impulses along it. The effect lasted about three quarters of an hour, and although there was a very bright moon, the aurora quite held its own in brilliance.[10]

Featherstonhaugh, like Anderson, had his own connections to the Canadian-American boundary. His father, George William Featherstonhaugh, and elder half-brother, James, had both taken leading roles in the surveying of the boundary between the state of Maine and Britain's maritime colonies in 1839.

His mother was a Virginian, but Featherstonhaugh himself had not visited her homeland until he made a brief and risky visit in 1864, during the Civil War. when he ran the Union blockade into the Confederate capital of Richmond. His observations, "Notes on the Defences of Petersburg," were published in the Royal Engineers' 1865 yearbook.

With Featherstonhaugh's camp relocated, Anderson and Herchmer returned to Dufferin, arriving early on the morning of Christmas Eve. Over their last few days on the line, and throughout the trip back to base, the weather had continued to deteriorate. Not only did the temperature continue to fall (the mercury finally bottomed out at −51° F on the night of the December 23), but the wind picked up and continued to blow in their faces as they pushed west toward Dufferin. If Featherstonhaugh had any regrets about deciding to stay in camp, he had not shown them. While Anderson was helping him shift his equipment to a new base of operations, "...he found the cold so piercing that he ran on ahead of every one else and I believe he never stopped till he reached his destination for the night, for when the main body reached there at 4 p.m. we found him comfortably established by a fire."[11]

Before he left for his tour of the camps, Anderson had tried to contact Forrest's survey party, then believed to be about 60 miles away and working west from Lake of the Woods. He had hired two Native men to carry a letter to the party. Equipped with fifteen days' worth of provisions (which they carried on their backs, along with their blankets), they were told simply to travel east in as straight a line as possible until they bumped into Forrest. And bump into him they did. It was an example of Anderson learning from his ambivalent experiences with Native cutting crews and deciding to use their natural skills in the most effective manner instead. Anderson had been back in Dufferin for several days when the tired and hungry couriers returned, carrying with them a letter from Forrest. Things were fine, he assured Anderson, and the work was progressing well. Nevertheless, Anderson decided he would pay the party a visit early in the New Year.

Despite the still-freezing temperatures, Christmas Day was, according to Anderson, "sufficiently festive." So the survey parties in the field could share in the joys of the season, Anderson had left some presents with Featherstonhaugh: "I left him with two turkeys, a supply of currants and raisins and suet to make a plum pudding for the whole party and some other luxuries. I believe they cooked the turkeys in pieces, but the plum pudding with rum sauce was a great success."[12]

The principal social event of the day was Anderson's first visit to Fort Pembina. It is hard to imagine that in the three months he had been at Pembina he had yet to make the five-mile trip to the American headquarters. Fort Pembina was still new, dedicated only in 1870, but it had a more permanent look to it than Dufferin. With its one- and two-storey white stucco buildings closely ranged around a central parade ground, it was a typical layout for a western U.S. fort of the period. The outward-facing walls of the barracks and stables con-stituted the fort's defensive perimeter (the familiar high wooden pali-sades, with their great swinging gates so often seen in western movie forts, were mostly a fantasy of the moviemakers themselves.)

Anderson's reaction to the fort was one of slightly condescending amusement. Noting that the parade ground was dominated by "... a prodigious flagstaff with the stars and stripes blowing themselves to ribbons at the mast head" he wondered, in mock concern, about what the Americans must think about the fact that no one at Dufferin had yet had the time to erect a flagpole. Slightly later photographs of the two establishments show both that the American flag was indeed a very large one, and that Dufferin still lacked one at all.

Christmas afternoon was given over to social niceties:

> We first paid a visit to the commanding officer and his wife, the only lady in the place. They received us most kindly and they made us take some refreshments in the American fashion. After this we had to visit each of the American officers in turn for they all live in different houses and the same programme had to be carried out at each house. This after the fifth visit was rather a bore, but they were all so hearty and really glad to see us that it was necessary to put up with it once in a while.[13]

Anderson's attitude toward the Americans seems a mix of admi-ration and pecksniffishness. His letters from the Pacific boundary survey of a decade before made little effort to conceal his disdain for their means and manners, while reserving a special venom for their accents and coarse speech. While his letters were obviously intended to be entertaining for their reader, the Anderson writing from Pem-bina is clearly a more mature, balanced and self-confident figure. That change of attitude may have been because the roles of the two commissions had reversed since the Pacific survey. Along the west-ern line, it was the Americans who had been better prepared and led the way into the field. The British were playing catch-up for nearly the entire course of the enterprise and ended up having to spend one more season on the line than their counterparts. This time, with the

British clearly the lead team, Anderson may have been tempering his criticism with an understanding of the frustrations being felt by the underfunded and undermanned American parties.

Although he exhibited a personal affection for many of the men— Campbell and Twining in particular—Anderson could not change his attitude on the American approach to social and military graces. His annoyance at having to visit each officer at Fort Pembina in turn, rather than meeting them all together in an organized military mess, was particularly revealing. When Anderson was out on the frontier, he was happily prepared to forego most of the traditional military pomp and circumstance. But if someone was determined to put on a show, he expected them at least to know how to do it properly!

New Year's Eve was marked by a soiree in the mess at Dufferin. At the charge of a pound or two from each of the senior officers to cover expenses, about thirty commission men and the same number of locals (including three women) enjoyed an evening of dancing and singing, including the accompaniment of two fiddlers. While Anderson thought the evening a success, Galwey took pains to note that nearly all of the local men managed to get drunk and, as a result, any thoughts of such events being repeated were abandoned.

Anderson's new, more even-handed attitude toward the Americans must have been severely tested by the news that Galwey brought back from the boundary line early in the New Year. Surveying and cutting west from Pointe d'Orme, he had connected with the tangent lines drawn by Lieutenant Greene the previous fall. According to Galwey's calculations, those tangents were more than fifty feet out. It was a mistake too significant to be ignored or glossed over.

Anderson reported the error to Cameron who, in turn, passed the information along to Campbell. One can imagine the mixture of annoyance and satisfaction with which Cameron might have greeted the news. As early as the first week in November he had been writing to London about problems with the American work on the line:

> Official decision with reference to the exact location of the Boundary here [at Pembina] was delayed when we started for Lake of the Woods because the astronomers had not then had sufficient time

to work out the calculations founded on their numerous observations. When we returned from the Lake Mr. Campbell's leavetaking was too hurried and unexpected as to preclude a possibility then of settling the point. Again eastward from here, one of the U.S. surveyors has committed errors in his work which necessitates a reference to Mr. Campbell before I can act on the authority he has given me to cut the line at our joint expense.[14]

Since Cameron's letter to London is dated December 21, concerns about the accuracy of Greene's work may have been in the air before Galwey's calculations showed the actual magnitude of the error. Cameron was happy to lay the problem at Campbell's door, suggesting that if the Americans had been in less of a hurry to leave, the consequences of basing tangents on unfinished calculations at Pembina would have been avoided. Clearly, though, the problem lay with what had been Greene's first major fieldwork assignment. The location of 49° North at Pembina may not have been officially agreed to by both commissioners, but it was certainly known with sufficient accuracy for Greene to have got closer than fifty feet.

For Anderson, the problem was one of time. He knew that his parties in the field could finish the work on the boundary from Lake of the Woods to Pembina—including the six-mile topographical survey—before spring, but only if the Americans agreed, in absentia, to accept the British corrections to Greene's tangents. Leaving the matter in Cameron's hands, Anderson set off to see Forrest, presumably still working the line west from Lake of the Woods.

With a pair of single-horse sledges, his servant and the teamsters, Anderson went first to Featherstonhaugh's camp, which by then was reachable in less than twelve hours of steady travel. It was another four days to the depot at Pine River where Anderson had his first contact with Forrest's survey party. Two men and a dogsled struggled into the camp just after Anderson's arrival. They had been sent out by Forrest to try to locate any other party that might have been working along the line. These men had no idea of the existence of the newly built depot, which they had been directed to by a party of

Natives who lived at Roseau Lake. They were already out of provisions and, without the guidance of the Natives, would certainly have ended up travelling at least as far as the station at Point d'Orme, if not all the way to Pembina. In another coincidence, the men at the depot had sent out a shipment of supplies for Forrest's party just that morning, but not being sure of the surveyors' location there was no guarantee they would even find them. Anderson determined to take the two men, the dogsled and his servant to meet with Forrest and see for himself how the work was progressing. He would also be able to inform Forrest of the existence of the depot and have him watch out for the supply wagons which were then headed his way. Since this was all something that the returning sled drivers could easily have done themselves, it is likely that Anderson just could not resist the lure of travelling across country by dog team, though as a good senior officer he would also have wanted those under his command to see him in person and know he was concerned for their welfare.

They left the next day on what had been estimated by the dog-sled drivers to be a trip of twenty-six miles. They packed very little—a four-day supply of food, some frozen pike for the dogs, sleeping robes and cooking utensils—and the three dogs amazed Anderson by pulling what he estimated to be a 250-pound load at a steady clip:

> ... and so the procession was formed; the leading man, the three dogs one behind the other, the sled, the driver, my servant and self last of all. The leading man started off at a good 4 miles an hour and every now and then I had to run to keep up... The pace at which these dogs travel is very trying for a man, as it is very irregular, and most of the time the dogs are running, sometimes they break into a canter, but never go at a walk. The leading man, as I learned afterwards was a wonderful walker and was selected to go on this trip on account of his extraordinary powers. He was said on one occasion to have walked two Indians to death, but I shall require to be furnished with the full particulars of this wondrous tragedy before I ask you to believe the story.[15]

The party went down Pine River to Lake Roseau and across it
to the woodlands at the eastern end. Once in the woods, crashing
through the brush and the deadfall, Anderson was amazed by the
way the dogs "... crawled along dragging their load in and out up
and down and occasionally becoming fixed in the fork of a tree from
which they had to be extricated by hand." From the woods, they followed a stream bed across yet another of the numberless swamps and,
finally, at about five o'clock in the afternoon, they crossed a snowshoe
track coming from the north. After three hours of following the track,
they found themselves standing at the clear-cut line of the boundary.
Forrest's party was just a little east along the cut, their camp sheltered from the wind in a stand of trees. It was 9:30 in the evening of
the same day they had left the Pine River depot and Anderson reckoned they had made about 27 miles, not including the meanders of
the stream bed they had followed for more than two hours.

Forrest's party had a huge fire going and were about to start eating the last of their supplies—a large kettle of pea soup. Anderson
contributed a little beefsteak, some salt and some sugar from his
own provisions. Although the survey party had been working for
the Boundary Commission since September, this was the first time
Anderson and Forrest had set eyes on each other.

The surveying party had been assembled in Ottawa during Cameron's organizational visit the previous summer. With Forrest in command, the men had left Ottawa in mid-August and travelled to the
Northwest Angle via the Dawson Route from Lake Superior. Once
there, they had done some preliminary work around the controversial
northwesternmost point and then, before Anderson arrived with the
astronomical parties, departed down the lake to Buffalo Point, where
they had begun a preliminary topographical survey. The first members of either commission they met were probably Galwey and Twining when they arrived at Buffalo Point. The party had been drawing
their provisions from the station at the Northwest Angle while they
continued to cut their line west toward the Red River, but that depot
was now too far away and, with their stores almost exhausted, they
had finally reached out to the west in the hope of finding some other
party working along the boundary.

First thing in the morning, Forrest sent his men out in a wide arc to make sure the supply wagons from Pine River did not pass them, and Anderson made ready to return to Dufferin. He was on his way before noon, intending to take a relaxed two days to reach the depot at Pine River.

The weather had been comparatively mild and they set off in high spirits, but within only an hour or so winter returned with a vengeance that Anderson had never before experienced. The temperature dropped quickly to −20° F and winds of unbelievable fury made continued travel impossible: they simply could not see where they were going. They found a small island of poplars and, making camp under the roots of an old tree that had been brought down by the gale, gathered what firewood they could and settled in to wait out the storm. But as Anderson later recorded, rather than abating, the storm only gained in strength and, as the night came on, the blinding snow drifted over their camp and, near the fire, it melted and soaked into their clothes and bedding:

> The night was painfully long, and when we had slept as much as we could it was only 11, and so we counted the wearisome hours till 5, when we all went to sleep again and did not wake till dawn... The storm was as bad as ever, but we were obliged to go on and to travel considerably south of our proper course to keep our faces from the storm. The worst part of the day's journey and which we all dreaded was crossing the lake [Roseau] where there was no escape from the fury of the storm. In many places the ice was swept perfectly clean, and many a tumble we got running over the black ice and being overbalanced by the wind. The poor dogs suffered greatly, for the wind and drifting snow stung their eyes and ears.[16]

With what few provisions they had packed either eaten or shared with Forrest's party, they were saved by the sight of a small Native settlement at the south end of the lake. The inhabitants treated them with great care and kindness, even sharing some of their limited food supplies. (Every member of the commissions who had encountered the Native populations in the area had commented on how little they had to eat.) Purely by chance, they were met at the settlement by one of their own supply parties, which had been heading for the Pine River depot and had also been caught in the storm. Anderson found it wonderfully strange to be handed a package of letters from home that someone at Dufferin had forwarded for him to read at the depot. Although loath to leave the comfort of the fire, the storm had abated a little and they all pushed on toward Pine River, about eight miles to the north.

The storm had hit every point along the boundary line, although each party had seen it coming in sufficient time to take shelter. One sleigh wagon with two men aboard, however, had been caught in the open just east of Dufferin and had been stopped in its tracks. The men had no choice but to turn their horses loose, wrap themselves in their robes and curl up in the bottom of the wagon box. They were there for two days. The horses managed to find their way back to Dufferin, where their appearance caused a rescue party to be sent out in search of the men. They eventually made it back to the post unharmed.

Many others were not so lucky. The storm, which raged over a broad area of the country for those three days in early January, has become part of Minnesota folklore. At least eighty people lost their lives, mostly from the effects of prolonged exposure to the terrible winds. The death toll included a great many children who got lost in the storm as they made their way home from school, and even an entire coachload of passengers together with their horses. It was also fortunate that the time-checks with Chicago had already been completed, for according to Anderson, the storm "... swept down hundreds of miles of posts and wires, and destroyed telegraphic communication for two months as effectually as if it had been done by the scouts of an invading army."[17]

As January ended, Anderson and Cameron took stock of what had been accomplished and what remained to be done. The accomplishments, forwarded in a letter to British minister Sir Edward Thornton in Washington, made for an impressive list. Five astronomical stations had been established—at Pembina, Pointe d'Orme, Pine River,

Buffalo Point and the Northwest Angle—and all observations and calculations at those points had been completed. The cutting and temporary marking of the line across the Northwest Angle had been finished (in the faint hope that reason would eventually prevail, the British Commission was still not referring to the line as a "boundary"). All of the tangents and the tracing of eighty-six miles of sight lines along which the boundary would eventually run had been completed from Lake of the Woods to Pembina, and the six-mile-wide topographical survey along the north side of the boundary line was half completed. Thornton was also told that the thirty-foot-wide clear-cut along the entire line of the boundary would be finished before the end of March, as would the balance of the topographical survey.

What is clear from the list is that the British Commission had decided, without waiting for agreement from the Americans, to resurvey Greene's tangents and complete work on the boundary from the Roseau River to Pembina. It was a decision driven by their winter experience. The stretch from Pembina to Roseau was mostly across open ground. While that would keep cutting and clearing to a minimum, it also meant that when the spring thaw finally came the ground would melt back to impassable swamp and the job would have to be left until another winter had set in. As Anderson bluntly put it in an early March letter to his mother: "If the Americans won't let us mark the Boundary this winter (and it can only be done in the winter) they must come and do it themselves next winter."[18]

The decision to finish with the boundary east of Pembina before spring put enormous pressure on Anderson. Despite his hope that the epidemic of equine influenza was on the wane, it finally infected the horse herd at Dufferin and nearly brought work on the line to a halt. He was forced to hire additional oxen and wagons from Winnipeg, further inflating what was already a huge bill. In mid-January Anderson had pegged expenses to that point at £25,000, and fully expected them to reach £30,000 by spring. In order to ensure that the cutting would not be delayed, Anderson had also been hiring additional axemen and teamsters. By the end of January, the British Commission numbered 138 men.

All this was being accomplished without the assistance of Cameron. Writing to his mother in mid-January, Anderson's attitude toward the chief commissioner showed a much more openly peeved tone than he had previously adopted:

> Capt. Cameron takes no charge of the work, in fact I don't know what he does except nurse his baby, but his unfortunate habit of finding fault without meaning it and making himself very disagreeable to everybody is a serious misfortune to the Commission. The progress of the work I am happy to say is not in the least impeded, as he expects that all the arrangements will be made without consulting him, but he reserves to himself the right of picking holes in everything. I don't take any notice, in fact I don't believe he thinks that one would, for he speaks without thinking and possibly forgets what he has said. [19]

In February, as the days lengthened and the temperatures moderated (at least somewhat; the thermometers would still be registering the occasional overnight –40° F as late as March 1), Anderson mounted his last great assault on the boundary. Three more parties, totalling 45 additional men, were put into the field to reinforce Featherstonhaugh, Galwey and the topographical parties, and a third supply depot was built between Pine River and Lake of the Woods. With the horses confined to their stables by the influenza, oxen would haul the supply wagons, adding the considerable trouble of feeding and watering them to Anderson's existing logistical burden. When the horses were working, they lived on oats, which the commission had stockpiled in prodigious quantities. But oxen required hay, and that was a commodity in very short supply around Dufferin. Hauling it out to the line camps was another problem (oats made for a more efficient load) and, although there was water everywhere underfoot, it was frozen solid, and thawing enough for the animals to drink was a major undertaking. Still, without the oxen the pace of the work on the line could not have been sustained. Even with the new personnel, it was a race against the thaw, and Anderson prayed that the previous fall's predictions of an easy winter and an early spring would continue to be wrong.

Anderson followed the new parties into the field in early February ("to see them all properly started," he said), but this time he did not join a supply train. He had so enjoyed his previous adventure with the dog team (blizzard notwithstanding), he decided to use them again to make his tour of inspection. With boundless self-confidence and not a little excitement, Anderson decided that the party would comprise only himself, his servant, one Native driver and four dogs. Mindful of the lessons of the blizzard, but determined to make the most of the limited load that the dogs could pull, he made sure the party would be travelling with more than the too-scant stores of his previous trip. Their provisions included three buffalo robes and six blankets, a small sheet-iron stove, a single three-man tent (which all would share), forty pounds of frozen bread, the same of beefsteak, sugar and tea, a small mess kit and, finally, more than fifty pounds of meat for the dogs. Altogether, the load would weigh less than three hundred pounds, which was comparatively easy for a four-dog team.

Anderson's confident and experienced preparations speak volumes for the attitude of the British Commission to the particular world in which it was working. From the moment they arrived at Pembina, the men of the Royal Engineers had immediately put to rest any question about their ability—or willingness—to adapt their military training to the local environment. With the possible exception of the Christmas visit to Fort Pembina and a few other social occasions in Winnipeg, there had been barely a sign of a red serge jacket or mirror-bright buttons. While every non-commissioned officer and sapper had been ordered to pack "the regimental clothing which he had in wear at the time, except his busby and knapsack," the balance of the men's clothing for the field had been drawn primarily from the stores of the Hudson's Bay Company and other suppliers in Winnipeg. Every man was issued with a "[seal] skin jacket & trowsers" and a pair of skin mittens, pairs of woollen mittens (to be worn inside the skins), a Hudson's Bay pattern hooded great coat, a buffalo robe and three pairs of Hudson's Bay blankets. They also spent most of their time out on the line wearing locally produced moccasins rather than the regulation knee- and ankle-boots they had brought from England. The Native footwear would only last a fortnight, but replacements were always stocked at the outlying depots. When other articles of clothing wore out, they were replaced locally and fitted by the Engineers' tailors.

From just after Christmas, as the snow began to build up in the bush, the men also took to wearing snowshoes. Anderson quickly adopted them without reservation from his first dogsled trip on, and while Featherstonhaugh found them useful, too, he was more guarded in his appraisal:

> ... the men soon [learned] how to walk in them; indeed there is little difficulty in doing so. It is a mistake, however, to suppose that these contrivances enable a man to travel over snow as easily as he would over grass. In some cases where a track is partially beaten, or in the spring of the year when there is a crust on the surface, very quick walking can be accomplished by their aid, but under ordinary circumstances, all that a snow shoe does is enable a man to progress slowly where, without them, he would not get on at all.[20]

While the snowshoes were prone to break in heavy deadfall, two pairs were sufficient to last most of the men through the deep winter months of 1873.

Dogsleds also came into general use among the survey and cutting parties along the line. After the permanent depots were constructed, the dogs provided the primary communication link between the outlying camps and the depots, and were able to ferry up to four hundred pounds of supplies through areas where horses and oxen simply could not go. They also required much less food, water and shelter than the other animals. While the Engineers more or less accepted that the dogs were working animals rather than pets, some were still troubled by what they saw as the unnecessary cruelty of the local handlers who, they thought, were much too liberal in the use of the whip.

While prepared, without question, to "go native" where such issues as transportation and clothing were concerned, few of the British liked the local foods. They expected, and received, their rations of beef and, more often, salt pork, but they ate little fish and simply would not touch pemmican—the high-energy, long-lasting mash of dried meat, animal fat and berries that was a staple of exploration parties, particularly in the north, where it formed a useful backup when fresh game could not be found. Pemmican was, however, kept in good supply at the depots. Anderson's "fifty pounds of meat for the dogs" was almost certainly bison pemmican, fed at a ration of one pound per day. The field parties would certainly have enjoyed a roast of venison, but there were few deer or moose to be found anywhere along the line, and no one reported seeing, let alone shooting, either animal.

As Anderson and his teams worked to finish marking the line east from Red River, other members of the commission seemed to be working to ensure that relations between the British and their absent American counterparts would become thoroughly sour. In mid-February, Herchmer and W.G. Boswell, the veterinarian, had travelled to St. Paul, Minnesota, on commission business and found themselves cornered by a reporter for a local newspaper. The reporter wanted to know what they thought about working hard on the line all winter while the American commission lounged in the comparative comfort of Detroit. The resulting article, which appeared in the *St. Paul Pioneer Press* on February 22, quoted Herchmer (and, by implication, Boswell) as being furious that the Americans were not pulling their weight, viewing them as slackers while the British did their work for them.

Reaction to the piece was immediate and far-reaching. Sir Edward Thornton wrote from Washington to warn Cameron of the impending storm. Someone had clipped the article and sent it to Secretary of State Fish, who had forwarded a copy to Archibald Campbell, demanding to know what was going on. Despite Thornton's attempt to understate the possibility of there being much long-term damage (he found American newspapers thoroughly contemptible), he clearly expected Cameron to accept full responsibility for the incident and do whatever it took to keep it from getting out of hand. An obviously embarrassed and blindsided Cameron immediately demanded a written explanation from Herchmer. The commissary seemed as surprised as everyone else by the contents of the article. While he admitted to talking with the reporter, he vigorously denied saying anything at all about the American withdrawal. Indeed, he insisted, he held no opinion on the subject.

When Campbell's letter to Cameron arrived, it was terse and to the point. The reason the Americans had withdrawn from the field was strictly as a result of their funding having run out. At that very moment, Campbell said, he was spending all of his time lobbying members of Congress to ensure that the money for the coming season would be approved and that, he went on, was very far from a sure thing. He would greatly appreciate it, he continued, if members of the British commission would not provide the annexationist forces in Washington (who resented spending money on a survey that would be redundant when, they believed, western Canada was absorbed by the United States) with any further reason to vote against extending the work on the boundary.

Campbell must have enjoyed the opportunity of taking a slap at Cameron. The two men had parted on less than cordial terms, and nothing that had passed between them during the winter had done anything to reduce the tension. There was really nothing Cameron could say in defence of the commission. Everyone knew that the *Press* (well known for its annexationist sympathies) had almost certainly invented Herchmer's response to what had been an unfairly leading question in the first place. Yet it would be unprovable to claim as much, so there was nothing to be done but for Cameron to swallow his pride and pen a sincere apology to Campbell. It must have been as galling to the British commissioner as it was satisfying for the American.

WITH MARCH CAME the repair of the telegraph lines, and over those lines came the first of a series of messages from the American Commission. Anderson did not like what he read. Campbell was not prepared to accept the British corrections to the line and wanted all work on the thirty-three-mile stretch east from Pembina to cease until they returned from Detroit. Anderson was also worried that they would object to the portion of the line that ran east from the end of Greene's corrected tangents toward Lake of the Woods. Anderson and Cameron had taken a huge gamble by putting two officers and full parties to work for six weeks on a portion of the line which they knew was likely to be disputed, and now it seemed it would end up being an expensive waste of time. The Americans were hardly likely to pick up half the cost of work they had not authorized in the first place. On March 8, Anderson vented his frustration in a long tirade to his mother:

> The American Commissioner for the last 3 months has not been able to give his mind or attention to anything except the engagement of his daughter to a Mr. Charlton, an attaché of the British Legation at Washington, the eldest son of a Northumberland gentleman of property, [and] a Roman Catholic... Yesterday I had to send a long telegram to Mr. Campbell with reference to the portion of Boundary where Galwey is working and if he Mr. Campbell takes a fortnight to answer this as he did the last communication, the work will be finished whether he approves of it or not, for I have authorized Galwey to go on, it being out of the question to keep the parties out in camp eating their heads off and doing nothing.[21]

When Anderson again wrote to his mother later that same month, he was in camp on the line just west of Lake of the Woods preparing to bring his parties in. Despite his all-out effort to see the work completed, the trouble with the Americans had finally brought it to a premature end. The telegram regarding Galwey's work to which Anderson had alluded in his previous letter had drawn a conciliatory reply from Campbell. While saying how much he appreciated the British efforts to complete the whole of the work, the final decision regarding the problem had been left to Chief Astronomer Farquhar. Farquhar then telegraphed to say that he wanted no further work undertaken until there had been a meeting of the two chief commissioners and the American party had been able to examine the line in person. While Anderson thought seriously about pushing Cameron to keep the work going for the few weeks it would take to complete everything, he finally accepted that the Foreign Office would never agree to cover the entire cost and, reluctantly, began to wind the operation down.

Even with the premature end to the fieldwork, Anderson had almost achieved his goal:

> The two astronomical parties under Captain F-H and Lieutenant Galwey R.E. will now be released a fortnight earlier than was expected, but we shall have left the work in such a state that it will be quite unnecessary for any of our officers to visit this section of the boundary again. We shall have done everything, but setting up the permanent Boundary marks and cutting a 30 feet lane thro' the forest. For these purposes we have made all the measurements, visited and marked all the points, completed our map of this section of the country, and the work that remains to be done might be carried out by any of the colonial contractors.[22]

Having managed to delay bringing in the parties for as long as possible, Anderson determined to supervise the retreat personally and prepared for another expedition with his dogs. For this last winter adventure he would take the same personnel and dog team he had used on his previous trip, plus two other teams and their drivers, with each sled carrying only a bare minimum of provisions in case they were needed to help with the moves.

While Anderson's greatest concern was the possibility of an early thaw trapping the men and the horses in the swamps, winter showed that it still had some bite as the teams ran into a blizzard on their second morning out. Half blinded by the driving snow and riding curled up on the sled, Anderson watched in amazement as his lead dog somehow recognized a shortcut they had used on their previous trip, took control of the sled and pulled it unerringly to the first depot. Dragging the other three dogs behind him, he burst into the depot, headed for the warmth of the hearth and was stopped short only when the sled jammed in the doorway.

The next morning, they were off through the deep snow with two men on snowshoes breaking a trail for the dogs. They were headed toward a topographical survey party working north of the line— unlike those cutting the boundary swath itself, who could be located simply by making a course along the parallel, the topographical parties were harder to find since they might be located anywhere within six miles of the border. Without a clear track to follow, Anderson, by now in full native mode, looked for traces of the party's passing by examinating the stunted brush, looking for any sign of a bent or broken twig. They finally found the party and spent the night, relaying the news about the end of work. This group, made up entirely of Royal Engineers, was under the direction of Sergeant Kay, a trained surveyor who was the only non-commissioned officer given responsibility for his own party, and the only non-Canadian to work on the topographical survey.

Anderson found another of his topographical parties working deep in an area of burned and fallen timber so inaccessible that he could only approach the camp by struggling on his snowshoes for seven miles through the wreckage. That party, too, was given their mail from home and told the news. To finish as much work as possible, Anderson also agreed to start another party working toward them from the west. When they met, they were all to turn for Pembina.

After a planning meeting with Featherstonhaugh near the second depot, Anderson pushed on toward Lake of the Woods and the two remaining field parties. Galwey was directing the clear-cutting of the boundary line. His had been by far the most mobile of the two main parties. As Featherstonhaugh worked primarily in the middle section, Galwey had worked everywhere from the shore of Lake of the Woods to Greene's line just east of Pembina and back again. He had been making good progress on the cutting, despite facing an abortive mutiny from the hired men. What had caused the problem is not clear (Galwey was not the easiest man to get along with, and the party had been in the bush for a very long time), but Anderson noted, "It is most fortunate that we have a nucleus of our own men in the different parties whom we can always depend on, and they make us quite independent of the hired men, and of course have no sympathy with the latter."[23]

While Galwey used the dog teams to move his camp farther west, Anderson remained with the main party, which had been left under the direction of one of the Canadian surveyors. George Coster had been attached to Galwey on his arrival in September and was to stay with him right through to the fall of 1874. Anderson took a liking to the enthusiastic surveyor, who was well-known for taking the place of any obviously tired man among his comrades, "hewing the trees as vigorously as the others." It was while Anderson was in camp, however, that a sad accident befell the party:

> He [Coster] and another man were some distance ahead of the others, as they were widening a line that had been cut the day before. He was felling a tree, and as it was tottering he told the other man to look out, but the latter placed himself behind another tree... and looked out... at the one that was falling. The top of the tree unhappily struck him on the head and knocked him senseless.[24]

The man was quickly brought into camp, but died in less than an hour. Anderson prepared to bury him near where he had fallen and had inscribed a wooden cross for the purpose, but the men in the camp insisted that he be taken to Winnipeg for a proper service. He was apparently a Freemason and the men felt he deserved the last rites of his order. Complying with their wishes, Anderson had the body (by then completely frozen) stitched up in a large green blanket and sent off by dogsled to Pembina. The deceased was escorted by two of the cutting crew and Coster, who had been terribly shaken by the accident and was not fit for further work.

A dog team from the last survey party came into Galwey's camp on their way to pick up supplies at the third depot, but Anderson gave them enough of Galwey's stores to tide the party over and went with them back to their base of operations. The men in camp were recovering slowly from a general attack of snowblindness and, after supplying them with some green gauze to wear over their eyes as makeshift sunglasses, Anderson ordered them to pull out.

With the last of his parties contacted, Anderson turned back to the depot at Pine River to wait for them to come in. The winter's work was done, and not a moment too soon.

As the parties moved back toward headquarters, they left their equipment and surplus stores at the depots from where they could be shipped out en masse by horse or ox team. By April 1, Anderson was waiting at the Pine River depot for the last eleven men to arrive. Their heavy equipment had already been sent on, and Anderson was to lead them out along with the last four dog teams.

March had ended with a three-day thaw and April had begun with heavy rains. Thinking he might have to leave the last of the horses at the Native settlement on Lake Roseau to be collected later, Anderson was counting on the still-cold nights to keep the swamps frozen long enough to get his dog teams back to the Red River. By the time he reached Dufferin on April 5, the winter road across the valley was quickly dissolving into an impassable sea of mud, and only a few nights of hard frost allowed the last of the horse-drawn supply wagons to come in from the Pointe d'Orme depot. By April 8, everyone and everything was safely back at Dufferin.

Anderson no doubt offered up a silent, grudging "Thank you!" to Farquhar. The American's intransigence about continuing with the boundary work had spared the British chief astronomer from becoming (quite literally) mired in a tactical nightmare of enormous proportions.

· 4 ·

SPRING

1873

The first shower that we had a week ago produced
a wondrous change. The prairie, charred
from last autumn's fires, suddenly became green.

SAMUEL ANDERSON

A s THE LAST of the winter parties
struggled back into Dufferin,
the ice of the Red River was
decaying under their feet. Although more than five feet thick at Christmas, as the temperatures climbed it quickly rotted, became waterlogged and finally cracked apart. On April 9, the river had risen by
eight inches; two weeks later, it was twenty-two feet over its January
mark and still rising. The great blocks of broken ice, pushed by the
steady pressure of a strong current, piled into the banks and into each
other at every twist and bend in the river, backing the water up and
out into the valley. By April 22, the river had flooded over half of the
200 yards between its winter banks and the commission buildings,
forcing a precautionary emptying of the cellars. Plans were made for
the Camerons to leave their cottage, which was closer to the river, and

move into the upper floor of the officers' quarters. Finally, by the end of the second week in May, the river had crested at thirty-two feet above its winter level, flooding the basement at Emmadale but stopping five feet below the headquarters.

It was a respectable enough show of force by the Red, but nowhere near the devastating floods which it was capable of generating. Because the Red River flows from south to north, a winter of heavy snowfall or an early thaw on its southern reaches can send huge volumes of water rushing downstream. When this wall of water, carrying its load of ice and silt and accumulated flotsam, hits the still-frozen river to the north, it has nowhere to go but to spill out across the valley. The Red River Colony was almost drowned out of existence in 1826, and everyone who had lived beside the river for even a few years could remember the number of times they had watched helpless from the high ground as their homes were submerged.

Just before the ice had finally begun to break, someone at Dufferin had the foresight to cut fifteen tons of it out of the river and pack it in one of the cellars, moving Anderson to observe that "... the lucky few who remain in charge of this place during the summer, will have the benefit of this."[1]

He was clearly being ironic about the "lucky few." His letters home during these few weeks of spring are full of anticipation and even a little excitement about the coming season's work and about what discoveries might await him out on the high plains.

Anderson reckoned it would be at least six weeks before the astronomical and surveying parties could take to the field. Though the snow was almost gone from the flatlands, and the night frosts were less frequent, the hollows were still clogged with drifts and everything else was a sea of mud. It was also too early for the new grasses to provide sufficient feed for the horses, a crucial consideration if the commission was to avoid transporting large quantities of hay and oats.

While the officers busied themselves with preparing reports and maps of their winter's work, the men turned their hands to farming. Dufferin occupied only a small part of the 360-acre parcel that had been acquired for the commission. "It will be a great triumph," wrote

Anderson to his mother, "if we can grow sufficient vegetables for ourselves and oats for the horses, for the whole winter." With four 3-horse ploughs at work, he thought perhaps 180 acres could be broken and planted before the animals were required in the field. But three weeks later only thirty acres had gone under the plough, and the work to cut and build more than two miles of post-and-rail fence to enclose them was proving more than anyone had anticipated. While his hopes for the farm had become less grandiose, he still believed in the fundamental soundness of the plan:

> The prairie is now being ploughed for the first time, and it is difficult to plough deep enough to get below the roots of the grass. There is some doubt of our getting a good crop of oats this year, but we are going to try. The soil is a beautiful black mould. The first shower that we had a week ago produced a wondrous change. The prairie, charred from last autumn's fires, suddenly became green.[2]

As April gave way to May, the floods peaked and began slowly to subside. On May 2, the first of the season's paddlewheelers came down the river from Minnesota. On board were twenty of Winnipeg's leading citizens who had been trapped at Moorhead waiting for the river to open for navigation. Sailing with them was Commissioner Cameron, returning from a month-long trip to Ottawa. Forced to spend five days in what Anderson called "a most wild and lawless place," Cameron's only activity was "to keep on sending... telegrams principally referring to the state of the floods."[3] Putting on a show for the cream of Winnipeg society cost the commission dearly. A dozen bottles of champagne and "... all that our larder and cellar could produce at the time"[4] had been devoured by the time the party reboarded and sailed off.

The steamers could run only between the worst of the spring floods and the low water of fall. Early in the season, they could make it all the way from Moorhead to Winnipeg, but as the water dropped, they abandoned the more southerly reaches of their routes and tied up at places like Frog Point, pressing wagons into service to keep them connected with the railway. While the return of the paddlewheelers was a welcome sight in the spring, they were neither the quickest nor the most reliable form of transport. As soon as the floods subsided and the mud tracks dried out, stage coaches became the preferred means for moving goods such as the mail. Forced to crash their way along the convoluted course of the river, the steamers had to travel twice as far as the stages to reach their destination.

After the Winnipeg business community's attack on the commission's depleted stores, the river brought a welcome supply of fresh food:

> A party of Americans suddenly appeared drifting down the river in a floating house, called a flat boat. This is a sort of box composed of planks of suitable length for building purposes, and the boat is so lightly built that it can be easily broken up, and the planks command a good and ready sale. The miniature ark is so clumsy that the crew have no power over it except to steer it clear of obstacles, as the current takes it down. We hailed the flat boat, and after much difficulty she drifted to the shore, half a mile below our Quarters. We went on board and found out she had potatoes, apples, butter, maple sugar, hams and eggs for sale.[5]

The new foodstuffs were an important addition to the commission's table at that time, not only for their variety and novelty, but as a blessed relief from the salt pork. After a winter of living on it, the officers had been looking forward to a change when they returned to Dufferin. What they found, however, was that the local butcher who had been supplying the mess with fresh beef and other commodities wanted a substantially higher price for them, and the commissary had refused to pay. That put salt pork back on the menu, much to the men's dismay:

> As you may suppose, no one took very kindly to this change, so we all go out in the afternoon for an hour or two before dinner to a little lake on the prairie about a mile and a half from the Quarters,

and by surrounding the lake we generally bring in 3 or 4 brace of wild duck. We have been living on duck for some days… Geese have been passing in large flocks, but only one has been shot by our party.[6]

The butcher was not the only one demanding a higher price for his services. Early in May, there was a general strike among the hired men from Winnipeg. Their winter wage had been £6 a month, all found, but they were asking for more. The economy was booming on both sides of the line and though winter had dampened demand, spring brought new opportunities for anyone with any level of skill in the building trades. So great was the need for workers on the Northern Pacific Railway, agents had approached Anderson's sappers as they disembarked in Duluth the previous fall, offering high wages to join the rail gangs. The well-trained carpenters and masons among the non-commissioned officers and enlisted men could have commanded top dollar, but none had defected. Dufferin's labourers may have thought they had the upper hand, but Cameron was simply not interested in negotiating wages or anything else. Fifteen of the twenty or so strikers were summarily dismissed and took passage on the next steamer to Winnipeg. Cameron went north on the same vessel, intent on finding replacements. The commission's hired men seem to have overestimated their value, as Cameron had little trouble hiring twenty-eight new recruits at the old rate. The replacements may have been the best available, but they were far from perfect: one man was suffering an epileptic seizure when he arrived. With Anderson and the commission's chief surgeon "weeding out the weak ones,"[7] the strikers were replaced without trouble.

That senior medical officer was Dr. Thomas Joseph Workman Burgess. Surprisingly young for such a responsibility, Burgess was only twenty-three when he arrived to take up his duties at Dufferin. Born into a Toronto merchant family, Burgess had been named after a close friend of his parents. Joseph Workman was a physician and teacher at the John Rolph School of Medicine (which eventually became the medical school of the University of Toronto). Workman was certainly responsible for interesting young Burgess in a medical career after he graduated from Toronto's prestigious Upper Canada College. Workman also provided Burgess with an internship at the Toronto Asylum after he finished his studies in 1870. Now, just two years after his graduation, Burgess was headed west to join the boundary commission as its senior surgeon.

While in Winnipeg, Commissioner Cameron had also been busy with recruiting of a different kind. The question of military escorts for the two boundary commissions had been a matter for discussion from the earliest planning stages—or at least, it had been in Britain. For the Americans, there was really nothing to talk about. Drawing the boundary was to be largely a military exercise and, as long as they were in the field, the American survey parties would be fully escorted by the army. In Britain, the issue was not so cut and dried. Hawkins had looked at the business of military protection when he made his original estimates, but there was never any suggestion that British soldiers would be sent into western Canada to accompany the Royal Engineers. It was generally felt that, if there were to be "Indian trouble," it would be on the American side of the line.

The British attitude was a reflection of there being no joint boundary commission, even though everyone regularly referred to the existence of one. Neither commission had consulted with the other about its appointments. Each commission was separately funded and each would make its own final report to its respective government. How the two commissioners co-operated in the actual fieldwork had been left mostly to their discretion. It was simply assumed they would deploy their resources in the most efficient and effective fashion and that each would agree on the final result of the survey.

The British and the Canadians felt the chance of serious trouble along the line was remote, and were apparently willing to bet on the U.S. Army automatically protecting the men of both commissions if there were an attack. But, hedging that bet, the Foreign Office told Cameron in no uncertain terms that he was to avoid walking into any trouble and immediately pull his men out of the field if he sensed any serious danger of attack.

From the British-Canadian perspective, there really wasn't much to worry about on "their" side of the line. The Red River Rebellion had been crushed and Louis Riel sent into exile more than two years before, and there was nothing in the way of obvious trouble west of Manitoba. The situation for the Americans was far more volatile, and it centred on the Sioux.

Since the late eighteenth century the increasing pressure of white settlement had been pushing the Sioux from their traditional lands at the western end of the Great Lakes and out toward the plains. A succession of treaties, beginning in 1815, had steadily reduced the Sioux presence east of the Red River and, in anticipation of Minnesota statehood, yet another treaty in 1851 had taken nine-tenths of the Sioux lands, leaving only a small strip of a reservation along the Minnesota River. As more than 150,000 settlers poured into the country in the decade before the Civil War, guarantees of access to hunting grounds and other promises went by the board, and the Sioux found themselves hemmed in on all sides. By the mid-1850s, with the final disappearance of the bison from Minnesota and the eastern Dakotas, the Sioux had become entirely dependent on treaty payments and agency stores.

As the Civil War focussed the government's attention elsewhere, the treaty payments of 1862 were either forgotten or stolen, and years of smouldering resentment and frustration among Little Crow's Santee Sioux erupted into a full-scale war. The string of skirmishes and pitched battles that swept across southwestern Minnesota left more than eight hundred men, women and children—white and Native—dead.

By the end of 1862, the Santee had been forced back onto their reserves, and over three hundred of the warriors deemed to have been most deeply involved in the attacks on the white settlements were tried and sentenced to death. Only an intervention by President Lincoln delayed the hangings. He reviewed the record of the trials and stayed the execution of most of the warriors. But, with his approval, thirty-eight Santee were sent to the gallows on December 26.

Little Crow and some of his followers managed to escape into the Dakotas. From there, anticipating a number of later, more famous, crossings, he went north to the Red River Colony to seek help from the British authorities. But other than providing some food supplies and, perhaps, a sympathetic ear, the Red River colonists wanted nothing to do with the Santee, though they made no effort to expel them. In June 1863, Little Crow made the mistake of crossing back into Minnesota, supposedly to steal horses, and he was shot dead by settlers.

By 1867 what remained of the Santee were forced to give up the last of their land in Minnesota. Sent west to join the rest of their nation in the Dakotas, they carried with them yet another promise that they could live their old ways and hunt freely across the still-unsettled territory. But three years later, the Northern Pacific Railway was preparing to bridge the Red River, and the whole bloody business seemed ready to start again.

It was Cameron who finally took it upon himself to provide the British commission with an armed escort, and his reasons for doing so were sound. If trouble arose, the British parties would be forced to conform their operations to those of the Americans. Accepting American protection meant accepting American direction, even if only in matters of security. Further, he argued, being seen as travelling under the protection of the U.S. Army would immediately compromise the historically kinder feelings of the Native populations toward the British crown. With the well-known Sioux antagonism toward the Americans, the British and Canadian effort would, in effect, find itself tarred with the same brush.

Meeting with Manitoba lieutenant governor Adams Archibald in September 1872, Cameron had proposed the creation of "a body of mounted half breeds [i.e., Metis] as a covering escort for the small detached parties of surveyors and astronomers." He recommended using the Metis on the grounds that the entire community would be "highly flattered by such duty... being entrusted to them." Beyond the public relations aspect, he also believed that Metis would be far less likely to stir up hostilities with the plains nations than any regular army unit. Cameron was also counting on the fact that the relatively modest cost of creating and maintaining a party of scouts—something under £4,000 a year—would forestall any Foreign Office objections to his proposal.

In consultation with Archibald, Cameron approached William Hallett to organize and lead the scouts. Hallett, a mixed-blood hunter, was well-known in Winnipeg. The son of a Hudson's Bay Company factor, he had been employed as a scout for McDougall's party during his ill-fated attempt to take office in 1869. Cameron, as McDougall's aide-de-camp, would doubtless have met him at that time. While Cameron was recruiting his replacement workers in Winnipeg, Hallett was signing up the thirty Metis who would come to be known as the 49th Rangers.

Anderson thought the rangers a generally good idea, though he believed any trouble with the Sioux would be minimal:

> These men will act as guides, and at times as hunters. They will hover about in advance and on the flanks of our working parties and will give due notice of the approach of Indian thieves, who would probably attempt no more mischief than stampeding our horses at night.[8]

While Anderson may not have thought the Sioux capable of much more than a little mischief, others—especially Cameron—took their presence in the eastern Dakotas more seriously. Early in May, the commission's veterinarian, Boswell, was in Moorhead preparing to bring a substantial herd of forty oxen and over a hundred horses to Dufferin. There had already been a dispute over ownership of one of the horses involving a gang of Fenians, and the Red was still sufficiently high to force the party well out into the Dakota Territory as they drove the animals north. It was then that rumours of a massing of the Sioux in the area were heard in Dufferin, and Cameron was not prepared to take any chances with losing the herd.

Since the 49th Rangers had not yet arrived at the headquarters, Cameron put Featherstonhaugh and Ward in charge of a party of twenty Royal Engineers, each armed with a standard-issue Snider rifle and Dean's revolver, and sent them out to escort Boswell back to Dufferin. They were to march south at the rate of thirty miles a day, and were expected back in camp in just over a week.

It is remarkable that a stickler for detail like Cameron would decide to send an armed party of British soldiers across the border into the United States without, apparently, the slightest concern for what could be seen as a serious breach of protocol. There is no evidence that he contacted the U.S. Army at Fort Pembina to seek their help or their permission. For the first and perhaps the only time, Anderson expressed his unqualified approval of the chief commissioner: "Capt. C. has shown wonderful energy in this last affair, and it augurs well for our adopting a bold policy throughout..."[9]

Cameron's bold stroke proved unnecessary, as word was received the next day that Boswell was within eighty miles of Pembina and well past any possible trouble from the Sioux. The Engineers were promptly recalled, but Anderson still thought the wasted march had been worth the effort: "This little excitement has done the whole of our little community good, as we were able to show our appreciation of the well-conducted men by selecting them for this service."[10]

While the "little excitement" may have been over for the Royal Engineers, it was anything but smooth sailing for Boswell. As his herd approached the boundary, the drovers balked at trying to cross the flood-swollen Pembina River. Their refusal to move, stiffened by an ample supply of liquor, led to fist fights, smashed equipment and a general discharging of pistols. Once again, Captain Lloyd Wheaton rode out from Fort Pembina to help settle his neighbour's problems, and a grateful Boswell brought his herd into Dufferin without further incident. Along with the animals, he also brought in fifty wagons, two field ambulances and a number of water carts.

The cool-headed performance of his veterinarian through the first potential trouble faced by the commission should have pleased Cameron immensely. William George Boswell was from Ontario but little else is known about his life either before or after his seasons on the 49th Parallel. In the group photograph taken at Dufferin just after his return from his Minnesota adventures, Boswell appears an unremarkable figure in a battered hat, squeezed between Featherstonhaugh and Burgess on the front step of the commission's headquarters. Indeed, even his correct name is uncertain, with some sources referring to him as "Walter." The man himself does little to clarify the matter, habitually signing his name "W. George Boswell." Nevertheless, as the commission's complement of horses and oxen rose steadily into the hundreds, Boswell's veterinary skills would be absolutely critical to the success of the mission. He would not disappoint.

While Cameron had finally found a meaningful role for himself—something in which his battle experience with the Royal Artillery gave him a real advantage over the Royal Engineers—one must wonder why he continued to keep his wife and child with him at Dufferin. Although Emma Cameron had managed to find a companion and helpmate in the commissary's wife, Mrs. Herchmer had two children of her own with her, which must have made for at least as much additional work as it saved. Emma's life at the post had been one potential disaster after another. She had been frostbitten at least once and her child had suffered terribly from an attack of ophthalmia, a dangerous eye disease. When Cameron had gone on his recruiting trip to Winnipeg, she had insisted on accompanying him and taking the child, only to rush back two days later to escape an outbreak of whooping cough. As soon as the snow had gone, the post was plagued by clouds of mosquitoes, and both she and her baby were badly swollen from the bites. When her husband left for an extended trip to Ottawa, she had remained behind, trapped in the cold and loneliness of a Manitoba winter. With the other officers out in the field, she was forced to entertain, as best she could, the various Winnipeg churchmen and business people who occasionally appeared, mostly unannounced, at the headquarters.

To add to her difficulties, Emma found that Cameron himself required a good deal of attention. For as long as he had been at Dufferin, he had suffered periodic bouts of agonizing rheumatism, and Emma was primarily responsible for trying to ease his pain. Anderson described one of the Camerons' home remedies to his mother: "He has had no rest for 2 nights, and the treatment he tries in the middle of the night is to have his shoulder blade ironed with a hot laundress' iron. The most successful palliative has been rubbing the arm and shoulder with a horse brush."[11]

AS THE COMMISSION continued its preparations for the western section of the survey, the four Canadian surveyors and assistant astronomers who had taken leave following the winter work came back from the east, and additional personnel began to appear at Pembina. A Mr. Almon and his wife came in from Nova Scotia to superintend the operation of the farm, while D'Arcy East, a former Royal Artillery officer, arrived from Britain to take command of a special survey party. Also arriving at about this time was assistant surveyor George Crompton. Both Crompton and East would later prove invaluable to the commission, though not in the capacities for which they had been appointed.

East's special survey party was yet more fallout from Cameron's politicking over the Northwest Angle. He still believed that the location of the northwesternmost point held the key to preventing the Angle from falling to the Americans and had pressured the Foreign Office to allow another full survey of the area. He wanted desperately to discredit the old crib marker once and for all. East would undertake the survey and then remain with the commission, taking on a variety of roles throughout the course of its western work.

Another important spring arrival was Dr. Thomas Millman. A student in his final year of medicine at the University of Toronto when he heard that the boundary commission was looking for an assistant surgeon, he had been chosen from among several applicants. While his appointment had been effective since the beginning of February 1873, he could not leave Toronto for Dufferin since the equine influenza epidemic had stopped the stages from Moorhead to Winnipeg. When the stages began running again toward the end of the month, Millman was given a special sitting for his final exams and, on passing them, left within a few days to join the commission. He went by train from Toronto to St. Paul, via Detroit and Chicago, in only three days; the rail journey from St. Paul to Moorhead, and then by stagecoach to Dufferin, took a further six. He arrived at headquarters just in time to join the inquest into the loss of the axeman at Lake of the Woods. The official verdict was accidental death by a transverse fracture of the skull.

Obviously bright and possessed of a flexible nature, Millman fitted quickly and easily into the commission's routine, and continued to keep the lively diary he had started the day he left Toronto. From the state of the accommodation at Dufferin—"my bed... consisted of two benches and a couple of boards stretched across them"—to his first visit to the infirmary—"one with frozen feet, one of tuberculosis and a few of chronic rheumatism"—the diary reveals a young man intrigued by his first visit to the west and excited to be beginning his medical career. When the first boat of the season stopped at Dufferin on May 2, bringing the mail, he was delighted to be able to write: "By the paper I see that I have received my degree. I am mentioned as 'Thomas Millman, of Manitoba, in his absence.'"[12]

Part of the equipment transported from Britain with the Engineers were "two complete sets, Messrs. Savory and Moore's medical field panniers."[13] Originally packed in woven baskets to insulate the bottles and instruments from the knocks and jars of travel ("pannier" derives from the French for "bread basket"), these standard-issue military kits formed the basic equipment for what would be known as the "Surgeons' Party." At the peak of the summer operations, this party would comprise Burgess and Millman, two sprung wagons and carts, two field ambulances and two water carts, five teamsters, twelve horses and a servant. Everything was duplicated so the surgeon's party could, if necessary, easily split up and operate as two fully independent units.

In addition, Burgess and Millman produced sixty "medical boxes" (what we would now call first-aid kits) to be sent out with the various field parties. Preparing the lists of contents, labels and instructions for the use of the various medicines and "appliances" occupied a substantial portion of Millman's time during his first month at the post. While the heads of the individual parties were expected to be able to deal with everyday cases of sickness or injury, the surgeon was directed to "take advantage of all available means to enable reference to be made to him without delay," and to "govern his movements so as to be equally accessible from the extreme points of the country under survey at any one time." The doctors were further instructed to pay special attention to "the prevention and treatment of scurvy, diarrhoea, fruit-poisoning [this might refer to casual browsing of unknown types of berries] and the treatment of cuts, fractures, shot wounds, bruises, sunstroke and apparent death from drowning."[14]

Considering the dangers and privations of the winter work, casualties among the parties had been surprisingly light. Forrest's cook, Charles Randall, had died from a bowel inflammation early in the work at Lake of the Woods, and there had been the fatal accident at Galwey's camp, but most of the other work-related injuries were about what would be expected: burns, frostbite, and the various self-inflicted wounds that come with wielding an axe. Most of these were treated in the camps, although a few men were sent back to Dufferin to recuperate. From Millman's diary, however, it is obvious that, in addition to providing medical care to many of the residents in the area, there were more than enough injuries to keep them busy. A teamster with a broken collar-bone, a broken hand and a split lip from a fist fight, a sapper with two teeth that needed pulling and a civilian who had a finger nearly torn off while trying to break up a dog fight were all a part of the young doctor's introduction to "emergency room" medicine. He appears to have retained his sense of humour, writing of the man and the dogs:

> It seems he was the worse for liquor and out with a gun. Two of the dogs were fighting and he tried to separate them. In doing so he received his injury... Afterwards it was found that he had a tremendous charge in the gun, so you might say it was a blessing the dog bit him.[15]

Only one of the injuries he treated was truly serious. At the end of April, a sapper named McCammon had, for reasons not explained, tried to fire an old flintlock rifle. It blew up in his face and he eventually lost his left eye. McCammon recovered sufficiently to take his place with the photographic party, but a year later he somehow conspired to shoot himself again (and again, he survived).

BY THE MIDDLE of May, as the livestock, men and matériel continued to pour into Dufferin, the British were ready to take to the field in force. All that was missing were the Americans. Commissioner Campbell had been assembling his men at St. Paul since mid-April, but there was no firm indication of when they would start for Pembina. Through the mails and the telegraph, however, the British were well aware of several significant developments on the American side that would bear directly on the season's work.

The good news was that Campbell's lobbying efforts had been at least partially successful. Congress had approved a budget of $125,000 for the summer and winter seasons of 1873. The bad news was that there had been a significant change to the American personnel. Chief Astronomer Francis Farquhar's request to be relieved of his boundary duties and to return to work on the Great Lakes had been granted.

Anderson put the resignation down to two factors. First was the issue of salary. He wrote at the time that while the Royal Engineers had been granted a special supplement to their usual stipend, "The United States Government have adopted a very short sighted policy in granting no extra pay to their officers on the Boundary Commission, and all those who were associated with us last autumn were ordered for the duty, and of course they did nothing but grumble."[16] In Farquhar's case, however, Anderson remarked "... I think the real reason [for his resignation] is that he prefers the work he had formerly on Lake Michigan, when he was able to have his family with him. The comfort and luxury of spending the past winter *en famille* at Detroit has quite unnerved him from facing the Boundary work on the plains."[17]

The Americans were fortunate to be able to promote Twining to the position of chief astronomer, but when they did so they declined to appoint a replacement for him. That left the U.S. commission capable of mounting only two of the three astronomical parties they had agreed to provide (Twining one, James Gregory the other). The young Lieutenant Greene would lead the crews that would draw the lines between the astronomical stations and undertake the six-mile topographical survey.

The news of Farquhar's departure was received at Dufferin in mid-April, causing an immediate review of the British plans. For Cameron and Anderson, it was a question of whether they should once again, as they had over the winter, undertake more than an equal share of the work. When the official notification of the American decision to mount only two astronomical parties was received in mid-May, the British responded in kind. While they would keep the three topographical survey parties ("...which are operating entirely in our own Territory and have nothing to do with the Americans"[18]), they would start the season with only Featherstonhaugh and Galwey's astronomical parties. Anderson, who would otherwise have had charge of the third party, came up with a new scheme that, in the event, proved far more valuable to the work of both commissions than the two lost astronomical parties could ever have been.

The chief astronomer would take charge of a new party, to include the 49th Rangers. With it, he would reconnoitre ahead of the main body, predetermining the best sites for the astronomical stations, looking for reliable sources of water and firewood, and, in general, trying to anticipate any sort of problem that might slow the progress of the other parties. He could also ensure that the rangers would respond quickly to any trouble with the Native populations. The commissions were moving into entirely new terrain and no one really knew what to expect. Anderson intended to keep the nasty surprises to a minimum.

By freeing himself to roam the line at will, Anderson would also be able to deal almost immediately with any difficulties that arose in the course of the surveying or astronomical work, especially as it might relate to the coordination between the two commissions. In this last role, Anderson had neatly usurped a duty that should have fallen to Cameron. While he had been impressed with Cameron's decisive action over Boswell's trouble, he still wanted to keep him away from any involvement with the fieldwork and, more particularly, from the Americans. This would prove to be the one part of an otherwise-inspired plan that achieved only modest success.

FINALLY, ON MAY 12, the first of the British survey parties left Dufferin and moved west. Sergeant Kay's topographical work did not depend on the American presence and there was no reason he should not be sent out. Indeed, there was at least one compelling reason to get as many parties as possible into the field: Dufferin was fairly bursting at the seams. At the end of the month, Anderson wrote to his mother:

> The waggons and horses are now collected in a square enclosure close to the Quarters on the open prairie, and the whole presents a formidable appearance... The resources of the Commissariat are now being severely tried, as we have 230 people to feed, and upwards of 250 animals, and our fresh stock of provisions and stores is only now beginning to arrive by the successive boats.[19]

Kay's party was not going far—only to the Moray River, about eight miles distant—but at least they were out of Dufferin and beginning the western work. Anderson could not resist recording that "the party went off in great glee."

Galwey's astronomical party was the next to go out, quitting the headquarters on May 26 to spend a week near the customs house checking their equipment and getting ready to start the first observations west of Pembina.

The special survey group that was bound for yet another study of Lake of the Woods would have headed out too, but there seemed to be some difficulty in getting a northbound paddlewheeler to put in at Dufferin long enough for the men to board.

As the commission began to spread out along the line, each of the parties took with it a firm directive from Chief Commissioner Cameron. Dr. Millman, whose job it was to make the necessary number of copies, recorded a substantial portion of it in his diary. Planting his diplomatic hat squarely on his head and writing mostly in the third person, Cameron wanted something clearly understood:

> ... the commissioner desires to bring most forcibly to the notice of each individual the necessity... for a most discreet bearing toward the Indians who may be met with during the progress of

the survey. It is presumed that all of those who may be encountered during the first three hundred miles to be passed over are prepared to tender us a friendly reception. Such being the case it is more imperative than were they hostilely disposed toward us, that nothing should be done to offend their susceptibilities, and the commission will not fail to take grave notice of any inattention to this point.

He strictly enjoins upon all to support him in maintaining friendly relations with the Indians, to show them every consideration and to avoid even the appearance of contempt toward them. He also enjoins that in case of Indians desiring to confer with any of the commission they will be glad to see them; that no authority has been deputed to members of the commission to discuss Indian questions; that the object of Her Majesty in sending out the commission was merely and purely to mark a line with a United States' Commissioner, to the North of which the United States agreed not to encroach and that nothing could cause Her Majesty greater dissatisfaction than that any of her servants should cause her friends the Indians to doubt her friendly feeling for them or to forget that they have always been at peace with her.[20]

In other words, be nice and don't say anything foolish. But hidden behind the triple negatives, the "susceptibilities" and the Great White Mother clichés, there is a sense that Cameron is almost hoping that something would happen out along the line. He would not have been wishing for gunfire or bloodshed, but rather for the opportunity to put on his best uniform, sit in solemn council with the Noble Red Man and assuage any fears about Her Majesty's intentions. Cameron was still a man looking for something meaningful to do.

AS CAMERON TALKED his men through the *what-ifs* and *wherefores* of diplomatic nicety, six hundred miles away to the west, almost within sight of the 49th Parallel, a small party of Montana wolf hunters was bedding down for the night. They were back to within an easy morning's ride of their home base at Fort Benton and, flushed with the success of their expedition (their wagons creaked under perhaps ten thousand wolf pelts, worth as much as $2.50 each to the wholesalers in Benton), they didn't bother to post their usual night herders or camp guard. When they woke up in the morning, they discovered more than twenty of their mounts were missing, probably stolen by a party of young Natives.

The wolfers tracked the horses until they were sure they had not simply run off and, noting the general direction in which they were being driven, they hitched up what was left of their animals and pushed on into Fort Benton. The next day, remounted and reprovisioned, they headed back north, intent on recovering their horses. It was a motley crew of about a dozen men, most of whom had been scratching about in the whiskey and robe trade since the end of the Civil War. Their leader, if they had one, was probably Tom Hardwick, also known as Green River Renegade, who had served in the Confederate Army and come north to Montana in 1864. He had been the principal instigator of a shoot-out with an Assiniboine trading party in the Sweetgrass Hills almost exactly a year before. Also riding with the party was John Evans, known across the territory as "The Chief," a veteran of the whiskey trade north of the border in the Bow River country of present-day Alberta. All in all, it was a not a pleasant party, but it was probably no worse than any of the other bands of drifters and hunters that inhabited the northern plains in search of anything from which they could trade a living.

Just what happened over the next few days is not entirely clear. As is invariably the case with stories of trouble between whites and Natives, the contemporary accounts range from the simply unreliable to the utterly outrageous, but it is possible to draw at least a broad brush picture of what came to be known as the Cypress Hills Massacre.

The tracks of the stolen horses led north, across the still-to-be-marked 49th Parallel, and up toward the Cypress Hills. Within sight of the hills, the men lost the tracks and decided to pay a visit to nearby local trader named Abel Farwell to see if he had heard anything of their horses.

Camped across the creek from Farwell's trading post was a large band of North Assiniboine under a chief named Little Soldier. The forty or so lodges would normally have been much farther north in Saskatchewan, but near starvation had driven them south into the shelter of the Cypress Hills. The Assiniboine immediately came under the wolfers' suspicion, but Farwell assured them that their horses were not there, and that no one in that part of the country had seen them.

As the men relaxed with a good supply of Farwell's bottled hospitality, another dispute about horses erupted in the camp. A Canadian by the name of George Hammond claimed that his mount had just been stolen and was, at that very minute, being hidden in the Assiniboine camp. Despite denials by Little Soldier and even some credible evidence that the horse had simply wandered off in search of greener grass, the combination of the wolfers' wounded pride and the Assiniboine's indignity at being wrongly accused, lubricated with large quantities of bad whiskey on both sides, led quickly to gunfire.

When the smoke cleared, one of the wolfers lay dead from a gunshot wound to the chest. Depending on which account you read, Assiniboine dead from the initial gunfight and the subsequent rage of the wolfers numbered anywhere from a too-conservative estimate of thirteen to as many as two hundred. The official Canadian count was forty.

Badly outnumbered by the Assiniboine and fearing what might happen next, the wolfers sobered up quickly, buried their dead comrade under the floor of a trading post building and burned it down around him (to prevent the subsequent mutilation of the body, they said). They then mounted up and headed west toward Fort Whoop-Up, still ostensibly on the trail of their missing horses. At Whoop-Up there was no news of their horses either, but they did hear of a large camp of North Peigans just a little farther to the west and determined to look it over for evidence of their missing stock horses. As they rode bravely into the middle of the camp, the wolfers realized they had made a huge miscalculation. Rather than the sorry gang of half-starved Assiniboine they had faced in the Cypress Hills, this camp held as many 150 lodges and anywhere up to 400 well-armed warriors. Luckily for the wolfers, the Peigan were in relatively good humour and actually let them look through their herds to prove the horses were not there. Relieved and happy, this time, *not* to find any of their lost mounts in the herds, the party gave up and rode back to Fort Benton. The stolen horses were never recovered.

As the wolfers rode west toward Fort Whoop-Up, Farwell and the rest of his crew, unwilling to risk remaining in the Cypress Hills, packed up their trade goods and headed south to Fort Benton. There they told their version of the great battle and were cheered for their bravery in the face of overwhelming odds. When Hardwick and his party rode back into Benton a few days later, they were treated to similar accolades, and no doubt a good deal of free whiskey as they told and retold their tale.

The first published account of the massacre appeared in the Helena, Montana, *Daily Herald* on June 11, 1873, and it presented Hardwick and his men in a mostly favourable light. As the story spread east and north, however, the coverage changed. Canadian papers vigorously denounced the wolfers as "American gangsters" and "American scum" (even though a number of the men were Canadians). Where the Montana papers presented a story of Indians getting no more than they deserved, Canadians were regaled with tales of American whiskey traders invading a sovereign nation and murdering Her Majesty's poor, defenceless subjects.

Each side had its reasons for presenting the story as it did. In the United States, the murders were just one more consequence of deliberate Native aggression toward the white settlers who were just beginning to flood onto the northern plains. If the law was ineffective in the American west, across the border in the Canadian west it was non-existent.

Since the Hudson's Bay Company had given up its title to Rupert's Land just three years earlier, there had been no real law enforcement anywhere west of the Red River. In Ottawa, Prime Minister Sir John A. Macdonald had already introduced legislation to create a national police force to patrol Canada's new western lands, but the incident in the Cypress Hills made it much easier for him to push the bill into law. Canadians were demanding that the American whiskey trade be stopped at once.

The surveying and marking of the 49th Parallel, just about to begin in earnest when the massacre took place, was to be the first step in making Canada's sovereignty a reality across the west to the Pacific Ocean.

· 5 ·

SUMMER
1873

The climate of the country in the vicinity
of the boundary cannot be surpassed. The days, though
sometimes warm, are always more or less tempered by a pleasant
breeze, and the nights in midsummer are cool and refreshing,
and sometimes exceedingly cool, even to the freezing point.
ALEXANDER CAMPBELL

O N THE FIRST DAY of June 1873, the paddlewheeler *Selkirk* came down from Moorhead, bringing the officers of the United States Northern Boundary Commission back to Pembina. There she unceremoniously deposited them on the west bank of the Red River in the midst of a torrential downpour. Most of their wagons and supplies were pinned down at Fort Abercrombie, unable to move north across tributary rivers and creeks still swollen from the spring runoff. Everywhere around them, the hardpan roads and tracks that had only just dried out sufficiently to support the wagons were, once again, dissolving into rich, brown soup. As the rain soaked into everything they owned, pooled up through the floors of their tents and clotted their boots and wheels with pounds of mud, it must have been hard to imagine that, no more than a long day's ride from where they stood, water would soon become a commodity prized above almost every other. Forty miles to the east, on the other hand, a single misstep in the Roseau swamp would plunge a man to his armpits in a vast, grass-covered lake. The parched land to the west began about forty miles from the Red River, where the broad river valley ended at the scarp of Pembina Mountain. From there to the Rocky Mountain foothills lay more than seven hundred miles of what some maps were still calling "The Great American Desert." In his final instructions to the medical parties, Cameron had cautioned his surgeons to be especially vigilant in cases of "apparent death by drowning." West of Pembina Mountain, that would be the least of their worries.

American Chief Commissioner Campbell would not arrive at Pembina for another two weeks, but the details of the work on the western line had already been arranged through a steady succession of letters and telegrams between Dufferin, Detroit and, later, St. Paul. The overarching principle that would drive the work of both commissions was simple: The 49th Parallel must be drawn and marked to the Continental Divide before the winter of 1874 set in. The parties would do everything heaven and earth would allow to avoid spending a third summer in the field.

Balancing the need for speed and accuracy against the vagaries of the weather (no one had forgotten the blizzard of the previous September), the work was to be divided into two roughly equal parts. By the end of September 1873, just four months away, the commissions intended to have a full four hundred miles of the line completed. From that point, most of the Americans would retreat once again to their firesides in Detroit. The British would find a likely place for a forward depot, stock it with head-start supplies for the second season's work and then return along the line to winter in Dufferin. This strategy would leave what both commissions believed would be an easily manageable 350 miles of largely open ground to be surveyed and marked in 1874.

In the fall of 1872, the two commissions had taken simultaneous observations at the Pembina and Lake of the Woods astronomical stations. Since their independent conclusions had been well within any reasonable margin of error, it was agreed there would be no need for constant checking of each other's work. After conducting joint observations at the first two stations west of Pembina (presumably to ensure all the instruments were working properly and their calculations were in harmony), the four astronomical parties would leapfrog one another along the line, establishing observation posts at twenty-mile intervals. Each party would then be responsible for running the tangents and marking the boundary from "their" station west to the next one.

A series of astronomical stations exactly twenty miles apart was the ideal, but a certain degree of flexibility had to be allowed. The stations required reasonably dry and level ground, a clear line of sight in all directions and an unobstructed view of the night sky, and maintaining intervals of exactly twenty miles might put a station at the bottom of a coulee, on the side of a hill or in the middle of a river. That the station should be as close to the 49th Parallel as possible was obvious, except that it would take a complex series of observations to determine just where that might be. An educated guess would have to suffice, and missing the ideal site by a mile or so in any direction would not unduly compromise the work.

The twenty-mile distance between astronomical stations was itself a compromise between accuracy and efficiency. The astronomers knew that they would rarely, if ever, be sure of hitting 49° 00′ 00″ on the head. Featherstonhaugh reckoned, though, that the average error in their observations should not amount to more than ten feet either way. Insignificant as that might seem, any error, no matter how small, would quickly magnify as the line was drawn between two stations. The farther the stations were apart, the larger the error accumulated and the more time would be required to correct it.

While moving the stations closer together would reduce the effect of the errors, it would also dramatically slow the progress of the work. Each set of astronomical observations required at least three cloudless nights. With the extra time needed to complete each set of calculations, the astronomers felt that an average of seven days must be allowed at each station.

Consideration also had to be given to the time needed to mark the boundary between each station. Featherstonhaugh was sure that the Americans could draw the line at the rate of about five miles per day, including construction of the actual markers. This was one place where the American organization showed an advantage. Greene's parties were doing double duty, not only carrying out the topographical survey alongside the boundary but also running the lines between the stations. The British had to assign surveyors from the astronomical party itself to make the connections, and that could easily take longer. If everything went according to schedule (and everyone knew that the whole plan was a potential house of cards), the twenty miles of boundary could be drawn before the astronomical parties literally pulled up stakes and leapfrogged along the line to their next position.

Twenty miles between the stations also meant that at no time would any party be farther than a day's quick march away from another. Although most of the men discounted the danger of a confrontation with the Native population, it was better to be safe than sorry.

With four astronomical parties at work, the line of boundary markers would extend west at a rate of more than twenty miles per week. Barring any serious delays, there would be just enough time to reach the four-hundred-mile target by early October. Continuing the work much beyond then, without leaving enough time to get the men back to their bases before winter came, would be courting disaster.

The commissioners also agreed that, in the eighty miles between Pembina and the western edge of Manitoba (which was then at 99° west of Greenwich, but now some 110 miles further west), the boundary markers would be cast-iron pillars and would be placed at one-mile intervals, making the line more visible (since this was the region in which settlement pressures were most immediately expected, on both sides of the border). Beyond that to the west, a stone or timber marker every three miles was deemed sufficient. But how would the astronomical parties go about the business of discovering exactly where the boundary was and in which direction it needed to go?

WITH A KNOWN longitude and a set of the finest portable chronometers, religiously wound and carefully checked, the boundary commissions' astronomers, surveyors and computers could carry the exact time out into the trackless high plains and, together with their instruments and almanacs, establish the precise latitude of any point upon which they stood.

Samuel Anderson and his Metis scouts led the way, not only selecting and marking the best place for each of the astronomical stations, but also taking the trouble to calculate a close approximation of its latitude, something that would save the astronomical parties valuable time when they arrived on site.

Moving steadily west in Anderson's footsteps, the British and American astronomical teams would follow essentially the same procedures at each of the forty astronomical stations between the Red River and the Continental Divide. Albany Featherstonhaugh, in his account for the Royal Engineers' journal, has provided a clear outline:

> On approaching the site selected for an astronomical station, usually at about 3 pm., though sometimes much later, the first step was to select, for the observatory tent, an elevated spot from which an uninterrupted sight line could be obtained to a distance of about three-fourths of a mile, either due north or due south. The camp was then pitched at a short distance off, so that neither the north or south nor the east or west lines from the observatory tent came within 100 yards of it.[1]

This distance between the observatory tent and the camp was crucial. So delicate were the instruments that the vibrations from horses, wagons and even men walking past could easily ruin a set of observations.

As Gregory pointed out in his final report, other local conditions also had a great impact on the smooth operation of the astronomical parties:

I rarely found it possible to put the [instruments] in perfect adjustment until after sundown, because of the rapid changes in temperature which occurred during the latter part of the afternoon. The difference between the highest temperature on July 6, 1874, and the lowest on the succeeding night was 56.3°; in many instances the changes inside of twenty-four hours were as much as 40° to 50°.[2]

It was for the same reason that the topographical and tangent parties spent much of the middle of the day shooting for the dinner pot or resting in their tents. The high-gloss shimmer that hovered over the plains beneath the midday sun made seeing the surveyors' targets through their transits all but impossible.

The key to finding the exact point of the 49th Parallel was the zenith telescope:

... this instrument is of American invention and is exclusively adopted in the United States Coast Survey for the determination of latitudes... The reasons which led to the adoption of this instrument for the work of the boundary survey were its portability, the simplicity both of the observations and subsequent computations, and the accuracy of the result.[3]

This assertion of Featherstonhaugh notwithstanding, it was actually the method for determining latitude with a zenith telescope, not the instrument itself, which was an American innovation. In 1834, while working on determining the boundary between Michigan and Ohio, Captain Andrew Talcott of the Army Corps of Engineers accidentally rediscovered a long-forgotten formula for determining latitude. Originally invented in the early eighteenth century by Danish astronomer Peder Horrebow, the formula allowed an accurate latitude to be deduced by observing the differences in the zeniths of a number of stars culminating (that is, reaching their highest point in the sky) within a short time of each other. In short, it allowed for a substantially quicker and only slightly less accurate calculation of latitude than previous methods.

Simply put, the zenith telescope allows an observer to establish the exact angle at which any particular star reaches its zenith during its nightly rotation. Knowing the exact time at which that zenith is reached, together with the angle of the star above the observer's horizon at that moment, allows the observer to calculate his precise latitude. It is all based on the brilliantly simple fact that the angle of Polaris, the pole star, above the horizon of an observer is exactly equal to the latitude of that observer. If the pole star is 49° above the horizon, the observer must be standing at 49° North. This is all true for the sun as well, but its blinding brightness make direct observations more difficult.

As for the zenith telescope itself, Featherstonhaugh's "portability" is a relative term. While nowhere near as cumbersome and heavy as the great instruments they could replace, the British commission's three telescopes—two from top American maker Würdemann and another from London's storied Troughton & Sims—including their wooden shipping crates, weighed in at two hundred pounds each. Their stands added an additional 150 pounds apiece, the heaviness contributing essential stability.

The instrument stands were another example of how delicate the work really was. Both commissions were forced to improvise new stands based on the realities of field observations on the high plains. For the British, the problem was vibration. The original stands required that a wooden post of a substantial diameter be driven deep into the ground at each station. But, as Featherstonhaugh pointed out, while these posts would certainly stop the instrument from falling over, they could do nothing to prevent the transmission of even the smallest vibrations. Indeed, they might even have amplified them: "A post inserted in the ground has its sides in contact with the soil and every footstep on the surface above is transmitted directly to them."[4] Featherstonhaugh's solution was simple and elegant: replace the heavy pole with a tripod of slim posts and insulate them from vibration:

This was done by digging a hole in the middle of the observatory tent, 2 feet square and 18 inches deep, the floor of the whole being levelled; the footplates were then bedded carefully, each in its proper place, and the stand placed upon them. Any tremor from the surface of the soil was caught by the sides of the hole, or, if it did go as deep as its floor it could hardly affect the foot plates, as it would travel laterally underneath them...Two posts, each eight feet long and two feet in diameter, would have weighed 1,600 pounds; whereas the two stands only weighed 310 pounds and being in parts they could, if necessary, have been carried wherever the men could climb.[5]

The Americans did not seem as bothered by vibrations as they were by the sheer physical labour of driving the poles—twenty inches in diameter and six feet long—four feet down into the rough western soil. In their replacement stands (devised by Twining and introduced at Turtle Mountain West, the sixth American station) the central post was replaced by a tripod of pointed iron rods, two inches in diameter and more than six feet in length. The soil was scraped from a patch of the prairie and a triangular oak framework some twenty-nine inches high placed on the levelled pad. The iron rods were then driven down through the three points of the frame a full four feet into the ground, fixing the framework and providing a solid base upon which the telescope could be mounted.

As soon as darkness had fallen, with the longitude accurately established and the zenith telescope mounted and adjusted, the parties could begin their observations to establish the precise latitude of the station. As the movements of selected stars were tracked and checked against the almanacs, other observations and calculations gave ever more precise fixes for local time, which allowed more refined measurements of longitude, which led to more accurate readings for latitude. It was a series of checks and rechecks, narrowing the focus and reducing the possible error with every step until the astronomer was satisfied that they had determined the latitude of the astronomical station to within a few feet of perfect. From the station they could then measure south or north along the meridian to mark a point on the 49th Parallel itself. With the point of the 49th fixed on the ground, they could then swing the telescope 90° from the meridian and begin to run the tangent line due west toward the next station, approximately twenty miles to the west.

In order not to be caught waiting around with nothing to do, the tangent parties began to anticipate the results. As soon as the observers could come up with a close approximation of the latitude (to within, say, twenty or thirty feet), they would begin to draw their line. If it remained cloudy, they might run it west for nine or ten miles before the observers could finish and issue a correction. For work on the open plains, where no clear-cutting was needed and the line consisted only of a series of discrete markers, it was far quicker to adjust a line in the field than wait for a perfect latitude before starting out.

While the intention was for the markers to be placed a mile apart along the border in Manitoba and three miles apart out on the open plains, flexibility was once again the watchword. Where a deep valley or steep hillside interfered with the placing of the markers, they were moved, often substantial distances, to more even terrain. As the parties approached the rough foothills of the Rocky Mountains, it often became impossible to build a proper marker of any sort. But it is interesting to note that even in open ground, with no trees through which to make a clear-cut, no continuous barrier was used to trace the course of the boundary between the three-mile markers. Today, the edges of fields running along the border tend to make its course clear, but when first surveyed there would have been few visual clues. Yet for anyone crossing the border on the prairies—rarely more than a mile and a half from the nearest marker—the flat nature of most of the terrain made it likely that the nearest cairn or post would almost always be visible.

Even the markers themselves varied greatly in their construction. Where there were rocks to be had, the markers were stone cairns. Where there were forests, stripped logs were bound together into solid tripods. Where there were neither trees nor rocks, the sappers dug and packed the thin, gravelly soil and sod into great conical mounds that would have been visible for miles across the dead-flat plains.

The long series of observations and calculations should have taken four days and five nights at each station, but that was rarely the case:

> The time of completing a station... was actually always more than this. Sometimes the first night could not be used for latitude observations, owing to the party having arrived too late at the station to make the necessary preparations, and one night out of three was generally cloudy or unfavourable to observation owing to thunderstorms or gales of wind. The average time to complete one station was seven days during the summer months. [6]

As soon as the tangent was well on its way, the observers had finished their work and the mound marking the 49th Parallel had been built, the whole camp was packed up and moved. "Shifted," wrote Featherstonhaugh, "to some spot where water was to be had, about half way to the next astronomical station."[7] From there, the tangent would be run the final ten miles or so to the next station. This usually added another four days to the process. Building the intervening mounds every three miles added yet another three days.

All this painstaking and complex work was at least predictable and presented no real problem for any trained surveyor. There was, however, yet another wild card waiting in the deck: the unpredictable "deviation of the plumb line." It had the potential to be far more troublesome.

As usual, Featherstonhaugh could be counted on to explain the problem in his confident, matter-of-fact manner. The only way to find a point on any parallel is:

> ... by finding a point [star] whose zenith is the required number of degrees from the celestial equator. It is then assumed that the plumb-line from the point in question to its apparent zenith is truly vertical, and that the point on the ground is the same number of degrees from the terrestrial equator that its apparent zenith is from the celestial one; but experience has shown that this is not the case.[8]

The reason for this discrepancy is a fact of life for any surveyor (and another of life's few certainties shattered for the rest of us):

The plumb-line can, strictly speaking, never be said to be truly vertical; local attraction, due to irregularities in the density and figure of the earth, pull it to one side or the other, and as there is no check on this, the absolute amount of the deviation at any one spot cannot be ascertained.[9]

The consequences are obvious:

… when a connection is made, by actual survey, between two points, situated at some distance, whose latitudes have been determined astronomically, the relative deviation of the plumb-line at the two spots is at once apparent… The parallel passing through one station would not, if continued with the proper curvature, be identical with the parallel passing through the next station, and so on.[10]

The line of the 49th Parallel across the high plains would encounter more than a few of Featherstonhaugh's "irregularities," each one capable of pulling the plumb line off centre to the north or south. Such physical features as Pembina and Turtle Mountains, the Coteau of the Missouri, the Cypress and Sweetgrass Hills, not to mention the front ranges of the Rocky Mountains themselves, would be a persistent presence all the way to the Great Divide. While a plumb line's microscopic drift off centre might not be a problem for a housebuilder or even a highway engineer, just how much trouble it could be for the boundary commissions was demonstrated as the surveys moved past the Sweetgrass Hills. Lying just to the south of the line, their huge mass was sufficient to create a distortion amounting to fourteen feet for every mile. To a surveyor, that magnitude of error is unimaginably far beyond what is acceptable.

It was the inescapable fact of plumb line deviation that was behind all the arguments about whether the international boundary should be an astronomical or a mean parallel. For Twining, it came down to choosing what he called "practical rather than mathematical considerations"[11]:

> [The line] must be clearly defined by visible monuments, and the positions of these marks must be such that, in case of their loss, the points can be easily and accurately recovered. The only simple method of recovery is by astronomical observation, and since the local deflections of the plumb-line are supposed not to vary for long periods of time, the process is easy and accurate.[12]

So establishing a series of exact measurements along the 49th Parallel and then, as it were, connecting the dots between them would not produce a perfect arc of impeccable accuracy, but it would produce a series of straight lines that, viewed from a larger scale, made a slightly irregular curve that was as close to perfect as it needed to be.

THAT CAMPBELL TRUSTED his officers' abilities was evident from the fact that the American parties were already in the field by the time he arrived at Pembina. There had been a lot of time for them to talk things through while they waited in St. Paul. His opposite number, however, was not so sure of his own subordinates.

Cameron's instructions to the surgeons, and his diplomatic directive about the Indians, were both part of a much larger document he had prepared earlier in the spring. With his men soon to be strung out along a four-hundred-mile front, he was attempting to establish at least some measure of control over their activities. The reason for this, he said, was that the officers had taken on more responsibility and been allowed a greater freedom of action than it was "considered to be in the interest of the service to continue."[13] He may have been thinking specifically of Featherstonhaugh, who had gone off into the Roseau swamp in September and had not returned to Dufferin until just before the spring breakup. Featherstonhaugh might well have retorted that he knew his job and had simply gone about doing it.

Anderson certainly never expressed any concern about Featherston-haugh's or Galwey's capacity for independent action.

To bring the commission under a tighter rein, Cameron announced that he had divided it into seven distinct departments: Headquarters, Intelligence, Medical, Veterinary, Commissariat, Natural History and, most important, Topographical. Each of the first five departments existed to ensure that the topographical group could accomplish its work with minimum delay. The natural history group was free to do more or less wherever it wanted and could draw on such additional support as might be spared, particularly from the medical department. Each department had its own head, reporting to the commissioner, but Anderson, in charge of the all-important topographical department, was also authorized to issue orders to any member of the commission.

Having apparently taken firm control, Cameron could not resist giving himself a way out of the very responsibilities he had just assumed. "While thus limiting the authority of heads of departments and members," he wrote, "... any responsibility they may incur which is plainly to the advantage of the service yet incompatible with previous reference for authority will not only be approved of but expected of them as a matter of duty."[14] What Anderson made of the new regime he did not say, although he probably found it (as he had already characterized an earlier directive) "perhaps not altogether intelligible."[15]

With Galwey on the trail to the season's first astronomical station at Pointe Michel, the other parties followed in quick succession. Under threatening skies on the morning of June 7, Featherstonhaugh tucked Cameron's directive in his pocket and took his twenty-five-man party out to establish the second station at the end of Pembina Mountain. At noon the same day, Greene put his men to work on the topographical survey. On the 9th, Gregory headed out to join Featherstonhaugh, followed just a day later by Twining, bound to Pointe Michel and his joint observations with Galwey.[16]

Finally, on June 11, Anderson swirled out of Dufferin with Hallett and his Metis scouts. With sufficient provisions for fourteen days

Senior staff of the British North American Boundary Commission.
Back row, left to right: George Burpee, William F. King, George Coster, Lawrence Herchmer, Samuel Anderson, George Dawson, Alexander Lord Russell, William Ashe. *Front row, left to right*:William Galwey, Arthur Ward, Chief Commissioner Donald Cameron, Albany Featherstonhaugh, Thomas Burgess, William Boswell, Dufferin, 1873 (NA-249-1).

ABOVE: Senior staff of the United States Northern Boundary Commission. *Back row, left to right*: James Bangs, Lewis Boss, Francis Vinton Greene, Edwin Ames, Charles Doolittle, Orrin Wilson, Valentine McGillycuddy. *Front row, left to right*: James Gregory, Elliott Coues, Chief Commissioner Archibald Campbell, William Twining, Montgomery Bryant, Sweetgrass Hills, 1874 (NA-249-2).

TOP RIGHT: The north–south clear-cut defining the Northwest Angle, 1872 (NA-249-9).

BOTTOM RIGHT: The rediscovered and rebuilt monument marking the northwesternmost point of Lake of the Woods. The figure next to the monument is George Dawson, 1873 (NA-249-8).

The United States Northern Boundary Commission under canvas
at Pembina, Dakota Territory, 1872 (NA-249-12).

The sternwheeler *Dakota* at Upper Fort Garry, Manitoba, 1872 (NA-249-11).

ABOVE: Cutting ice on the Red River, Dufferin, 1873 (NA-249-14).

TOP RIGHT: William F. Butler, author of *The Great Lone Land*, and his famous dog, Cerf-vola, visit the boundary commission camp, Dufferin, 1872 (NA-249-27).

BOTTOM RIGHT: Packed earth and sod-covered boundary marker, west of the Souris River, 1873 (NA-249-25).

Captain Cameron in his buckboard, 1873 (NA-249-26).

loaded into two light wagons, he originally intended to reconnoitre some 180 miles of the country. Even with the drag of the wagons, it is hard to imagine Anderson leaving Pembina at a stately pace. He must have delighted in the sheer magic of riding out at the head of such a party. The dark-skinned, weatherbeaten hunters, with their rough ponies, knee-high buckskin boots, traditional multicoloured sashes about their waists and shiny new Spencer carbines crooked in their arms, were every young Englishman's imagination made flesh. Over the next three decades, thousands of them would cross the Atlantic to live out their cowboy fantasies, but few would ever experience the dream so fully realized.

Anderson ranged west past the two joint astronomical stations and turned north along an old Metis trail to skirt the steep face of Pembina Mountain. Turning south back down toward the boundary, he crossed the Pembina River and established the site for the seventh astronomical station on the west bank. The need for flexibility in positioning the stations was already in evidence. Featherstonhaugh's station was only fifteen miles west of Pointe Michel. Station 7 at the Pembina River crossing would be just another 12 miles farther west. The distance beyond that to number 8 was thirty miles, but from that point on, the spacing of the stations was, with few exceptions, remarkably close to twenty miles.

Pembina Mountain is a mountain in appearance only, and only when viewed from the floor of the Red River valley. Pembina's face is, in fact, an escarpment; the exposed eastern edge of a broad, sloping sedimentary plane that extends nearly three hundred miles into the heart of the continent. As Anderson moved out onto the plateau, the true nature of the western high plains quickly began to reveal itself. "We travelled across an open prairie," he wrote, "& at one period saw no wood for 3 days."[17] This must have been quite a shock after establishing the site for the seventh astronomical station, where he had noted that the dense cover of poplars on the "summit" of Pembina Mountain would require an eight mile clear-cut. In work more reminiscent of the boundary marking in the Roseau swamp, the axemen would likely chop down more wood on Pembina Mountain than they would see over the next eighty miles of the plateau. The wood was just the first sign that this was a world of extremes, where there was no baseline of predictability, or even of reasonable expectation.

Barely four months before, on his inspection tour of the eastern line, Anderson had been buried under a mound of blankets and bison robes, shivering at –40° F. Now, in mid-June, he was riding in temperatures which hovered in the mid-80s F and, in another month, might easily eclipse 100° F for a week at a stretch. There are really just two true seasons on the plains: high summer and deep winter, separated only by a few weeks of chronic instability. Modern data for North Dakota show the state's all-time record high and low temperatures both occurred in the same year—1936—in two towns little more than a hundred miles apart. On the morning of February 15, the few residents of Parshall awoke to a temperature of –60° F. Less than five months later, on July 6, the town of Steele was baking under a relentless sun that pushed the thermometer to 121° F. Few other regions of earth are subject to such meteorological wrenching.

Beyond the wild swings of temperature, almost everything else about life on the plains was lived in a series of short, violent outbursts. It was (and still can be) a place where no report could be dismissed as just a tall tale. Travellers who had gone for days with nothing to eat ended up running for their lives as thousands of stampeding bison rushed out of nowhere to trample their camp into the dust and disappear as quickly as they had come, leaving nothing behind but sharply whetted appetites. Men who had run out of water could feel their thirst intensify as a brief, violent thunderstorm flooded the creeks with undrinkable mud or bombed them with golfball-sized hail. Patient hours spent scouring the ground for enough scraps of brush to cook a meal could turn to a mad panic in the face of a towering wall of fire sweeping through the grass with the speed of the wind, burning days of precious forage for the animals and covering the plains with a choking blanket of soot for miles in every direction. In short, it seemed in every way a land of either too much or nothing at all.

This was the world into which the boundary commissions were about to move, and it was Anderson's self-appointed task to try to mitigate the dangers and pre-empt the delays that could quickly leave even the most carefully considered plan in ruins. In this, the experience of the scouts would be beyond price. It was not enough simply to find reliable sources of wood and water, establish the sites for the stations and be on the lookout for any trouble from the Natives. There was also the matter of the supply wagons. It was one thing to sweep across the plains on a horse or pull a light cart, but both commissions' heavy wagons would require a clear, hard-packed trail with shallow fords and as little climbing and descending of hills as possible. At the height of the work, there would be nearly a hundred wagons moving back and forth along the line from Pembina. After only the briefest rainstorm, the succession of hooves and wheels from even a small train would churn the wet soil into a mud gumbo that could render the trail impassable for days.

By the time he cleared Pembina Mountain, Anderson had already discovered that where the Pembina River crossed the boundary it was running in a three-mile-wide canyon some 350 feet deep. Scouting back up the trail for eight miles, he found a reasonable crossing (as long as the water stayed at its usual summer levels) and marked it for the big wagons to follow.

There was one problem that even Anderson's careful explorations could do nothing to avoid or even minimize: the mosquitoes. If anyone thought that leaving the muskeg and the Red River for the high, dry plains would put the swarms behind them, they were immediately disabused of the idea. If anything, the plagues on the Pembina plateau were the equal of anything they had experienced in the Roseau swamps. Anderson, his men and their animals were "terribly tortured"[18] almost without relief, and nearly every correspondence from the boundary through the spring and summer was filled with references to life with the mosquitoes and the hopelessness of trying to find even a small measure of respite. The men had learned a great deal from the local populations about how to live and work through the winter. If there was a home remedy for the mosquitoes (other than making as much green wood smoke as possible) no one made any mention of it.

BACK AT THE headquarters one man was conducting field tests of what was purported to be an effective insect repellent. The new U.S. medical officer, Elliott Coues, had faced the swarms before, but they paled before what he found at Pembina:

> My first lesson in mosquitoes was learned in Labrador in 1860; it was retaught me in 1873 on the Red River of the North—where horses, cattle and caribou are sometimes killed by breathing mosquitoes till their nasal passages are plugged solid—where in walking across a piece of prairie, colored gray with a veil of the insects settled on the herbage, one leaves a trail of bright green grass, over which a gray cloud hangs in the air.[19]

Soon after his arrival, the young captain had made several trials with something called Persian Insect Powders, after which he was able to report only that "the article is a perfect failure."[20] But Coues had not come to the Red River to test insect repellents, nor did he even count ensuring the health of the American parties as his first priority. What had drawn him to the 49th Parallel was his concurrent appointment as commission naturalist, and he fully expected it to occupy the vast majority of his time. It was an attitude that would cause him no small amount of trouble with at least one of his fellow officers.

Although barely thirty years of age, Coues was already emerging as one of the leading ornithologists in the United States. It was a reputation that had been greatly enhanced the previous fall with the appearance of his first major work, the *Key to North American Birds*. Its scope was enormous—according to its subtitle, it contained "a Concise Account of Every Species of Living and Fossil Bird at Present Known from the Continent North of the Mexican and United States Boundary"—and its organization revolutionary. It was one of the first of what today might be called a "field guide." Rather than being aimed at the professional scientist in his laboratory, the book was designed to allow the student or amateur ornithologist to identify birds quickly and, just as quickly, put them into their correct family, genus and species. The book immediately became a great success with students and, among teachers, it influenced a whole generation of scientific textbooks.

Like Twining, Coues was no stranger to the great American west. At the end of March 1873, when he received his orders to join the commission in St. Paul, he was serving as surgeon at Fort Randall, a cavalry post in the southeastern corner of the Dakota Territory some three hundred miles up the Missouri from Sioux City. Nearly a decade before, as the Civil War was drawing to a close, the young Coues had spent more than a year in the far west as medical officer at Fort Whipple in the Arizona Territory.

Born to a prosperous New Hampshire merchant family in 1842, Coues moved to Washington D.C. in 1854 when his father took a job in the Patent Office there; for the rest of Elliott's life, the city would be his home. He was educated at Columbian College, ancestor of today's George Washington University, where in quick succession he earned a series of degrees, beginning with his Bachelor of Arts in 1861. Later that year, he entered Columbian's National Medical College, and in 1862, while simultaneously earning his master of arts degree, he became a U.S. Army medical cadet and was assigned to Mount Pleasant Hospital in Washington. In the nearly fourteen months he was resident there, the sick and wounded from a series of battles were brought into the hospital and Coues's front-line medical education came quickly to include amputations and the treatment of a variety of wounds and contagious diseases. By March 1864 Coues received his army commission at the rank of assistant surgeon (equivalent to first lieutenant) and was assigned immediately to active duty in the Arizona Territory.

The appointment, safely distant from the front lines and the field hospitals, was probably engineered by Coues's mentor Spencer Fullerton Baird. Baird, assistant secretary of the Smithsonian Institution and one of America's best-known naturalists, had first met the precocious young ornithologist soon after the Coues family moved to Washington. It was Baird who had arranged for Coues's first field trip—the 1860 voyage to Labrador where he encountered his first plague of mosquitoes—and Coues expressed his thanks by naming the first new species he identified "Baird's sandpiper."

On the last day of 1865, Coues returned from his western posting. Immediately upon reporting for duty in Washington, he was assigned to the Smithsonian to catalogue the substantial collection of birds, mammals, reptiles and every other sort of living thing which he had shipped back from Fort Whipple. It seems Baird had intervened again to secure a posting for Coues that was, to say the least, unusual. After a few months at the Smithsonian, he spent the next seven years on postings in South Carolina, North Carolina and Maryland.

The one constant among all his diverse postings was his steady stream of published observations, notes and articles on ornithology. In such comparatively unknown territory as Arizona, it had been easy to discover and describe any number of new species and subspecies, but even in the Carolinas and Maryland, where ornithologists had been beating the bushes for two centuries or more, Coues still found enough new material to keep his mind and his pen active.

The hand of Spencer Baird was once again at work in Coues's appointment to the boundary commission. Coues himself wrote to a colleague, "Congratulate me! I have got my appointment as naturalist of the British Boundary Survey... Baird seems to have got it for me, as he does everything."[21] To Baird himself, Coues wrote "You have laid me under a load of obligation from which I see no possible escape except by systematic ingratitude—and that would come harder to me than to stay in debt..."[22] Baird's active support of Coues's career (indeed of a whole generation of young American naturalists) was motivated by more than simple philanthropy. The Smithsonian Institution was less than three decades old and still far from holding anything like the comprehensive natural history collections that would have marked it as one of the world's great museums. The opening of the American west provided a grand opportunity to see those collections dramatically enriched, and Baird was quick to act. Although the new boundary survey was far smaller and much more narrowly focussed than some (such as Ferdinand Hayden's 1870 "Survey of the Territories" of the American West), it was still a chance for Baird to build his collections, and he was not shy in pushing for the appointment of a man he knew could be counted on to make the most of the opportunity.

During his relatively brief stay in Arizona, Coues had identified one new species—the gray vireo—and five new subspecies, but he knew that the high plains country through which the boundary commission would be travelling would not prove nearly as fertile for new discoveries. A number of naturalists, including Audubon, had travelled the Upper Missouri, and their observations had identified most of what one could reasonably expect to find. Still, the picture was far from complete in every detail, and Coues was excited by his prospects. Also, while his speciality was birds, he would be expected to collect as widely as possible from among the mammals, fish, reptiles and plants he would encounter, knowing enough about each field to recognize specialities when he saw them. When those collections were shipped back to Washington, they would be farmed out to other experts for analysis and final cataloguing. Any number of eminent scholars had a vested interest in what a sharp-eyed Coues might find along the 49th Parallel.

Following his disappointing experiments with the Persian insect powders, Coues got down to the serious work of collecting. Throughout June he habituated himself to the sloughs, streams and woodlots surrounding Fort Pembina. By the beginning of July, without travelling much out sight of the fort, he could write to a colleague that, despite the mosquitoes and the lack of decent assistants, he had already collected "...some 550 skins, nests and eggs...Besides I have perhaps 1500 insects in alcohol, other alcoholics and an herbarium."[23]

WHEN ELLIOTT COUES and the other officers of the American boundary commission stepped from the steamer *Selkirk* onto the west bank of the Red River on June 1, they were accompanied by the small, brittle figure of what seemed to be a boy of no more than nine or ten years old. His name was George Mercer Dawson and only a thin moustache and wispy beard hinted at his true age of twenty-three. Dawson was Coues's opposite number—the Canadian-appointed naturalist and scientist to Her Majesty's commission—and rarely could the word "opposite" be applied more appropriately.

Coues was barely out of his twenties, but he had already developed a solid scientific reputation on both sides of the Atlantic. Described by an acquaintance as "... tall, well-formed, [with] classic features, straight as an arrow, with the air of the scholar without the student's stoop,"[24] Coues was also gaining a reputation as something of a womanizer. Dawson, by contrast, was small, sickly, fresh out of school and a virtual unknown to everyone outside his immediate family and a few of his father's professional colleagues. While Coues had a broad grasp of most things in the natural world, he evinced almost no interest (or knowledge) on the subject of geology. Dawson, on the other hand, was first and foremost a geologist, already well on his way to developing one of the most brilliantly intuitive minds of his generation.

George Dawson was born in Pictou, Nova Scotia, on August 1, 1849. His father, John William Dawson, was a brilliant, Edinburgh University–educated teacher, geologist and naturalist. The year after George's birth, William was appointed Nova Scotia's Superintendent of Education and then, in 1855, moved his family to Montreal when he assumed the office of principal of McGill University. It was a chair he would fill admirably for the next 38 years, turning the university into an internationally recognized centre of learning. Before his death in 1899, Principal Dawson would found the Royal Society of Canada and serve as the head of both the American and the British Association for the Advancement of Science. For his enormous contributions to Canadian letters, he was knighted in 1884.

Early in his education, George showed he had inherited much of his father's love of learning, especially where it came to the sciences. Then, when he was just nine years of age, he contracted a debilitating disease which kept him bedridden for several years. The affliction—probably Pott's disease, a tuberculosis of the spine—left George a stunted hunchback with a caved-in chest and a respiratory system so delicate that, for the rest of his life, something as simple as a common cold could have killed him. The disease had no effect on his mind, however, and, after a succession of private tutors during his convalescence, he studied briefly at McGill before going on to Edinburgh, then London's Royal School of Mines, from which he graduated at the top of his class, winning, as one writer has put it, "...almost every honour that institution could bestow."[25]

Although he had intended to join the Geological Survey of Canada (GSC) immediately following his graduation, Principal Dawson prevailed upon his son to accept the position of geologist and naturalist with the boundary commission, and delay joining the Survey. The arrangement would certainly have received the prior approval of the GSC's director, Alfred Selwyn.

That there was even to be a professional scientist with the commission was uncertain almost up to the moment of its departure for the west. The Foreign Office had initially approved the position of "veterinarian/zoologist" and was loath to entertain any suggestion that the already inflated number of commission personnel should be further increased. However, Cameron petitioned the Foreign Office with the fact that W.G. Boswell, while a fine veterinarian, "... does not pretend to any knowledge or experience of zoology"; an additional position was reluctantly authorized.[26]

So it was that George Mercer Dawson came to begin his journal on the first day of June, 1873:

> Arrived at Dufferin, Manitoba, per steamer "Selkirk" about 1 P.M. & landed on the muddy bank of the Red River amidst torrents of rain. Great confusion during landing of baggage, during which missed three out of my nine packages. Introduced to members of Boundary Commission. Got room, &c. &c.[27]

Often in the company of Doctors Burgess and Millman, and a sapper named Duckworth who had been assigned to him on a more-or-less permanent basis, Dawson went to work immediately. Where the floods had receded, he explored the broad valley of the Red River and began his collections of plants, animals and birds.

Like his fellow scientist Elliott Coues, Dawson was expected to know something about mosquitoes, and he too was conducting some informal field tests. Obviously in possession of some sort of alleged repellent sent to him by his sister Anna, Dawson sent her a brief report on its effectiveness:

> ... if you smear yourself with [the oil] no mosquito will light for about half and hour. At the end of this time it loses its effect & you have to repeat the dose from a small bottle carried in the pocket. The remedy at best is worse than the disease & its frequent application destructive of comfort & clothes. [28]

Like Coues, Dawson also had his literary aspirations and was a regular producer of florid (and invariably awful) high-Victorian verse. He would later turn his pen to the subject of the dreaded insects:

> The air is full of murmur and of song
> That rounds the solemn stillness of the waste
> As gay the light mosquito oars along
> "In God and in his sword" his trust is placed—
> Oh smudge Oh glorious smudge! let me entrench in thy sweet
> noxious cloud
> And nose and eyes all smarting with thy stench, there curse the
> winged crowd!

Except for the terrible predation of the mosquitoes—something that continued to rate a mention in nearly every letter and journal entry—Dawson seemed happy and entirely at home with his first field experience. To his sister (who had obviously expressed some concern about his health) he wrote: "So far I have never ceased to enjoy myself."[29] When he was not rushing down to the jetty to meet any incoming steamers in hope that some of his lost luggage might be on board, he continued his daily forays out across the plain of the Red River and planned for his first major expedition. However, as Anderson and the astronomical teams were preparing to head west, Dawson was making ready to go east to undertake a natural and geological survey of Lake of the Woods.

ON JUNE 13, with his scouts ranged out ahead of him across a five-mile front, Anderson pushed west from the Pembina River. He established astronomical sites at Long River, at a place that would come to be known as "Sleepy Hollow" and at the east end of Turtle Mountain, 115 miles from Pembina. At that point, the scouts split into two groups and circled the mountain to the north and south, meeting on the far side to compare notes on the topography and settle the location for the next station.

For Anderson, Turtle Mountain was another of the plains' mixed blessings. The name is misleading, for it is not a mountain but a fifty-mile-wide, broadly circular upland area a few hundred feet above the level of the surrounding plains. While there was water everywhere, much of it was not safe to drink. There was so much water, in fact, the succession of lakes and swamps through which the line passed forced numerous detours, and the building of several lengths of corduroy road for the wagons. All this slowed the work terribly. As for firewood, it might be a scarce commodity out on the plains, but marking the boundary across Turtle Mountain would take thirty-five miles of clear-cutting through impossibly dense timber, brush and deadfall. Still, all that wood and water—the very things that would make so much extra work for the topographical and astronomical parties—made Turtle Mountain the perfect location for the first of the western depots. Sensing the opportunity to bring his builders and supply trains forward, Anderson abandoned any thoughts of continuing west and rushed back to Dufferin.

He arrived at the headquarters on about June 24, having made a round trip of some three hundred miles in less than a fortnight. As for the possibility of trouble, Anderson wrote, "We saw no Indians tho' our Scouts tried very hard to find some."[30] Anderson did see something else worthy of note: "On my return I met Captain Cameron with his wife and family encamped two days journey from here [Dufferin]. They are moving about the country in a picnic style and will return in about a week."[31] What he thought of the commissioner taking more than a week of holidays at the height of the season's work he does not say, but he was probably relieved to have him out of the way. In any event, Anderson did not intend to be waiting when the Camerons returned from their extended picnic: "I have only come back here for a few days and I shall join the parties in the field and remain with them for the rest of the season..."[32]

Having seen for himself that the work on the line was progressing smoothly, Anderson immediately dispatched the last of his support parties from Dufferin. On June 24, Dr. Burgess went out to meet with Featherstonhaugh and accompany him to Turtle Mountain, while Millman took the second medical party out with orders to join Galwey as he left the Pointe Michel station and swung out around Pembina Mountain toward the site of his next observations.

The logistical challenge in organizing men and matériel involved in the apparently simple act of drawing a thin line along 49° North was becoming clear. For the 1873 season, Her Majesty's commission would deploy a total of 270 men, including 18 officers and 23 noncommissioned officers and staff. They would move with the aid of 100 horses, 59 ponies and 48 oxen pulling 112 vehicles of every sort and size. Other than those wagons being used to carry the instruments or additional water, nearly every other vehicle would be dedicated to carrying huge quantities of food for the men and forage for the animals. All these provisions were to be stored along the line at a series of four principal depots. Built at intervals of about ninety miles, each of the depots would involve the construction of at least one log storage building and perhaps basic workshops for the carpenters or blacksmiths. Some would even have rudimentary stables. In addition to the main depots, three subdepots would eventually be established where they were deemed necessary. These were primarily to store oats for the horses and small quantities of rations for the supply train teamsters as they moved steadily back and forth between the main depots and Dufferin.

Part of the men's daily allowance of meat would be provided by a small herd of cattle driven along the boundary to the principal depot at Turtle Mountain. Anything the men could shoot along the way— bison, pronghorn, ducks or geese—was considered a bonus. Perhaps *almost* anything would be more precise. On his way to Turtle Mountain, young subassistant astronomer William F. King wrote to his father that one of his party had killed a badger, "which we tried without success to eat."[33]

The wisdom of Ottawa's intention to have its appointments form the core of a homegrown scientific community was proven in the case of English-born William King. He was barely eighteen but had already graduated from the University of Toronto with highest honours and a gold medal in mathematics. The boundary work would be the first step in a career that would see him emerge as one of Canada's most significant scientists of the early twentieth century. Within two years of his boundary service, King would be confirmed as both a Dominion land and topographical surveyor and then go on to serve as the Department of the Interior's chief inspector of surveys and, in 1890, to become Canada's chief astronomer.

By mid-June, as the British were moving west in strength, the American commission had still not been joined by either its supply wagons from Fort Abercrombie or its cavalry escort. Since this left Twining and Gregory short of stores, it was agreed to keep them close to Pembina—and to each other—for as long as possible, and the alternating of astronomical observations was modified. After finishing their joint observations with the British at Pointe Michel and the east side of Pembina Mountain, the Americans would take the next two stations (7 and 8, at Pembina Mountain West and Long River respectively) while Galwey and Featherstonhaugh, with their superior reach, would take stations 9 and 10 at Sleepy Hollow and the east end of Turtle Mountain. By the end of the month, however, both the American wagons and the cavalry had arrived at Pembina and almost immediately headed out to join their field parties.

It is hard to make direct comparisons between the two commissions' efforts. From the scale of the respective operations, it seems either that the British were spending far more in men and supplies than was really necessary, or that the U.S. commission simply could not have been doing its rightful share of the work. In fact, neither assumption is fair. Certainly the British complement was considerably larger, both in working parties and in the armada of hired wagons and teamsters that supported them. It must be remembered, however, that there were three fully equipped parties, each with about fifteen men, working on the topographical survey along the north side of the line, and only one of these was staffed with Royal Engineers. The other two were made up entirely of Canadian appointees, their costs paid for by the Canadian government as an investment in the country's own future surveying needs.

With the relative strength of the astronomical parties, too, comparisons are difficult. The British had two parties, each with a complement of twenty-three or twenty-four men. U.S. Assistant Astronomer James Gregory was usually accompanied by about fifteen military and civilian personnel:

> ... the organization of my party, which was retained throughout the season, was as follows: [a] computer, [a] recorder, a foreman, an observatory attendant and meteorological observer, a cook, waiter, three laborers, a mounted man to serve as scout and messenger and five teamsters.
>
> For transportation of party, instruments, equipage, and generally twenty to thirty days' rations and forage, I had one four-mule spring wagon, three six-mule Army-wagons, one two-mule Minnesota wagon, and a horse for myself.[34]

It is reasonable to assume that Twining had a similar complement under his direction. The presence of so many civilians with the American parties, in contrast to the previous year, was a result of Washington having dropped its original insistence that the commission use U.S. Army personnel wherever possible.

The difference in strength can also be accounted for by the different roles that each side assigned to its parties. Galwey and Featherstonhaugh were responsible for running the lines between the stations; the Americans assigned that task to the topographical unit under Lieutenant Greene and staffed it accordingly. Greene had about fifty men under his command to run the lines and accomplish the survey.

In his contributions to the later published report on the British commission's activities, Featherstonhaugh detailed the full weight of the British effort, including the medical and veterinary parties, the commissariat, the chief commissioner's party and the depot crews. While most of these substantial operations may seem to be missing from the records of the American effort, they are simply not identified as separate activities. Rather, any and all field support to the commission—including the supplies, wagons, teamsters, veterinarians and so forth—was provided as a matter of course by the U.S. Army and, as a result, not "billed" to the commission's account.

In the final analysis, despite an apparently overwhelming superiority in resources, the British were never held up waiting for the Americans as the two parties progressed westward in parallel, indicating that any real differences in commitment were far less significant than they might appear.

Indeed, the only area where there was a clear and real difference between the two commissions was in the American provision of escorts. The thirty men of the hurriedly organized 49th Rangers, who had arrived at Dufferin from Winnipeg at the end of May, were no match for the show of military might that arrived at the American headquarters toward the end of June 1873. Joining Captain Abram Harbach's Company K of the 20th Infantry from Fort Pembina were two full companies of the 7th Cavalry: Captain Thomas B. Weir's Company D and Company I under Captain Myles Keogh. Major Marcus Reno was placed in overall command.

Not wanting to be held up by the clear-cutting at Pembina Mountain, Featherstonhaugh left a party of axemen with one of his Canadian assistants and prepared to move to station 10, some eighty miles away at the east end of Turtle Mountain. At the same time, Greene began to chop his way east from the American station at the Pembina River.

After finishing up at Pointe Michel on June 25, Galwey swung north around the mountain and spent an adventurous three days covering the eighty miles to station 9. Daytime temperatures were in the high 80s, but still falling to within a few degrees of frost at night. There were problems with water, too, but not in the way Galwey might have anticipated:

> We have had no less than thirteen bad [thunderstorms] since the 4th of the month. They are always accompanied with a violent gale and rain. I had to rush out of my tent with nothing on but my night shirt, could not even wait to find my boots, to save my tent from being swept away. I found it held by only two guys and did not the mosquitos take an unfair advantage. They completely outflanked me.[35]

Another storm found Galwey again standing in the rain with his nightshirt blowing in the wind like "an old woman struggling with an umbrella turned inside out,"[36] and he resorted to desperate measures: "I have found out a very good way of making my tent stand up, *viz*, by turning out all my men whenever it blows down. It is wonderful the care they bestow in pitching it now."[37] For Dr. Millman, it didn't seem to matter whether his tent stood up to the wind or not: "The new Hudson's Bay tents are perfectly useless in keeping out rain. During a heavy shower you can soon catch a basin of water."[38]

The foul weather, mosquitoes and lack of sleep gave station 9 its official name. Galwey christened it Sleepy Hollow "... as all the men slept I think for at least eighteen hours on the stretch."[39]

All along the line, a steady stream of traffic was moving between Dufferin and the new depot at Turtle Mountain. Anderson had passed through Sleepy Hollow on July 8, heading west on the second of his explorations and, by the 16th Galwey had finished with his observations and was running the line toward Featherstonhaugh at station 10. With Dr. Burgess detained at the depot treating the victim of a logging accident, Millman was sent back to the small subdepot at Pembina Mountain to deal with a Royal Engineers corporal who was reported to be seriously ill. He was joined on the trip by commission secretary Arthur Ward who was returning to Dufferin. Along the way, they met with Canadian surveyor W.F. King and commissioner Cameron, both of whom were headed independently for Turtle

Mountain. It was as if the horses and ox carts were nose to tail along the entire 130 miles between headquarters and the depot.

THE AMERICANS, too, were converging on Turtle Mountain. With their escort and supply trains fully operational, Twining and Gregory finished their joint observations at stations 7 and 8 and, with their lines run all the way to Sleepy Hollow, they prepared to make their first great leap along the boundary. Gregory would move more than 115 miles in one manoeuvre to set up station 13 at Antler Creek, while Twining would direct the work at station 11 on the far side of Turtle Mountain, of necessity some thirty-five miles west of Featherstonhaugh's station 10. While the American parties were happy to use the astronomical sites that Anderson was identifying on his reconnaissances, they did not join their British counterparts on the well-used trails west from Pembina. From the outset, the U.S. commission had tended, wherever possible, to stay on their own side of the line—even before that line had tangibly come into existence. There had certainly been no restrictions on cross-border operational mobility coming from Washington, London or Ottawa. It may have been that the Army teamsters and cavalry were anxious to avoid any confrontation with "Canadian" Indians, but a more likely explanation is that Greene's topographical parties were working across a five-mile swath of land to the south of the line and there was little to be gained by moving their supply trains significantly northward, no matter how much easier the terrain might be. In one of the few exceptions to that rule, the entire American commission, cavalry and all, would stop at the British depot on Turtle Mountain for a grand parley before pushing any farther west.

U.S. Commissioner Campbell, Secretary Bangs and Elliott Coues had remained at Pembina until well into July, no doubt organizing the last of the supply parties and ensuring that the military escort was well on its way. Bangs and Coues left Pembina on July 10 and Campbell followed a day or so later. They would not be coming back to the Red River. At the close of the season's work, the main body of the commission would swing southeast across the Dakotas toward

St. Paul, and the following spring they would make use of the rapidly extending Northern Pacific Railway to reach the Missouri and, from there, move directly up toward the line. Only Lieutenant Greene would have reason to return to Pembina. There were still more than eighty miles of unfinished American business waiting in the great Roseau swamp.

Campbell caught up to Bangs and Coues on July 13 and together they joined up with Gregory and Greene, all moving toward Turtle Mountain. By the 18th they were camped with Twining near Featherstonhaugh's station at the east side of the mountain. With substantial parts of the British and Canadian parties already having arrived, the American presence contributed to what must have been a remarkable sight in such a lonely and isolated place. As an amazed Galwey observed: "the place presents the appearance of a town, two of the American parties being camped there with an escort of 70 infantry and 160 cavalry... There must be 500 men here."[40]

TWINING'S PREVIOUS sortie into the Turtle Mountain country gave him a perspective that no one seeing it for the first time could have shared. To many of the commission's men, the area seemed perfectly suited to settlement; a place that could not help but reward the diligent application of modern farming methods. Wood, water and good grass were all around, and everyone seemed to believe that the snows and the cold were not as severe as they were farther to the north and the east. Because he had seen so much of it, however, Twining knew enough not to fall for such first impressions.

Twining believed that the boundary commission's job was not simply to draw a line across the high plains. He also saw an opportunity to add to America's understanding of what had been, until after the Civil War, a mostly unknown and largely ignored part of its territory. "Within the last few years," he would write in the commission's final report:

> the rapid growth of the great States of the Northwest has given
> an impulse to the more distant territories beyond, so that now the
> lines of settlement are stretching out, up the rich valley of the Red

River, and rapidly extending to the west... The survey of the northern boundary... by giving the results of careful examination along a continuous line, has already contributed largely to the actual knowledge necessary to form a correct judgement in regard to the resources and probable future of a vast tract of country.[41]

In calling for some clear-headed analysis, Twining is unable to resist at least one shot at both the naysayers and the boosters. That "vast tract of country," he wrote, has been "... at one time classed, by unthinking and careless writers, as part of the 'Great American Desert' and a few years later exalted by the same class of authorities into something little less than a paradise."[42]

Twining's cautionary analysis of the country around Turtle Mountain and, by implication, of everywhere to the west of it, provides strong evidence that he was already conversant with the steady stream of reports flowing into Washington from the many survey expeditions sweeping across the American west. In particular, John Wesley Powell's unflinching analysis of the northern plains' ability to support a huge, sudden influx of homesteaders is echoed in Twining's thoughts about the lands that lay, both literally and figuratively, on the border line. Nowhere is this more evident than in his thoughts about water:

> There is... a limit to the extent of the arable lands fixed by the amount of the annual rain-fall. Commencing with the valley of the Red River, where the annual deposition amounts to from seventeen to nineteen inches, the amount of the rain-fall decreases until in longitude 106° it will scarcely exceed seven inches. Here we find a fact which sets a limit to the western extension of the cultivated area of the United States.[43]

That limiting "fact"—Twining puts it at a longitude of 102° West, for Powell is was at 100°, and a succession of American historians and environmentalists have seen it everywhere between 98° and 100°—has remained at the heart of the longest-running and most contentious debates about the future of the high plains. Just where, by the prevailing standards of careful stewardship and contemporary practice, does the land simply stop being habitable?

Turtle Mountain provided the perfect venue for Twining's ruminations. It represented the last truly rich environment they would see until they reached the Rocky Mountains. From Turtle Mountain westward, across the Missouri Coteau and the badlands of the White Mud River, simple survival could be a challenge even to the best prepared of expeditions, let alone for waves of inexperienced homesteaders. Longitude 100° West runs straight through the heart of Turtle Mountain.

FOR COUES, the ride toward Turtle Mountain had been marked by several interesting discoveries. Although he was not expecting to find any completely new plants and animals, there was still much to be learned about the geographical range of many species, and the possible existence of identifiable subspecies—a field of particular interest to Coues.

He found Baird's sparrow to be "the most abundant and characteristic species" between Pembina and Turtle Mountains, although it was rare anywhere else. The Sprague's pipit—Lewis and Clark's "Missouri skylark"—was common too, although Coues saw it as another example of "... the curious fact that a very abundant bird, and one inhabiting no inaccessible region, may by mere accident remain for years almost unknown."[44] Both birds had been named by Audubon following his trip up the Missouri, but their range was poorly understood.

Most important for Coues was that he continued to see evidence to support an observation he had probably first made during his time in the southwest and later confirmed during his stay at Fort Randall: "The general *facies* [appearance] of the birds of this region may be summed up in a word. They are characterized by a *pallor* of plumage, the direct result of the low annual rain-fall."[45] In fact, Coues and others would go on to realize that the generally pale coloration of the birds of the high plains was also characteristic of its small mammals and reptiles too.

While most of his observations were expressed in carefully objective terms suitable for the scientific publications in which his steady stream of essays would appear, on occasion Coues could not help drifting into the sort of mawkish or morbid sentimentality that characterized so much Victorian natural history writing. He was moved to write of the sound of the common poor-will (a small relative of the nighthawks and another Lewis and Clark discovery):

> In places where the birds are numerous the wailing chorus is enough to excite vague apprehensions on the part of the lonely traveler, as he lies down to rest by his camp-fire, or to break his sleep with fitful dreams, in which lost spirits appear to bemoan their fate and implore his intercession.[46]

Any birdwatcher who has heard the brief, simple onomatopoeia of the poor-will's call would have a difficult time trying to vest in it any hint of moaning spirits.

ONE MAN WHO was not at Turtle Mountain for the grand assembly was Anderson. He had left the depot long before Cameron or Campbell arrived, intent on locating the sites for the next three astronomical stations and pushing his preliminary survey of the boundary to more than two hundred miles west of the Red River:

> The last reconnaissance extended for 100 miles beyond the point of my first trip, and with a very light and easily handled party of 25 mounted men (natives), and two lightly loaded waggons, we advanced fearlessly at the rate of 25 miles a day, scouring the country and surveying it as we marched. I generally got observations at noon and at night, to fix accurately our course, and to keep us in the right line. We were not interfered with by Indians, nor do I think there were any Indians in reach... All the same we took all precautions by day and night. We travelled across open plains and at long intervals saw no wood and very little water, so we carried both wood and water some days.[47]

Anderson may not have seen any sign of the Indians, but nearly everyone else had. On his way to Turtle Mountain, James Bangs had written the words "Indian Scare" in his diary entry of July 18 (apparently a false alarm) and, a week later, had met two men he identified as Wahpeton Sioux on his way west after the rendezvous. Dr. Millman, setting off from the depot to rejoin Galwey along the line after a medical call, saw a number of Sioux teepees at the north end of Turtle Mountain.

The Wahpeton were a branch of what were generally known as the "eastern" Sioux, who had only recently become a presence in the Dakota Territory, a consequence of their involvement with the troubles in Minnesota of a decade before. There was no indication that they were anything more than simply curious about the large party of soldiers and other whites that had descended on Turtle Mountain. None of them had sought an audience with Cameron.

Anderson came back to the depot on July 19, having "selected routes for our transport trains, fording places across the rivers, and points for the different parties to proceed without delay." "All this," he wrote to his mother, "has been equally acceptable to the American Commission who are sadly in arrear, but I have given them the benefit of all our explorations, as the progress of the work interests us both equally..."[48]

While Anderson was still enjoying the freedom that his expeditions afforded him, his travels were not without their troubles, and the miseries which befell the scouts were being shared by every other party in the field, no matter which side of the line they were working:

> This is a terrible place for storms. Every two days we have most terrific thunder and lightning storms... I was almost eaten up by mosquitos when taking the observations at night, as they swarmed to where the lanterns were burning, and it was necessary to nerve ones self up to stand a certain number of minutes torment without moving. After the fatigues of a long march in the heat of the day these were minutes of great misery. About 11 p.m., the nights became very cool, and the mosquito plague abated, so

that one slept in peace, under 2 or 3 blankets, but these terrible storms generally came on about 2 or 3 a.m., and if one was actually turned out of the tent, we were generally so roused and wet that we were glad to get up. The rain pours thro' the light tents like water thro' a sieve.[49]

Finding the Americans still at the depot waiting anxiously for his news, Anderson "... gave them my map and am thankful to say they moved forward today [July 24], but not before our parties had got 5 days ahead of them."[50] An exhausted Anderson had one more annoyance at the end of his long ride: "Captain Cameron appeared here like a comet the night I returned, and after talking to me for two hours while I lay in bed very tired, went off to Pembina at 6 the next morning, and I don't know when he will appear again."[51]

What Cameron was talking about grew from a disagreement with Campbell, which had surfaced during their meeting at Pembina at the beginning of the month. The problem had grown from a request by Cameron that there be a substantial change to the manner in which the location of the 49th Parallel was being drawn. Briefly stated, the boundary had been marked according to what was called an "astronomical parallel" (in effect, a series of short, straight lines connecting points on the parallel.) Cameron wanted to create a "mean parallel" which would form a more perfect curve but would require the relocation of the markers that had already been established (a mean parallel could only be drawn after the astronomical parallel had been completed.) The idea had so infuriated both Campbell and his chief astronomer that they had declined to sign the Cameron-prepared minutes of the meeting. Anderson, although he does not say so at the time, was equally angry, and that anger would eventually lead to a near-breach of the already difficult relationship with his commissioner. The issue would finally be resolved at Dufferin during the winter hiatus and, for the balance of the 1873 work, the boundary would be marked as it had been for the previous two hundred miles.

With Cameron gone and the survey parties back in the field, Anderson was able to relax for the first time since he had left Dufferin in mid-June. He settled in at Turtle Mountain depot with Dr. Burgess and Boswell for company, and tried to do as little as possible.

Just beyond the depot, Featherstonhaugh's party, supplemented by seven additional hired men, had begun to cut the line across the mountain. Lieutenant Greene was supposed to have begun chopping and sawing toward him from the west side at about the same time, but he did not start the work until nearly a month later. Seeing that at least the British portion of the cutting was well under way, Featherstonhaugh left his young assistant, W.F. King, in charge and, taking ten men and the instruments with him, he headed west toward station 16, a leap of some 120 miles.

Greene, hacking through undergrowth so thick that he could report "I could hear but not see a motion of a man cutting twenty feet from me,"[52] it took nearly three weeks to cut just ten miles of the line into the west slope of Turtle Mountain. When Greene and his men ran up against the shore of a mile-wide lake stretching across their path, they named it Lake Farquhar (for their former chief astronomer). They then promptly abandoned the cutting and went back to the far less demanding work of the topographical survey.

What seems a precipitous action could not have been undertaken without authorization from either Campbell or Twining, and neither of those gentlemen would have approved it without first checking with Anderson. What was obvious to everyone was that the clear-cutting on Turtle Mountain could finish the Americans' chances of keeping up with the British all the way to the four-hundred-mile mark before the season's work had to come to an end. While Anderson suspected that both chief commissioners were willing to consider a third season in the field, Anderson and Twining had already agreed between themselves that they wanted at all costs to avoid such a necessity. Despite the tension with Cameron, Twining was still getting along famously with his British counterpart. So it was probably with Anderson's blessing that Greene went back to the survey and left the cutting to the British. King's men finally connected to the aborted American line after slashing through nearly twenty-four miles of brush and timber, but it took them until the end of September to do it.

While Featherstonhaugh and his party were struggling with impossible undergrowth, he was also genuinely moved by Turtle Mountain:

> The interior of the mountain is... singularly beautiful, owing to the graceful outlines of the hills, covered with leafy poplars, and the perfect stillness of the lakes, the shores of which are clothed with foliage down to the water's edge. From a high point in the cutting about three miles from its commencement, the mounds, marking the 49th parallel on the prairie to the eastward could be seen stretching in a gentle but well defined curve for a distance of 15 miles, thus giving the spectator a very graphic idea of the size and figure of the earth.[53]

AT THE END of June, as the astronomical parties pushed their way west, George Dawson, with a party of two sappers (his regular preparator Duckworth and a man named Spearman), two teamsters and a pair of Red River carts, headed north out of Dufferin toward Winnipeg and the Dawson Route. It was Dawson's first look at the inhabitants and settlements of the Red River valley and his journal (for all its choppy shorthand and awful spelling) is filled with a detailed commentary that does not appear in his final report:

> Travelled on over country as before, & of the usual prairie character to Stinking R[iver]. An R.C. church here with pretty sounding bell, & quite a little village of houses. Stopped for dinner at the N. end of bridge. Saw half breeds returning from church. A Very motely assemblage. The men in peculiar fitting Sunday clothes & moccasins. The women in bright coloured dresses, & shawls often worn blanket-wise. All shades of colour, & none remarkable for beauty. Most seemed about as dark as the "Indians" of the lower St. Laurence, &c.[54]

Dawson did not stay in Winnipeg any longer than necessary and on July 1 he left the town and turned east onto the Dawson Route. It was not long before he discovered for himself the truth of all the tales he had doubtless heard about it:

> Followed E. to place where road branched, a new trail through the grass, to the left. Here found a split stick with a paper on which written "This is the *write* road"... Found considerable difficulty as even when going on unbroken sod the horses often plunging in mud up to knees, & cart wheels sinking. Found an old woman & boy with two carts stuck fast, but by taking the horses out and lightening the loads were managing to get them out.[55]

His party also managed to encounter a horror of the road that his fellow members of the commission seem to have missed: the horseflies.

They were told by the men at the rest stations that at least three oxen had been killed by swarms of the huge biting insects (also known locally as "bull-dogs") and that most traffic along the road was moving only at night. Dawson continued for another day, and then the wisdom of the locals became obvious:

> After getting on sandy ground the horse-flies began to be very troublesome & teased the horses much. I could hardly get mine to go along even when occupied the whole time sweeping them off with a bush. Horse kept running sideways into bushes and altogether showed great signs of distress... the horses were each surrounded by an immense swarm of flies, just like a nest of disturbed hornets. Patches as large as a plate on horses sides so covered with flies that could not see the hair, & when swept off they constantly renewed themselves. Kidd [one of the teamsters] swept off at one time a large double handful of flies.[56]

After this encounter the party travelled mostly at night and, after suffering the usual spate of lost horses, broken axles, thunderstorms and mosquitoes, Dawson arrived at the Northwest Angle on the afternoon of July 5. No doubt he would have been quick to point out to anyone he met that the Dawson for whom the road was named was in no way related to him.

For the next month, Dawson, in the company of Duckworth and two Native paddlers named Albert and Begg (who also served as translators, guides and general factotums) explored the perimeter of Lake of the Woods. Moving counter-clockwise past the Northwest Angle, Buffalo Point and the War Road River, they camped for a day or two with D'Arcy East and his special topographical party, and also met a Mr. Harris, who was on his way to explore the region west of the lake to determine its timber-producing potential.

Other than East and Harris, the only people Dawson encountered between the Northwest Angle and the mouth of the Rainy River were thinly scattered bands of Natives. Although obviously interested in their ways (his journal is riddled with phonetic renderings of the local words for nearly every bird, fish or plant he collected), Dawson was also quick to become annoyed with their constant begging for tobacco, pork or tea. In his attitudes, Dawson was not so different from most of his colleagues, tending to view the local population with a shifting mix of curiosity, indifference and disdain. He was willing to trade a little tobacco or flour for some fresh fish, or to sit politely and listen to a long, rambling monologue from a minor chief, but he would just as soon be left alone to conduct his survey and move on.

Dawson's survey of the lake, as it develops in his journal and finds full expression in his final report, is a portrait of a place that no longer mattered. With the fur trade a thing of the distant past, the trade routes that were once alive with the great freight canoes of the North West Company lay abandoned and overgrown. At the mouth of the Rainy River, Hungry Hall had once been a major post for the Hudson's Bay Company. When Dawson arrived there to pick up the supplies that had been forwarded directly from the Northwest Angle, he found the place reduced to nothing more than "... 2 ruinous looking log shanties & a rough landing about 20′ long for tug. M. Couture in charge & only white man here."[57] Confirming his low opinion of the place was the fact that his promised supplies had not arrived.

From Hungry Hall, the party paddled up the eastern shore of the lake, dodging through the myriad islands and seeking shelter from the frequent, violent thunderstorms as they circled back toward the Northwest Angle. Along the way, Dawson continued to produce an ad hoc lexicon of the local tongues and to take note of such customs as the "sweating bath," which he describes in some detail and accompanies with a quick ink sketch. By noon on July 28, the party was back in its old camp near the government buildings at the Northwest Angle.

Dawson began to write up his notes and went exploring a little around the Angle, continuing to build up his collections of plants and rocks and anything else that struck his interest. East and his party came in from their topographical work around the mouth of Rainy River a day or so later, and everyone settled in to wait for the promised appearance of Commissioner Cameron.

On August 4, two sappers from Dufferin—a photographer and his assistant—drove their Red River carts into camp, and Cameron, travelling as usual in his buckboard with only a single attendant, finally arrived from Winnipeg on the 5th. Bright and early the next morning, the commissioner put Dawson and East in a large boat and took them out to the much-disputed reference monument. He was determined to take one last shot at preserving for the new Dominion as much of that waterlogged, mosquito-infested country as possible.

For Dawson, the question seemed clear:

> The old reference monument is stated to have been placed on the nearest firm ground to the actual angle, but taking the angle as determined last year, the point last described is very much nearer than the place where the monument is said to have stood & is drier & a far better camping place. It therefore becomes of interest to determine if by any chance the point mentioned can have been formed in recent years.[58]

So, did Thompson and Tiarks build their monument where they said—on the nearest solid ground to the northwesternmost point—or had there been another monument, since lost, built closer to the actual point and, therefore, the real benchmark from which to determine where the international boundary ought to run? Dawson's approach to answering the question was solidly practical. He sawed through a number of the oldest deadfall poplars and counted their growth rings:

> Found 4 trees. 36 years (about), 31 years, 32 years, 30–33 years. Another very large & rotten poplar lying about 4 chains N of the monument, gave at least 48 annual rings at 27 feet above the roots. All of the above logs were more or less rotten & burned & many with fungus growing from them. Most have lain at least 4 years from their appearance.
>
> These observations show that the point of firm ground was there when the boundary was formerly determined, & that it must, in all probability, have been missed in the search for a camping place.[59]

There was solid ground that lay closer to the true northwestern-most point of the lake than did the original reference monument. And, according to Dawson, it had been solid ground—above water—when the original monument had been constructed. The original survey-ors had simply missed it when searching for a good camp site in that God-forsaken swamp. But there had certainly never been another reference monument. It should have been the end of Cameron's fight—a fight that everyone else had given up on long before.

Over the next two days, Dawson and Duckworth made sure that the photographers had fully documented the land around the monument before beginning to pack up for the return to Dufferin. Cameron had disappeared as quickly as he had arrived, and East was beginning to wind down his survey. The special party's heaviest baggage was being loaded for shipment, and sapper Duckworth would ride with the wagons, taking Dawson's precious collections with him. Dawson himself would be returning to Dufferin by a different route, but not before he had made one more excursion around Lake of the Woods.

Dawson was back at the Northwest Angle again by August 16 and began immediately to finalize arrangements for his return to Dufferin. Desperate to steer clear of the Dawson Route, he had decided to canoe back to headquarters via the Roseau River. It was a curious thing to do. Although Dawson said he intended to explore the potential of the Roseau for providing a navigable route between Lake of the Woods and the Red River, that potential had already been examined countless times, including by the boundary parties, which had spent the entire previous winter going over nearly every inch of the Roseau's watershed.

It took his small party of three men nine days to paddle and drag their three-fathom canoe from the Northwest Angle back to Dufferin. According to Dawson, they travelled nearly 300 miles to cover a straight-line distance of barely 120. Along the way, they discovered nothing in the way of new plants or animals, and the rocks—where they were elevated above the muck—revealed little in the way of interesting minerals. In his final report, Dawson's opinion of the country is no different from that expressed by his boundary commission colleagues or any of the other recent explorers: this was a country that had once mattered a little, and now mattered not a bit.

Dawson arrived at Dufferin on August 28 to find only commissary Herchmer and Almon, the farm manager, keeping the lights on. Everyone else had moved west to the depot at Turtle Mountain. Dawson immediately began making plans to join them.

BY THE END of July, the stocking of Turtle Mountain depot was nearly completed and, for the first time, the British commission made a significant reduction in its manpower. None of the other officers of the commission mention it, but Dr. Millman, writing in his diary on July 27, says that fifty or sixty men were to be let go. He took it a little personally since he lost a teamster to the layoffs and would probably have to give up some of his freedom to range out across the country in order to spend more time helping with the wagons. It would have been primarily hired teamsters (and their wagons) who were no longer required by the commission, since there was certainly no reduction in the number of other contract tradesmen. Indeed, additional axemen had been hired to cut the line across Turtle Mountain. At about this time, the commission also lost the services of A.L. Russell, in charge of the second surveying party. He resigned his position for "personal reasons" and returned to the east. His place at the head of the party was taken by Corporal Malings, a qualified Royal Engineers surveyor who had been working with Sergeant Kay.

Despite the layoffs, with little in the way of serious medical problems to deal with (sick stomachs from stagnant water seemed to be the most common ailment), Millman was able to enjoy the excitement of what must have been the first real adventure of his life. When he was not attending to his few patients, he was required to assist George Dawson, and such comments as "I was botanizing in the forenoon" or "botanizing this morning with Mr. Dawson" occur in his diaries with sufficient frequency to show that he hardly considered the assignment a chore. In fact, his work with Dawson led to a lifelong interest in Canadian plants.

Millman was fascinated by nearly everything he saw in the west, although he is not always the best informed of observers: "We saw some antelopes... This is the first of the deer tribe I have seen running at large."[60] By the early 1870s it was firmly established that the pronghorn antelope of the western plains was in no way a part of the deer family (or, for that matter, of the antelope). He was not much of a botanist yet either. He records having "... a feast of berries. They are the same as are put in pemmican of a bluish black color and very sweet when ripe,"[61] and later refers to "... those berries previously mentioned,"[62] without once identifying them as Saskatoons, a widely known and common staple of the Native diet.

Along with such observations, Millman's diary is also a charming and informative account of daily life along the line. Soon after leaving Dufferin he tackled something he may never before have had to do for himself: "I attempted my first washing of clothes. Washed three shirts, one jersey, two pairs of socks, two handkerchiefs. Before I got through I succeeded in taking nearly all the skin off my fingers."[63] Later he made another attempt at personal hygiene: "Had a bath in the arrangement I made yesterday, consisting of my ground sheet laid in a hole in the ground of the tent six or eight inches deep, two feet long and about one and a half feet wide. It can be as long or wide as one wishes and takes up very little room in the tent."[64]

Like everyone else along the boundary that first summer, Millman was both intrigued and worried by the increasingly regular presence of the Sioux. Following one encounter, after travelling with only a small-gauge shotgun used to collect specimens of birds and small mammals, he checked a Spencer carbine and fifteen rounds of ammunition for himself and another for his teamsters out of the sub-depot near the Souris crossings.

His interest in the Native population could be either intense or almost perfunctory—sometimes in the same entry. On July 31, he wrote, "While botanizing I got an Indian skull out of a grave. It appears to have been about twelve years of age. A few trinkets were also found in the grave. Prairie chickens are plentiful."[65]

Two weeks later, while camped with Galwey's party at the first Souris crossing, he joined what had become almost a mass pilgrimage to a Native burial site:

> In the forenoon, I rode over to the American camp and to an Indian grave about half a mile on [the] east side of the river. The grave was protected by sticks stuck up endwise and interlocked at the top. But some animal had torn the grave open and dragged out part of the body. The bones of the head were on top bleached as white as snow.[66]

This grave site was probably visited by most of the boundary parties in the area at the time. American secretary James Bangs tried to visit too, though with less success: "Rode out in evening to desecrate supposed Indian graves—found nothing."[67] Elliott Coues was so impressed by the site he wrote a mournfully elegiac "fragment" about it that he published a few years later in *Forest and Stream* magazine (the forerunner of today's *Field and Stream*). Entitled "The Bivouac of Death," it is Coues at his high-Victorian best:

> The widow crouches by the grave, and all night long cries of the bird of darkness echo her despairing lamentations; the rest is silence, gloom and fear. But her dim vision reaches into spirit

land, beyond the black river, where the ghostly brave on a phan-
tom steed still urges the chase, and still conquers his foes on the
voiceless shore.[68]

ANDERSON COULD NOT bring himself to relax for long at Turtle
Mountain. At the beginning of August, he was off again with his
armed scouts and his light wagons. This time, however, the party
carried an ample supply of its own water and firewood. On the second day out he also finally managed to get his first look at the Sioux.
"They were very friendly," he wrote. "I got a good photograph of their
camp and group."[69] Passing quickly by the astronomical sites he had
identified on his previous sweep, Anderson pushed his survey to a
point nearly 170 miles west of the depot and fully three-quarters of
the way to his season's goal.

No matter how confused and erratic the watercourses along the
boundary from Dufferin had seemed, they all had one thing in common. Whether they flowed down off the Pembina plateau to the north,
south, east or west, no matter what circuitous route they followed,
they all eventually found their way into the Red River and, from there,
into Hudson Bay. Now, almost exactly three hundred miles west of
the Red, Anderson recognized the enormous significance of the place
where he brought his third sortie to a halt: "We have now penetrated
into the desert lands of the Missouri."[70]

He had reached the Great Coteau of the Missouri and, from where
he stood on its crest, all the way to the Rocky Mountain foothills, the
waters he crossed would be flowing south, down toward the Missouri
and on to the Mississippi and the Gulf of Mexico. What lay behind
him was Rupert's Land and its two-hundred-year history with Britain and the Hudson's Bay Company. What stretched out before him
were the northern limits of the equally old French lands that La Salle
had called Louisiana. Both were relics of a time when men in great
palaces, half a world away, divided entire continents not with the cool
precision of the zenith telescope and the surveyor's chain, but according to the grand vagaries of the way the waters moved.

· 6 ·

AUTUMN
1873

From the hill at sunset an immense prospect
of prairie perfectly trackless & with an edge purple & perfect
as the sea round the whole horizon.

GEORGE DAWSON

R ETREATING FROM the Coteau after marking the location for astronomical station 18, Anderson found a perfect site for the last principal depot the parties would need to support their push toward the four-hundred-mile mark. Tucked into the Souris River valley about ten miles north of the boundary, Anderson named the depot Wood End, a wry celebration of the fact that, from his vantage point on the crest of the Coteau, he had not discerned as much as a stick of firewood for as far as the eye could see. Leaving thirty men at the depot with instructions to cut and stack as many cords of firewood as they could, Anderson rode back along the line toward Turtle Mountain, stopping briefly to spend time with each working party, including Gregory and Twining, to give them the hastily sketched (but remarkably accurate) maps he had prepared directing them to their next stations.

Using the established traders' trails wherever possible, Anderson had come upon a Metis family making its way east. While the track was obviously used regularly, traffic must have been light since he was surprised to see them:

> Strange to say, [we] met a native trader on his way from the Rocky Mountains to Fort Garry. He had a caravan of carts loaded with dried meat, for sale at Fort Garry, and in front of the caravans in a spring wagon were his wife and family, all of a very dusky hue. There was a young Englishman with the party, who had lived for 9 years with these people, and was just like an Indian. From these people I learned many interesting particulars concerning the country they had travelled over…"[1]

By mid-August, all four of the astronomical parties, together with the headquarters for the U.S. military escort, were concentrated along the boundary line between the two crossings of the Souris River. The river rises in the flatlands of what is today south-central Saskatchewan and runs southeast along the edge of the Great Coteau. It crosses the 49th Parallel just over two hundred miles west of the Red River, and flows south into present-day North Dakota for nearly sixty miles. At a point no more than forty miles from the Missouri River, the edge of the Coteau blocks the river and turns it back toward the border. It becomes a Canadian river once again some forty-five miles to the east of its first crossing. From there, it winds north by east toward its junction with the Assiniboine. Together with the upper course of the Red River, the great loop of the Souris marked the southern edge of Rupert's Land before the Convention of 1818 neatly severed it along the line of the 49th Parallel. Like the Red, too, the valley of the lower Souris no longer held any interest for the British directors of the Hudson's Bay Company, and they let it go with barely a token complaint.

Where the Souris flows south across the boundary (the commissions' "second crossing" as they moved west along the line), it is a thin, small stream in high summer, as it meanders through a deep, rough valley. Millman says his party came to within half a mile of the valley edge before they realized it was there. Even the tops of the poplars that grew along the river were well below the level of the plain. The steep-sided valley walls, cut with countless coulees and side canyons, conspired to tip Millman's ambulance into the river as he attempted a crossing. Neither the ambulance nor its four passengers were damaged, or even got very wet, as the stream was no more than two feet deep.

On August 10, Greene's party was finishing building the boundary markers between the west side of Turtle Mountain and the first crossing of the Souris (the crossings being numbered in the order the parties came to them—in this case the opposite of the order according to the flow of the river). On the 13th Gregory was nearing the end of his observations at station 13 on South Antler Creek. By the end of the month, he would be moving west toward the Great Coteau, 312 miles from Pembina. Twining, meanwhile, chose to observe at a station close to the American cavalry headquarters on the Souris. This would be Twining's last station for the season, and he assigned Gregory the task of making the observations at all the remaining U.S. sites.

On August 16, Galwey was observing at station 14, the second Souris crossing, while Featherstonhaugh was working at Short Creek, only ten miles east of the new depot at Wood End. Galwey was on the verge of leapfrogging everyone to take up work at the Grand Coteau station marked by Anderson at the end of his third sortie. With almost no natural obstacles to impede the running of the lines between the stations, the pace of the astronomical parties was accelerating.

There is some confusion in the official naming of the astronomical stations (other than the fact that the Americans habitually referred to the Souris by its English translation—the Mouse). Station 17, for example, is identified in both British and American reports as being at the third of four Souris crossings. As would quickly become clear to the Canadian topographical parties, however, the third and fourth crossings were actually made by a stream called Long Creek. A major tributary of the Souris (if there could be such a thing in that bone-dry season), the creek parallels the river just to the west and makes a brief, shallow foray across the line before turning north to join the Souris at the site of Wood End depot.

When Millman made his slightly damp second crossing of the Souris and set up his camp near Galwey's astronomical station and the British subdepot, he was impressed by what he saw: "From here we had a splendid view. The 'Stars and Stripes' waving on one side of the river and the 'Union Jack' on the other, presented the appearance of two enemies encamped."[2]

The loop of the Souris was the ideal location for the Americans' Camp Terry (named for Brigadier General Alfred Howe Terry, the senior officer in the Dakota Territory), their only equivalent to the string of depots that the British were obliged to build every ninety miles or so along the line. Easily able to supply the working parties wherever they happened to be between Pembina Mountain and the westernmost stations, the site also offered easy access to the American commission's source of supplies. Using trains of six-mule wagons (the Americans harnessed military-issue mules, rather than horses or oxen, everywhere along the line), the commission's provisions could be brought up from any one of the series of cavalry forts that stretched across the Dakota Territory and up the Missouri.

Built in the years just after the Civil War, the forts were primarily intended to protect the mail routes and Missouri steamboats. At its peak in the late 1860s, that Missouri traffic was principally bound for Alder Gulch and Virginia City, the western Montana boom towns where gold had been discovered in 1863. The string began on the Red River at Fort Abercrombie (the source for supplies to Fort Pembina and the eastern end of the boundary work). From there, the military trails led to Fort Ransom (near present-day Lisbon, North Dakota), Fort Seward (near Jamestown) and then north to Fort Totten. From there they led west to Fort Stevenson on the Missouri and on up the river to Forts Buford, Peck and Benton.

Throughout the late summer and fall of 1873, small escort parties of infantry would continue to move east and west along the line from Camp Terry, covering the topographical and astronomical parties.

With most of the commission's stores coming up from Fort Stevenson, barely a hundred miles to the south, it was the cavalry's job to pick up the wagon trains and bring them north to the depot. Other than performing this occasional duty, however, the main body of Reno's men rarely left the base, counting on a great show of strength to discourage any trouble from the small, scattered bands of Sioux.

In his two years of command on the 49th Parallel, Major Reno's relationship with the members of the commission (especially with its civilian appointees) was never more than barely civil and often failed to reach even that level. First and foremost, Reno was a cavalryman. Born in Carrollton, Illinois, in 1834, he had graduated from West Point in 1857 and served with the 1st Cavalry in Washington and Oregon before the outbreak of the Civil War. During the war, he was variously promoted and breveted from first lieutenant all the way through captain, major, colonel and brigadier general before he was mustered out in mid-1865. In 1868, Reno rejoined the army with the rank of major in the 7th Cavalry and spent the next two years at various postings in the west. A series of staff postings followed until 1873, when he was assigned to head the boundary commission's escort. He was stiff, rather formal and a great believer in discipline—characteristics that were not going to endear him to his more easygoing fellow officers.

Reno's principal concern was the way in which the field parties made use of his soldiers. While he seemed less troubled by the commission's treatment of the infantry companies (though they were also under his command), he was adamant that his cavalrymen were not there to be surveyors' helpers, as he put it in his report at the end of the 1873 season:

> [My men were] used virtually as assistants by the parties for which they were escorts. This was particularly so with the topographical parties, when, in addition to the generally regular march of twenty miles, they would be sent a distance of five miles south of the line, and be used as flag bearers, to station themselves as sight at the head of ravines, etc., consuming that time that care and attention to grazing renders necessary, when the allowance of forage is reduced.[3]

Reno might have been genuinely concerned with the condition of the horses, in case the half-expected trouble with the Sioux had materialized, but his men may not have entirely appreciated his complaint. Like most of the non-scientific members of both commissions, the men of the military escort passed the better part of their days with very little to do. After moving to a new location, there was almost no official activity to occupy them for as long as it took the astronomers and surveyors to complete their work, and it was once again time to break camp and move on. On the British side, nearly every non-scientific member of the commission willingly and cheerfully spent time helping out with the survey work. Whether they were satisfying their curiosity about the instruments, learning something of the methodology or just escaping the general boredom, Dawson, Burgess and Millman all thoroughly enjoyed their time hauling the chain, holding the targets or squinting through the transit. There is no reason to suppose that the American infantry and cavalrymen were any different. In fact, in his final report, Lieutenant Greene had nothing but praise for the co-operation he had enjoyed from his infantry escort during the brief fall season of 1872:

> Captain A.A. Harbach's company of Twentieth Infantry remained with me when the rest of the commission went to the Northwest Angle. We met no Indians in the short distance which we penetrated eastward, but when we came to an impassable swamp, and had to make a corduroy-road, Captain Harbach at once ordered out his whole company to assist in it.[4]

Anderson, who had constantly been urging both his own and the American parties forward, was now in danger of being outrun by them, and he quickly planned a fourth and final sortie. He left Turtle Mountain some time after the middle of August and returned to Wood End depot. His goal was to have the season's work finished and the parties moving back toward Dufferin by mid-October. Barring any unforeseen problems, he believed they might actually achieve their four hundred miles west as much as a fortnight earlier than that.

While Anderson was preparing to set out, Cameron appeared:

... driving an American trotting gig, having made a curious journey of 14 or 15 days across country from Fort Garry, and being
in a great hurry as usual drove onwards to one of our advanced
camps... since which time he has not been heard of. He says he
must be back at Pembina in the course of a fortnight so I expect
he will vanish as he came.[5]

Anderson's fourth sortie party was his smallest to date, involving
only ten men, twelve days' food and ten days' worth of firewood. He
would also be taking a fifty-gallon water cart and—the largest item of
all—a thousand pounds of oats for the horses.

At the end of his previous reconnaissance, Anderson had discovered a traders' wagon road running generally along the line of the
boundary, and he determined to follow it west. He was hoping it
would provide a line of least resistance for his supply trains across
the confusion of canyons and coulees that marked the Great Coteau,
an area Dr. Millman had described as having "the appearance of a
rough sea suddenly petrified."[6] But the road went northwest and, by
the time he found himself twenty-six miles north of the boundary,
Anderson gave up and called a halt. Retreating down the same trail,
he realized he had no choice but to confront the Coteau head-on.

He made for a small subdepot (constructed by the men from Wood
End) out on the Coteau and there, on September 8, he discovered Galwey, ready to start his observations at station 18. Featherstonhaugh
was not far behind, coming forward toward his next position—which
Anderson had yet to locate. At the subdepot he was also informed that
Cameron had come through a few days earlier. Driving a light wagon
with three days' provisions and accompanied by one other man, the
peripatetic commissioner had gone west to see the country.

Resting only overnight at the subdepot, Anderson pushed out
across the Coteau, looking for a route that the wagons could follow. In
the afternoon they met the returning Cameron and, after just a few
minutes of conversation, the chief commissioner drove away toward

Wood End. Anderson's account of the meeting almost drips with sarcasm: "…we met Captain Cameron returning from his picnic, bringing information sufficiently alarming about the want of water…"[7] Anderson also discovered that Gregory had just occupied station 19, the aptly named "Mid-Coteau." In a bid to continue pressing the American effort forward, Gregory had hit upon an innovative way of taking his astronomical fixes. At Mid-Coteau he left most of his party camped at the nearest source of fresh water and took only his assistants and a small escort up to the actual observation site. While making his observations, he had water and cooked food brought forward daily from the main camp. He would repeat this approach again at his next station. More significantly, for the first time since the work began, the Americans were in the lead.

It was about this time that the field parties faced their most serious threat to life and limb. The lack of wood and water could be countered with careful planning, and the mosquitoes, while aggravating, were not fatal. But altogether beyond their control were the grass fires.

The fires began to sweep across the plains in mid-August in a succession of burns that lasted well into September. There was not a party anywhere on the line between Turtle Mountain and the Coteau that did not find itself running for its life at least once. Some were started by lightning, others by causes unknown. At least two of the biggest and most dangerous burns were started by the men of the commission themselves, one of them deliberately. The most dangerous feature of the fires was their unpredictability. As Anderson wrote:

> The course of the fire was most capricious, and often turned by a ravine, or by a slight change in the wind, into a new course… A surveying party working in one of the ravines 5 or 6 miles from their camp, found that the fire had swept round behind them and threatened their camp with destruction. They had just time to reach their camp, and to tear down their tents, and to plunge everything into an adjoining pool…[8]

The deliberately set fire began as a perfectly sensible response:

At one of the astronomical camps one of the officers, seeing the onward progress of the fire, employed all the men in the camp to meet the fire and save as much grass as possible by burning a strip; this was so far successful that about 400 acres of grass were saved, which were of incalculable value to the transport animals on the final retreat; but the fire that had been started with this object at last got out beyond control, and swept back upon their own camp and nearly destroyed it.[9]

There was only one act of incredible stupidity (at least that was known about) and it was responsible for the worst fire of all:

On one occasion one of the labourers thoughtlessly struck a match on his boot in a patch of long grass, and in an instant the fire flew, and though the camp was saved, the effect of that fire was afterwards ascertained to have destroyed the grass for 150 miles of longitude, and then to have turned southwards, when it is probable its progress in that direction was not arrested until it reached the Missouri River.[10]

There was little enough grass for the animals before the fires. After they had swept through, as Anderson grimly reported, "the general appearance of the country was now changed from the universal yellow tint to a dismal black, and the whole surface of the plains was as bare of herbage as the sand on the sea-shore." But for the occasional patch of sheltered ground or the wet margins of a pothole lake, there was barely a blade of grass left standing between the Coteau and Pembina Mountain. Anticipating a late-season shortage of grass, hay had been cut and stacks built at several places along the wagon routes. The fires took all but a few of them, too.

ON SEPTEMBER 5, Commissioner Campbell, Secretary James Bangs and Elliott Coues broke camp on the Souris River and moved the fifty miles to Wood End. According to Bangs, the weather had become increasingly unstable over the past week or so. In late August, it had been "Terrific winds all day like hot air blasts." By the end of the month it was "Wind, rain, and hail as large as a hen's egg. Terrible blow! Tents barely stand—*Dust*, DUST, DUST."[11] The previous day had been "cold and mean," while on the following one they had pulled out on a "Morning cold and rainy. Dismal indeed!"

The move to Wood End was to be brief—a chance to see the new depot and assess the progress of the work. They ran into Twining and Greene, and the chief astronomer joined them for the trip. They were in camp at Wood End by September 8 and, three days later, the two chief commissioners held another of their infrequent meetings, as noted in Bangs's diary for the 11th:

> Cloudy—Twining leaves and goes back to Mouse River Depot. Commissioner decides to return in morning—Capt. Cameron calls in morning and has an interview with Mr. Campbell—lively time. Plain talk—Invite him and Ward to dinner. He comes but not Ward. Very pleasant time—Duck, Beef, all the luxuries of the season. He stays till 9—*buzzing* Com'r. To bed early but restless and not able to sleep.[12]

It is not clear whether a meeting with the British chief commissioner had been on the agenda for their visit. Cameron had lately been enjoying his "picnic" out on the Coteau and it is not likely that he could have returned to Wood End much before he paid his visit to the Americans. Bangs does not give any details about what the commissioners discussed, but it is almost certain Cameron was continuing to press his case for a mean parallel. It is just as certain that Campbell still wanted nothing to do with it.

With the exception of his infrequent encounters with Major Reno, Elliott Coues had been thoroughly enjoying his high summer on the 49th Parallel. He collected several examples of Le Conte's sparrow, another of the pale-coloured grassland specialties that were found in substantial numbers along the boundary line while remaining a rarity elsewhere. In addition to all the shooting, he managed to capture a couple of young Swainson's hawks and a pair of great horned owls, which he kept with him for the rest of the season. Although the male owl was later burned to death in a grass fire, the female survived at least as far as the autumn return to St. Paul.

Along with the birds and mammals, Coues also collected as many examples of reptiles and amphibians as he could. He even believed he had discovered a hitherto-unknown subspecies of the plains garter snake, and named it for William Twining, in appreciation of his "cordial cooperation in the scientific interests of the Boundary Commission, and in expression of our personal consideration."[13] Unfortunately, the tribute did not survive closer examination, and the snake was subsequently reclassified and renamed.

GEORGE DAWSON wasted no time at Dufferin. Within four days of finishing his canoe trip from Lake of the Woods, he was packed and ready to head west. On September 3, armed with Herchmer's directions, he set out for his first look at the western high plains: "The morning dull & misty. Road muddy. Party consists of self, Duckworth, Spearman, Paul (teamster), two Red R. carts & my grey mare."[14]

For Dawson, the geological survey of the 49th Parallel was by the far the most important element of his work. It was the real reason he had been appointed. Although he spent a good deal of time studying the rocks and plants of Lake of the Woods and the Roseau swamps, that was already yesterday's country. In his final report, he was reduced to making the almost mandatory upbeat suggestion that certain areas were worthy of further study, but he was vague on which areas they might be, and what more detailed examination might uncover.

As he expressed it in the introduction to his final report, the 49th Parallel was paramount:

> In working up the geological material, I have found it necessary
> to make myself familiar with the geological literature, not only of
> the interior region of British America, but with that Western por-

tion of the United States to the south, where extensive and accurate geological surveys have been carried on. It has been my aim to make the region near the boundary line as much as possible a link of connection between the more or less isolated previous surveys, and to collect by quotation or reference, the facts bearing on it from either side. In this way it has been attempted to make the forty-ninth parallel a geological base-line with which future investigations may be connected.[15]

As far as the Canadian west was concerned, the geological literature—the accounts of those "more or less isolated previous surveys"—was painfully thin. As Dawson himself suggests, "... the geological biography is as yet quite small, and the knowledge of some districts has not been extended since the date of the first observations, made many years ago."[16] A good case in point was Sir John Richardson's *Arctic Searching Expedition: A Journal of a Boat Voyage through Rupert's Land and the Arctic Sea... with an Appendix on the Physical Geography of North America*. First published in 1851, it contained the sum of what Richardson had learned of the geology of the Canadian north during his time with Franklin's two overland expeditions of 1819–22 and 1825–27, and the failed search for Franklin of 1848 that was the book's main subject. But the work dealt mostly with regions far to the north of the boundary country, and was thus seriously limited in its usefulness for understanding that region.

D.D. Owen's *Geology of Wisconsin, Iowa and Minnesota* (1852) incidentally touched on some areas above the international boundary, but only where certain prominent features extended across the line. Dr. John Bigsby, an English-born geologist with long experience in eastern Canada, had published two significant papers on the geology of the Lake of the Woods area. Dawson cites them often, but like the other sources they were, by then, more than twenty years old, and Bigsby had never travelled any farther west than Lake of the Woods.

While the Geological Survey of Canada was just beginning, literally and figuratively, to take the measure of Canada's new western lands, the fieldwork it had done, while at least up to date, was still preliminary and related primarily to the Saskatchewan River water-sheds, again well north of the 49th Parallel. That left Dawson with only two truly useful studies of the lands through which he was to pass. The reports, one British-sponsored and the other Canadian, were the result of expeditions mounted almost simultaneously in the late 1850s. The purpose of both expeditions was ostensibly the same— to look for a viable, all-Canadian transportation corridor from the Great Lakes to the Pacific coast, and to analyse the potential of the prairie lands to support large-scale settlement—but their respective scales were quite different.

The Canadian expedition made two modest forays into the west in the summers of 1857 and 1858. Although nominally under the direction of retired Hudson's Bay Company trader George Gladman, the key members of the party were a young University of Toronto chemistry professor named Henry Youle Hind and Simon J. Dawson, the civil engineer from Quebec for whom the dreaded Dawson Route would eventually be named. The British expedition, jointly sponsored by the government and the Royal Geographical Society, was led by Captain John Palliser. It lasted more than two years and explored huge areas of the country all the way from Lake Superior to Vancouver Island.

Both expeditions eventually published the results of their explorations, and George Dawson knew both accounts almost by heart. While Hind and Simon Dawson produced a report that "furnished much information, both as to the geology and general character of the country traversed,"[17] it was Palliser's companion, the Scottish medical doctor and geologist James Hector, who drew most of Dawson's admiration. "To him," wrote Dawson, "the first really trustworthy general geological map of the interior portion of B.N. America is due; and he has besides accumulated and published a great mass of geological observations, the significance of many of which appears as the country is more thoroughly explored."[18]

George Dawson would have both Hind and Hector for company until he reached Turtle Mountain—both earlier parties had travelled west from the Red River up the Pembina and out across the so-called second tier. At Turtle Mountain, however, both had turned north-west and followed the well-established trader trails toward Fort Ellice, Fort Qu'Appelle and the old fur trade routes of the Saskatch-ewan River country. From Turtle Mountain west along the 49th Par-allel for more than five hundred miles, Dawson would be breaking entirely new ground for the discipline of geology. He was the perfect man for the job.

Despite his youth, he had already demonstrated an almost pre-ternatural grasp of his chosen field. According to one historian of the Geological Survey:

> His work was always careful and precise. The acid test of any geol-ogist is how well his work will stand up when it is re-examined later on the ground by a geologist equipped with new tools and informed with new scientific knowledge. Dawson meets this test better than any man of his generation.[19]

As a case in point, Dawson made very few geological notes in his diary when he was passing Pembina Mountain on his way west. Nev-ertheless, his final report contains the following astute analysis of the area:

> I was unable to trace the rumours of the occurrence of gold, coal and other valuable minerals, in this locality, to any authentic source. That fragments of lignite, or even traces of gold, should exist in the drift deposits of this region, is not impossible; but it is more probable that the reports concerning the latter, have arisen from the discovery of iron pyrites in the Cretaceous clays.[20]

His conclusion—a gently but firmly stated mix of both theoreti-cal and practical interest—is typical of the tone that informs nearly every page.

With Dufferin and Pembina depot all but deserted, Dawson was looking forward to the comforts of the new western headquarters at Turtle Mountain. By the afternoon of September 9, he and his party arrived there only to find it, too, was almost empty. All the officers had moved west three or four days before his arrival, leaving only the depot manager, some haymakers and firewood cutters. It would be several more days of hard travel with his diminishing supplies and rattletrap carts before he would come across the main body of the commission, strung out along the 49th Parallel west of the Souris River.

Dawson continued to scribble quick notes in his diary as he hurried west, pausing only long enough to collect those plants, insects and, especially, birds that caught his interest. He was particularly interested in the large numbers of sandhill cranes and tried on more than one occasion to "collect" an example or two. Although the great birds were "exceedingly shy,"[21] Dawson's marksmanship was probably not what it should have been for a field naturalist. His diary regularly records his attempts to bring down a wide variety of prey—whether for the scientific collections or for the pot—most often without success. He was especially anxious to bag one of the great white cranes that strode through the reed beds surrounding the pothole sloughs and alkaline ponds.

Even then, the stately whooping crane, standing nearly six feet tall and with a wingspan approaching seven feet, was much less common than its smaller grey cousin, the sandhill. Dawson had managed to collect at least one whooping crane skin soon after he had arrived at Dufferin, but it had died from causes other than the shotgun and was already in sorry shape by the time he and Duckworth tried to preserve it. Dawson does not record whether he succeeded in taking another specimen; he only seems to list his misses.

Coues, too, was intrigued by the whooping crane, and included a lengthy essay on them in his *Birds of the Northwest.* While a large portion of the essay is given over to a detailed discussion of the whooper's peculiarly convoluted trachea (something Coues had been able to study in a St. Paul museum) there is also a good deal of discussion about its supposed range. "I have never seen it alive," he wrote, "excepting in Northern Dakota, where I observed it in August, September and October, and where, probably, it breeds." He goes on to speculate that "... here [on the northern plains] it seems to be chiefly migratory, but there is every reason to believe that it breeds in Minnesota and, as just said, in Dakota, as it does further north."[22]

In fact, by the time Coues and Dawson saw the stately white crane, its numbers—never great at any time—were already in precipitous decline. Recent estimates suggest that by the time the boundary commissions arrived at Pembina, no more than 1,500 whooping cranes survived. While there may still have been scattered nests in the ponds and sloughs along the 49th Parallel, none of the commissions' naturalists and collectors found solid evidence for them, and neither did they see any new chicks in either year they were on the plains. By the turn of the century, there would be no breeding pairs left anywhere south of 60° N and, by the mid-twentieth century, fewer than fifty birds remained.

The great ghostly constant in Dawson's diary (and in every other journal that has survived from the boundary commissions) was the bison. Although the record of its presence was scattered everywhere west of the Red River, living animals were impossible to find. While still within fifty miles of Dufferin, Dawson was recording the sight of "... many old rotten Buffalo horns ... & other indications of an old pond in which the large animals mired no doubt during their migrations"[23] At the same place, he met three or four bison hunters in a wagon who were returning from a hunting trip to Devil's Lake, some eighty miles to the southwest near Fort Totten. They had found nothing.

As he moved west, Dawson continued to take note of the evidence: "Passed many horns of Bison," he wrote from just east of Turtle Mountain. "These remains are rapidly becoming more numerous & in better preservation. One skull found today so good that I had it put on one of the carts."[24] At Turtle Mountain itself, he began to get a real sense of how huge the herds must have been: "Saw today very many deeply worn ruts in the prairie sod crossing the road. Thought at first that cart tracks but soon found out that could not be, but really old buffalo paths & probably indicating pretty well the direction of their migrations. The ruts were nearly parallel, generally ran along the low ground & all tended to the N.W."[25]

Elliott Coues, too, noticed how the bison signs changed the farther west he went. Having noted "I saw no signs whatever until the vicinity of Turtle Mountain, where an occasional weather-worn skull or limb-bone may be observed,"[26] by the time he crossed the Souris, he was reporting that "... the bony remains multiply with each day's journey, until they become common objects; still, no horn, hoof, or patch of hide."[27] By the time he reached his farthest west for that year—at the eastern edge of the Coteau—in mid-September, Coues was able to report seeing the most recent evidence of the animal. There were skulls that still showed "horns, nose-gristle, or hair, and portions of skeletons still ligamentously attached."[28] Dawson's observations closely paralleled Coues's, although the Canadian pushed out well west of the Coteau and almost as far as the terminal depot at Wood Mountain. In late September he reported seeing a bison skull "... with the whole of the skin attached & which probably belonged to an animal killed last year."[29]

But scatterings of last year's bones were as close as any member of the either commission came to seeing bison during the summer of 1873. Even those relatively fresh remains were few and far between, and both Dawson and Coues noted that the concentrations of skeletons and the nearby teepee rings that marked several major kill sites were many, many years old. The bison were long gone from Rupert's Land and the Red River watershed, and they would never be coming back.

AFTER THEIR VISIT to the Wood End depot, the Americans set out for their main camp on the Souris while Cameron, heading back for Dufferin, paralleled their course on the north side of the line. By September 13 they were back in camp, and with Cameron under canvas just above the boundary, Twining and Reno went off to pay him a visit. Bangs reports that they came back "full of spirits." If the two officers had enjoyed their time with Cameron, Campbell was still in a vile mood, and in Bangs's diary, entries such as "Grand Council on the official status of Commissioners," "Mr. Campbell and I have a long talk about Cameron" and "... long talk about Cameron, etc." appear on a regular basis. Campbell's mood certainly did not improve on September 19, as Bangs reported that he had "Received account of expenses of cutting line East of Pembina from Ward."[30]

The British cutting bill was for more than $7,000, and over the next few days secretary Bangs, and anyone else unfortunate enough to be in camp, bore the brunt of Campbell's anger, though we cannot now tell whether he had any good reason to suspect the bill was inflated, or whether he was simply unaware how much cutting had been required on Turtle Mountain. On the 29th Bangs wrote: "Mr. C. expatiates on the enormity of Cameron's bill for cutting. He may kick, but of course we'll have to take their word for it" and, on October 1, "Commissioner takes the day to 'interview' me... [it was a] long conversation in which Cameron, Farquhar, Twining, Coues and everybody generally gets a good scoring." By "good scoring," the secretary does not mean "high marks." The two commissioners would not see each other again before the end of the 1873 season, but the rancour generated by their last meeting would define their working and personal relationships until the final reports were signed more than two and a half years later.

AFTER ENTERTAINING the American officers at the Souris, Cameron finally got what he had long been anticipating: a chance to put on his diplomatic hat and meet with the Natives. On September 13 Millman recorded, in some detail, the arrival of a large party at Turtle Mountain:

> A band of fifty Sioux Indians arrived to-day. They intend to remain in the mountains all Winter to hunt. We could see them as they marched across the prairies. The squaws had to carry the baggage as well as the young ones. They had one or two horses which carried loads by means of "travails." This consists of two poles about twelve feet long, one end of them fastened to the horse; the other drags on the ground. By means of strips of skin they make a netting between the poles on which they lace the goods to be conveyed. When on the march a party will average twenty to thirty

miles a day. This one would think impossible for the old squaws with the loads they carry and for the children five to eight years of age. Both Indians and squaws have a blanket which they get from the Hudson's Bay store in exchange for skins. Men wear a pair of leggings, a sort of fixture around [the] loins and some of them a skirt. The squaws wear a skirt made of blue material which they get from [the] Hudson's Bay store, also leggings of same. They have a jacket on the body, over which is the blanket. Both wear their hair long, but the former plait theirs and wear a band around the head. They paint their faces with all kinds of hieroglyphics. One or two of them could speak English fluently. Their wigwam, which they call "tepee" is similar to others. These Indians had a hand in the Minnesota Massacre [of] 1862. I believe they have two or three white girls with them whom they captured at that time.[31]

When the diary was published by his wife in 1925, Millman's speculation about the white captives is footnoted with the following: "Afterwards in conversation with some of the tribe he was confirmed in this belief." If true, this marks the band as Wahpeton or Santee.

On September 18, after buying a pair of moccasins from a Sioux woman for $1.20, Millman recorded their meeting with Cameron:

. The Indians had a pow-wow with the commissioner. They were jubilant on seeing him. Expecting a liberal present from him, they all shook hands. He ordered depot-man Ellis to give each of them two plugs of tobacco, two pounds of flour and three of beans.[32]

How the Sioux reacted to these gifts, which by the informal standards of the time would have been thought less than generous, Millman does not say, but they probably had to listen to an extended lecture on the peaceful and friendly nature of Her Majesty's boundary commission in order to get even those. Ever true to form, "the commissioner left in the morning."[33]

On September 9, Anderson was out on the Coteau, filling his water wagon at every opportunity and fighting his way across forty miles of closely spaced ridge tops and narrow, precipitous valleys. Stopping along the way only long enough to mark the site for station 19, he finally emerged on the west side of the Coteau. Expecting to find water and firewood in the comparatively flat land that stretched out from the edge of the Coteau, Anderson was disappointed to discover "plenty of lakes but all salt."[34]

The standing water of the Pembina plateau was often swampy and foul, but at least the horses would drink it and the men could disguise its taste by boiling up a strong tea. But this was something different:

> Most of the places where Lakes had existed during the summer were now dry, and the bed of the Lake covered with white crystals of salts of soda, and the ground had a brilliant whiteness as if it was covered with snow. Around the margin of these white crystal deposits a beautiful blood red plant flourished, the colour of which was striking in contrast to the white lakes it bordered. Unfortunately for our botanist we were too late to secure this plant in flower.[35]

Two things mark Anderson's correspondence from his fourth sortie: the constant references to the tormenting plagues of mosquitoes are gone, and he has begun to note the changing colours around him. The *Salicornia* (as he later identified the plant) surrounding the lakes is green when in flower, only taking on its blood-red colour at the end of its growing season. Just a day or so later, in a wooded valley to the west, Anderson rode through poplar, elm, cedar and cherry, waxing that "The sudden burst of even this scant growth of wood, with foliage in autumns brightest and most varied colours was as refreshing to us as is the sight of a spring of water in travelling thro' an eastern desert."[36] The sight may have briefly recalled his earlier days of surveying in the Holy Land, but there, out on the high plateau of the Missouri in early September, another thought would have quickly pushed the reminiscence aside: summer was over and the brief, dangerous instability of fall was upon them.

With his wagons able to move more quickly across the flat ground, Anderson left the dry salt lakes behind and, fifteen miles to the west, came upon another lake. Although about a mile long and a rich, deep blue in colour, the lack of any vegetation around its margin suggested to Anderson that it, too, might be strongly alkaline. But he needed water for his horses and brought them forward:

> In descending to the Lake, we came to a little ravine... and in this ravine there was a little pool of water not in actual contact with the waters of the lake. To our great delight we found that not only would the horses drink it eagerly, but that it was only slightly alkaline, and not bad to drink. However, I thought it desirable to drink half a pint of it to be able to judge of its properties; and feeling no ill effects was able to recommend it for those who were coming after us.[37]

Later that same day, at another spring-fed pool, he found a site for station 20 ("Big Muddy"), 340 miles west of Pembina. Beyond station 20, after "double-hitching" his teams and mustering his men to help push the wagons up out of the steep valley, they descended almost immediately into another and crossed the first significant stream (unnamed in Anderson's account) they had come to that was flowing south toward the Missouri.

Another steady spring of clear water provided the site for station 21 and, twenty miles further along through the now-characteristic mix of steep, dry shoulders and verdant valleys, he marked station 22 at the east branch of the Poplar River. There, 385 miles from Pembina, he turned his party back toward Wood End:

> As this was the principal remaining object of my journey... it was necessary to return with all speed, and bring up the surveying parties, for only another month remained for work. At the place where we halted I could see ahead 8 or 10 miles further, and altho' there was no wood, it seemed a fine open country with no impediment for travelling with waggons and with an abundant supply

of water and grass. I saw a good many antelope but I had no time to stalk them, as we travelled from morning to night... and were anxious as we travelled to mark the Easiest road, so that the waggon trains that were following and were loaded far more heavily than my own would be able to reach their destinations with the greatest economy of time and labour.[38]

Anderson got back to Wood End on September 18 and immediately began to ready his party to make one last reconnaissance. He was convinced there was time to mark the sites of perhaps two or three more astronomical stations, as well as find a suitable site for the first depot of the following season. He knew it was a risky proposition and, on September 21, wrote to his mother: "I am now going out on the next journey tomorrow in the same leather suit I wore last winter when travelling with the dog trains, and do not expect to find winter clothes too warm."[39]

The three remaining astronomical parties had all cleared the Coteau and were taking their first fixes in the Missouri country. Featherstonhaugh was at Big Muddy and Galwey had already reached Anderson's furthest station at the Poplar River. Gregory, now moving faster than anyone, was beginning observations at West Poplar. Each party was at its farthest reach and Gregory would have the honour of occupying the last station of the season, 408 miles west of Pembina.

At the Big Muddy, Featherstonhaugh was joined by a new assistant astronomer, Lieutenant Valentine Francis Rowe, a thirty-two-year-old Royal Engineer fresh from Britain. He had landed at Dufferin at the end of August and immediately made his way west, arriving in camp toward the middle of September.

Early that spring, facing special surveys of Lake of the Woods and the loss of several enlisted men, Cameron had requested additional staff to be sent from England. Anderson was convinced the Canadian government would never allow it, preferring to make any additional appointments from Ottawa, but they had apparently raised no serious objection. George Crompton and D'Arcy East had arrived earlier in the year, while Rowe brought three additional sappers to replace those who had been lost—two had been invalided by rheumatism while another had deserted and gone to the United States. Rowe was well known to his fellow Royal Engineers. He and Galwey had graduated together from Woolwich and he had met the rest during his posting to Halifax from 1867 to 1872. Indeed, Anderson had mentioned Rowe specifically by name in his request for additional men.

ON THE MORNING of September 23, Anderson was at Wood End, packing his leather suit and mustering his scouts for a final sortie. Suddenly, with almost no warning, Nature celebrated the first anniversary of her equinoctial blizzard of 1872 by delivering another one, this time far more intense.

George Dawson had just left the depot on the Great Coteau and was headed west toward Wood Mountain:

Left camp by 8 o'c. Morning dull & doubtful looking... Steady wetting rain with S.W. wind... Shortly after noon the wind very suddenly went round to the N.N.W. & became cold. As we went on it continued increasing in violence till it blew a perfect gale, the rain at the same time changing first to sleet & then to snow. Found it impossible to ride, the horse being frightened by the storm and unmanageable. Tied it behind the carts & walked on. Reached Featherstonhaugh's old camp with much difficulty & discomfort. Found a good sized wood pile with which made free. Got tents up. The ground soon white with snow. Horses very cold & crowding round the tents for shelter. A Wolf seen near the camp about dark.[40]

The scattered astronomical and topographical parties sought shelter in nearby ravines and tried to calm their horses as the wet, wind-driven snow piled up around them:

By placing the waggons in a horse-shoe form, and stretching canvas sheets on the interior side, shelter was afforded to the horses from the driving sleet, which now set in with great violence from the north-west. The light canvas tents formed but a poor protection for the men, and, in the absence of fuel there was no help for it but to huddle together and get under their blankets. The storm continued, with scarcely any intermediate lulls, for seven days, during which period it was impossible to get the horses to graze, for as soon as they were turned out they would all come back again to the shelter of the waggons. During these seven days of forced inactivity, the horses lost flesh sadly, and many were incapacitated from work for the remainder of the season.[41]

All of this was hearsay for Anderson, who was fortunate not to have left Wood End when he intended. Although there were no serious injuries among the commissions' men, several became separated from their parties and got lost in the confusion of canyons and coulees. West of the Coteau, Forrest's topographical party had lost several horses during the blizzard, and then lost two of the men who had gone off to find them. Everyone in the area—including both Featherstonhaugh's and Dawson's parties—joined in the search, and the men were finally located, not much the worse for wear after two days with nothing to eat. Others were not as lucky. According to Anderson, "...the half-breed hunters, who were in temporary camps hunting buffalo to the west...were also caught by the storm, and some of them were unable to find their way back to the camp, and were afterwards found frozen under the cover of some buffalo hides, which they had stripped from the animals they had just killed."[42]

By the time it reached the Souris crossings, the fury of the storm had diminished substantially and the snow was mixed with heavy rain. But the wind still had a bite. Twining, then observing at station 15, once again noted the sight that had augured the storm of 1872: "Throughout the day flocks of ducks and other aquatic birds had been winging their way towards the south, while at night the air was filled with wild-geese urging their flight before the tempest, and piercing the sky with harsh cries and the rushing of wings."[43]

With supplies running short, Dawson did what he could to supplement his men's diet. "Shot a number of blackbirds of which great quantities haunting the camp," he reported, "& had them stewed for dinner." There is no record of what his men thought (although it is easy to imagine the "song of sixpence" which must have accompanied the dish's appearance) but Dawson pronounced "They turned out pretty good but rather tough for so small a bird."[44]

More seriously, in the face of the cold, wet weather and the severe shortage of firewood, Dawson also experimented with burning the local lignite. While the soft, brown near-coal was plentiful enough nearly everywhere along the line, it was hardly a replacement for even the greenest of wood:

> The lignite does not... form a very good fire to cook with as it crumbles under the action of the heat, or this together with the copious production of ash soon clogs up the heap which continues to burn within in a smothered way. It would burn very well on a grate through which ashes might fall & which would allow a draft from below & through the mass. No iron or any material for constructing grates being at hand, must do as the rest... burning it on a mass of pebbles.[45]

The whole experience of the blizzard was best summed up by a man named Kingston, one of Forrest's party. At the height of the snowstorm, Dawson heard him exclaim "Oh, ain't it romantic to think that we're 500 miles from the nearest house!"[46]

Anderson, refusing to be beaten at the last minute, waited for the weather to settle and then raced his small party west over the Coteau and out toward the end of the line.

On October 2, he reached Gregory's camp on the West Poplar River, but the American party had already pulled out. In his final report, Gregory says that the blizzard came down on him when he was "about half done" with his observations and kept him pinned in his tent until September 29. By the end of the next day he had retreated as far as Galwey's Poplar River camp (where he had bumped into Dawson, still out exploring) and, by October 6, he had covered the 150 miles back to Wood End.

Beyond the camp at West Poplar, Anderson pushed on along the projected line until, from the summit of a high ridge, he looked out across a broad swath of what his scouts called *les mauvaises terres,* the "badlands." The wagons could go no farther and, without time to locate a passable road for them, Anderson went ahead on horseback. After about ten miles of winding through the convoluted canyons of dried white mud, he found what he thought would be a suitable place from which to begin the astronomical observations in 1874. Leaving his mark at Little Rocky Creek, 432 miles west of Pembina, he turned toward a low range of hills about twenty miles north of the line. He was looking for a site for the first principal depot for the next season's operations.

For some reason, Anderson's regular letters to his mother and sister break off at the time he left Wood End for his final reconnaissance. To follow his activities during this exploration, one has to rely on Featherstonhaugh, who included an account in his 1876 paper for the Royal Engineers' journal, and Anderson himself, who described his journey in a paper for the *Journal of the Royal Geographical Society.*

From a ridge at the edge of the Woody Mountains (known today as Wood Mountain), Anderson could look out over the broad ravine that marked the western limit of the mountain, and north toward a broad, level plain that continued to the horizon. Featherstonhaugh wrote:

> The ravines below the feet of the party were well wooded, but now filling up with drifted snow, and some buffalo were seen taking refuge in them. Turning eastward from this wild spot, Captain Anderson proceeded to explore the hills, in order to find the camp of the Half-breeds, who were known to spend the winter in one of the valleys. Some Sioux Indians, who were met travelling toward the south, pointed out the right direction, and place was reached after a day's journey. About eighty families of Half-breeds, who migrated from the Red River valley, form a sort of settlement here in the winter time residing in huts... Having found a suitable

site, with wood and water for a large depot for the next season's work, Captain Anderson started for the Red River on the 8th of October.[47]

Anderson confirmed that he would never have discovered the Metis camp without the help of the Sioux. That he even knew it was somewhere there in the hills was due to the family trading party he had met on the road to Fort Garry at the start of his third sortie in early August. The family lived in the Woody Mountains when they were not off hunting far to the west.

Hidden in the ravines on the north side of the mountain, the "rude and desolate huts" of the Metis village were 25 miles north of the boundary line. As Anderson and his men worked south from the village in brilliant sunshine, through snow that lay eighteen inches deep on the high ground and clogged the valleys with drifts, the glare caused a number of cases of snow blindness, but Anderson eventually found his ideal depot site in another ravine just three miles below the settlement and 416 miles west of Dufferin.

On October 3, Featherstonhaugh left Rowe in charge of his astronomical party while he rushed back to check the progress of the cutting at Turtle Mountain. Farther west, Galwey was trying desperately to finish the connection between Poplar station and Gregory's final position twenty-three miles along the line. As temperatures plunged and their few remaining sticks of firewood ran out, the men burned the tables, stools and wooden floor of the observatory tent. They even reduced the doctor's stretcher to kindling in order to cook their final dinner. By the time the party had returned to the depot on the Coteau, five of Galwey's horses had broken down, and one eventually died.

As the astronomical parties began their trek back to Dufferin, the topographical parties remained in the field, determined to take advantage of the return of good weather and complete their six-mile-wide surveys all the way to Wood Mountain. Dawson stayed out, too, moving about the country at his own excited pace, drawing his supplies from whichever party was closest or had the most to spare.

After the blizzard, the weather had improved dramatically. Although the nights were still cold, on Sunday, October 5, Dawson

could write: "The weather today delightful & thorough indian summer. Sun shining bright & warm in the vallies. Air beautifully clear
& the distant hills very distinct & purple tinted. Wind gentle S.W.
Patches of snow where drifts have been still on the hills & uplands."[48]
On the afternoon of October 7, under a sun "almost oppressively
warm," the temperature reached a high of 83° F.

Although he was slowly moving generally east, Dawson had only
been out on the plains for a month or so and was in no hurry to get
back to Dufferin. He always rose early and was moving within a hour
or so, but by lunchtime he was ready to camp again in some interesting spot, having travelled perhaps no more than ten miles.

In the Pyramid Valley, 350 miles west of Pembina, he climbed the
spectacularly shaped hill for which both the valley and the creek that
flowed through it were named. From the top of the pyramid he could
see what he thought was a hundred miles, but what he found at his
feet interested him more:

> Found a portion of a neatly made stone pipe on the side of the pyr-
> amid hill. Made of the celebrated "red pipe stone." Many indian
> graves on the hills near & this probably washed out on the hillside
> by the action of the weather. Must belong to an old interment as a
> little patch of calcareous crust from the soil appears on one end of
> it. It seems very probable that the peculiar Pyramid hill capped by
> flat blocks of hard sandstone has been an object of superstitious
> veneration with the indians & the pipe may have been deposited
> there as an offering.[49]

Everywhere he stopped along the Parallel, Dawson looked for
Native burial sites and, nearly everywhere, he found them. Where they
were particularly numerous or seemed more recent, he would dig his
way enthusiastically into the mounds, although he rarely found anything of real interest, or value. He even remained unsure as to exactly
whose remains he was dealing with. The Sioux, he was told, usually
left their dead above ground on raised platforms of interwoven sticks,
and the Engineers did manage to photograph at least one such site in
the Souris valley. The men of the 49th Rangers were always willing

to offer advice on matters of Native lore and custom, although their individual credibility varied widely. Based on the scouts' information, Dawson concluded the burial mounds were likely to be Assiniboine or Plains Cree. He was probably correct, although by the 1870s there had already been such extensive influence from white missionaries that the Sioux, too, could well have begun using in-ground burials.

Of most interest to Dawson was an extensive Native site along the banks of South Antler Creek, midway between the two Souris River crossings. A ranger by the name of Pruden claimed the area was a long-abandoned Mandan village, complete with the collapsed, overgrown foundations of several large communal houses and other assorted earthworks, some of which Dawson was certain were gravesites. Chief scout Hallett agreed that the site was probably Mandan, based on what he had seen of their remnant villages down along the Missouri.

Dawson felt the site was worth a fairly detailed sketch in his journal and a lengthy written description. "The whole," he wrote, "bears the mark of very great antiquity, especially when the permanence of any disturbance of the prairie level is considered."[50]

The Souris River valley and the innumerable canyons and ravines that flowed into it represented what had clearly once been the Native heart of the far northern plains. It was here the boundary parties found the richest concentrations of burial sites, teepee rings, pictographs and bison bones, but little of what they saw was of recent origin. Save for the occasional individual or small band of Sioux, there was little of a Native presence in the valleys, and no living sign of the bison at all. The Metis crossed the Souris country often on their old trails between Wood Mountain and Fort Garry, but there was no sign of any permanent settlement. What had once been a land rich in bison and the hunters who lived off them was, by the 1870s, largely abandoned.

There were two particularly well-known attractions in the Souris valley, both of which were just north of the boundary line and a few miles west of the second Souris crossing. There is little doubt that almost every member of both commissions and every man in their escorts would have taken the time to clamber over the dramatic erosions of the Roche Percée and to climb the Hill of the Murdered Scout.

Roche Percée, the most spectacular of a line of eroded rocks found for some distance along the Souris, had long been known to travellers across the west. John Palliser and James Hector had been drawn down to the area from Fort Ellice in August 1857, and were impressed enough with what they saw to make detailed sketches of the most fantastic examples of natural architecture. Although they had visited the valley less than twenty years before the boundary commissions, Palliser and Hector found a place that was still full of life. They encountered a large band of Assiniboine camped along the river, with more in a village just to the south, on the edge of the Great Coteau. It was near the Souris, on the same side trip, that Palliser had seen (and promptly shot) the two bull bison that were the first of their kind he had encountered on the expedition.

What Dawson called "the remarkably castellated, fantastic and picturesque rock scenery"[51] of the Roche Percée—caused by the varying hardness of the many layers of sandstone and their differing rates of erosion—had long been a place of spiritual fascination for the Native populations. It was not possible for them to pass by without leaving some sort of offering, and the crevices in the rocks were packed with strings of beads, knots of tobacco and other small personal objects. The rock faces themselves were covered with rubbings of vermilion pigment and hundreds of carvings representing every kind of bird and animal.

The temptation to leave a similar record of their passing was too much to resist for many of the men of the boundary commissions, and they scratched their own graffiti into the soft sandstone. Most remarkable of all was the work of two British soldiers. They carved into the rock—and then photographed—the message "J.M. & G.P. Photographers B.N.A.B.C.S. Sept. 10, 1873."[52] The initials can only belong to the accident-prone sapper McCammon and to another private named Parsons. It is the only clue to the identity of any of the four Royal Engineers who created the nearly two hundred wonderful photographs of the commissions' progress along the 49th Parallel.

The Hill of the Murdered Scout received its share of visitors too. A little to the northeast of the Roche Percée, it is one of a series of not particularly spectacular low buttes that cover the area. Today it is hard to find, but for the nineteenth-century traveller it was a must-see. Depending on who was telling the story—and for the British commission, that was probably one or more members of the 49th Rangers—an Assiniboine scout had either killed, or been killed by, a Sioux or a member of some other tribe. Every surviving journal and diary records some variation of the legend, but William Twining's version, as he included it in the American commission's final report, contains most of elements common to most of the stories:

> Late in the fall of 1830, a party of Assiniboines, extending their wanderings far to the east of their own country, camped on the point of the lake to the north of the butte. One of their number, ascending the hill to watch the surrounding country for traces of hostile occupation, discovered a camp of Sioux close under the hill on the south. Cautiously approaching the crest, he came suddenly upon a Sioux warrior lying rolled up in his buffalo-robe, and apparently overcome with sleep. Seizing a large fragment of granite rock, the Assiniboine approached his foe with stealthy step. With one vigorous blow he struck the Sioux... In memory of this deed... he dug in the gravelly soil the figure of a man lying at full length, with outstretched legs and uplifted arms. He also scooped out each of the footprints marking his path as he fled. These marks, though only a few inches deep, were still distinctly visible when I visited the spot in 1873, and will probably remain for many years. In the hollow representing the head of the murdered man there was a red granite stone, smooth, oblong in shape, and about eight inches in greatest diameter, which was said to have been the stone used.[53]

As Dawson wandered about through the middle weeks of October, the rest of the men were moving steadily east. Greene and his parties, together with elements of their infantry escort, passed by on their way back to the main American camp at the Souris. As the British topographical parties continued to explore the canyons and coulees and refine their maps, they were slowly edging their way back toward their winter headquarters, ready to pack up and move fast should the weather finally break. While supplies were still being sent west from Wood End to support the parties, word was received that every one of the cattle from a herd intended to supply enough meat for the return trek to Dufferin had escaped and strayed on the same day they had arrived at the depot. While the scouts were out scouring the country, all non-essential personnel had been sent east, and anyone left at Wood End was subsisting on little more than bread and tea.

Slowly, the weather grew more and more unpredictable. October 14 was "overcast & threatening. Cold wind in morning & early afternoon. Evening calm & mild with a little rain,"[54] while the 15th saw heavy rain and sleet with "a very heavy hoar frost & water frozen more than an inch thick" overnight. By October 22, Dawson had crossed the Souris and was headed for Turtle Mountain. It was a freezing cold day with intermittent snowstorms, and most of the men found themselves walking to save their animals. Making matters worse, most of the country had been ravaged by late-season grass fires and, where there was no snow, the soot and ash came up in blinding clouds with every step or breath of wind.

Long after dark, Dawson's party found its way to the Turtle Mountain depot and discovered Forrest's topographical party and a small wagon train already in camp. Corporal Malings and his men came in later that same evening. Dawson decided to take the next day off to rest his men and animals (and himself), reporting that the thermometer read 16° F in his tent at 8:00 a.m. and that he had "extemporized a stove, thawed ink & wrote up diary."[55]

On the morning of October 24, Dawson, Malings, Forrest and the wagon train all headed out together onto the trail toward Pembina Mountain. Dawson's diary records one last curiosity:

About 8 miles E. of Turtle Mt. found two carts side by side near a frozen swamp. On examination turned out to be abandoned. A lot of baggage, provisions, &c. in them, also two guns, & an old tent between the carts as if to make a shelter. A tin pan & some dough & a spoon frozen in on top of one cart, & a lot of gophers running about examining things. On one of the carts scrawled "Wood Mountain or Bust" & after this in a bracket "Bust by G-d." No horses or men near. Heard afterwards that a man had turned up at depot in the morning asking shelter, saying that their horses had gone off & he & comrade separated during the snowstorm in search of them.[56]

By the evening of October 28, Dawson, Forrest and the rest camped for the night at a stopping place known as Grant's, hard by the eastern base of Pembina Mountain. It was, according to Dawson, "A very merry camp... all hands having been imbibing as freely as their pockets would admit of, but fortunately not much ready money among the crowd."[57] The next morning they were back on the trail: "Morning mild with snow showers. Roads heavy & slushy. Many of the horses 'played out' & barely able to move along. Rode ahead of carts & arrived at Dufferin about 3 p.m. New buildings going up on all sides for stores, &c."[58]

Galwey had been the first to return to Dufferin. He had arrived on October 20 after covering the four hundred miles from West Poplar in just twenty days. To spare the horses, he had walked at least three-quarters of the way. Anderson, who had been the first to push over the Pembina plateau, the first across the Coteau and nearly the first to see four hundred miles west, was the last to start for home. Keeping company with Dr. Burgess, he picked up the third survey party on October 20 and, herding any remaining astronomers, surveyors, depot keepers and teamsters ahead of him, finally reached Dufferin on the last day of October.

With his customary quiet pride, he wrote to his mother from the warmth of his room at the headquarters, "we have been travelling in snow almost continuously since the 24 Sept. but this did not stop our finishing all the work we had to do..."[59]

AT CAMP TERRY on the Souris the Americans were also preparing to pull out. Campbell and Coues were the first to go, leaving for

Fort Stevenson on October 8. They were both bound for Washington, D.C., where Coues would be spending the winter with his family and working on the results of his season's collecting from an office at the Smithsonian. Campbell would doubtless be reporting on the season's efforts too, but a good deal of his time would be dedicated to lobbying the secretary of state and other senior officials. The appropriation for the next phase of the work had still not been secured (in fact, the money for the 1874 season would not be safely in the bank until just days before the parties took to the field).

Coues and Campbell had barely left camp before Major Reno was registering yet another complaint. In a letter of October 11 to the assistant adjutant general in Washington, he all but accuses the commission's medical officer of dereliction of duty. While Reno couches his charge as if he were actually seeking clarification of Coues's role with the commission, he cannot entirely hide his dislike for the man:

> I have the honor to report that Asst. Surgeon Elliott Coues U.S.A. left this command with Mr. Campbell (U.S. Commissioner) and six men belonging to the Commissioner, on the 8th inst.
>
> He is Asst Surgeon of the Escort and Commission as well as naturalist, but his medical duties seem to be confined to attendance on one person, since he has left the Command and the parties under the Engineers, without other medical attendance than the Act'g. Asst. Surgeon attached to the troops.
>
> I report the preceding for information at superior Headquarters, as I do not understand Doctor Coues position with regard to the troops having no copy of the War Dep't order under which I assume he is acting.[60]

Whether they had met before is not clear, but the trouble between Coues and Reno had been building almost from the moment they both arrived at Fort Pembina three months earlier. When Reno first took command of the escort he discovered, much to his annoyance, that Coues had obtained an order allowing off-duty enlisted men to leave the garrison to help collect specimens. At that time, too, Reno had been forced to dismiss his own troops' surgeon for drunkenness and had asked if Coues could fill in until a new doctor was assigned. Coues had told him in no uncertain terms that he was strictly a member of the boundary commission and would not act as physician for the cavalrymen. It was the kind of selfish arrogance that would have galled the spit-and-polish 7th Cavalry major, and not something he was likely to forget.

In Coues's own correspondence, it is not hard to find examples of just the sort of attitude that Reno found so difficult to take. Writing to a fellow naturalist in July 1873, Coues reported on the great success of his specimen gathering and closed with a mock complaint: "The only thing that troubles me is the cruelly stringent orders I am under. The commissioner directed me to 'get what I want, go where I please, & do what I like.' Too bad, isn't it?"[61] Reno would not have found any part of such a letter even remotely amusing.

In the end, Coues's attitude bought him a reprimand from the surgeon general's office, but Reno did not get to savour his little victory. By the end of the year, he was in serious trouble of his own with the adjutant general, and only a personal appeal to his old Civil War comrade General Philip Sheridan saved him from a court martial.

Twining had been out at Wood End since some time in late September and, on October 6, Gregory and his men came in from West Poplar station. According to Twining, he was in rough shape, "... his animals worn out and totally exhausted with fatigue and hunger, they having been for three days without forage." As Gregory explained, since the blizzard, the animals had been on a ration of only three pounds of food per day, half of which had been flour or hard bread. Even that ration had given out and, with the whole of the Coteau a blackened wasteland from the grass fires, the animals had had nothing to eat. He lost two mules on the journey. After Commissioner Campbell had left, James Bangs relocated his tent to the cavalry camp and began to assemble the men who would be going out with him and the other officers. Two days later, on October 10, Twining and Gregory crawled in from Wood End, and on the 12th they all began moving southeast toward Fort Totten.

On his way back to Wood End, Gregory had passed Greene and his parties, still toiling away at their surveys and boundary markers. But by the time he reached East Poplar on October 3, Greene had abandoned the idea of trying to complete the final twenty-four miles of the topographical survey and he, too, turned back toward the Souris.

Arriving at Camp Terry on October 13, Greene found a letter from Twining and Gregory saying they had gone on ahead the previous day and instructing him to meet them as soon as possible at Fort Totten.

Twining was the only man with any previous experience in the country between Wood End and Fort Totten (a distance of about two hundred miles as the crow flies), and he took the lead:

> I felt certain that there was no part of the country in which occa-
> sional pools of water could not be found, and I only feared that we
> might be caught in another heavy storm while on the open plains.
> I therefore directed the march toward what I supposed to be the
> head of the Cut Bank Creek, which we reached after a march of
> twenty four-miles, having suffered much for want of water.[62]

At this point, the party was cutting diagonally across the loop of the Souris, following another of the numerous "half-breed trails." Once he had crossed the river, Twining had two choices: either follow it to the bottom of the loop and then turn east, or strike out directly across country. On the longer route along the river, there would at least be some assurance of water for the animals. On neither route was there any guarantee of forage:

> The prairie fires, which for some days had been burning brightly in
> every direction, had swept every vestige of grass from these plains,
> except in the immediate vicinity of the ponds, leaving the ground
> covered with a light film of ashes... A strong east wind raised the
> dust and ashes in clouds, filling the eyes, nose and mouth with an
> irritating alkali, which bit and smarted with undying zeal.[63]

Not wanting the trip to take any longer than absolutely necessary, Twining struck directly east, hoping to hit Devil's Lake and, hard by it, Fort Totten.

After eight days of short rations and foul water, the party arrived at the fort. Twining would retain only one pleasant memory of the march:

> We reached Fort Totten on the 20th October, the only notable camp being that on the Hurricane Lake. This lake, of which I had never heard before, although tolerably familiar with that part of the country, is a beautiful sheet of water, perhaps a mile in width. The north and west banks are covered by a heavy forest... The water is green and clear, and a perfect delight to the traveler wearied and disgusted with the usual alkaline or offensive fresh water of the plains... I am quite certain that it had never before been visited by white men.[64]

The tireless Greene followed them into Totten two days later, but not before he had undertaken yet another survey (he seemed incapable of marching more than a day without measuring or mapping something). He had taken his party along the Souris to the great loop, "in order to make a reconnaissance of its course," and then turned east "across the burnt prairies and salt lakes."[65]

Leaving Greene and his men to recuperate and repair their equipment, the rest of the officers and men left Totten on October 24 to march the eighty miles south to Fort Seward. It was bitterly cold and snowing, the ponds and creeks were frozen, and they had no proper winter gear. After their four-day march to Seward, those men not assigned to drive the animals on to St. Cloud, Minnesota, were put on the train for St. Paul, where they would be formally discharged. The animals were in such poor shape that any of the wagons not required to carry forage were left at Seward, to be recovered the following spring.

As Twining and Gregory headed off to the comforts of their winter quarters in Detroit, Lieutenant Greene and his men turned their faces into the wind and marched back toward Pembina.

· 7 ·

WINTER
1873 – 74

A more dismal holiday-week I have never passed.

FRANCIS GREENE

RUE TO THE local belief that the first storm of fall would be followed by several weeks of fine weather, there had not been a repeat of the mid-September blizzard. Nevertheless, the snow that had fallen held on, and the temperatures never fully recovered. Winter was coming sooner than it had in 1872, a fact confirmed when the Red River froze over on October 28, ending the steamboats' season more than two weeks earlier than the previous year.

At Dufferin there had been more construction, adding two storehouses and new stables for up to two hundred horses and oxen. According to Millman: "They think they will have sufficient stores to last till the end of the commission, which they suppose will be in the summer or fall of 1875."[1] There is no indication here as to who "they" are, but the summer's success would have given Anderson no reason to rethink his plan to have the line completed by the fall of 1874.

Cameron had left Dufferin for Ottawa in mid-October, before any of the field parties had come in. He was taking his wife and child back to her father for the winter. Whether Cameron had agreed to reconsider his domestic arrangements or not, Charles Tupper would not allow his daughter and grandchild to spend another dismal winter in the Red River valley. Before he left Dufferin, however, Commissioner Cameron made yet another rather odd move. He opened a trading post in the commission depot on Turtle Mountain.

The reasoning behind the project is not entirely clear. In his letters and reports to the Foreign Office, Cameron suggested that it was intended to be a profit-making venture—a way to recover some of the Boundary Commission's expenses. At the same time, however, he was telling the men who would be staffing the post (the depot's regular keeper, a civilian named George Hill, and at least one other individual) that their real purpose was to ingratiate themselves with whatever Native groups appeared at the post (or wintered anywhere on Turtle Mountain) and gather whatever intelligence they could about the possibility for trouble over the coming months. Cameron also seems to have believed that fair trading with the Natives would gain their trust and reduce the likelihood of raids and petty thefts from the commission's supply depots the following summer.

Just what goods the post was expecting to trade with the Sioux is not reported, but it was probably bison robes and other more valuable furs (not that the Sioux were particularly renowned for their skill as trappers). But the commission records do contain a detailed listing (including the wholesale price) of everything Hill took with him when he returned to Turtle Mountain in late October. Designated "Indian Notions," some of the items he signed for were:

> 34 cotton handkerchiefs ($3.21)
> 1 dozen bead necklaces ($0.80)
> 3 dozen combs ($3.60)
> 2 dozen mirrors ($1.20)
> 31 yards of cotton ($3.41)
> 136 yards of print ($14.96)

In a more practical vein, he also took:

> 1½ dozen pocket knives ($1.35)
> ½ dozen guns ($35.00)
> 2 dozen boxes of caps ($2.40)
> 16 dozen ½ pound tins of powder ($36.00)
> 165 pounds of shot ($24.75)

Just what the American military might have thought of these last items as trade goods for the Sioux, we can only speculate.

Early in November, Galwey, Featherstonhaugh and Rowe left to winter at the British garrison in Halifax where, no doubt, they still had friends from their years of service there. After most of the Canadians had retreated to their homes in the east, only Anderson, Ward, Millman and Boswell remained at Dufferin.

Millman had found his room filled with stores, and he moved first into the harness shop and then set himself up under canvas nearby. With a small stove installed, he was comfortable and happy to be out of the general bustle. Before Burgess and Dawson left for the winter, he shared with them a number of the plants he had collected, and was pleased to receive nearly 350 different botanical specimens in return. He took over administration of the post library, carefully listing which books had been lost during the summer and which were "no longer fit for use." He also went back to treating patients from the surrounding area, dealing confidently with a variety of tumours, infections and burns. The wide-eyed young doctor who had arrived at Dufferin was maturing quickly. He had thoroughly enjoyed his first months in the west and was already looking forward to the spring and another full season on the boundary.

Millman, too, described the summer as less than successful:

> The farm was a complete failure. I don't think it was managed properly. It has been a favorable year for agriculture, there being no grasshoppers—or very few—and no other insects to destroy the grain.[2]

Mr. Almon may have discovered something that many other outsiders would learn in the coming years: being a successful farmer in eastern Canada (or even eastern Europe) was no guarantee of success in the west, where few of the old rules applied.

Anderson had briefly hoped for some leave as well. Writing to his mother in mid-November, he outlined a plan he had already abandoned:

> I had an idea of going to Canada during the winter, and visiting Toronto, Quebec, Philadelphia, Washington and a few other places. But at present I do not like to be away, as there is great deal of office work on hand connected with the maps and Field notes. Moreover all the others want to go, and they have worked so magnificently throughout, that I should not have liked to make any difficulty. It is possible however I may have to go to Toronto to examine some old documents referring to the initial point of our work at the Lake of the Woods, tho' I do not anticipate it would be any use...[3]

The final sentence makes clear that the whole business of the Northwest Angle was far from settled. Indeed, it would remain the principal aggravation of Anderson's life at Dufferin for the entire winter. D'Arcy East had already spent most of the summer resurveying the entire area, and was still working there with his special party at the end of October.

Cameron's continuing obsession with the location of the northwesternmost point of the lake defies reason. Some senior Foreign Office officials might have believed that ensuring free access to a shabby steamboat landing was still a matter of some importance. They may even have sincerely believed that the Northwest Angle itself was an important piece of real estate—though that, too, was probably due to Cameron's constant prattling on about it. Colonel Hawkins had said the Angle "should, *if possible*, be preserved to the Dominion of Canada." One word from Cameron and the matter would have dropped from the agenda in an instant. Commissioner Campbell half-heartedly claimed the place had great economic potential, but allowed his assistant, Twining, to dismiss the notion out of hand in the same official report. Only Campbell's personal acrimony toward Cameron could have stayed him from the obvious recommendation that the Angle be turned over to Canada. If Twining and Anderson had been the chief commissioners, they would surely have done the sensible thing.

Following on from the officers' departure, there were dramatic reductions in the workforce at headquarters. Ward paid off most of the seasonal workers and, according to Millman, only 106 men were to be retained through the winter—including the two who had been sent off to operate Cameron's trading post at Turtle Mountain. With no surveying work to be done, life for the men at Dufferin quickly settled into a predictable routine of feeding the animals and keeping the woodboxes full.

LIEUTENANT FRANCIS VINTON GREENE and his party arrived at Pembina on October 29. While they had made good time from Fort Totten, it had been far from a pleasant march:

> The greater part of this journey was over an open prairie from which the grass had been burned, and was made in the face of a northerly snow-storm. As we were insufficiently clad, having only the ragged remains of the summer's outfit, we suffered considerably—more perhaps than during the rest of the winter.[4]

From the moment Greene began to assemble and equip his parties, it was obvious that he had taken a good deal of time to learn from the experiences of the British and Canadian men who had spent the previous winter between the Red River and the lake. He must have quizzed them about it whenever their paths crossed during the summer. It is also likely that he had been asked by his superiors to provide as much information as possible about the effects of sustained outdoor work at extremely low temperatures, as his submission to the American commission's final report contains a wealth of detailed analysis of the effect of cold weather on men, animals and equipment. With the purchase of Alaska only five years before, Washington seemed to recognize that there was much they needed to learn as they began to take more than just legal possession of their new territory. Or, in Greene's words: "The experience gained in carrying on a survey in the depths of winter, in a locality where the temperature reached a point 50° below zero, was of such a novel character that I think a somewhat detailed account of it will not be out of place."[5]

The preamble to Greene's report contains another interesting piece of information. In it he acknowledges that he was directed "... to proceed to Fort Pembina with my parties, and complete the geodetic and topographical work between the Red River and Lake of the Woods; and to adopt, without examination, the intermediate astronomical stations observed by the British parties during the preceding winter."[6] Farquhar had insisted that the U.S. commission could not agree to the British calculations without carefully checking them. Now, Twining (obviously with Campbell's blessing) was willing to accept the British fixes sight unseen.

Several factors might have been involved in the American about-face. Perhaps Farquhar did, as Anderson had suggested, bear a personal grudge against Cameron after their last meeting at the Northwest Angle. If so, his resignation may have removed the greatest objection to the British position. While Campbell certainly shared Farquhar's distaste for the British commissioner, perhaps he could not see the advantage in spiting him by spending large sums of American money to resurvey something which he already knew was probably correct. As for Twining, the subject of the eastern line must have come up more than once during his meetings with Anderson over the previous summer, and the two men may have come to an understanding. Twining must have asked himself whether anyone would really want to go back into the depths of the Roseau swamp and measure it all again, when the existing line was surely very close to accurate.

The most likely reason for the change in the American position could well be related to Cameron's constant agitation for a mean parallel. If it were discovered that there was a major problem with the line in the Roseau and nearly ninety miles of the border had to be resurveyed, it might give the British commissioner the opening he needed to force the refinement of the boundary line across the entire 853 miles. Anything that thwarted such an outcome would have had the unqualified support of Campbell, Twining and Anderson.

Even without the burden of checking the British line, Greene had more than enough work before him. Not only was he to finish the work he had started the previous fall, but there was also the five-mile topographical survey east to Lake of the Woods, the building of boundary markers every mile where they did not already exist (courtesy of the British) and a new assignment: a survey of the south shore of Lake of the Woods from the astronomical station at Buffalo Point to the mouth of Rainy River.

After acquiring proper winter gear for his topographical and survey crews, Greene began to take on the additional men he would need to drive the wagons and stock the depots. He hired eight teamsters, seven dogsled drivers and sundry other support. He would move out with a complement of forty-seven men, divided into three parties: one to run the tangents and two for the survey. The topographical parties would be led by Alfred Downing, a twenty-five-year-old English-trained surveyor who had been with Greene since the beginning of the work, and Charles L. Doolittle, a thirty-year-old mathematician from Bethlehem, Pennsylvania, who had been hired as an emergency replacement for another man in September 1873. Assisting Greene with the tangents would be recorder and computer Orrin S. Wilson, a new, though not inexperienced, addition. The twenty-one-year-old engineering graduate of the University of Michigan had worked for a year on the Great Lakes geodetic survey before joining the boundary commission.

Greene had hoped to provision his party from the Army stores at Fort Pembina, but the commissary could provide only a part of his forage and none of his food stores. He was forced to buy everything else from the Hudson's Bay Company and other suppliers in Pembina: "The supplies were of excellent quality, but the rations cost 15 per cent. and the forage 60 per cent. more than the government price."[7]

For $24 each, he was able to acquire a set of the appropriate clothing for each man. While the clothing was of local manufacture and well suited to the country, its sheer bulk must have made such precise work as surveying doubly difficult. Greene's report contains both detailed description and critical analysis:

> Head-gear—a close-fitting skull-cap, made of two thicknesses of blanket, and lined with flannel. Sewed to this was a havelock, also of blanket, reaching to the shoulders, and fastening under the nose. This left only the eyes and nose exposed. In addition to this the men generally wrapped around the face and ears a heavy scarf of some kind, as it was found that in a wind, on the open swamps, the ears were frozen through the blanket cap.
>
> Sack-coat—of buffalo-leather, made loose, and fastened around the waist by a scarf.
>
> Trowsers—of buffalo-leather, made "barn door" fashion to keep out the wind. The coat and trowsers for myself and my assistants were made of moose-leather, which is closer and keeps out the wind better. Its cost is about double that of buffalo leather.
>
> Mittens—of moose-leather, lined with blanket, with gauntlets reaching to the elbow. These were made large so that a pair of gloves might be worn inside of them, but this was not found desirable. The mittens were suspended from the neck by a string. The trowsers were always tied tightly around the ankle to keep out the snow, and, in addition, we sometimes wore leggings made of moose-leather or of blanket—the latter being preferable, as the snow did not soak into it as into leather.
>
> The leather clothing was worn over a suit of woolen clothes and two or three suits of woolen underclothes. In the woods where the wind could have no force, it formed a perfect protection, and men worked cheerfully and lustily in temperatures of 20° and 25° below zero. But on the open swamp, a temperature of –5° accompanied by a wind was sufficient to put a stop to all stationary work.[8]

Greene rightly devotes by far the most time and care to the crucial matter of footwear:

I...procured moccasins for the whole party. They were made after the Sioux pattern, and several sizes too large. The ordinary covering for the foot, throughout the rest of the winter, consisted of one or two pairs of woolen socks, then a pair of "neeps" (slippers made of blanket), then a square piece of blanket wrapped several times around the foot from heel to toe; finally the moccasin was put on, more to keep the blanket and slipper in place than for any other purpose. This method of covering proved to be a perfect protection to the foot, provided care was taken to always have a dry pair of moccasins and stockings on hand. The feet often got wet in moving about a fire, and to start out on a journey with wet stockings was to insure the freezing of the feet.[9]

He experienced the same problems with snowshoes that had plagued Anderson the previous winter. Manufactured in Montreal, the snowshoes were well made, but far too light for working in Roseau's heavy brush and windfall. Like Anderson's shoes, Greene's tended to break behind the foot where the two sidebars met to form the "tail." "At the close of the season," he wrote, "not one in fifteen pairs was fit for use."[10] Unlike Anderson, who soldiered on with his broken frames, Greene found an alternative. The snowshoes made by the Natives around Lake of the Woods were, he found, far superior in every way. While the Montreal frames were about forty inches long and weighed just over a pound each, the Native equivalent was between sixty and seventy inches in length, slightly narrower and, weighing in at nearly four pounds each, of much heavier construction. Greene found it nearly impossible to break them with even the heaviest use.

Greene's penchant for experimentation came out in his choice of transportation. He had been advised by the British officers to acquire dogsleds immediately to avoid the difficulties of moving large animals through the swamps. Although he intended to use dogs for some work, Greene was not ready to give up on the huge loads that could only be moved by wagon. From the local settlers, he learned that winter freighting was usually accomplished by a wagon bed mounted on large runners or by a sled drawn by a single ox. Greene was also not inclined to abandon his army mules without a fair trial so, after a difficult search through Pembina, he managed to find a sufficient number of the sled runners known as "Maineite bobs" and, by modifying the tongues to handle the long mule teams, he mounted them to his vehicles. In total, Greene went into the field with four six-mule army wagons, a four-mule ambulance and three hired teams, two of which were drawn by a pair of mules and one by a pair of oxen.

Even Greene seemed impressed by the fact that his six-mule teams could easily draw a sled-mounted wagon loaded with upward of six thousand pounds of freight not only on hard roads but, as long as they could find firm footing, through soft snow as well. But there were drawbacks:

> In following the winding roads through the woods great care was required in driving the long teams, and even this was not always sufficient to keep clear of the trees. At the end of every trip one or more bobs would be broken; fortunately there was plenty of oak and ash available for repairs, for during the winter the wood-work of every set of bobs had to be replaced.[11]

Using the big animals, however, also meant a large percentage of what they were hauling was their own feed and, to work in extreme cold, they needed even more of it than usual. As a result, the mules were allowed forty pounds of hay per day (for feed and bedding), supplemented by a daily ration of more than twelve pounds of oats, wheat or barley. This was more than a third higher than the standard army ration, and more than twice what they had received during the summer. Quite apart from the weight, the sheer volume of the material Greene had to haul was reduced by a series of haystacks, which had been cut and stacked at twenty-five-mile intervals by a summer contractor.

As long as they got enough food, the mules more than justified Greene's faith in them:

> I could detect no sickness or signs of weakness among the mules, and at the close of the season they were in nearly as good condition as at the beginning. Their superiority over oxen was clearly

proved, as I had an ox-team with Mr. Doolittle's party. Their greatest daily travel was eighteen miles, against forty-four for the mules. At the close of the season they could only make eight miles a day and were abandoned by their owner, whereas the mules carried us from Pembina to Georgetown, one hundred and forty miles, over a heavy road, in five days.[12]

With his mules and his sleds, Greene efficiently restocked the abandoned British depot at Pointe D'Orme with 20,000 pounds of supplies and then, brimming with confidence, he walked straight into his first big mistake.

Believing in his mules' ability to advance as easily to the next depot at Pine River, he "tried an empty sleigh on this swamp, and, in doing so, mired the mules to their bellies. To [his] great surprise it was found that the swamp was not frozen at all, in spite of the fact that [they] had already had the thermometer down to 35° below zero."[13] Even if his discussions with Featherstonhaugh, Galwey, and the rest had not been quite as comprehensive as he suggested, it is hard to understand how Greene missed the British officers' single most significant discovery about the Roseau swamp: that the snow on the heavy grass insulated the water and kept it from freezing.

Retreating to Pointe D'Orme, Greene was forced to take his wagons onto the ice of the Roseau River and follow its course up to the lake and, from there, north to the Pine River depot. He was now fifty miles east of Red River but still not in a position to deploy his working parties. Another experiment was in order:

> I had the carpenters make in camp three "tobogans" or flat trains, each to be driven by a single animal. These tobogans were made of two pine boards, fastened side by side with transverse cleats and sprung up in front by hot water. This made, in fact, a rude sledge, twelve by two feet. Its load was packed after the fashion of a dog-sled.[14]

The sledges worked well enough, as long as the men went ahead of them and made a sort of road. Walking back and forth in their snowshoes, they packed the grass and snow down into the water where they froze instantly and, according to Greene, could easily support several tons within a few minutes. Discovering how strong the "road" really was, Greene had it widened and run back to Point d'Orme, from where he brought his heavy wagons up to Pine River. However, the innovative Greene was forced to admit that what he had gained with the wagons, he had lost to the weather:

> It was not a very safe road, however, for the drifting snow soon filled it up to the level of the surrounding country. It was not distinguishable by the eye, and had to be followed by feeling, the road being hard, and the rest being very soft snow. If, by any carelessness, a sleigh got a runner off the road and in the soft snow, the whole was instantly upset, and it required several hours to right it again. This mishap occurred two or three times.[15]

Greene now had his heavy wagons at Pine River, but the heavy deadfall along the line stopped him moving them any farther east. The sledges were not much better, but by taking advantage of the ribbon of creek beds that riddled the swamp, he was able to move forward to establish another depot on the Roseau River just thirty miles from Lake of the Woods. From there, even the toboggans were defeated by the deadfall: "Beyond this depot dog-sleds were absolutely necessary, and I procured six of them from Pembina, at a cost of about $80 for each train complete, including dogs."[16]

Getting so much heavy equipment so far across the Roseau swamp in winter was certainly a triumph of sorts. One has to wonder, though, if Greene had given any thought to what would happen if spring came as early as the winter had. Getting six-mule sleds into a frozen swamp had proved difficult enough; getting them out if the ice had melted would have been almost impossible.

IN MID-NOVEMBER, as Greene pursued his experiments in the Roseau swamp, Anderson, comfortably ensconced in his rooms at Dufferin, received what he took for an early Christmas present:

News has just reached us that there has been a change of government in Canada, which will affect us in as much as Capt.
Cameron's father-in-law a certain Dr. Tupper is no longer a Cabinet Minister. We shall get on all the better for not having any
back stairs influence at work, but no doubt it will make a great
difference to Capt. C. There is no probability of its making the
least difference to me, or to the prosecution of the work...[17]

Sir John A. Macdonald's government had fallen as a consequence
of the Pacific Scandal, a volatile mix of alleged influence-peddling
and backroom politics driven by the vast sums of money that would
come with the awarding of the contract to build the transcontinental railway. Anderson was right about the change of government not
directly affecting the work of the commission, but the importance of
the railway in dictating both the pace and the timing of the boundary
work cannot be overstated.

It was British Columbia joining Confederation on the promise
of a transcontinental railway link which had finally pushed Canada,
through Britain, to finish with the marking of the 49th Parallel. It
was a botched attempt to survey the new province of Manitoba that
had precipitated the rebellion at Red River and pushed the building
of the Dawson Route to bring in the troops that quelled it. It was the
location of that road—an all-Canadian route to the west—that had
reignited the whole issue of the Northwest Angle and the division
of Lake of the Woods. All these things, and more, had conspired to
bring the Royal Engineers to the banks of the Red River in the fall of
1872. While Anderson's work was not directly affected by any of them,
he must have been aware of their broad implications.

By the time Anderson first arrived at Pembina, the land surveyors were back in Manitoba, this time without opposition from the
broken Metis Council. Over the next few years, they would run their
lines and grids everywhere across the former Rupert's Land. Railway
surveyors were in the field as well, strung out across the impossible
maze of rock, water and muskeg that lay northwest of Lake Superior,
looking for a route that would bring them onto the plains somewhere

near the new town of Winnipeg. West of the Great Divide, exploratory surveys of British Columbia were well underway, although the path the railway would follow to the Pacific coast was still years away from being decided. Nevertheless, everyone seemed to be poised and ready, waiting only for the boundary to be drawn before moving out to take possession of the new lands.

Just two months before the boundary commissions arrived at the Northwest Angle in the fall of 1872, the crude landing had received another visitor. Sandford Fleming was engineer-in-chief of the Canadian Pacific, and he was headed overland to the west coast, seeing for himself the land through which he believed his railway would run, talking with the survey parties and generally trying to grasp something of the sheer scale of what he had undertaken. Fleming's small party—which included secretary Rev. George M. Grant, naturalist John Macoun, a doctor, a cook and Fleming's young son, Frank—had come along the notorious Dawson Route.

Although Fleming's position ensured that the managers of the road would treat them with far more deference than the usual customers, the party avoided most of the problems by travelling in their own canoes with their own Native paddlers. Nevertheless, at nearly every juncture where they had to rely on wagons to move their baggage, the wagons were either late or unavailable. Where they were to board steamers or tugs to cross the larger lakes (with the canoes towed in a line behind), the boats were invariably out of commission for one reason or another. In the end, Fleming's party had to rely almost entirely on their own canoes to reach the Northwest Angle.

That Fleming so enjoyed his journey from Lake Superior, moving at an unimpeded speed of five miles per hour in his canoes, reveals the fatal flaw in the Dawson Route. Fleming had travelled it as the Natives, and later, the voyageurs of the North West Company had. It was a near-perfect route for light canoes and strong backs, but completely unsuited to steamboats and wagons. Open, at best, only six months of the year and, by the nature of its construction and operation, constantly on the verge of complete collapse, the Dawson Route was never a viable link between the Great Lakes and the west, and no amount of government subsidy could ever have made it so.

Grant called the Angle "the dirtiest, most desolate-looking [and] mosquito-haunted of all our camping grounds" and they stayed only one miserable night. By 5:30 the next morning, they were on their way to Winnipeg. Before he left, however, Grant recorded his thoughts about the whole controversy over the location of the boundary through Lake of the Woods:

> It seems that this point, though far north of the 49th degree, or the boundary line between the Dominion and the United States, is claimed by the Republic, and that their claim is sustained by an evident verbal mistake in the Treaty that defined the boundary. "North-west" has been inserted instead of "South-west." If so, it is only another instance in which the diplomatists of the Empire have been outwitted by the superior knowledge and unscrupulousness of our neighbours.[18]

Grant's notion that the Americans had cleverly and deliberately engineered a land grab on the western shore of the lake seems paranoid, though if he had in mind the simple taking advantage of a mistake, or a refusal to "play fair," he may not have been so wide of the mark (the British had agreed to an adjustment of the Vermont–Quebec border in 1842 to prevent the creation of a similar Canadian exclave in Lake Champlain, but the Americans had refused to reciprocate over Point Roberts during the Pacific survey). But leaving that aside, Grant's suggestion that the long confusion over the Northwest Angle was, in fact, the consequence of a simple clerical error—since the southwest corner of the lake does indeed intersect neatly with the 49th Parallel—is intriguing.

The 1783 treaty that first introduced the northwesternmost point of the lake also tied that point to the source of the Mississippi. While no one had yet located the true source of the river—not its main course, but the head of the smallest, most distant stream which could actually be followed to the river proper—the geography of Lake of the Woods was far better known. There might have been a chance that the source of the Mississippi was close to the southern edge of the lake, but no one thought it was anywhere north of that.

It is easy to imagine an error in transcription during the grand confusion of dialogue between two parties, neither of whom had ever been anywhere near the land they were so cheerfully dividing up. But, even assuming that the treaty makers had indeed agreed upon a northwesternmost point, the men who prepared the Convention of 1818 certainly should have recognized it as an absurdity. By then they knew perfectly well where the Mississippi was, what Lake of the Woods looked like and, generally, where the 49th Parallel lay. Why the British did not press for a change to that single word is a mystery (though if they overlooked it, there is no mystery as to why the Americans would not have raised the issue). Even harder to explain is why none of the subsequent British visitors to the site—all hard-nosed, practical men of science—seem to have challenged the wording either. They simply fell into a series of obtuse arguments about exactly where that northwesternmost point actually was, even though they all knew that such a place might not really exist in any meaningful sense or, at least, could have been any one of a dozen equally valid candidates.

Sandford Fleming's appearance at the Northwest Angle was really the *coup de grâce* for the northwesternmost point, for the Dawson Route and for most of the reasons anyone had ever cared about the impossible confusion of rock, swamp and water between Lake Superior and the Red River. The Americans had already given up on it. The future wealth of Minnesota would come from railways, not ancient canoe routes. The biggest town in the area was Duluth and Duluth was a railway town, a place where the state's wood and wheat and, eventually, iron ore would be gathered and loaded onto Lake Superior freighters to be sent east by the thousands of tons per ship.

When Fleming finally built his railway, it would bypass the Northwest Angle, the great Roseau swamp and the centuries of life in that country. The boundary, no matter where it happened to wander, would no longer control access to the Canadian west. Water had once been the measure by which the continent was carved up, and access to navigable water still mattered where the Great Lakes and the Mississippi were concerned. But the west was being built by the railway, and railways were hugely indifferent to the meandering courses and unpredictable levels of the western rivers. For the railways, rivers meant only the expensive inconvenience of building bridges.

In addition to Fleming and his party, there had been other significant travellers moving through the territory. When Galwey left Dufferin for Halifax at the beginning of November 1873, he was in the company of Alfred R.C. Selwyn, successor to the great Sir W.E. Logan as head of the Geological Survey of Canada. Selwyn's appointment as the survey's second director coincided neatly with the Hudson's Bay Company's sale of Rupert's Land and the birth of Canada's new transcontinental reach. His presence at Dufferin in the fall of 1873 marked the end of his third significant trip into Canada's new western lands. As he was planning to order a massive series of geological explorations in the new lands, he believed it would be best if he was at least somewhat familiar with their general nature and potential complexities.

Selwyn's arrival in Dufferin would have been of great interest to one member of Her Majesty's North American Boundary Commission in particular. George Dawson had taken his position with the commission only on the assurance that a job with the Geological Survey would be waiting for him when he was done. That the Dawson family was already well acquainted with Selwyn is clear from a letter George sent to his sister Anna soon after the director had left Dufferin:

> I was much surprised by the advent of Mr. Selwyn the other day. He was on his way to Montreal from the Saskatchewan region, but having been frozen up on the Red R. hired carts from some half-breed and gone on this far. He was here a couple of days.[19]

In fact, Selwyn was already working on plans to have Dawson return to the west almost as soon as he could finish writing the final report on his discoveries along the 49th Parallel.

On December 11, 1873, Captain Cameron finally returned from his extended visit to Ottawa; he had been travelling with important company. Lieutenant Colonel George Arthur French, first commissioner of the newly formed North-West Mounted Police, was on his way to Winnipeg to take command of his first recruits. The two men would have had a lot to talk about. Both were Royal Artillery officers and Cameron, before he was turned back from the Metis barricades in 1869, was supposed to have created the new police force to patrol the Red River Colony and what would become the North-West Territories.

The first 150 Mounted Policemen had arrived in late October and bivouacked near Winnipeg. In just seven months, the still-green forces would follow the boundary commission's tracks almost to the foothills of the Rocky Mountains. There, they would announce the Canadian government's presence with regular patrols along the newly marked 49th Parallel, putting paid to the Montana whiskey traders and preparing the new country for the transcontinental railway and the coming waves of immigrants.

In the absence of his family, Cameron moved into the officers' quarters. There was a great deal of work waiting for him, but he stayed only three days before he went up to Winnipeg to visit friends. Anderson, who now complained bitterly and at length about the man in every letter home, must at least have been pleased to hear one piece of news. The commissioner was finally giving up his fight to preserve the Northwest Angle and was willing to accept the drowned reference monument as the key to the location of the northwestern-most point. Perhaps it was seeing the results of D'Arcy East's special survey party, which had looked long and hard but failed to find anything else that could possibly have been the marker. Perhaps it was the fact that the government and the Hudson's Bay Company were in the process of moving their buildings at the landing to a place that was safely within Canadian territory. Perhaps the new Canadian government had simply told him there would be no more time or money spent on a lost cause.

Whatever the reason, at least Cameron had finally abandoned the Angle. He was now free to concentrate solely on his fight for a mean parallel, a cause that would do nothing to narrow the divide between him and the other commission officers on both sides of the boundary line.

WITH HIS DEPOTS finally stocked, Greene began to deploy his working parties. On November 4 Doolittle had started his topographic survey at the edge of the Red River valley. With instructions to work his way east to the Roseau River and then, after making a special survey of the course of the river, to continue toward Pine River, Greene expected to meet him there in mid-December.

Over the next few days, Greene moved the rest of his men into the field. With his supply parties re-establishing the abandoned British depots, he began, for a second time, to run tangent lines from Pembina east toward the end of the British work. Leapfrogging along the line with Wilson's party, Greene eventually hit the last British mark almost perfectly. In doing so, he proved two critical points. First, that his initial work the previous year had indeed been in error and, second, that the American decision to accept the British demarcation east to Lake of the Woods had been the right one. What Greene had planned to do if the two lines had not matched up he does not say.

By the time his parties reassembled at Pine River on December 15, Greene had learned a great deal more about winter work:

> The thermometer had already been down in the minus twenties, and winter was fairly begun. Nearly everything in the commissariat line was frozen hard. The beef had to be sawed off in slabs like limestone; vinegar, if left in an open vessel, had to be chopped out with a hatchet; several novices attempted to drink out of metallic cups without first warming them in water, and, as a result, left the skin of their lips on the cups; the dark mules were white and glistening with frost in the morning; and various other novel and amusing effects of a minimum temperature were observed.[20]

One of the effects of the cold that Greene found neither novel nor amusing was the havoc it played with his instruments. Fully three pages of his report are given over to the travails of trying to take his fixes at anything below −20° F. Anticipating that the lubricants in his instruments would freeze solid, he carefully removed every trace of oil, hoping the clean, smoothly machined plates would not stick to

each other. It was, at best, a marginally successful strategy. His recommendation to the army's instrument suppliers was to substitute
graphite (which he knew as "black lead") for the oil, something he
wishes he had been supplied with before he set out. He learned to
keep two sets of lanterns going—one to light his work in the observation tent and another near the fire. In the tent the lamps, once
away from the fire's warmth, would glow for perhaps fifteen minutes
before the oil congealed, the flame went out, and the lamp had to be
exchanged for the fire-warmed backup. When doing the delicate work
of taking readings, he learned to resist the instinctive act of reaching out with his ungloved hand to tighten a screw on his instruments
(the cold contracted and constantly loosened them) since "the instan-
taneous result was a 'burn,' and not a temporary sensation, but one
like that from a hot iron."[21]

The topographical observations, which were carried out in the
daytime, remained accurate (due to temperatures some 20 or 30
degrees higher than at night). However, Greene discovered that,
where it required perhaps three or four sets of astronomical observations to take an accurate summer fix, anywhere from eight to more
than a dozen such sets were necessary in the winter due to the inaccuracies brought on by the extreme conditions. Add to that the tendency
of his chronometers to become unpredictable (another consequence
of congealing oil) and Greene was forced to conclude: "Our experience, then, proves that fair topographical work can be done in a semi-
arctic climate, and that astronomical work of a certain sort can also
be done, but that refinements are out of the question." "These poor
results," he went on to say, "were all the more discouraging from the
fact that they involved so much labour, and such great personal discomfort."[22] None of the British teams expressed any concerns about
the accuracy of their winter fixes, which may demonstrate the overall superiority of their instruments. The Americans had certainly
viewed them with envy when they had first seen them come out of
their cases at the Northwest Angle.

With the line not only defined but clear-cut and marked all the
way from Pine River to Lake of the Woods, Greene took stock of his

situation and made a final division of his parties. Wilson and Down-ing would work on cutting a ten-foot-wide line of sight, and the place-ment of a marker for every one of the fifty-six miles back to Pembina. Doolittle would take his one-mule toboggans forward to the point where the eastern branch of the Roseau River met the boundary before pushing his topographical survey to Lake of the Woods and, from there, around the southern shore to Rainy River. When the dog teams arrived from Pembina, Greene would bring them along, together with a couple of toboggans and enough supplies for a month, and establish a new subdepot at East Roseau. From there, all the work would be done with the dogs. The stage was set for what would prove to be a wilderness adventure that Greene would likely never forget, nor ever wish to repeat.

Back at Dufferin, Millman and the rest of the British commission were enjoying a Christmas dinner of "two rounds of beef... a splendid plum pudding, drowned in brandy and then set fire to, liquors with-out end and several kinds." On December 26, nothing whatsoever was accomplished "on account of the men not having recovered from their indulgence of the previous day."[23] Out at East Roseau, Greene and his men were accomplishing nothing either, but it was no excess of Christmas spirits that kept them in their tents, but a storm that lasted from the 23rd to the 30th:

A more dismal holiday-week I have never passed. There were six of us in all... [and] our camp, of two little tents, was pitched in an opening of windfall, close to the post marking the junction of the tangents. Under the intricate lacing of fallen logs, and the three feet of snow in which they were imbedded, was a frozen swamp. My own tent floor was composed of ice, and in order that the stove might not melt through this and disappear, it was supported on a scaffold of logs run out under the tent... It snowed fiercely during the greater part of the week, and our efforts at cooking... over an open fire were not the most successful... The appearance of the camp, with a smouldering fire, the dogs curled up in the snow, and the whole shut in by cold-looking pines, was lonely and desolate in the extreme; to add to its weirdness, at intervals a wolf would approach camp and utter a low moan, which would be taken up by all the dogs.[24]

The image of the stove disappearing into the swamp was no over-statement. The party had been issued the army's standard "Sibley stove" to heat their tents, which had been in use since the Civil War and served its purpose well on hard ground. But neither the designer nor the army quartermasters had anticipated anything like the conditions at Roseau. The stove was a fifty-pound cone-shaped arrangement of iron plates with the pipe emerging from the top. The firebox was at the very bottom, sitting almost on the ground. In the Roseau swamp, this arrangement guaranteed that the intense heat from the firebox would melt the ice and snow underneath and flood the tent with water, which would douse the fire before refreezing, trapping anything that happened to be lying on the floor. To counter the problem, Greene had the Fort Pembina blacksmith build eight box stoves of light sheet iron. Although more difficult to transport, they were raised off the ground on legs and, unlike the conical Sibley, provided a flat top where pans of snow could be melted for drinking water. More efficient than the Sibley they might have been, but safer they were not: "In spite of our caution, during the winter two tents were entirely destroyed, with a considerable amount of clothing and bedding, and every tent we had was more or less punctured with spark holes."[25]

When the storm abated, Greene took two of his men and a pair of heavily loaded dogsleds and set out for Lake of the Woods. He still had a lot to learn about packing and the limitations of travelling with dogs. After spending four hours to cover the five miles to Doolittle's camp, with his top-heavy sleds upsetting every hundred yards or so, he borrowed an additional sled and sent back for another man, but even with the loads redistributed it took sixteen hours to make the seventeen miles to Lake of the Woods. Although disgusted by the performance of the snowshoes and the sleds (which were clearly still not packed properly), Greene was obliged to admit that, but for the dogs, he could never have made the trip at all. He passed New Year's

Day at the site of the Lake of the Woods astronomical station and then, with the temperature hovering just above 0° F under a bright sun, set off across the ice of the lake toward Rainy River.

Greene stayed at Rainy River for more than a week, checking latitudes and generally confirming Doolittle's survey work. The local inhabitants were not pleased to see him:

> The Indians did not receive me very cordially, and there were several pow-wows and a good deal of "bluff" and threats on both sides. They did not succeed, however, either in inducing me to go away, nor in getting any rations (I barely had enough for myself), nor did they molest me.[26]

At the root of the Natives' hostility toward Greene was their insistence that he was a trespasser. They told him that they had not given any of their land to the United States (with whom they had no treaties) and had no intention of doing so in the future. It was theirs and they did not want it surveyed. In his final report, Greene provided an assessment of the people he had encountered around the lake, and although the families at Rainy River had proven the least compliant, he reserved for them what little enthusiasm he could muster:

> The Indians residing in this neighbourhood are small tribes of the formerly great Ojibway nation. There are about twenty families around Lake Roseau, as many more at the mouth of the War Road River [at the southwestern corner of Lake of the Woods], and about fifty families at the mouth of Rainy River.
>
> Several families also pass the winter on the islands in the lake. They are generally peaceable but, extremely indolent. Those about Rainy River live on lands which have never been ceded, and they are the only ones that show any spirit. They have several log houses, and make feeble attempts at agriculture, but many of them live in birch "teepees," and their principal sustenance is fish… Those who survive the age of ten years seem to be a healthy race of people, but many children perish from lung diseases and exposure to the cold.[27]

Just after midnight on January 11, with his work at Rainy River done, Greene was waiting in his tent for a storm to abate before returning to the East Roseau depot when he was abruptly woken up:

> ... our only tent [was] in flames over my head. All our efforts to extinguish it were unavailing, and we were glad to save our bedding and clothes from more than partial destruction, and to have pulled three pound-cans of powder from the edge of a burning mass of leggins. The bright fire lit up the woods... and revealed the spirit thermometer fixed to a neighbouring tree. It stood at 18° below zero, and plainly told us that, storm or no storm, we could not remain where we were... With this accident to our tent began a week of misfortunes.[28]

The party went out onto the lake ice and, following the shore, headed toward the astronomical station on the opposite shore. After losing one lead dog, and with another suffering from an increasingly painful injury that made his behaviour unpredictable, they pushed across the lake into a building storm. Stopping at a promontory to rest and eat with one of Doolittle's men, Greene then made the mistake of trying to reach the astronomical station, still some fifteen miles away across Buffalo Bay. In the blinding blizzard, they were soon out of sight of land and trying to navigate across the bay by compass. With darkness coming on, they finally reached the shelter of a small patch of trees on the shore and felt their way north along the shore to the astronomical station. There they located a man named Macey, the fourth member of their party, left behind to wait for them with food supplies and, most importantly, a tent. At ten o'clock in the evening, they were finally able to sleep after travelling forty miles in twenty-one uninterrupted hours.

The four men were up at five the next morning and ready to push on to the depot, but their guide, a Scottish dog driver named McKenney, convinced them not to repeat their experience with the nearly impenetrable deadfall along the boundary. Instead, he took them south to the War Road River and then west across the swamps toward the East Roseau depot. When they stopped just before dark,

McKenney assured them it was no more than eight miles farther to the depot. Greene then made another miscalculation:

> As I was anxious to get on as fast as possible, and had only enough provisions to make two half meals, I decided not to camp, but to consume all of our provisions in a hearty supper, and then travel on during the night... By eight o'clock we had finished our supper, put on dry socks and moccasins, packed up and started. Midnight did not find us safely at the depot, but only three or four miles from our resting place. The sky had clouded again; we had lost the road, and had broken through some shell-ice in a little brook whose existence McKenney did not know.[29]

One of the men had sunk into the creek to his shoulders and was soaked through to the skin while the others were only briefly dunked to their waists. At –20° F the men and both the sleds were instantly encased in a thick coating of ice. By beating each other with sticks, they managed to free their legs, but could not dislodge what Greene believed was about two hundred pounds of ice caked to the sleds. Abandoning everything in the sleds save the instruments, notes and blankets, they pushed on with King, the man who had gone most deeply into the creek, riding on McKenny's sled, and Macey with Greene on the second.

When the sleds became separated, Greene lost sight of McKenney, the only man who claimed to know the country (though he had not proved a terribly reliable guide to that point) and soon the sled was stuck again and the dogs refused to pull another foot. After running nearly 70 miles and with only one meal in the past 24 hours, Greene and Macey abandoned their sled at 2:15 a.m. (Greene had noted the time as he wound the chronometers before leaving them) and set out to find the depot. After a few short rests, during each of which the deadly desire for sleep almost overpowered them, the men stumbled into the depot just after noon.

The depot keepers went out and retrieved the dogs and the instruments. McKenney and King, after their own close brush with hypothermia, finally came in as well. Knowing they were safe, Greene collapsed into sleep and did not rouse himself from under his bison robes for a full eighteen hours.

The next morning Greene was up and about and ready to leave on the next leg of his trip. His report gives only the barest hint that he was aware of how close he and his men came to losing their lives. He had badly underestimated how quickly the lack of even rudimentary shelter and a shortage of food could conspire to rob a man of every ounce of energy and leave him wanting nothing more than to curl up in the snow and fall into an endless sleep.

Driving a dog team west along the line, Greene covered the twenty-five miles to Pine Ridge in only six hours and found Downing's party well on their way to finishing up. Switching to a one-horse sled, he tracked down Wilson and his mound builders and, having satisfied himself that there, too, the work was almost done, he began to organize the retreat to Pembina. Sending word to the East Roseau depot to leave enough supplies for Doolittle and move everything else to Pine River, Greene gathered the wagons, sleds and animals and took them west to Pointe D'Orme on January 20. There he camped, working on his computations and waiting for the other parties as the coldest weather of the winter set in. Daytime temperatures did not rise above –15° F, and he recorded at least one nighttime temperature of –51° F. He must have reflected long and hard on what would surely have happened had he seen –51° just one week earlier.

On January 26, the men finally came in from along the line. After sending Doolittle ahead to complete a topographical survey of the course of the Red, and leaving Wilson to finish the last of the cutting and mound-building, Greene took his dog team and an empty sled and raced the forty miles to Fort Pembina in just nine hours.

As he warmed himself by a good fire and began to read through the stack of messages, orders and correspondence that no doubt awaited his return, he would have come across the official notification of his promotion to first lieutenant, signed in Washington on January 13. Apart from some final monument-building, the demarcation of the 49th Parallel between Lake of the Woods and the Red River was finally a hard fact.

Greene gave most of his dogs and sleds to the British to be sold off, and when Wilson finally came in on February 6 Greene was able to discharge all but three of the hired men. With a foreman and two dogsleds, these three were sent west to complete the American portion of the mound-building on Turtle Mountain. It had originally been postponed due to the slow progress of the clear-cutting the British had taken on for the Americans the previous summer, but by March 5 the small party had it finished.

On February 7, Greene left Fort Pembina for the last time and drove his mules and six heavy sleigh wagons down to Fort Abercrombie. The wagons would go on to St. Cloud where they would be refitted and, along with the rest of the commission's transport, wait for the start of the next season's work. Greene went on to St. Paul and from there to Detroit where he and his assistants, clutching their hard-won records, made their final report to Chief Astronomer Twining.

· 8 ·

SPRING
1874

It is impossible to say what amount of mischief has
been done, as the whole success of our work
this year depended on our having good men who could be
trusted when troubles arose. We shall now have
to start on a march of 460 miles with a rabble of strange men.

SAMUEL ANDERSON

T HE WARM GLOW of Christmas
faded quickly at Dufferin as
the men settled in to the
numbing routine of waiting. They waited for the mail from home,
they waited for the supplies to come in from Winnipeg or Minnesota,
and they waited to see what the weather would bring. But mostly they
just waited for the faintest sign of spring.

January had been mild, or at least not nearly as bad as it could
have been. At mid-month, Anderson found it "altogether too hot at
present for any special winter clothing such as was used from the
first last winter,"[1] but he fully expected February could (and almost
certainly would) be much more in character. There were dog teams

out in all four directions, tying up various loose ends for the topographical surveys and, even if the work was not particularly crucial, the men enjoyed any opportunity to escape the daily drudgery of headquarters.

Even Anderson, whose self-proclaimed sense of duty and consideration for his fellow officers had kept him from fleeing Dufferin, must have wished he was anywhere but there. With only Millman, Ward and Boswell for company, there was barely enough companionship for the habitual after-dinner rubbers of whist. The carefully observed rituals of what was, in effect, a Royal Engineers officers' mess must have paled quickly with so little variety in either diet or conversation. There was certainly no shortage of reading material. The field library was there, neatly catalogued and arranged by Millman (whose terse diary entries through this period show a man fighting his own battles with boredom), while from Toronto Dr. Burgess sent a steady stream of new books and reasonably fresh Canadian and British newspapers. The news probably succeeded only in making home seem even further away.

In the face of the unrelieved grey of winter, Anderson's letters to his mother became more sporadic and less focussed. They are filled with speculation about the coming summer season and, increasingly, with frustration about the amount of work there was to do and how little was getting done. But most of that work was paperwork and Anderson, for all his organizational and motivational strengths, was not at his best as a paper-pusher. To make matters worse, rather than seizing any opportunity to get out of camp for an occasional dogsled trip or to enjoy the limited social charms of Winnipeg, Anderson continued to decline any and all invitations (including one to a grand pre-Christmas ball hosted by Manitoba's new lieutenant governor), choosing instead to pass the time at his desk heaping vitriol on his chief commissioner.

When Cameron was absent, Anderson wanted him back at Dufferin to take on his share of the work. When Cameron returned, Anderson wished he would just go away and stop interfering. When the commissioner would not make a decision, he was damned for his waffling. When he issued an order, it was attacked as ill-informed or wrong-headed. He was, by turns, either too headstrong or too weak, too involved or too removed, even too friendly or too distant. For Anderson, Cameron simply could not do anything right, and where in the past, the chief astronomer had seemed able to rise above the vexations in the higher cause of the work, by February 1874 he was in danger of becoming the very things he so despised in Cameron.

At the end of 1873, Anderson had been supremely confident in the commission's ability to complete the work in one more season. By February 1874, however, he had begun to have his doubts:

> We have every expectation of finishing our work as far as the Rocky Mountains this year, and of returning to Pembina before the winter is sufficiently advanced to make travelling on the plains dangerous. At the same time one cannot shut ones eyes to the fact that the work we have planned can only be executed if everything is favourable.... As a matter of precaution I think it will be necessary to make arrangements for wintering 50 men at some convenient spot near the mountains, in case it is not practicable for all to make good their retreat to Pembina at the last.[2]

While he would repeat this caveat several times in later letters, he would also begin to assert that, while it might be necessary to overwinter men at the far end of the line, he himself, would not. Neither did he intend that any of his Royal Engineers officers would spend another winter in the west. He was adamant that the astronomical and topographical work would be finished, and that any followup, like clear-cutting or mound-building, could be accomplished by hired men under the direction of the Canadian surveyors.

In early February Cameron finally reported to the Foreign Office on the subject of the Northwest Angle. Referring to the special survey, he grudgingly accepted the old crib as the official reference point, but he could not resist making it clear that he still believed it to be in error. He even tried once again (albeit without much enthusiasm) to discredit the boundary line through Lake of the Woods. As it was drawn up the narrow arm to the northwesternmost point, the boundary was crossed several times by the line running straight south toward the 49th Parallel at Buffalo Point, creating small "loops" of water that were, in effect, a part of neither country. While the loops did in fact create a geographical absurdity, it was of so little consequence to either the United States or Canada that it would be 1925 before they bothered to iron it out.

Unfortunately, Cameron also used the report as an opportunity to seek clarification of whether the 49th Parallel should be drawn as a mean or an astronomical line. He estimated the cost of creating a mean parallel at £50,000 (equivalent to about US$271,000 at that time) but felt that even such a staggering sum, "however it may affect the public interests, does not bear upon the merits of the question," and "appears beyond my province to consider."[3]

While the Foreign Office did not look kindly on the idea, there was, surprisingly, some influential support for it in Ottawa (even though Canada would certainly be asked to pay a part, if not all, of the huge additional cost). But Anderson was not prepared to rely solely on the influence of his superiors in London to carry the day. Almost in self-defence, Anderson risked a bold and very undiplomatic manoeuvre. Just a few days after learning the contents of Cameron's report, he wrote to an old friend and colleague in the War Office.

Believing that Major Charles Wilson, a veteran of the Pacific Boundary Survey and a fellow Royal Engineer, would be able to exert some influence at Whitehall, Anderson went straight to the point:

> We have already run the astronomical parallel for 500 miles, built the mounds, and I have estimated that in conjunction with the Americans we can complete the demarcation of the astronomical parallel to the Rocky Mountains this season... To mark a mean parallel will involve another season's work over the whole ground again, and it is altogether opposed to the views of Mr. Campbell and his chief astronomer, with whom I am in perfect accord. Surely the Foreign Office would never consent to this most unnecessary waste of public money, merely to move the boundary mounds a few feet north and south and still be no nearer the truth.[4]

Wilson's response was quick and wholehearted in its support. He forwarded a copy of Anderson's letter to several people with influence in the cabinet, and attached some comments of his own:

> The question of a mean parallel is no new one; it was often discussed by the members of the Oregon Boundary Commission of which I was the Secretary and the opinion of Colonel Hawkins, Major Haig and the other officers was opposed to it on the ground that the mere adjustment of the boundary at certain points in a country unsuitable for settlement or pasturage would certainly not justify the enormous expense of running a mean parallel.[5]

It happened that the man to whom Cameron's report was finally submitted was different from the one to whom it had been addressed. The Liberal government of Prime Minister William Gladstone had fallen to Benjamin Disraeli's Conservatives, and Lord Granville had been replaced as foreign secretary by Lord Derby. An uncertain Derby sought guidance on both outstanding boundary questions. He sent the matter of the Northwest Angle to Charles Wilson and, on the subject of the mean parallel, he consulted Sir George Airey, the astronomer royal.

As to whether the Northwest Angle should be accepted as proposed, Wilson was unequivocal.

He pointed out that moving the northwesternmost point to the place Cameron thought it should be would not avoid creating a boundary loop, but it would result in the north–south line to the 49th Parallel running more than a hundred feet farther to the west. Rather than hand the Americans even more territory, Wilson recommended accepting the results of the special survey and putting the matter to rest.

For George Airey, the question of a mean or an astronomical parallel was simpler still. Before the Royal Engineers left England in 1872 he had told Anderson that an astronomical boundary would satisfy both the letter and the spirit of the treaty. In his opinion to Lord Derby, Airey took the position that everyone save Cameron already accepted: that the small increase in accuracy to be gained from creating a mean parallel was simply not worth the cost of doing the work. Before he had even received Airey's report, however, Derby had cabled Cameron and told him to take no further steps toward tracing a mean boundary. The issue was as good as dead.

Why Cameron had continued to carry the flag for a mean parallel is not at all clear. Everyone agreed it would be more accurate, but, as Anderson had said, it would still be "no nearer the truth." What he meant was that any fix—even a mean parallel—contained within it a certain degree of error. At Pembina, when the American and British survey teams had made the same calculations at the same place and under the same conditions, their results had varied by 32 feet. Had they repeated those calculations a dozen times, the disagreement would have varied to a certain degree every time, but it would probably always have been there. The important question was whether the error fell within a range that was acceptable to both parties. What Cameron was proposing would certainly have made a more elegant curve, but where it gained a foot or two for Canada in one place, it would give the same to the United States somewhere else. On average, across the whole eight hundred miles of the line, the alterations would not amount to very much. Or, as Airey put it, the difference would be "less than the breadth of a London square."[6]

Having submitted his reports, Cameron left for Ottawa on February 9, giving no indication of when he would return. Before he left, however, he did authorize a significant and very practical alteration to the commission's working strategy for the 1874 season. While the fieldwork would continue on the alternating station model that had worked so well the previous year, the matter of keeping those parties and the men of the topographical survey supplied with food and forage would be substantially more difficult. Anderson put the problem succinctly:

We have to march 460 miles before we can do any work, our supplies have to be taken that distance before we can begin to distribute them... This shall make our progress somewhat slower, and at the last we shall have 40 or 50 miles of work in the heart of the Rocky Mountains, where we cannot take waggons and where we shall have to depend for transport on pack animals... After the work is accomplished, we shall have to retreat 850 miles to get back to Pembina.[7]

Recognizing that the American parties had benefited enormously by their ability to supply their camps from the cavalry forts along the Missouri, the British sought to cut the length of their supply lines and avail themselves of those same Missouri settlements. At the end of January, Cameron dispatched W.G. Boswell to western Montana to arrange for the purchase and forward delivery of certain crucial supplies.

Travelling by railway and wagon, Boswell took a long, circuitous route through the United States to reach the mining boom towns along the east slope of the Continental Divide. Once there, he contracted with a grain dealer, probably in Helena, to have a substantial part of the British commission's forage requirements delivered first to the depot at Wood End and, later in the season, to an advanced depot closer to the Rocky Mountains. The first shipment of grain, comprising some 29,000 bushels of oats, would be moved north to the depot from Fort Benton.

While relieved of the responsibility for transporting the huge, bulky cargoes of oats all the way from Dufferin, the commission never seriously considered entrusting the *men's* food supplies to American contractors. It was simply too risky. There was still a fundamental belief among the British that the Sioux and, farther along the line, the Assiniboine and the Blackfeet, had no quarrel with Her Majesty's agents. As Anderson put it, "... we shall have to keep closer together for protection against Indians, who altho' not hostile to English people, cannot resist the temptation of stampeding horses if they have a chance."[8] However, no one was willing to bet that American wagon trains, alone and exposed in the open country north of the Missouri, would not be a target for raiding parties. The main weight of the British supplies would still be brought out along the line from Dufferin.

That it was possible to contract for supplies from the far western edge of the high plains points to one of the profound differences between the relative state of development on either side of the 49th Parallel at that time. The Red River valley was thriving from top to bottom. In Minnesota, settlers continued to pour in and the best lands were quickly being taken up. There was even talk that some of the prime woodlands in the northern parts of the state had already been stripped of their most valuable timber. Above the border, after years of neglect and uncertainty, the Red River Colony was being transformed. Fuelled by the promise of the transcontinental railway, the new city of Winnipeg was growing up fast around the old Hudson's Bay post of Fort Garry. Once renowned only for its rough shacks and mud streets, the city quickly sprouted street lights and even a rudimentary sewer system. There were also plans to give it a railway of its own. As Anderson wrote to his mother in mid-February, "This year will see great changes in this remote part of the world, as they propose to complete the railway which now comes to an end at a place 180 miles south of us, to Fort Garry, and this will no doubt make Manitoba much more inviting."[9] In this, Anderson has perhaps been caught up in the promotional hyperbole that was part and parcel of the booming economy. In fact, the American railway builders would not get around to building north to the border until the end of 1878. By then, the Manitobans had already completed a line from Selkirk (north of Winnipeg) through the capital and down to the 49th Parallel, but riding the jury-rigged tracks of the Pembina Branch railway was, like the Dawson Route, an experience that few people ever wished to experience for a second time.

That the good burghers of Winnipeg would so value a railway running south to the United States was a crucial consideration in Ottawa's push to secure its new western territories. The earliest settlers in 1812 came to the Red River colony on Hudson's Bay Company ships, which landed them at ports on Hudson Bay itself. Those first settlers, mostly from Scotland, had no allegiance to the Canada which lay far to the east along the Great Lakes and the St. Lawrence. The already established native-born Metis, of mixed indigenous, Scots and French ancestry, felt no affinity with Canada at all. Quite the contrary; their first encounter with their new Canadian masters had led to bloodshed and exile. For most of its sixty years, the Red River Colony had grown only through the settlement of men retiring from the fur trade.

With such a vast, inhospitable expanse of land between Canada and its new territory, which had until recently been the private domain of the Hudson's Bay Company, Canadians did not share the American dream of conquering the west. Even the great popular flood across the Mississippi in the early nineteenth century did not trigger a similar wanderlust in the residents of the British colonies to the north. Manifest Destiny was a purely American idea. It was only with Canadian Confederation and the appearance in the early 1870s of such best-selling travelogues as Butler's *Great Lone Land* and George M. Grant's *Ocean to Ocean*, an account of the Fleming expedition, that Canadians really began to pay any attention to the west.

When the pressures of settlement finally began to build, there were only two ways for the new immigrants to reach the Canadian west. They could test themselves against the well-publicized horrors of the Dawson Route or, if they could afford it, go directly from southern Ontario through the United States by the comparatively comfortable and predictable railway. And it was not just Canadians who wanted to go west. Most of the good farmland in the U.S. Midwest was already taken up, and land prices were too high to allow the average man to buy his way into the game. North of the boundary, however, there was still promising land to be had in the Red River valley, and an increasing number of the new settlers were Americans. Europe, too, was beginning to take notice. As Anderson wrote to his mother early in 1874, "300 or 400 of the Russian Menonites from Odessa are coming this summer, and the land has already been staked out for them…"[10]

It was not just the spread of development along the Red River valley that gave the Canadian government cause for concern. The Americans were also quickly becoming a major presence in the lands just east of the Rocky Mountains. While the Dakota Territory and eastern Montana were still largely deserted, the discovery of gold in places like Helena and Virginia City had brought fortune hunters north from California and Oregon, as well as from the eastern states. Along with the gold-seekers came the loggers, farmers, ranchers and whiskey merchants. From the thriving towns they created, the prospectors spread out, looking for promising rock in every direction, including the unclaimed land to the north. If gold were to be found in the creeks and valleys above the 49th Parallel—as it had been a decade earlier west of the Divide in British Columbia's Cariboo country—there would be no authority on the ground to say it was not the prospectors' or the speculators' land to do with as they wished. It was a thousand miles from anyone who could tell them different.

All of these factors, along with the continuing agitation for annexation coming from south of the border, pushed the government in Ottawa to begin its surveys for an all-weather, all-Canadian route to the west. If it did not undertake to establish its sovereignty as soon as possible, it was increasingly likely that the west, as Ulysses S. Grant had expected, would simply fall to the Americans by the sheer weight of their numbers.

AT THE END of February 1874, Anderson finally came out of his shell. The enlisted men at Dufferin had hosted a party and invited twelve regimental bandsmen down from Winnipeg for the occasion. While the musicians were still at Dufferin, Anderson and the other officers took the opportunity to organize a dance for their American counterparts from Fort Pembina.

They took great pains to make as grand a show as possible, decorating the hall with swords and flags, planing and waxing the dance floor and covering the stairs and sitting room floor with colourful Hudson's Bay blankets. Mrs. Herchmer and Mrs. Almon cooked up soups, jellies and ices, and supplied crockery and silverware from Emmadale. With eight couples up from Fort Pembina, it was a grand night of dancing that went on from eight o'clock in the evening until four o'clock the next morning, when the Americans were packed into their hay wagons, covered with buffalo robes and sent on their way.

Although Anderson's attitude toward the Americans had improved considerably since he had first been exposed to them on the Pacific boundary survey, he could not resist the temptation to have some fun at their expense when he wrote to his sister the next day:

> It was quite marvellous every one had contrived to produce a pair of white kid gloves for the party. The only thing we could not get for the American ladies was sugar plums (or candies as they call them) and I am afraid they consider this as a grave omission, for I hear that some of the bachelors at the American fort are going to give a party but they have to wait till the Candies, they have sent for, arrive from New York.
>
> [One lady] was immensely delighted with my album, and she said there was one picture of a Miss Anderson in it that was lovely...Americans really appreciate the freshness and robustness of an English face, seeing that these qualities are so notably deficient even among their own beauties. This state of things among Americans is not to be wondered at when you consider that they live in heated houses, on a diet of pickles and candies and gobble their food at such a rate that it has been calculated that the average time an American takes for his dinner is 6½ minutes. About the only things the ladies ate heartily at supper last night were first course, Crosse & Blackwell's pickles, 2nd course ice creams. It was with fear and trembling that I pictured to myself the appalling results that might be reasonably expected from such a meal as this, followed by violent exercise...[11]

After the dance, Anderson went back to writing his reports, plotting the summer's work and complaining that the Americans were, once again, dragging their feet:

> If the Americans were not such dilly dallying people we could arrange our programme now to finish up every thing, but they care very little how long they spin the affair out and of course we are affected to a certain extent. They have not been able to keep us

back very much yet, no thanks to them however, but it is difficult to foresee now what the future course of events will be.[12]

It is hard to know exactly how the Americans might have been delaying the work. There had been tacit agreement on both sides that the second summer would proceed like the first—alternating astronomical parties and occasionally meeting for checks on each other's calculations. For all Anderson's complaining over the previous year, the U.S. parties did manage to keep up quite well and, even if he believed he could have done more work, it was still a two-season job. If anything was holding back the American commission's commitment it was that their appropriation had still not received congressional approval, and no one was yet sure if they would be out on the line at all in 1874. It is strange that Anderson would begin to question whether the Americans really intended to finish the line in one more season. He certainly had no reason to believe that Twining and Campbell had developed such a love for life on the plains that they wanted to prolong the work. He did, however, have something of a case for thinking that Cameron was trying to drag things out.

On his return from Ottawa at the end of March, Cameron announced that a number of the Canadian surveyors and their assistants would not be coming back. While Anderson called it a summary dismissal and believed there would be problems with Ottawa as a result, it was not a decision that Cameron would have taken on his own. He must have discussed it during his visit to the capital. For Anderson, it meant a significant reallocation of his resources.

For the coming season there was to be only one topographical party in the field, under the direction of Lieutenant Rowe. Canadian subassistant astronomers Burpee and Coster were to remain with Galwey, while Featherstonhaugh would keep his assistant, King. The fourth subassistant, William Ashe, had already been detached from Featherstonhaugh the previous season to take over Russell's party. With that party eliminated, he would act as Rowe's assistant. The old Metis hunter William Hallett had died that winter, and since D'Arcy

East's special topographical party would no longer be required, he was reassigned to lead the 49th Rangers. The only party to be disbanded in its entirety was A.G. Forrest's.

For Anderson, the news was another annoyance, but not of terribly great concern: "Fortunately, we can do the whole work with the officers and men of the Engineers, whom he [Cameron] cannot get rid of, but of course this summary reduction necessitates either skipping a good deal of work, or giving those that remain a great deal more to do."[13] This is perhaps more than a little disingenuous since Anderson had, after all, always felt that many of the Canadians were little more than extra mouths to feed. It did, however, play to his growing conviction that the chief commissioner intended to make a career of drawing the boundary. That feeling was only compounded by the news that Cameron's wife would soon be returning to Emmadale with three children, and that Cameron intended to make another attempt at farming the land around Dufferin.

Realizing that perhaps he had gone a little overboard in his criticism of the chief commissioner, Anderson added a postscript to one long letter of complaint: "I have mentioned many little matters of difficulty with Captain Cameron which need not go the rounds in the family reading."

Just before Cameron got back to Dufferin (bringing Galwey, Rowe and Burgess with him), the officers at Fort Pembina had made good on their promise of a dance. Three officers and the two Dufferin ladies sledged down to the fort, to be greeted by "all our friends... about 24 people,"[14] and to dance until past 3 o'clock in the morning. In addition to the long-awaited New York candies, the midnight meal was a prodigious affair:

We had a capital dance till 12, when a procession was formed and we marched thro' the passage round the supper table out again round the dancing room & passage and round the supper table again, by which time it was presumed that our appetites were sufficiently sharpened by looking at the good things provided, and we were then requested to settle down, and begin supper. There was no mistake about the appetites of the ladies, they began on fried oysters, continued with chicken salad, followed by turkey and ham, then two or three helpings of ice cream (a great American dish) cake almonds raisins and coffee. The meal seemed interminable and the supply inexhaustible.[15]

By the time of the dance, the first sure signs of spring had finally come to the Red River valley.

The thaw began on March 14 with three days of rain and a warm southerly wind. The snow almost disappeared from the prairies and the roads became quite bare. Before the breakup, the men again cut huge blocks of ice out of the river and packed them into the straw-insulated storage house and, while the roads were clear but still frozen hard, the first of the endless loads of hay had been taken out to the first two campgrounds on the long trail to Wood End.

The mood at Dufferin changed dramatically for the better. But it did not take long for the optimism to evaporate. Less than two weeks after cutting the size of the commission, and barely a week before the first of the new season's parties were to go into the field, Cameron reduced the food allowance. What had been one-and-a-half pounds of meat per day was reduced, without apparent reason, to one pound. There were other cuts as well. Millman, ready to go out with a party of Engineers to check the condition of the trails, scribbled in his diary, "... no butter and no cheese on the line this summer, meat consists of one pound of bacon per day per man."[16] Anderson must surely have thought back fondly to the oysters and ham at Fort Pembina.

The effect of the reduction was immediate and, for Anderson, potentially disastrous:

... we have lost 33 of our best (hired) men... This most unwise reduction induced the hired men to address a most respectful application to Capt. C. that their allowance of meat might be increased, on the ground that they were living in camp and being employed out of doors all day required more animal food than 1 lb. per diem. Capt. C. without consulting a soul immediately ordered the whole of the men to be discharged. They were picked men, who had worked with us, many of them from the beginning…

It is impossible to say what amount of mischief has been done, as the whole success of our work this year depended on our having good men who could be trusted when troubles arose. We shall now have to start on a march of 460 miles with a rabble of strange men.[17]

By the end of April, Dufferin seemed wholly in the grip of what could only be diagnosed as an epidemic of cabin fever, and the only thing that it seemed could prevent an outright mutiny among the men (if not the officers as well) was to get out of Dufferin and onto the trail to Wood End. But that seemed unlikely at any time in the near future. All the predictions of an early end to winter had proved well off the mark as bitterly cold winds kept the thermometer pegged near the freezing point in the daytime and hard frost remained a certainty every night. As a result, the new grass so essential to graze the oxen and the horses on their trek had not even begun to sprout. The only things that did not seem troubled by the cold were the clouds of mosquitoes, which had already begun to swirl around the headquarters.

Even George Dawson, who had enjoyed the luxury of spending the winter at his home in Montreal, was already fighting boredom:

Breakfast is generally about 9 o'c. Then those who have anything to do go off & do it & those who have nothing set round the stove in the upper hall (our drawing room) & smoke. Lunch about 1 or 2 as the case may be. About 4 go for a walk, or to shoot, or to look at the river or any other excitement. Dinner generally about 7PM. Then ajurn to the *Drawing room* again & cards & chess, & talk & reading & whisk toddy [*sic*] & smoking occupy the remainder of the evening.[18]

Apparently determined to prove that full spring was more than just a faint hope, the chief commissioner decided it was time to get to work on his farm.

The frost is not yet out of the ground, but Captain Cameron insisted that it was, and that ploughing should commence, so 30 horses were sent out to work 5 ploughs, and in a very short time, 3 ploughs out of the five were broken. It will take all our smiths now for a day or two to repair the damage caused by that little experiment.[19]

For Anderson, it was almost the last straw. "Were it not for the misfortune of having to abandon the work when it is within 6 months of its completion," he wrote to his mother, "I should certainly throw the whole thing up and come home."[20]

· 9 ·

SUMMER
1874

I do not recollect ever to have heard of a single
case of accident by explosion of boilers, or by fire on the
Upper Missouri. I am disposed to class this, also,
among the special providences, rather than to attribute it to
any skill on the part of the builders or owners.

WILLIAM TWINING

ALL APPEARANCES to the contrary, spring was coming slowly
to the Red River valley. On
April 20 the river ice went out at Moorhead and, within days, it was
cracking up and drifting downstream as far as the border. The first
flatboat came in at Pembina on the 27th, and only two days later the
river had broken open all the way to Winnipeg. Despite the icy winds
and frozen ground, the British commission could wait no longer to
begin its long trek to Wood End.

On April 22 a reconnaissance party of Engineers under Sergeant Major Flower set out to check the state of the trail and repair
the bridges and fords that would soon be assaulted by a hundred

heavy wagons. Millman went with them, and his attitude must have reflected the views of nearly everyone at Dufferin: "I love camp life and am glad it has begun again."[1] With no meat, cheese or butter in their supplies, Flower's party took every opportunity to buy eggs from the settlers, and always kept a shotgun at the ready for the ducks and geese that crowded every ice-free pothole, lake and slough. Part of the dreaded bacon ration was traded to an old Metis for a supply of venison, and any prairie chicken unfortunate enough to find itself near the trail was bound to come under heavy fire.

Back at Dufferin, trusting that the Engineers had done their work on the road, Anderson sent his first train of twenty ox-drawn wagons out toward Wood End on May 2. It was a start, but he still did not think he could follow with the main parties until at least the middle of the month. Although the benign winter had not produced any of the flooding that characterized the previous spring, there was still plenty of water in the creeks and rivers. Away from the river banks, however, there was already evidence of what could be a dry summer. The trails were in good condition, but only because there had been so little snow to melt and dissolve them into mud. There was almost nothing in the way of forage along the trails owing to the late frosts and the previous year's wholesale burning of the prairie. What grass had managed to sprout was immediately threatened by the first of the new season's fires. It swept down toward Millman's camp on May 1, and evidence of its passing could be seen everywhere to the west along the Pembina River.

By May 6, Anderson had moved the main parties out onto the valley floor just outside the barracks for a week of planning and equipment checks. This brief bivouac was known in the country as a "Hudson's Bay start," and had always been standard practice for anyone embarking on a long overland journey. It gave the field parties the opportunity to set up their camps and discover, while they were still within easy reach of the barracks, what equipment or supplies might have been left behind, or what could be sent back as surplus to their needs. Millman (probably from general excitement) had foregone the ritual the previous spring, and found himself a long way from Dufferin with a dozen bottles of wine on board his ambulance rather than the six each of brandy and wine that was standard issue. It was not a major gaffe, but a good indication of how easily essential items might be forgotten or misplaced in the rush to leave home base.

Everyone was still waiting for the arrival of fifty heavy ox-drawn supply wagons that Cameron had acquired in Minnesota. They would take fifteen days to reach Dufferin and then, with little rest, they would be turned west along the line toward Wood Mountain. Anderson, who had been so impressed by the prodigious strength of the oxen when he had first encountered them, and who had no reason to complain about their performance over the previous summer, was convinced that using the lumbering beasts for this final push was a mistake. His concern was based entirely on the calendar: while the summer of 1873 had been a series of short, steady pulls to depots only two or three hundred miles from Dufferin, 1874 would be different. The season was shorter, and the first depot to be provisioned was more than four hundred miles out from headquarters. Even assuming the weather co-operated, it would be five weeks before Wood End could be properly stocked and ready to supply the forward depots. With no sightlines to cut or muskeg to cross, the survey parties would be moving much faster than they had the previous season. And what Anderson had glimpsed of the country west of Wood Mountain told him that even horses would be hard pressed to move wagons through the badlands, let alone oxen. The only advantage he could see for the oxen was that (quoting Napoleon): "When the army can no longer nourish the oxen, the oxen can be made to nourish the army."[2] And so they eventually would.

Lieutenant Rowe caught up to the road maintenance party just west of the Pembina River and took command. Now keeping company with the twenty wagons of the advanced train, the party arrived at Turtle Mountain on May 19 and found the two winter keepers safe, well and no doubt happy to be relieved. Directed by Cameron to collect as much information as possible about the Sioux in the area, the men reported that only seven lodges had wintered at the mountain and, furthermore, none had shown any signs of hostility. Apparently the Natives' only concern was that the British might be planning to force them south across the new line and into the hands of the American cavalry. Although more than a decade had passed since they fled the United States in the wake of the troubles in Minnesota, they still feared for their safety.

Whatever the Turtle Mountain keepers might have reported about their winter experience with the Sioux and the trading post, it was not sufficient to change the tone of Captain Cameron's annual directive concerning the Native populations. Largely a rehash of the 1873 rules, the directive once again asserted the need to avoid confrontation at any cost. If the Natives attempted to stand in the way of the commission's progress, "no force must be used to remove the hindrance." "Should the Indians assume a decided objection to the progress of the expedition," he wrote, "the parties will return toward Dufferin," and, "do so without causing an open rupture."[3] Typically, the dictum was firm but flexible, allowing the parties to return "toward" Dufferin, presumably until the trouble could be sorted out by another grand parley.

It is another indication that the British continued to treat the marking of the 49th Parallel as a co-operative rather than a joint exercise with the Americans. It is inconceivable that the U.S. Army had been deployed along the line in such force with the idea that their survey parties would withdraw at the first hint of trouble, but the British continued to rely on their belief that the Natives' antagonism toward the Americans did not extend to Her Majesty's soldiers. In the final analysis, it is surprising that Cameron did not order the Engineers into their red jackets to distinguish them from the U.S. Cavalry blue.

Finally, on May 20, with the arrival of the heavy transport from Minnesota, the main body of the commission moved out of its temporary camp and plodded west toward Pembina Mountain. Altogether, there were eleven officers and nearly 130 men, accompanied by more than a hundred wagons of every size and description. For the first 250 miles or so, everyone would move at the speed of the oxen—everyone, that is, except Featherstonhaugh's party (including Dawson), which was detached in order to mark pickets for a string of permanent boundary markers to replace the temporary mounds built during the previous season. These iron markers, spaced one mile apart, would eventually stretch from Lake of the Woods to the original boundary between Manitoba and the North-West Territories at 99° West. Featherstonhaugh would then round Pembina Mountain on the American trail to the south, and reconnect with the main body somewhere near Turtle Mountain.

The construction of the depot buildings at Wood Mountain was completed by the end of May, and the scouts continued out along the trail to begin identifying sites for the astronomical stations beyond Anderson's farthest west of the previous fall. It must have been enormously frustrating for the chief astronomer to have been reduced to the office of wagon master, forced to keep a slow-march pace with the oxen as his Metis rangers swept ahead across the open plains. Despite all of Anderson's concerns, however, the beasts were doing yeoman service. When the commission arrived at the first Souris crossing on June 2, they had covered the 170 miles from Dufferin in only thirteen days, an almost high-stepping average of thirteen miles per day.

AS THE BRITISH approached that first Souris crossing, the American commission was still waiting for its money. Although Twining wrote that "As the parties could not be organized before the passage of the appropriation... there would be only four months in which to reach the ground, complete the survey, and to return,"[4] there must have been a great deal of unofficial preparation taking place. When Twining was formally notified on June 5 that the appropriation had passed, he was already waiting in St. Paul together with all of his officers. The wagons and mules that had overwintered at St. Cloud had already been loaded onto the Northern Pacific Railway and sent off to the Missouri river town of Bismarck, with a stop to pick up the rest of the wagons at Fort Seward along the way. Within twenty-four hours of getting the go-ahead, Twining and his men had boarded a train. Two days later, they had rejoined their supplies in Bismarck.

It did not take long for some unfinished business from the previous season to bubble to the surface. Whether Major Reno had been travelling with the rest of the party or waiting for them in Bismarck is not recorded, but he was certainly not happy about being ordered back to the boundary for a second summer. Almost from the moment Elliott Coues stepped down from the train there was trouble between the two men. Although Coues charmingly referred to it as a "difficulty" with the major, it was obviously much more than that. At one point Coues actually challenged Reno to a duel!

While cooler heads prevented any gunfire, Coues was smarting from the reprimand he had received as a result of Reno's complaints about him. Even so, one army officer issuing such a challenge to another in the 1870s was something of a stretch even for a man as short-tempered as Coues, and he must quickly have realized the ridiculousness of his situation. There is no evidence that anything more came of the trouble, and the two men managed to stay out of each other's way for the rest of the season.

Being challenged to a duel must have seemed to Reno the perfect climax to what had been a very difficult eight months. After leaving the line the previous October, he had taken his men, their bedraggled mounts and their worn-out equipment south to Fort Stevenson on the Missouri before turning east toward their assigned barracks at Fort Totten. What happened along the way is open to speculation, but Reno never appeared at Totten, and the next news anyone had from him came by mail from Harrisburg, Pennsylvania. He claimed to have hurt his ankle on the march south from the Parallel and taken thirty days' sick leave to recover. Reno's superiors were not amused and, since he had not forwarded a surgeon's certificate with his report, the army's paymaster general stopped his pay and reported him "absent without leave."

He was next heard from in January 1874, when he wrote to the adjutant general from New York to report that he was going to Chicago to see General Philip Sheridan in an attempt to iron out his problems. Reno had served as Sheridan's chief of staff for cavalry in the Shenandoah Valley in 1864 and, according to his letter, "I only hope I can arrange matters so as not to resign."[5] Whatever Reno had to say in his own defence must have been successful, since he was back with the boundary commission when the officers and men arrived in Bismarck at the beginning of June.

Reno's explanation to Sheridan has not been recorded, but it is possible to speculate about what took him to Harrisburg and kept him there without official leave long enough to risk a court martial. His wife died on July 10, 1874, and it is reasonable to suppose that he had gone home to be with her during an illness that would eventually prove fatal.

ANDERSON HAD ENVIED the Americans their smooth, easy passage to the boundary and, for the first part of the trip at least, it had indeed been quite luxurious, with the American officers invited to ride in the Northern Pacific superintendent's official car. At Bismarck, however, Twining and his men were brought quickly back to earth:

> [We] found the steamer *Fontenelle* waiting, but, contrary to the spirit of the contract made at St. Paul, the boat had been loaded with two hundred tons of [non-commission] freight. This, with our wagons and animals, crammed the steamer to its utmost capacity and made a rapid trip to Fort Buford an impossibil- ity. The river was high, running with a strong current and it was manifest that five days was too little time for the boat, loaded as it was, even supposing it possible under any circumstances, which I very much doubted. There was nothing else to be done but to resign one's self to a week of utter weariness and discomfort.[6]

The *Fontenelle* was typical of the Missouri river steamboats that supplied the Dakota forts and western Montana gold-rush towns. A two-hundred-foot sternwheeler with cabin accommodation for twenty passengers (in theory), there was always room for a few more travellers or a little more freight. In addition to the two hundred tons she had already loaded, the steamer somehow found space for the commission's 140 horses and mules, 110 men, 38 wagons and 270 tons of stores. The animals were packed into two pens on the lower deck so they could be fed and watered from above. The officers and civilian assistants took some of the cabins, while the enlisted men camped in the wagon boxes or on the deck, cooking their meals on one or two small stoves.

To push such a huge load against a strong Missouri current, the *Fontenelle*'s three boilers swallowed twenty cords of wood a day and could make no more than seventy-five miles out of it. That fuel, nearly all of it green, energy-poor cottonwood or pine, was purchased from private cutters—the "woodhawks"—who lived perilously along the banks of the river. If they managed to avoid being killed by the Sioux, they could command $5 a cord for their labour. For the privilege of having the men of its Northern Boundary Commission travel the 385 miles to Fort Buford in such circumstances, the United States government paid the steamboat company $4,300.

An envious Galwey, too, had written home that the Americans got to "travel like gentlemen by steamer up the Missouri,"[7] but Twining would quickly have disabused him of that notion. While writing his contribution to what was expected to be a straightforward final report, the chief astronomer could not resist recording an acid-etched account of the true state of navigation on the upper Missouri:

> In other and more civilized lands the word "steamer" conveys an idea of speed, as well as a certain assurance of comfort, and at least a semblance of the ways and practices of ordinary life. But no one in search of the amenities need look on the deck of an up-river boat. The hull is a shallow box over which is thrown a light deck and small cabin supported on upright posts. The machinery is rough, primitive in design, and constantly suggestive of unpleasant accidents. The high-pressure engines, exhausting in the open air, thumping over the centers, with leaky cylinders badly packed, or, as in this case, cracked and rudely banded with iron, can hardly be called reassuring. The light, thin upper works, burned in hundreds of holes by the sparks which are constantly flying in clouds over the deck, suggest an alternative scarcely more inviting. As an actual fact, however, I do not recollect ever to have heard of a single case of accident by explosion of boilers,

or by fire on the Upper Missouri. I am disposed to class this, also, among the special providences, rather than to attribute it to any skill on the part of the builders or owners. Certainly no thought of anything so worthless as human life entered into their calculation. The power of the machinery is apparently calculated with reference to down-stream work in a swift current, for, by the kindliest estimate of its performance, I have not been able to figure an up-stream speed so great as three miles an hour.[8]

So poor was the progress of the *Fontenelle* that when the supply of feed ran out after five days (by which time the boat was supposed to have reached Fort Buford), Twining took the mules and horses off at a place called Tobacco Gardens. Even allowing the herd time to graze while he pushed them along the river bank to the fort, he arrived only a few hours after the steamer.

Since the earliest days of the American fur trade, the confluence of the Yellowstone and the Missouri had been the great crossroads of the northern tier. In 1829, agents for John Jacob Astor's American Fur Company had founded Fort Union on the banks of the Missouri, and for the next twenty years everyone and everything coming or going from the heart of the continent had to pass through Fort Union. The Sioux and the Assiniboine, the Plains Cree, the Blackfeet and the Metis came in to trade their robes and skins for whatever was on offer. But as the Native trade declined, Fort Union declined with it, and only revived briefly when the Montana gold rush began in the early 1860s. For Coues, it was "... formerly a somewhat noted locality, now a mere heap of rubbish."[9]

After the Civil War, in an act that perfectly symbolized the end of that first brawling era, the U.S. government purchased the dilapidated fort and salvaged the precious boards and beams from its storehouses and once-grand governor's mansion. With them, they built Fort Buford barely a mile away. It would have no trading floors or great stocks of blankets, trinkets and musket powder. Buford was designed to protect the steamboats, the gold seekers and the coming railways from the very people that Fort Union had once worked so tirelessly to draw to its palisades from every corner of the high plains.

When Twining, Reno and the rest arrived at Buford on June 15, they found their army escort assembled and ready to leave. The previous year's 20th Infantry from Fort Pembina had been replaced by five companies of the 6th, resident at Fort Buford. They had been joined by two familiar companies of the 7th Cavalry, up from their winter base at Fort Totten. Captain Thomas B. Weir's Company D was back for a second season, as was Company I, but Captain Keogh had taken an extended leave to visit his family in Ireland, and his men were under the command of Lieutenant James E. Porter.

The American commission was lucky to have even two companies of cavalry in its escort. When they arrived in Bismarck, everyone immediately sensed a heightened level of excitement and activity in the new railway town. Across from Bismarck on the western bank of the Missouri, Fort Abraham Lincoln, too, was jammed with men and matériel. George Armstrong Custer had been ordered to take the 7th Cavalry into the Black Hills. Officially, it was nothing more than a military reconnaissance. In fact, as everyone well knew, Washington wanted to confirm or disprove the widely circulating rumours that the creeks and rivers of the Black Hills were positively sparkling with gold.

Whether it was simple reconnaissance or semi-official treasure hunt, the expedition was enormous in every respect. Custer would lead a full ten companies of the 7th, with additional support from two companies of infantry. Along with a large contingent of Native scouts and guides, there was a scientific corps that included two experienced prospectors, a geologist and his assistant, a naturalist, a botanist, a zoologist, a civil and a topographical engineer and a medical officer. Any discoveries would be immediately recorded and reported by a photographer and a newspaper correspondent. Also along for the adventure were Colonel Frederick Grant—the president's son—and Custer's two younger brothers, Tom and Boston.

The whole bloated enterprise of over a thousand men (and one woman—a black cook named Sarah Campbell) was supported by more than a hundred supply wagons, each drawn by a team of six mules, and a substantial herd of beef cattle. In order that no one should become bored, the mile-long procession would move to the strains of a 16-piece military band, all mounted on matching white horses.

While every cavalryman in Companies D and I must have wished he were riding out with Custer instead of watching over a small, dull group of astronomers and surveyors, Lieutenant Greene looked at it with a different attitude. Writing to his parents from Bismarck, he seems almost relieved to be heading north and away from the Black Hills:

> About the 20th of this month [June] Custer takes 10 companies of cavalry... and starts on an expedition southwest into the Black Hills. The Indians are collecting down there in large numbers to oppose him and he will probably have some hard fighting, but he has a fine regiment of several years' experience with Indians and as an Indian fighter Custer has no superior in the Army. His expedition will benefit us by drawing the Indians away from our scene of operations.[10]

As it turned out, Custer did not manage to get his travelling circus under way until the beginning of July and, despite Greene's dire predictions, the expedition hardly saw a Sioux. Mostly, they picked wildflowers, climbed the highest peaks and listened to evening concerts by the band. The hospital tent became a large dining hall and the ambulance a menagerie for the naturalists' collection of owls, cranes, prairie dogs and rattlesnakes.

By the end of August, Custer and his entire contingent had returned triumphantly to Fort Abraham Lincoln and but for one small moment of discovery, the whole expedition might have proved nothing more than a lark. Not realizing he was setting in motion a series of events that would, over the next two years, lead him to the Little Bighorn and one of the seminal moments in American history, Custer was pleased to report that the Black Hills were indeed filled with gold "from the grass roots down."

FOR FRANCIS GREENE, the scene at Fort Buford was a huge (and rather amusing) spectacle:

> A large post, with garrison of six companies, on the plain under the bluff near the river… up on the bluff are the pickets (Indian scouts) and around the post are camped between 500 and 600 men, and herds grazing near the hills of 200 horses, 500 mules and 200 beef cattle. And all this to find a line, which doubtless the framers of the Treaty imagined would be the most simple and economical boundary ever agreed upon![11]

After five days of shoeing the animals and organizing the six weeks of stores they would carry with them, the whole party moved off along the north bank of the Missouri on June 21. The last of the spring runoff was still pushing the creeks out over their banks and the Big Muddy was running 125 feet wide and 5 feet deep. The commission paused for only a day and a half to span the creek with a trestle bridge—no more than a mild annoyance to a party of military engineers—even though, in only a month or so, that same broad stream would be reduced to a mere trickle. By the 25th they had reached the mouth of the Poplar River, and there Greene's topographical parties took their leave. Together with two companies of the 6th Infantry, they turned north up the Poplar toward the place they had stopped work the previous fall.

The main body continued along the Missouri to its confluence with the Milk River at Fort Peck and, from there, up the Milk to the Little Rocky Creek, where Gregory's astronomical team and the 6th Infantry's Company D detached and turned north to establish their first station of the summer—number 25—at Frenchman's Creek, 462 miles west of Pembina.

Twining, with Reno's cavalry and the remaining two companies of infantry, stayed in the valley of the Milk River, angling northwest past Fort Belknap before turning south back toward the Missouri. They finally went under canvas on Big Sandy Creek about forty-five miles above Fort Benton.

AT THE FIRST SOURIS crossing, the British encountered a river much different from the shrivelled remnant they had seen the previous summer. Seven feet deep, 165 feet across and running a strong current, the place where they had previously forded their wagons so easily was well under water. Like their colleagues to the south, the Royal Engineers decided it was easier to throw a bridge over the stream than it was to scout the valley for another crossing. This one was on a somewhat grander scale than the American construction on the Big Muddy and, due to the scarcity of decent timber in the area, it took a good deal longer to complete. Still, by the evening of June 6 more than a hundred heavy wagons and miscellaneous transports had crossed the Souris bridge. One wagon at a time.

Despite the weather turning suddenly cold ("overcoats and caps over ears came into requisition," wrote Millman), the second Souris crossing was made without incident (or the need for another bridge), and the commission made steady progress to Wood End and the east slope of the Great Coteau. Once there, the three field parties would draw a fortnight's provisions from the main train and race ahead toward their first stations of the season, leaving Anderson and the wagon train to pick their way slowly and carefully across the Coteau. Featherstonhaugh, taking Millman with him, would set up at Little Rocky Creek, the most distant site identified by Anderson before he retreated the previous October. Galwey would be going on to Cottonwood Coulee at 480 miles west of Dufferin.

Before they reached Wood End, however, the commission was stunned by an accident that befell Valentine Rowe. On the morning of June 11, just after leaving camp at Short Creek, Rowe's horse stumbled at a full gallop and threw him violently to the ground where he landed headfirst. Fortunately, both doctors were still with the main party, and he received immediate care. Dr. Burgess, in fact, was considered something of an expert on head injuries, having had three years of surgical experience in an Ontario lunatic asylum. Rowe had been knocked senseless; even when he finally came around, he continued to drift in and out of delirium. Too sick to be moved any distance, he was placed on a cot in a tent and, with Dr. Burgess and Lieutenant Ward to watch over him, left behind to recover.

On June 13, the three field parties finally left the wagon train and advanced to their stations. Just a month after leaving Dufferin, Featherstonhaugh was taking his first fixes at Little Rocky Creek.

Still, it was not all smooth sailing. Featherstonhaugh somehow ended up on the wrong trail:

> We had to go back once three miles. Another time we got stuck. We could not get the waggon out till unloaded and then by aid of two teams and that after breaking several whipple trees, etc. At seven we came across the other parties, camped and having killed a wild ox. There were four of these but the rest got away.[12]

The "wild ox" to which Millman refers seem to have been a regular sight in the border country between the west side of the Coteau and Wood Mountain. However, while they may have been beasts of burden escaped either from the Metis or from American teamsters, Dawson reported that he was sure they were beef cattle, and possibly longhorns at that:

> I saw a band of cattle in the vicinity of the line, south of Wood Mountain, which had strayed from one of the U.S. forts to the south. They were quite wild, and almost as difficult of approach as the buffalo; and notwithstanding the fact that they had come originally from Texas, and were unaccustomed to frost and snow, they had passed through the winter and were in capital condition.[13]

Galwey's men had killed one by "... riding it down and shooting it like a buffalo."[14] Everyone agreed it made a nice change from the bacon.

By far the most important sight to greet Anderson when he arrived at Wood Mountain on June 22 was a huge cache of oats. Sixty tons had arrived on June 1, brought up from Fort Benton in the huge freight wagons of the Montana grain dealer. Anderson was impressed (and not a little surprised) that the dealer had fulfilled his contract, coming up without escort through unfamiliar, hostile territory, but he was positively amazed by the scale of the train that had made the journey:

The method of freighting adopted by the Americans in the Western plains may be considered worthy of passing notice. Each vehicle is mounted on four broad-rimmed wheels of unusually broad gauge, and the body has nearly vertical sides, the whole height being 12 or 14 feet. Into this huge car 4 tons of grain are packed in bags; two of these wagons are linked closely together as in a railway-train, and to the foremost van are yoked nine pairs of oxen, the pair at the pole and the leading pair being thoroughly broken animals, while the intermediate pairs of oxen are more or less wild and untaught. One teamster manages this formidable charge. The waggon-train is made up of pairs of vans in the same fashion, and the whole makes its way slowly across the unbroken plain at the rate of about 1½ mile per hour.[15]

And this was from a man who, despite his earlier enthusiasm, had been skeptical of the idea of using oxen at all during the 1874 season. Indeed, he almost brags of his own train's performance in reaching Wood Mountain: "We arrived at this site on the 22nd of June, the oxen with loaded waggons having accomplished the journey of 450 miles in 32 days, inclusive of six days' halts or detention."[16] That worked out to more than seventeen miles a day, exclusive of the rest stops and bridge-building.

Nevertheless, he manages to retain a healthy emotional distance from his charges. On arriving at Wood Mountain, he wrote to his mother, "We shall soon have to begin eating the oxen that have served us so well, but they still chew the cud in happy ignorance of our intended ingratitude."[17]

Two days later, Anderson left Wood Mountain to check on the progress of the field parties. By the end of the month he intended to begin moving even more supplies up to a second subdepot some 130 miles to the west. He had still seen no sign of the American commission, and was beginning to worry.

IN FACT, THE CHIEF astronomer just missed the first hard evidence that the Americans were fast coming up to the line. After his inspection of Featherstonhaugh's astronomical camp and the progress of the topographical party, he turned back for Wood Mountain on the morning of June 27. That very afternoon Millman and Dawson, out "botanizing and geologying," met an American scout exploring along the line. He was looking for a place where Gregory's party could camp and begin the season's observations at Frenchman's Creek, thirty miles west of Featherstonhaugh. Gregory himself finally arrived on July 6, one month to the day since the American commission had left St. Paul.

Unbeknown to the British, Gregory was not the first of the American commission to begin work. Lieutenant Greene, with his tangent party and three topographical parties, had detached from the main body of the commission on June 26 and branched off the Missouri up the Poplar River, a tributary. For 1874, in addition to the field parties, Greene had with him a number of scouts and teamsters and a party of mound-builders, totalling about seventy men. His escort, under the command of Captain E.R. Ames, comprised two companies of the 6th Infantry and a dozen Native scouts.

Where the forks of the Poplar met, Greene sent two of his topographical parties (under tried-and-true winter assistant Doolittle and a new man, the magnificently named Dr. Valentine Trant McGillycuddy) up the west fork to the place where Gregory had stopped work the previous fall, 408 miles from Pembina, while he took the remainder up the east fork to Galwey's final 1873 station. Arriving there on the June 29 he set his men to establishing a camp and then rode along the line to his parties on the West Poplar. Doolittle and McGillycuddy arrived shortly thereafter, and on July 1 the American commission got down to business.

While Greene's march to the boundary had been largely uneventful, Gregory was not having such an easy time of it. His summer party would comprise twenty-three men, including assistant astronomers Lewis Boss and Addison Edgerton, a foreman, two cooks, a waiter, five labourers, six teamsters and a scout named George Boyd. It could well have been Boyd whom Millman and Dawson met near Frenchman's Creek. Also travelling with Gregory were Elliott Coues and three assistants. The infantry escort, under the command of Civil War veteran Captain Montgomery Bryant, included forty soldiers and three Native scouts. The whole effort would move with the aid of three six-mule Army wagons, a four-mule spring wagon, a pair of two-mule Minnesota wagons, a horse and buckboard for Coues and a horse for Gregory himself. Counting on the creation of a main supply depot farther along the line, the astronomical party began its work with forty days of rations and forage.

Even without Coues and his assistants, Gregory's party was considerably larger than that deployed the previous summer. Gregory explained why:

> From the experience of the preceding season, in regard to the relative rapidity with which the various parties of the survey could accomplish their work, it was believed by the Chief Astronomer and myself that one astronomical party, with an organization somewhat stronger than that of my party of the preceding season, would be able to accomplish, in the allotted time, what astronomical work remained to be done, and to keep it at all times in advance of that of the line and topographical parties... In order, however, that no untoward accident to the *personnel*, or instrumental outfit of my party, should compass a failure to attain the purposes of the expedition, the Chief Astronomer kept with him a complete instrumental outfit, a copy of the ephemeris, text and note books, and, in fact, the means of organizing another astronomical party.[18]

What Anderson would have made of this decision had he heard of it in the spring can only be imagined. He had already expressed serious misgivings about the American's ability to keep pace with him. It is likely the decision was taken sometime later, while the parties were waiting in St. Paul for the approval of their appropriation. Campbell would obviously have had to authorize the change, but for once he certainly did not consult with either Cameron or Anderson.

Gregory turned north up the east bank of Rocky Creek on July 2, and quickly found himself in trouble:

I soon found, however, that we were getting into a country of bad-lands, impracticable for wagons, and therefore turned about, and followed the stream down to a practicable crossing near its forks. Thence we marched across the broken country which is the dividing ridge between the Rocky and Frenchman's Creeks, to the east bank of the latter. As it was impossible to reach the bed of Frenchman's Creek in the vicinity of the point where we approached the bluffs, and as an inspection revealed the same rough bad-lands for several miles farther north, I turned southward again, and made for the known crossing about three miles below the trading-post, Fort N.J. Turnay.[19]

From the crossing below Fort Turnay it was only a day's travel up to the boundary, but while the British had been pulling out their winter gear only three weeks earlier the temperature was now above 100° F all day and there was no drinkable water to be found anywhere along the route.

Fort Turnay also alerted the American commission to the first serious threat of trouble with the Sioux. Turnay was a private trading post, built about 1872 by Francis Janeaux, an enterprising French-Canadian originally from Montreal. Turnay was a small, rough accumulation of cabins surrounded by a ten-foot palisade, and it had never proved especially profitable. Accused of trading with the Sioux (something then being actively discouraged everywhere across northern Montana) and involvement in the illicit whiskey trade, Janeaux could not expect much protection either from the U.S. Army or from the few white settlers along the Missouri, and he was constantly being raided by the Sioux.

Just the day before Gregory's party arrived, there had been another incident:

We found Fort Turnay... occupied by two independent traders [probably Janeaux and his sometime partner, the Metis Ben Kline]. They informed me that they were so much annoyed, and subjected to so much loss of property, by raids upon them, by the Indians, and were also kept so much upon the alert for their personal safety, that they purposed burning the buildings and leaving the country, which purpose was, I believe, carried into effect later in the season. Only the day before our arrival, a party of Sioux, from Fort Peck, had been entertained by them at a propitiatory feast, after which the guests displayed their gratitude for favors received by running off nine of the eleven horses belonging to their hosts.[20]

Still, Fort Turnay's reputation did not prevent Gregory from using it as a temporary subdepot for his supplies. Perhaps he even left a few of his military escort to guard the surplus—a move that would have been welcomed by the traders.

THE SUMMER OF 1873 had provided little in the way of excitement as far as the commissions' contact with the resident Native populations was concerned. Along the first four hundred miles of the line west from the Red River, they had seen only the small bands of Sioux that were congregating around Turtle Mountain in anticipation of the coming winter. While these bands had carefully avoided any confrontation with the American parties, they had approached the British and Canadian surveyors with what seemed like an almost fawning deference. The reason was clear: they did not wish to do anything that might have them sent south across the newly drawn boundary to face the charges still pending in the state of Minnesota. The Sioux raiding parties who had been terrorizing the Metis traders at Fort Turnay in the spring of 1874, however, were a different matter entirely.

From the moment the American commission passed the point where the Milk River comes down to meet the Missouri, they had been travelling through "Indian Territory." According to the treaty of 1855, the whole of northern Montana, from the lower Milk to the Great Divide and south to a line well below the course of the Missouri, belonged to the Blackfeet. It was a truly enormous reservation—far larger, in fact, than anything the Blackfeet could have hoped to hold. The deepest southwestern corner of their land had been designated a "common hunting ground," a hopelessly idealistic idea of a preserve where all tribes, whether from the high plains or the inter-mountain valleys, would be free to pursue the bison without fear of attack from any other nation—the dreaded Blackfeet in particular. The reservation's long southern boundary was subject to constant penetration by the Blackfeet's age-old rivals from the various and populous Crow nations. At its eastern end—marked by a line that ran from the confluence of the Missouri and the Milk north to the 49th Parallel—Assiniboine, Plains Cree and Sioux would all have mounted constant challenges to the rights of the Blackfeet. Any of these nations had a perfectly legitimate claim to the lands east of the Cypress Hills. Even at the height of their power, the Blackfeet would have been a rare sight anywhere near the mouth of the Milk River, and their trading visits to Fort Union would have been fast, in-and-out affairs, with everyone on constant lookout for Sioux or Assiniboine raiding parties. It was a testament to the shifting realities of Native power along this stretch of the 49th Parallel that it was the Sioux, not the Blackfeet, who were tormenting Fort Turnay.

Indeed, not twenty years after scratching their marks on the 1855 treaty, the Blackfeet had begun to lose huge blocks of their grand allowance. In 1873, Congress had taken away the southwestern corner of the reservation, including the common hunting grounds, leaving the nation with no legal claim to anything south of the Missouri. As the boundary commission worked its way west toward the Great Divide in the summer of 1874, Congress was busy again, this time pushing the southwestern limits of the reservation up from the Sun River to Maria's River. Eventually, the railways would take almost everything east of the upper Maria's River country and, before the century was out, the Rocky Mountain foothills and the eastern slope of the Divide would be taken to create Glacier National Park.

Regardless of which band or nation happened to dominate the northern tier at any given time, the fact that the whole area was classified as an Indian reservation meant that any trade in rifles, ammunition or, most especially, in liquor was strictly prohibited. Since these three commodities were among the few things the Natives had any interest in trading for, and the fact that enforcement was at best sporadic (the presence of the U.S. Army notwithstanding), the rules were obviously more honoured in the breach than the observance.

There is no doubt the Fort Turnay traders were violating these prohibitions, and little doubt, too, that the Sioux knew that for this reason the traders had little recourse to recover any horses, guns or liquor that could be grabbed during a raid. It was the same story at a long string of trading posts and "whiskey forts" stretching along both sides of the 49th Parallel between Fort Turnay and the Rocky Mountain front. Below the line, the string of army forts along the Missouri was intended primarily to protect the people and freight moving up the river toward the gold-mining towns of western Montana. On the rare occasions that the troops actually took to the field to combat the whiskey trade, the traders simply moved up across the border, beyond the reach of the army and into a country that, as yet, had no police presence whatsoever. Indeed, it really had no significant white presence of any sort.

WITH CLEAR SKIES at night to speed his observations, and Greene pushing toward him at breakneck speed, Gregory took no more than two days to finish his observations at Frenchman's Creek. Unhampered by the need to run tangents or build monuments, he moved quickly ahead to his second station of the summer at the unimaginatively named "Pool on Prairie," exactly five hundred miles west of Pembina.

Frenchman's Creek (or the White Mud River as it was called in several of the commissions' accounts) lay at the heart of *les mauvaises terres*, the broad strip of badlands that runs from northwest to southeast across the line. For Twining:

> These bad lands... set at defiance all rules of topography, as well as all adequate description. Lacking even the continuous lines of drainage on which the eye may rest, and which give form and system to an ordinary *terraine*, they stretch in an endless and tiresome succession of arid and treeless hills and ridges, a tumul-

tuous expanse of baked mud. A large part of the country from the western edge of the Coteau to Frenchman's Creek may properly be called "bad lands."[21]

While the tangent and topographical parties struggled along the boundary with their light spring wagons, the nearest crossings for the heavy supply trains were at least sixteen miles to the north or south of the line. Featherstonhaugh, who traversed the country in early July, found the valley of the White Mud itself an "... immense trough... 6 miles wide and 320 feet in depth below the prairies on either side; its eastern edges are precipitous [with the] whole floor of the valley... cut up into gullies and slopes of shale." "At this time of the year, in the height of summer," he wrote, "the direct heat of the sun, aided by the reverberation from the soil, was oppressively great, and the aspect of the country was more like a desert than any that had been previously traversed."[22] There was water flowing in the White Mud, but it was so strongly alkaline that neither the horses nor the oxen would drink it. Even the army mules, which had a reputation for being able to swallow almost anything, were loath to touch it.

Despite cutting as much firewood as possible wherever there were small clusters of poplar around the few waterholes, the supply was so unreliable that every party was reduced to burning *bois des vâches* (literally "cow wood"), the Metis term for the chips of dried bison dung that lay everywhere across the floor of the valleys. Featherstonhaugh thought it odd that it should be in the middle of such a desolate land that they first found more than a memory of the great herds. The small groups of bison they saw in the twisted canyons were just a tantalizing glimpse of what was to come just a few miles to the west.

Millman and Dawson wandered the coulees and canyons of the White Mud, collecting new plants and a wealth of fossilized oyster shells and ammonites. Although the meat allowance had been restored at some point during their trek to Wood Mountain, they still took the opportunity to shoot at anything that might be edible. In the badlands, that meant either the occasional bison or the pronghorn, which they saw in substantial numbers. Dawson's diary records any number of errant potshots at distances of anywhere from two hundred to four hundred yards, but the other members of the astronomical parties were adept enough with a rifle to keep at least some pronghorn on the table. While they all liked roasted pronghorn well enough, it was the wild oxen that remained the most welcome addition to their larders. At one point Dawson recorded that someone had actually succeeded in herding four oxen into one of the camps. They had even managed to keep them tied up for a short while before the animals panicked and broke away. Before they escaped back into the canyons, however, the men managed to shoot two of them and, for Millman, it meant he would "enjoy the relish of fresh meat again."[23]

One living thing no one relished was beginning to appear everywhere across the valley of Frenchman's Creek. West from Dufferin it had been the torment of mosquitoes; in the White Mud country it was locusts. Dawson had been seeing outbreaks of grasshoppers since he crossed the Coteau in mid-June, noting that, although they were still too young to fly, they were "rapidly destroying what little grass there is."[24] In the badlands, he saw the plague at its peak:

> The grasshoppers for the last few days very numerous. Now well able to fly and may be seen passing along in the direction of the wind in that part of the sky near the sun at great heights. When rising from the ground and flying with the wind in one's face inflict painful blows, especially when they happen to light in one's eyes. Their appearance in passing before the sun are more like drifting snowflakes than anything else.[25]

He later likened the flying swarms to "the distant sound of surf or a gentle wind in [the] trees."[26] What he was seeing was the beginning of a very bad year for grasshoppers. Over the rest of the summer, they would blow eastward on the constant winds and inflict massive damage on the grain fields of the Red River valley.

Dawson would devote several pages of his final report to the problems presented by *Melanoplus spretus,* the Rocky Mountain locust, and he considered it one of the greatest barriers to the successful settlement of the west. In the end, he would be proved wrong, but only by one of the west's great mysteries. By the 1890s, the vast swarms were a fading memory and in 1904, a Montana entomologist could report that he had not collected a single locust in more than five years. By 1914, the Rocky Mountain locust was extinct. Only a century later have entomologists begun to understand something of what happened to it: as the homesteaders spread deeper into the west, they eventually ploughed the foothills grasslands that, it seems, were the insect's breeding grounds. It seems the Rocky Mountain locust became the victim of the very thing it had victimized.

If the biblical plague of locusts was bad news for the farmers of the Red River valley, Coues noted that it was manna to many of the high plains' other inhabitants:

> These insects, which appear sometimes in almost inconceivable numbers, seem to be the natural source of supply for a variety of animals. Wolves, foxes, badgers, and even rodents, like gophers, supposed vegetarians, come down to them. Sand-hill Cranes stalk over the plains to spear them by the thousands. Wild fowl waddle out of the reedy pools to scoop them up. We may kill scores of Sharp-tailed Grouse, in September, to find in every one of them a mass of grasshoppers, only leavened with a few grubs, beetles, leaves, berries and succulent tops of plants. It is amusing to see a Hawk catching grasshoppers, skipping about in an awkward way, and looking as if he were rather ashamed of being seen in such a performance.[27]

It was in the badlands that Millman and Dawson saw something else that fascinated them: "In the evening," wrote Millman on July 2, "we saw a comet in the Northwest. It appears to be Caggia's comet and an entirely new one. The tail extends upwards, not very large at present." Dawson, too, recorded the sighting in his journal on July 4.

The comet was visible in the night sky for nearly two weeks. Dawson saw it "beautifully half-enveloped in a faint auroral arch"[28] on July 14, but the next evening Millman wrote: "The comet Caggia's is getting quite large. But is rapidly approaching the sun and also the earth. In a few days we will not be able to see it as it will set before dark."[29] These would be their last references to the phenomenon.

What is most curious about the sightings is that, although they were surrounded by astronomers, these references by a physician and a naturalist are the only mentions of the comet made by any of the members of either commission. That cannot be because the other men were unaware of it. It was a bold presence in the summer skies, visible to the naked eye everywhere across the northern hemisphere. First identified and tracked only in mid-April of that year by the French astronomer Jérôme Coggia (not "Caggia" as Millman styled it), the comet was extremely well documented, and the scientific literature of the day holds a substantial store of information about it, including several early attempts at spectrographic photography. It is interesting, too, that Millman refers to the comet by name even though it had been known for less than three months and was indeed, as he suggested, "an entirely new one." That speaks well for the speed of communication between eastern Canada and the commission's camps in the remotest reaches of the western high plains. Someone's letters or newspapers had obviously brought word of the new discovery.

ON JUNE 19, the American boundary commission had just ridden out of Fort Buford, and Samuel Anderson was pulling his lumbering, ox-drawn wagon train into the depot at Wood Mountain. Back at a largely deserted Dufferin, some new tenants had just arrived. Canada's North-West Mounted Police were finally ready to take to the field.

The troops, which had spent the winter drilling and marching and freezing near Winnipeg, arrived in Dufferin the day before. They were just settling in when the balance of the force, with more than 200 men, nearly 300 carefully selected horses and nine carloads of wagons, supplies and farm implements, rode up from the railhead in Minnesota after their long train ride from Toronto.

So began one of the greatest chapters in Canada's emerging national mythology, and it would prove to be a chapter as rich in absurdity as it was in glory; every bit as foolhardy and reckless as it was colourful and proud.

Following a terrible thunderstorm and general stampede of the livestock on the night of June 21 and a fortnight of hurried preparation, the force began its great adventure on the morning of July 8.

It should have been easy, but from that day forward, popular historians and dedicated nationalists have been rationalizing what went so wrong. This was unknown country and the few available maps were next to useless; there were no truly knowledgeable scouts for hire; no one seemed to be able to speak the right Native tongues; the mosquitoes and the grass fires and the lack of water and firewood were surprises no one could have anticipated, and on and on. All these excuses would make some sense save for one glaring fact: the Mounties' commanding officer had spent the better part of a week travelling west from Ottawa in the company of the chief commissioner of the British boundary commission and should have known exactly what lay ahead.

Whatever else he might have been, Donald Cameron had proved himself a master organizer. Faced with those same unknowns, he had marshalled the right resources in the right proportions and applied them to the job at hand. All French had to do was follow Cameron's lead. In fact, all he had to do was, quite literally, follow Cameron's road out onto the high plains. Why he chose not to remains a mystery.

The boundary commission sent its supply trains out along the line long before the field crews left camp so that the slow-moving wagons would not impede the progress of the lighter field parties. This also gave the axemen and carpenters time to build the depot cabins and stables, to cut and stack the priceless supplies of firewood and even to cut and stack the hay to feed the incoming horses and oxen. The commission would not be using those depots again in 1874 and they were free for the taking and restocking. All the Mounties had to do was send their wagons out in the spring, stock those depots and cut the firewood that the 300 raw policemen would need when they set out for the far west.

As it was, the Mounties and their supplies all left Dufferin together, and within 48 hours the troopers had outrun their own supplies and were facing the first of a succession of cold, hungry nights as their supper and the feed for their horses lumbered slowly up the trail some 10 or 15 miles back. Their beautifully groomed eastern mounts took one sniff of the alkaline prairie water and refused to drink it. They would have none of the tough but nutritious prairie grasses either. It was just the beginning of a terrible ordeal.

· 10 ·

LATE SUMMER
1874

*Sometimes the water which we were compelled to
drink was so impregnated with buffalo urine as to partake of
its color, and to be altogether disgusting to the stomach.*

JAMES GREGORY

BY MID-JULY the astronomical and survey parties of both commissions broke out of the badlands and emerged onto the broad, open expanse of the shortgrass plains. Immediately, the pace of the work accelerated dramatically. The British had established a forward subdepot near what they called the East Fork of the Milk River (now known as Battle Creek) as Featherstonhaugh and Galwey were finishing their observations and running tangents west from stations 28 and 30. Gregory had come out onto the plains too, and was pushing hard to catch up. By July 13 he was moving toward his fourth camp of the season at Milk River Lake, some 590 miles from Pembina.

The quickening of the work was only partly due to reaching open country. At some point between Wood Mountain and the western limit of the badlands, Anderson, Featherstonhaugh and Galwey had made a significant change in the procedures they had used since the earliest days of the work. With the end of the line almost within their grasp, and the fair weather holding, Anderson was more determined than ever that neither he nor his Engineers would be spending a third season on the line. The British stopped building the grand stone and earth mounds that marked the boundary every three miles, and paused only long enough to mark their future location clearly. If the weather continued to favour them, they could bring the full weight of the commission—including the topographical party—to building the mounds as they retreated at the end of the summer. Should there be an early start to the winter, the Engineers could return quickly to Dufferin (and from there back to Britain), leaving the construction of the permanent markers to Cameron and the Canadian assistants, whether in that season or the next. Anderson was betting on the weather—always a dangerous thing, as the two previous falls had proved—to keep him ahead of the Americans in what he now viewed as a flat-out race to the Continental Divide.

As the American parties pushed west through the badlands, Twining and the main body of his military escort were still stuck down on Big Sandy Creek, nearly eighty miles below the line. Assistant astronomers Gregory and Greene were expecting to find a fully stocked depot at the Sweetgrass Hills, and Twining had heard nothing about the fate of the commission's main supplies. Of particular importance were the tons of corn essential to keep the mule teams fed. Tired of stewing, Twining rode down to Fort Benton on July 12, only to discover the hired wagons still waiting for the paddle-wheeler *Josephine* to come up from Fort Buford. He waited with them until July 24, when the steamer finally arrived, only to be told that most of his supply of feed was not on board. Falling water levels in the Missouri had forced the *Josephine* to leave fifty tons of the commission's forage at a landing place known as Cow Island, a full 125 miles back downstream. Loading the twenty-five tons of corn that had been delivered, Twining sent one train and a company of infantry off toward the boundary immediately and dispatched another, in the care of the last of his infantry, to Cow Island. From there, they would haul the feed overland nearly 150 miles up to the line. It would be first day of August before the Americans' main depot was finally established at the Sweetgrass Hills.

In mid-July, with the White Mud behind them, the men of the boundary commissions saw the country transformed, almost in an instant, from a desolate, largely deserted wasteland into the vibrant stage set of a Great West that was everything they must all have hoped it would be. The narrow, twisted canyons of the badlands gave way to a broad, rolling ocean of rich grass. Where there had been a few scattered bands of bison along the White Mud, suddenly there were thousands of them, spread across the plains in herd after immense herd for as far as the eye could see. And where there were bison, there were men to hunt them.

The commissions had seen little more than the occasional small band of Sioux at Turtle Mountain or along the Souris River, but the summer plains west of the badlands were home not only to substantial numbers of Sioux, but also to large concentrations of Assiniboine and Plains Cree. Beyond the Sweetgrass Hills, the Montana Peigan and the Bloods were out in force, shadowing the westernmost herds. To the north and west, the Blackfeet of the Bow and South Saskatchewan river valleys were also out among the herds in substantial strength. Rumours of trouble among the various bands and threats to the boundary commissions quickly became daily fare in the astronomical and topographical survey camps on both sides of the line and, while the American parties were under the protection of their infantry escorts, by mid-July Major Reno and the main body of his 7th Cavalry had still not made their appearance on the line.

As the land opened and gentled, Anderson was thrilled finally to be able to quit his job as nursemaid to the oxen. Between the depot at Battle Creek and the foothills of the Rocky Mountains, there was nothing to impede the progress of the supply wagons. Earlier reconnaissances by the 49th Rangers had clearly identified the sites for the subdepots and the astronomical stations. It was further understood by all the parties that the last pause before the final assault would take place at the beginning of August in the shadow of the Sweet-grass Hills. There, just a hundred miles short of the final goal, both American and British parties would mass their stocks and stores, double-check their instruments and their calculations, and launch their run to the Divide.

Writing to his mother from a camp on the Milk River on July 21, Anderson was delighted to report that he had been out again with his scouts and that they had pushed the reconnaissance just beyond the Sweetgrass Hills to within ninety miles of their goal. His reward had been his first horizon-stretching view of the Rocky Mountains, and his excitement was palpable: "I have now come back about 70 miles to communicate the good news to all the people in [the] rear who are coming on as fast as possible, and I am now again moving westward to get as near the end as possible."[1]

As the parties moved closer to the mountains, the scale of the operation was continually being cut back. With only a single topographical party surveying just three miles above the border (a reduction in the width of the Canadian survey that seems to have been in effect since the beginning of the season) and the astronomical parties no longer required to complete their mound-building before moving ahead to the next station, the emphasis had shifted from the slow, steady hauling of huge volumes of food and forage—nearly half of which was required to feed the men and the animals who were doing the hauling—to faster, more flexible supply lines that focussed on horses and light wagons to keep the field camps supplied.

In mid-July, Anderson was still gloating about being "about 100 miles" ahead of the Americans, but he was exaggerating his lead by at least sixty. In fact, Featherstonhaugh was still at station 28 on Goose Lake when Greene arrived, having finished running the line west from Gregory's previous station. While Galwey had already advanced, so had Gregory, and the real difference between the British and American positions by this point probably amounted to no more than twenty or thirty miles.

The American parties were still entirely reliant on the supplies they had brought up with them from the Missouri, and those must

Royal Engineers photographers camped somewhere west
of Turtle Mountain, 1873 (NA-249-24).

The depot at Turtle Mountain, 1873 (NA-249-28).

British commission ox-train near Wood End, 1873 (NA-249-42).

Royal Engineers sappers building a boundary marker near the Milk River, 1874 (NA-218-1).

British commission ox-train, near Wood End, 1874 (NA-65-4).

TOP LEFT: Mummified remains of an ambushed party of Crows, Sweetgrass Hills, 1874 (NA-65-1).

BOTTOM LEFT: Metis hunting camp, south of the Cypress Hills, 1874 (NA-249-71).

ABOVE: Survey camp below the east slope of Mount Wilson (now Mount Boswell), 1874 (NA-249-108).

Native burial scaffold near the Souris River, 1873 (NA-249-80).

have been running low. It would still be more than two weeks before they could avail themselves of the new main depot at the Sweetgrass Hills (provided, of course, their comrades had managed to get the supplies there at all). They did have a small herd of cattle with them, but Greene and Gregory were more than happy to see the herds of pronghorn and, especially, of bison, as they cleared the badlands and came out onto the Milk River plains.

While they were out of the worst of the badlands, the parties were still travelling through country that was not entirely hospitable. Gregory recorded that the country "had been very dry... Water was scarce, and usually unpleasantly alkaline. We found no wood along the line, and were therefore obliged to place our dependence for fuel upon buffalo-chips, which were everywhere abundant."[2]

With no water wagons, the American parties were counting on what they could find along the line each day. In the heat of mid-July most of the streams had already dried up, and where there was standing water, it was often foul and probably a serious health hazard to man and beast:

> The buffalo find every pool of water existing upon the prairie, and are in the habit of standing in them to rid themselves of the flies which are their peculiar pests. Wherever, therefore, the buffalo had preceded us, we found the pools were mud-holes, which were loaded with buffalo *excreta*. Sometimes the water... was so impregnated with buffalo urine as to partake of its color, and to be altogether disgusting to the stomach.[3]

Even the better-prepared British were finding the country a severe test of their resources. Anderson wrote from the banks of the Milk River in mid-July:

> I was afraid we were going to be put to much trouble and incon-venience on acc't of the scarcity of water, and on the Reconnais-sance we carried 3 and 4 days supply of drinking water along with us in a water cart, and trusted to finding swamp holes for

the animals to drink from. As the summer advances these pools are nearly dried up, and we have found it necessary to change the line of the route so as to pass by the larger pools which are likely to last the longest... The river where I am writing when I first crossed it eight days ago, was a good running stream, today it has disappeared, and water can only be found in pools.[4]

It had not rained for three weeks, and while the parties were not troubled by mosquitos, they were still dealing with clouds of locusts, which not only covered their equipment and tormented their animals but, in combination with the buffalo, devoured what little native forage there was for miles in every direction.

The young Francis Greene managed to retain a more enthusiastic attitude toward the new country. Dividing his time between directing the topographical party and running the tangents, he was free to indulge his taste for adventure in a way that officers like Gregory and Featherstonhaugh, tied to their tables and telescopes, were not. This was especially true when it came to bison running. For Greene, it was "the wildest and grandest sport [he] ever saw or engaged in."[5] Regularly rousting out his Native scouts and infantry officers, Greene rarely missed the opportunity for a chase. He wrote to his family after one hunt, describing how he had quietly approached a small herd of about eighty animals:

> The old bull in front soon saw us and with a snort threw down his head and up his tail and started off; the herd looked around at us, threw down their heads and rolled after him—and away we went. It seemed at first a slow lumbering gait like a lot of black cows frightened by a dog, but we soon found out that they were going a good 12 or 15 miles an hour with lots of wind inside their black hides.[6]

It was all great fun, and while Greene managed to wound one of the old bulls with his revolver, the party's scouts dropped two young cows for the dinner table. In the excitement, one of the escort officers,

Captain Ames, succeeded in shooting his own horse out from under himself, provoking Greene's good-natured derision: "Evidently the looking after horse, self, rifle, pistol, buffalo and badger holes at a gallop had been too much for him—an Infantry man."[7]

For Gregory, although the bison running allowed them to keep their larders full and their spirits high, he knew its obvious attractions outweighed the real demands of the camps. As he later reflected: "[We] killed more perhaps than our needs justified."[8]

Not every encounter with the bison was such grand sport. While bringing up supplies to an advanced depot, Anderson and his wagon train narrowly avoided a major disaster as they crossed a narrow ravine just east of the Milk River:

> ... the buffalo [that] extended over the plain on our left hand for many miles took fright and all rushed toward us, and were drawn into the little ravine that we were crossing, as into a funnel. I was afraid our horses and wagons would be swept away, but we were able to stop in time, and thousands of the terrified buffalo swept past us just in front, smothering us with their dust. It was no good firing into the midst of them, altho' they were quite close, 50 yards off, so we waited 10 minutes till they had all passed. As ill luck would have it they afterwards turned away from us, and charged thro' the only pool of water that we had seen for miles, and where we were obliged to make our camp for the night, making the water in such a mess that the horses only drank very sparingly of it.[9]

Even amid the great bounty, Featherstonhaugh managed to keep his perspective, observing with a sniff, "... the different parties obtained ample supplies of fresh [bison] meat, which, although not equal in quality to the flesh of the deer and antelope, was preferable to the hard beef that the much-travelled oxen afforded."[10]

With the bison came their indigenous hunters, and it was at station 28, some 527 miles out from Pembina, that Featherstonhaugh and Millman first encountered the Assiniboine. According to the assistant surgeon, it was an occasion for careful curiosity on both sides:

July 11th... Camped on a lake a mile north of the line called Lac des Marons [Goose Lake]... and on the line is a large salt lake. At this place we met with some Assiniboine Indians. They accompanied us to camp. We gave them a present of bacon, flour and tea. They appeared to be very friendly. There were about thirty all mounted on very good ponies and appeared to be well armed. Some had Winchester repeaters or sixteen shooters.[11]

The next day, Millman reported:

The Indians shifted their camp near ours. They had sixty tepees or wigwams. In the forenoon I visited these. Found the women as usual busy putting up tents, cleaning skins, etc. The Indians are making a great slaughter amongst the geese on the lake as they are now not able to fly, having shed their feathers."[12]

When Featherstonhaugh later published his own account of the meeting, he not only confirmed much of what Millman recorded in his diary, but added several details of considerable significance:

With the buffalo were found their constant attendants, the Indians, both Sioux and Assinebonies [*sic*]. These people were well clothed and armed and appeared to have plenty of food; they always begged for a small quantity of tea, sugar and flour, and were particularly keen after matches, which they evidently valued highly. They asked numerous questions about the objects of the expedition, and appeared relieved to hear that no idea of a railway lay at the bottom of it. As far as could be known, the fact of a boundary being marked between the British and American territories seemed to be welcome to them, and it is said that they were rather disappointed that a wall or continuous bank was not set up across the plains, a thing which they had been led to expect.[13]

Featherstonhaugh's observation about the Assiniboine's particular love of matches is an indication of something deeper than a simple desire for something to make life a little easier. One western writer, an expert in the history of firearms, suggests that the Natives used the matchheads as an element in reloading their Winchester cartridges. Although it is difficult to see how that might have been accomplished, it does square with the idea of the limitations of technology and supplies with which the plains tribes lived. Those nations that the commission encountered—the Sioux, the Assiniboine and, later, the Blackfeet—seemed, for the most part, well clothed, well fed and well armed. Still, they were all extremely careful about their use of firearms. While they lacked the technical know-how to repair a badly damaged rifle (they had no knowledge of smelting or metalworking by which they could have manufactured replacement parts), ammunition would have been particularly difficult and expensive to acquire. One of the sappers reported that a band of Peigan that came to his depot would have happily traded him "a moderately good pony" for about forty Spencer carbine shells. As George Dawson observed, such a price, with the ammunition worth around $1.20, "... could not be considered dear."[14]

According to Dawson, those same Peigan were loath to use their firearms even for hunting:

[Four hundred Peigan] killed about 800 buffalo in three days. Generally killed with steel pointed arrows. The arrow sticking in the flesh stops the animal very effectively. Also a great saving of ammunition. Even those possessing good rifles were armed also with bow and arrow for buffalo hunting.[15]

That the Assiniboine should be pleased to hear there was to be a clearly marked boundary between Canada and the United States— that they might even express disappointment that it was not to be a real wall—flies in the face of the conventional wisdom that the plains nations found the idea of any artificial border both laughable and unenforceable. Under normal circumstances that might have been true, but over the previous two years the Assiniboine had suffered enough death and indignity at the hands of the Montana traders to make any wish for an impervious border seem perfectly sensible.

The men of the two border commissions viewed the various Native populations of the western plains somewhat differently. The Assiniboine they both seemed to find fairly predictable and generally trustworthy (as far as they were inclined to trust any of them). That perception was perhaps based on the Assiniboine's long association with the white trading companies, and the lack of serious raiding or other hostilities associated with them. The Americans seemed not to know or care much about the Assiniboine—whom they probably considered largely "Canadian"—and, as long as they caused no trouble south of the line, they would remain of little interest. That was a situation with which the Assiniboine themselves were probably quite comfortable.

As for the Sioux, the attitudes of the two commissions differed dramatically, again based largely on previous experience. The British knew little about them first-hand, and generally seemed to find them interesting, perhaps regarding them as the archetype of the proud, independent Native spirit. This impression was never challenged by the Sioux themselves, who were usually on their best behaviour while on Canadian soil. But for the Americans, the Sioux were not to be trusted under any circumstances, and it was because of the Sioux, more than any other plains nation, that the boundary commission never strayed far from its escort.

Interestingly, though, it was not the Assiniboine or the Sioux who sparked the commissions' greatest interest and curiosity. Nor was it the widely feared Blackfeet, whose territories lay just ahead across the Milk River. It was the Metis.

A society unique to the Canadian plains, the Metis were the mixed-blood descendants of Native women and the French-Canadian voyageurs from Quebec who had come to the west with the fur trade in the eighteenth century. Their culture was a fusion of this double heritage: largely French-speaking and Roman Catholic, their lifestyle was nomadic and, traditionally, based on hunting bison. The men of the boundary commissions were familiar with the Metis from riding alongside the 49th Rangers through two seasons in the field, but they had also been meeting individual families or small travelling parties on the wagon trails between the Cypress Hills, Wood Mountain and the Red River. Nothing had prepared them, however, for the sight of a full Metis summer hunting camp. Every account— official or unofficial—every letter home and every journal entry contained lengthy descriptions of the spectacle. Samuel Anderson wrote:

> On this remote spot were encamped... 150 families of half-caste hunters, cut off entirely from the civilized world, and depending for food on buffalo meat. They were assembled and organised as one community for mutual protection. Their home-made carts were arranged in a circular form and packed closely together, forming an enclosure 150 yards in diameter, into which their ponies were driven at night and guarded. Around and outside the circle of carts, the skin-covered tents or wigwams were pitched where each family had its home and lived separately. Great order and regularity prevailed in the camp, principally due to the influence of a French priest who lived with them and seemed to be their chief adviser in temporal as well as spiritual matters. Business was transacted by a council who met daily and decided where they should hunt. On the hunting days, the women and children driving the pony-carts would follow in the rear of the hunters to carry home the meat. Each hunter would probably kill six or eight animals early in the day and for the remainder of the day his whole family would be employed cutting off the meat, the best pieces only being taken, the hide and the forequarters being left. For many miles the air was soon poisoned and in every direction could be seen evidence of the reckless slaughter and wanton waste of the hunters. The half-breeds are in constant collision with the Indians and no quarter is either given or received.[16]

Featherstonhaugh was struck not only by the scale of the camp and the presence of a Roman Catholic priest living among them (everyone who wrote about the Metis mentioned the priest) but also by what he saw as "... a sort of military discipline founded on mutual consent... [where] outlying videttes are regularly maintained at some miles from the camp, so as to give early notice of the approach of any party sufficiently numerous to be formidable."[17]

George Dawson thought the Metis sufficiently important to include a lengthy analysis in his final report:

> They live under no law or restraint other than that imposed by necessity and by the general consent, or by the priest who accompanies them. Spending the summer at large, in the neighbourhood of any district which happens to be well stocked with buffalo, they fall back eastward for winter quarters. A few of them going to Wood Mountain, but most to the White Mud River, south of the line, near a trading post known as Fort N.J. Turnay. A comparatively small proportion of the robes obtained by these people, find their way to Winnipeg; most of the trade being carried on toward the Missouri. The summer hunt is chiefly to obtain *pemican* meat, the skins of the buffalo killed being frequently wasted. In the autumn and early winter, when the skins are *prime*, robes are the chief object. The Indians, though some of them are friendly to these half-breeds, and glad enough to trade with them, are naturally jealous of their hunting, and slaughtering buffalo for themselves.
>
> The 'Big Camp' consisted of over two hundred tepees, most of them dressed skin, like those of the Indians, but some of canvas. Every family owns carts, at least equal in number to that of its members; and when the camp is made, these are arranged in a circle, to form a 'corral' for the horses; the tents being pitched round the whole. The total number of horses was stated to be about 2,000, valued at from $20 to $100, according to their aptitude in buffalo running... The camp is assiduously guarded, to prevent surprise or horse stealing.
>
> A few weeks before our arrival, the half-breeds had been in the Cypress Hills, and had there assisted, or countenanced, the Sioux in a fight with the Blackfeet, in which eight of the latter tribe were killed.[18]

Only William Twining seemed less than impressed:

Cut off almost entirely from communication with the outer and
progressive world, the forms of civilized life finally gave way, and
were superseded by the manners of a nomadic semi-barbarous
people, though, even in this stage of decay, the natural polite-
ness of a French ancestry and the teachings of a few pious priests
of the Catholic Church had left their impress on the succeeding
generations.[19]

What all the observers agreed upon was that they were witness-
ing a way of life that was fast disappearing. At home in neither Native
nor white society, and wholly dependent on the bison, as the herds
declined the Metis had been drawn farther and farther away from
their home bases in Manitoba. It became easier to trade with the
Americans at Fort Benton, but the fort, too, had already begun its
steady decline. The market for Metis pemmican had been severely
curtailed when the Hudson's Bay Company sold off its territory, but
that did not slow the killing. The bison were about to face their final
threat.

As Dawson observed, the Metis (and all the other hunters, Native
or white) had restricted their hunting to certain times of the year.
Summer was for pemmican, fall and early winter for the big prime
robe skins. The animals had not been much use for anything else, but
that was about to change. In 1872 eastern inventors finally discovered
a method for tanning bison leather that would leave it strong and
flexible enough for industrial belting as well as a host of other uses
for which it had previously been considered ill suited. Hard as it is to
imagine, the United States had been suffering serious shortages of
industrial leather for many years, and imports were growing prohibi-
tively expensive. When the patents were issued for this new form of
tanning, the fate of the bison was truly sealed. Young or old, male or
female, regardless of the season, the guns would be trained on them
and the already fierce rate of slaughter would increase dramatically.
And when the herds finally disappeared (as nearly everyone knew

they must), it would not be just the great plains Indian nations that
would suffer; the nomadic life of the Metis, too, would be finished.

Twining, usually so perceptive in his observations about the true
nature of the high plains, got his reading of the bison completely
wrong. In the great northern herd that swept down through the
broad pass between the Cypress and the Sweetgrass Hills he seems
to have almost willed himself to see not the last of their kind, but
rather some hope for their future. Writing in the U.S. commission's
final report, he offered a guarded, but basically upbeat, prognosis:

> This herd, which ranges from the Missouri River north to the Sas-
> katchewan, made its appearance, going south, about the last of
> August. The number of animals is beyond all estimation. Look-
> ing at the front of the herd from an elevation of 1,800 feet above
> the plain, I was unable to see the end in either direction. The
> half-breeds, Sioux, Assiniboines, Gros Ventres of the prairie, and
> Blackfeet, all follow the outskirts of this herd; but, with all their
> wasteful slaughter, they make but little impression upon it.[20]

He closed his analysis with a remark that cannot be seen as anything other than wishful thinking: "It is even said by the traders at
Fort Benton that the number of buffaloes is increasing, owing to the
destruction of the wolves in late years."

George Dawson did not agree:

> From what I could learn, I believe that at the present rate of exter-
> mination, twelve to fourteen years will see the destruction of what
> now remains of the great northern band of buffalo, and the termi-
> nation of the trade in robes and pemican, in so far as regards the
> country north of the Missouri River.[21]

As it turned out, even that estimate was overly optimistic.

BY THE BEGINNING of August, nearly every man, mule, ox and wagon
from both commissions—so recently strung out across more than
a hundred miles of the northern tier, or stranded down on the Mis-

souri—were gathered at the Sweetgrass Hills making ready for the final push into the Rocky Mountains and up onto the Great Divide.

The great peaks of the Three Buttes (as the hills were often called) had been clearly visible since the parties passed Goose Lake in mid-July. Towering between 6,500 and nearly 7,000 feet above sea level, the hills soared some 3,500 feet clear of the surrounding country—and all, as it turned out, to the south of the line. For Anderson, they were "the most prominent and important feature of the western plains," and the occasion for one of his rare flights of poesy:

> The first view of the Buttes was obtained when standing on the high ground overlooking the sandy cactus-plain. From this point of view, the nearest Butte is 100 miles distant to the west, and its conical peaks, which stand out mistily against the sky-line when viewed in the early morning, are quite lost in the haze of the afternoon sun. Thus, to a traveller approaching the three Buttes from the eastward, they seem to recede during the day's travel, and though invisible at sundown, at sunrise the next morning they appear to have advanced close to the camp.[22]

By July 25, Twining and Reno, together with the two companies of 7th Cavalry and a company of the 6th Infantry, had left Big Sandy and followed the main supply train north toward the parallel. Lieutenant Ladley and his troops had made a remarkably quick dash back downstream to Cow Island and then wasted no time in loading the precious forage and whipping their mules northwest toward the Sweetgrass Hills. As Reno's cavalry went under canvas in the shelter of the East Butte, the supply trains carried on toward their main depot, thirty miles away against the broad shoulders of the West Butte. Their arrival could not have been better timed. Both Gregory and Greene were quickly closing on the Sweetgrass Hills, and just as quickly running out of crucial supplies.

The ride up from Big Sandy to the Three Buttes would not have been pleasant for any officer or enlisted man. While the escort was waiting on the Missouri for the supplies to come up from Buford, Reno learned that his wife had died on July 10. He had ridden into

Fort Benton and telegraphed to his superiors for permission to take a leave and return home to Pennsylvania. That permission had been denied. It might have been caution about the rumours of increasing tension with the resident Natives along the boundary line that caused his superiors to deny Reno what might otherwise have been a routine request. More likely, however, Reno had simply burned too many political bridges in the past year or so, and no one among his superiors was disposed to grant him any favours. Never the most approachable individual at the best of times, Reno would certainly have been a man to avoid on the ride north to the Sweetgrass.

In the two months since he had come back to the line, Gregory had moved 175 miles west from the White Mud, observing at four stations along the way. This he had accomplished—in a country where there was almost no firewood or drinkable water and precious little feed for his mules and horses—with only the supplies he had brought with him from Fort Buford. Greene and his parties had come even farther, beginning their season east of Wood Mountain by completing the topographical and tangent work that had been abandoned the previous fall. On the last day of July, both Gregory and Greene were waiting at the East Butte astronomical station when Twining and the cavalry came up from Big Sandy.

There was still one significant member of the American commission who had yet to make an appearance during the 1874 season. Chief Commissioner Campbell had been stuck in Washington trying to move his long-delayed appropriation through the halls of Congress but, by early July, he was finally headed west to join his men. He and commission secretary James Bangs arrived at Fort Buford on July 15 and, picking up a small escort of one officer and fifteen infantrymen left for him by Reno, they set out immediately for the Sweetgrass Hills. Eighteen days later, on August 3, the chief commissioner caught up with Twining at the West Butte depot.

MAINTAINING THE LEAD they had established during the first few weeks of the season, the British were the first to arrive at the Sweetgrass Hills. The 49th Rangers had identified the location for the thirty-fourth station just beyond the West Butte, some 650 miles west of Pembina. It would become the last major depot before the parties moved into the Rocky Mountains.

West from Goose Lake, the land had grown steadily drier and less hospitable. "I sometimes wonder," wrote Francis Greene, "if the original geographer who left an immense blank in the middle of the map of America and labelled it 'Great American Desert' was so far wrong."[23] Anderson called the fifty-mile stretch an "arid cactus-plain," and all of the various diaries and journals for the month of July refer to the dried-out waterholes, the prickly pear and, with no small amount of fascination, the large rattlesnakes that began to appear everywhere along the route. Millman collected the rattles from several specimens killed by the men.

While the field parties were able to make good time with their light wagons, Anderson found it nearly impossible to move his ox-drawn supply train through the deep cuts and eroded coulees. The greatest barrier of all was the Milk River. Although the river itself had been reduced to a bare trickle, near the boundary it meandered through a great canyon nearly half a mile wide and five hundred feet deep. With its precipitous walls and deep-cut side canyons, the Milk seemed to present an impassable obstacle. It took Anderson three separate reconnaissance trips along almost forty miles of the river before he found a crossing his oxen could manage. That route took the twenty-five heavy wagons nearly ten miles south of the line and then kept them in American territory for another sixty miles before they could swing northwest again under the shadow of the Sweet-grass Hills. The supply train, under the direction of Lawrence Herchmer, finally drew up on the slopes of the West Butte on July 24. On that same day, travelling by a more direct route, Galwey's astronomical party arrived to begin observations at station 34, just 114 miles from the Continental Divide.

With the last main depot fully established, Anderson turned the oxen out to graze on the rich grass and began to organize his final reconnaissance. From the shoulder of the West Butte he could clearly see the peaks of the Rocky Mountains, "a rugged and snowy outline… in full relief against the western sky-line."[24] It was a week before the beginning of August and, barring anything but a catastrophic change in the weather, Anderson was convinced he would be leading his men back toward Pembina before the middle of September.

Early on the morning of July 25, Anderson assembled a small party of rangers, packed enough rations for two weeks and headed west toward the mountains. He had gone only fifty miles when his worst nightmare came true. A messenger raced up with an order that he return to the depot immediately. Chief Commissioner Cameron had arrived at the West Butte and wanted a meeting with his chief astronomer.

Anderson made no effort to hide his annoyance—or his deep disdain—in a long letter to his mother on the first day of August:

> ...I had to return [to the West Butte], but I took only two or three men with me, as I sent on the party to finish the Reconnaissance and return when their work was accomplished or their provisions exhausted. If I had only been left to me own devices for a few days I should have been able to explore to the end, and form a better estimate of what remained to be done.[25]

Cameron, as he seemed almost pathologically determined to do in his dealings with his men, proceeded to heap insult on injury. As Anderson continued in his letter:

> I got back to this camp (where I am now writing) three days ago, and had my interview with Captain Cameron and he disappeared the following evening, starting on a journey westward to go to the end of the Line and return immediately to Pembina. I have no expectation that he will succeed in getting to the end of the Line, which is in the very heart of the Rocky Mountains, and not easy to find.[26]

Not only was Cameron apparently determined to steal the modest honour of being first to reach the Continental Divide, but according to Anderson the chief commissioner was willing to employ deceit and abuse of his authority to do it:

During the last two days all the working parties have carried the work as far as this camp, and have gone on, so that for the first time this season I now find myself in rear, being obliged to stop, to make payments to a Contractor who is bringing us supplies of oats from Fort Benton. This was imposed on me by an order left by Capt. Cameron, and not delivered to me till after he had started (according to his own arrangement) so I cannot hand over the blank cheques...to anybody else.[27]

The oats for which Anderson had been ordered to wait were the second instalment of the huge order placed by W.G. Boswell when he had travelled to Helena and Fort Benton the previous winter. This second delivery had been arranged on a visit to Fort Benton from the base at Wood Mountain earlier in July.

Anderson had not seen the chief commissioner since May, and he was clearly convinced that nothing had happened in the intervening weeks to ameliorate the problems between them:

...[Cameron] was as usual out of temper and had not a civil word to say to any one, Altho we had made twice the progress than had been either calculated or expected, not one word of congratulations or satisfaction at the progress of the work fell from his lips. I can only conclude that he is greatly put out at being compelled to wind up the work so soon... He asked me if Ottawa would do for finishing our plans in the spring, and I said we should finish them during the winter, so it is quite possible we may move our office to Ottawa and work there all this winter. The little work we have to do at Lake of the Woods will not require the presence of any of our officers, so if we finish everything out here, there will not be any reason for detaining any of the officers or men at Pembina this winter.[28]

"I took little or no notice of his intemperate language," Anderson concluded, "...and I am thankful to say he has now disappeared and left us alone for a time."[29]

The timing of Anderson's departure and Cameron's arrival at the West Butte depot are crucial in any attempt to understand how poisoned the relationship between the two men had become, since it hints that the chief astronomer may not have been as free from responsibility for the problems as his letters home suggested. It is almost too much of a coincidence that Anderson quickly threw together a reconnaissance party and left the depot on the morning of the same day on which Cameron appeared (just before midnight). The fact that most of the Rangers were still at the West Butte, but preparing to leave the next day, strongly suggests that Anderson left earlier than he had planned, specifically to avoid a meeting with Cameron. There is no way to know how Anderson had discovered Cameron was on his way, but it would not have been the first time he had deliberately ducked his chief commissioner. Nor would it be the last.

As for Cameron, his actions were hardly free from personal animosity toward Anderson. It is easy to imagine his annoyance at discovering the chief astronomer had packed up and left camp just ahead of his arrival. He may also have been justified in issuing his recall (although he could just as easily have sent word for Anderson to wait for him at some specific location along the boundary). His decision regarding the method of payment for the oats, however, was simply mean-spirited. There was no reason to make Anderson wait for the contractor to arrive from Fort Benton. Not only did the depot have a resident manager, but Lawrence Herchmer, the man who was ultimately responsible for all matters relating to supplies (and who had ordered the oats delivered in the first place) was also still at the West Butte.

By July 30 Featherstonhaugh had finished his observations at station 32 and run his lines twenty miles west to Gregory's camp at the eastern edge of the Sweetgrass Hills. The next morning he and his party began the long trek to their next station some sixty miles to the west. That day, as they passed across the north shoulder of the West Butte on their way to the depot, they ran into Dawson, Boswell and the commission photographers in the process of recording what was certainly the most striking and bizarre of their contacts with the Native peoples of the northern high plains.

Ranged in a rough circle at the base of the butte were the mummified remains of perhaps twenty Crow warriors. Every journal and diary contains at least some description of the scene, and it is unlikely that any member of either commission missed visiting the site. How long the bodies had lain there no one, not even the doctors, could be certain, although the general consensus was that they had been there no longer than since the previous summer. It was rumoured that a party of Crows had passed near Fort Benton the previous fall, headed north on a horse-stealing expedition, but that none of them had returned. Anderson's description of the site is typical:

> The deadly combats that have occurred between the Blackfoot and Crow Indians, when meeting in this region in pursuit of the buffalo, have in some degree made it a neutral ground, but a recent battle must have been fought, as the bodies of twenty Crow Indians were found on the plain a few miles from the depôt camp. They were all scalped, and in consequence of the intense dryness of the atmosphere, the bodies were completely sun-dried and well-preserved.[30]

Featherstonhaugh added a few more details and changed the emphasis of the story from bison to stolen horses:

> It appears that the vanquished party had stolen some horses from the others, and, being pursued, had been overtaken before they had reached the shelter of the hills; small rifle pits had been scratched up by them in haste when they had to turn and fight, but they had been overpowered. The bodies had been stripped, scalped, and hacked about a good deal; there were one or two very large men amongst them.[31]

The idea that the land around the Sweetgrass Hills was some sort of "neutral territory" was a popular one among the men of both commissions. Certainly it was something they could have heard from their scouts, and their own personal observations seemed to bear it out. Despite the fact that the bison seemed more numerous near the

Three Buttes than anywhere else, no one had seen a Native for more than a hundred miles. Featherstonhaugh had been told that the Sioux and Assiniboine never crossed the Milk and that the Blackfeet stayed well to the west of the Sweetgrass. He also believed it was the very neutrality of the hills that explained the large number of bison that inhabited the area.

While Anderson had no hard evidence, he was sure there were at least a few Natives—probably Peigans—in the surrounding ravines:

> ...the first day I came to this place I rode up in the hills a little way
> and an Indian dog somewhere beyond me started barking, tho'
> I could not see where he was. There cannot be more than a few
> families, as our people have now been wandering all over the hills
> and have seen no recent signs of Indians.[32]

The Peigans—indeed, the whole of the so-called Blackfeet Confederacy—had long bred a mixture of curiosity and fear in any white trader or settler who had approached their foothills territories. They were the reason for the strong American military presence along the eastern slope of the Rockies, but, as a force to be reckoned with on the northern plains, the Blackfeet were a fast-fading memory. What smallpox epidemics had begun, Major Eugene Baker and the U.S. 2nd Cavalry finished. In January 1870 he had swept down on a winter camp along the Maria's River and, when he was through, nearly two hundred Peigan—mostly women, children and the aged—were dead, and the Blackfeet were finished as a threat to the railways, to settlement or to anything else.

When Featherstonhaugh brought his party into the West Butte depot late on the last day of July, Anderson and Herchmer were still there, but Cameron, East and Crompton had already gone on ahead. Galwey had finished his observations near the depot and was running his tangents west toward Red Creek. Within a few days, he would be on his way to his final astronomical station.

Featherstonhaugh, Millman and the rest stayed at the West Butte for just one night and, by seven o'clock on the morning of August 1, they were back on the trail heading west toward station 36. They passed Galwey ten miles out, and went another twelve before camping for the night. As they left the depot and rode across the shoulder of the West Butte, the party got its first clear glimpse of the Rocky Mountains. It was Anderson who had pointed out that as one climbed the side of the butte from the depot, the mountains came into view at precisely 49° North.

If Cameron was disappointed that the work would be over in less than a month, Anderson must have been pleased to hear that Twining and Campbell still intended to finish as soon as possible: "The Americans arrived yesterday [August 2] and pitched camp close to mine. They seem very positive about finishing everything out here this season, and are most anxious to co-operate with us in every way to save time and help on the work."[33] But he could not resist pointing out who was really helping whom: "We have of course saved them great trouble and expense, as all they have to do is follow our track and take up the work at points that we leave for them, so that they lose no time in going straight to the scene of operations and commencing the work at once."[34]

Anderson finally escaped the West Butte depot on August 3. "Everything is packed up and I am writing on my knee while the horses are pawing the ground impatient to be moving on,"[35] he wrote to his mother, concluding the long letter he had begun as he waited at the depot for the oats to arrive from Fort Benton.

For Dawson, seeing the arrival of the wagon train was something worth delaying his departure for the mountains and, just before noon on August 2, the whole huge operation finally groaned and roared into the West Butte depot:

A most extraordinary sight! Huge Missouri freighting waggons like Noah's arks with canvas covers. Two and in some cases three of these fastened together like the cars in a train and furnished with powerful lever brakes, eight or nine yoke of oxen attached to each set of waggons. Stretched out to enormous length and all hitched to a strong chain.[36]

Dawson and the remaining scouts left the West Butte with Anderson, a final ox-train of supplies and the pack-horses that would be needed to haul those supplies up into the Rockies. Herchmer had already turned back to his base at the Wood Mountain depot, where there was much to organize in advance of the return march. He would see no more of the Rocky Mountains than the view from the slope of the West Butte.

WHILE THE BRITISH pushed on toward the foothills, the Americans relaxed at the West Butte looking after repairs to their wagons, reshoeing their horses and mules and letting them fatten a little on the rich native grasses and imported corn. Dr. McGillycuddy went off to see the dead Crow warriors and proudly recorded that he had "got three pairs of femurs, one head and one infer max."[37] If any of the other visitors collected souvenirs at the site, they made no mention of it in their letters or diaries.

Commissioner Campbell, who had found the Missouri River country largely "monotonous and uninteresting,"[38] was charmed by the Sweetgrass Hills. The peaks of the buttes presented "... a most agreeable relief to the eye in contrast with the tameness of the country... recently passed" and the abundant cold spring water was "a great luxury after the unpalatable and unwholesome water [they] had been obliged to drink on the route."[39] Despite his sixty-one years, Campbell joined Francis Greene for a trip to the top of the West Butte, describing the ascent as "... steep toward the summit, but practicable. From that elevated point the Rocky Mountains in all their grandeur were in full view, while beneath us it required but little imagination to convert the rolling prairie into an ocean."[40]

Elliott Coues continued to collect and catalogue everything and anything that walked, crawled, flew, swam or flowered. His small group of assistants had been supplemented by Joseph Batty, a trained taxidermist and hunter who joined the party at the Sweetgrass Hills. Coues collected examples of resident small and medium-sized animals such as the porcupine and, especially, the local "gophers"—the Richardson's ground squirrel. So numerous were the creatures in the

vicinity of the Three Buttes that Coues was moved to note that "If
Montana and Dakota were the garden of the world (which they are
not, however), either the gophers or the gardeners would have to
quit."[41] Coues sent his man Batty up into the hills in search of the bighorn sheep, which were common enough but wary and hard to shoot.
He seemed as interested in their culinary potential as he was in their
scientific interest. Batty managed to bag one old ram, but then found
himself obliged to "sleep all night alongside of the meat to keep [his]
share from the wolves."[42]

Although Coues was dutifully recording and collecting as many
samples of every kind of living thing, birds were still his first love,
and he continued to make detailed notes on every type he saw. The
country yielded no particular specialties, but the area around the
Sweetgrass Hills was rich in the pale-coloured dryland sparrows
and longspurs he had been noting everywhere west of the Red River.
Where the potholes and alkaline pools had not dried out, they were
host to a huge variety of ducks, waders and other water birds, all
dutifully noted as to number, colour, location and particular habits.
Some—such as the elegant and beautiful avocet—he singled out for
special attention. His comments on the long-billed curlew, common
in the dry uplands, were typical of his colourful note-taking. At night,
he wrote, "their piercing and lugubrious cries resounded to the howl-
ing of the wolves."[43]

However, nothing occupied his attention as much as the Milk River
country's birds of prey. Golden eagles were common enough, building their huge, rough nests on the rock ledges and stunted trees, raising their young on a diet of the plentiful cottontails, jackrabbits and
gophers. The birds could also make an easy living from the carrion
scraps of bison that littered the plains below the hills. He took note
of the three common buteos—the soaring buzzard hawks of the open
country—paying special attention to the Swainson's and the great
ferruginous hawks. Unlike their cousins the red-tails, which seemed
more able to adapt to a variety of habitats, the Swainson's and the
ferruginous were tied to the harshest, most remote areas of the high
plains. Of the former, Coues wrote admiringly "[it] occurs in great

numbers over large areas of almost unbroken, arid and cactus-ridden prairie, where, even along the water-courses, there may be no trees or bushes for many miles."[44] Noting a peregrine falcon's nest—even then an uncommon site—Coues lowered a man down on a rope to collect it. Later, finding another "on the bare face of a perpendicular embankment," Coues tried to capture the three young it contained. While the male falcon watched from "a respectable distance," the female repeatedly swooped to the attack and Coues finally felt compelled to shoot her. The young birds continued to elude capture and Coues eventually abandoned the effort, leaving the young to the care of the father, "who, it is to be hoped, has since done more for his family than he did on the occasion just mentioned."[45]

On August 6 a photographer from the Royal Engineers carefully posed the American officers and civilians with their folding camp stools and instrument tripods. It was the only time in the entire duration of the mission the American commission would be photographed together; only Reno is missing. That morning he had mustered his troop of 7th Cavalry and ridden west along the line in response to what he described as "many rumours of anticipated troubles" from the Blackfeet.[46] Later the same day Captain Gregory assembled his party and followed in Reno's tracks toward his next set of observations at Red Creek. Twining, Campbell, Coues and their 6th Infantry escort remained in the hills until August 12 when they, too, packed up and headed for the Rockies.

· 11 ·

AUTUMN

1874

Clear and impetuous streams took the place
of muddy and stagnant pools, and the eye once more
rejoiced with the sight of trees and foliage.
ALBANY FEATHERSTONHAUGH

FEATHERSTONHAUGH wasted no time moving to his fourth station of the season, number 36, on the banks of the Milk River; as darkness fell on the evening of August 2, he was ready with his zenith telescope. The weeks without rainfall had dried the waterholes and parched the land, but they had also given clear skies and almost no observation time lost to cloudy nights. The teams of astronomers, calculators and surveyors had been together long enough that working in unison had become second nature. After only four or five days at any given station, it was time to pack up and move on. Featherstonhaugh had made his first observations of the 1874 season at Little Rocky Creek, 432 miles west of Pembina. Now, just six weeks later, he was 265 miles farther west, and within a few days he would be moving into the mountains toward his final station.

Station 36 quickly became a busy place. D'Arcy East brought his scouts out of the foothills on August 2 to meet Anderson and the supply train. They pulled into camp, with George Dawson in tow, on the evening of the 4th, followed the next morning by Galwey's crew and William Ashe's topographical party. Boswell the veterinarian was travelling with them too.

Then, almost as soon as they had arrived, everyone was gone. Galwey, Boswell and Ashe stayed just long enough for a quick parley before continuing west. Galwey was on his way to the St. Mary River to begin his final set of observations. Ashe would be continuing his topographical mapping, but the three-mile wide strip of the survey that had been the rule for the 1874 season would be widened again to its original six miles once the party had crossed the St. Mary. Hard on Galwey's heels, Anderson, Dawson and most of the supplies followed East and his 49th Rangers along the trail they had blazed for the oxen and the heavy wagons. They were pushing on to establish a final subdepot, and the thirty days of provisions they carried in the wagons would be more than enough to see the fieldwork completed. As soon as the wagons had been unloaded at what was to be known as the Rocky Mountain depot, they were to turn for home, the first significant element of Her Majesty's North American Boundary Commission to begin the retreat.

As they moved west from the Milk River the parties would drive up and over a low ridge, about 720 miles out from the Red River. Barely distinguishable in the increasingly broken country, the ridge peaked at 4,700 feet above sea level before descending into yet another river valley. Marked on today's Montana maps as the Hudson Bay Divide, it pushes out from the front range and trends northeast across the 49th Parallel, where it is called the Milk River Ridge. For more than four hundred miles, since they had come out onto the Great Coteau in early September 1873, the commissions had been moving through old Louisiana, the northern limits of the Missouri River country. From the crest of the Milk River Ridge, they would descend into the valley of the St. Mary River and find themselves, once again, in what had been Rupert's Land. The St. Mary, the Belly and every other stream they would cross between the ridge and the crest of the Great Divide flowed north and east toward Hudson Bay.

Anderson's mood had improved dramatically since leaving the Sweetgrass Hills and, in a celebratory fit of generosity, he left Featherstonhaugh's party well supplied from his main stores. Millman's diary reads, "We got some luxuries such as canned peaches, damsons, whortleberries, strawberries, corn and tomatoes—quite a treat! for lately we have been living on bread, bacon and tea.": In closing his entry for that day, the assistant surgeon, perhaps with his spirits lifted by the sweet pleasure of canned peaches, took obvious delight in recording that "My tent is standing directly on the line so that when I go to bed one half of me is in Canada, the other half in Uncle Sam's domain.":

With the continuing clear weather, Featherstonhaugh finished observing at the South Branch of the Milk River by August 8. As they drew their tangents, the party moved to a new campsite at a small lake seven miles to the west. Along the trail, they had a brief run-in with the Blackfeet. According to Millman:

> [We] saw about one hundred of the North Piegan Indians—very poorly clad. They were quite friendly and two or three had credentials. They were to the effect that they were going north to join their tribe—"good Indians," etc. One of them had an English Testament... [and] a book of sermons in French.[3]

These were not the first Blackfeet that Featherstonhaugh's party had encountered. On their way to the Milk River station a few days earlier a smaller band had crossed their path. Millman thought them friendly enough. "All they ask," he wrote, "is that we wipe those whiskey traders out of existence, for they are robbing them—getting all their ponies, etc."[4]

It was these two parties of Blackfeet that must have constituted the threat to which Major Reno had responded, and the cavalry troop swept into Featherstonhaugh's camp on the morning of August 9 (erasing any doubt as to whether the American cavalry could be counted on to protect the men of both commissions).

Reno's unsuccessful search for "hostiles" was the 7th Cavalry's first—and last—action on the 49th Parallel. By the middle of August the astronomical and surveying parties were well to the west of the Three Buttes and there was no reason to suspect any further threat from the Sioux. Soon after the reconnaissance to the Milk River, Reno and his two companies of cavalry, together with a substantial part of the 6th Infantry, broke camp at the East Butte and rode back toward Fort Buford.

The relationships that had developed between the officers of the American commission and those of their escort are easy to describe. With the infantry, they were strong and cordial. With the cavalry they were, at best, strained and, at worst, non-existent. In their final reports, each of the commission's officers took the time to express his thanks to the various individual infantry officers who had accompanied them over the two years of the work, but there is almost no mention of the cavalry, and certainly no compliments paid to Major Reno. Chief Commissioner Campbell, who might have been expected at least to make some formal expression of gratitude, no matter how strained, chose to ignore him as well.

Greene wrote that infantry leader Ames "... did everything in his power to facilitate the work of the survey, and I feel the more grateful to him as his interests were entirely opposite to mine."[5] Nevertheless, in Greene's opinion, "[Ames's] force was inadequate and his instructions too circumscribed to have allowed him to materially aid us in case the Indians, who hovered about our trail, had at any time proved troublesome."[6] Further, the young lieutenant hinted at some deeper trouble that may have remained just below the surface of his relationship with Ames and Reno:

> The question of the relations between an officer in charge of a surveying-party and the officer in command of his escort, is at best a vexed one, and particularly so when the surveying-officer, who must necessarily direct the movements, is the junior, and I am glad to be able to record my appreciation of the forbearance and kindness exhibited by all the officers who were detailed with me.[7]

JUST AFTER DAWN on the morning of August 12, Chief Commissioner Campbell, Chief Astronomer Twining and Elliot Coues left the depot at West Butte and headed out along what was becoming a well-worn trail along the boundary line toward the Rocky Mountains. With the cool, clear heights of the Sweetgrass at their backs, and despite the snow-white peaks of the Rockies shimmering on the horizon ahead, the trek across the last eighty miles or so of the Milk River country was, for Coues, a "tedious march through... monotonous country."[8] Despite its wealth of bird life, it was all too much of a muchness: "the eternal sameness of flat, dusty, treeless prairie, where the ground and the water and the air are loaded with Glauber's salts and other vile saline compounds."[9]

By the afternoon of August 13, Campbell and Twining had set up an overnight camp on the North Branch of the Milk River. Finding the site would have been easy; it had been well marked by D'Arcy East and his 49th Rangers during their earlier reconnaissances. If that were not clear enough, they had only to follow Featherstonhaugh's tangent line. He had crossed the North Branch of the Milk and reached the site four days earlier. By the 13th he was already thirty miles further west, on the banks of the Belly River, getting ready to take his last set of observations.

That evening, as he settled in after a long day's travel, Commissioner Campbell was more than a little surprised to receive a visitor:

> Captain Cameron, the British Commissioner, unexpectedly made his appearance among us, having just returned from the summit of the Rocky Mountains, where the survey was rapidly progressing to a conclusion. As this was the last opportunity before the parties would be withdrawn from the field, we held a meeting of the joint commission at our camp.[10]

MUCH HAD HAPPENED to Cameron in the fortnight since he had slipped out of West Butte depot. Travelling in his familiar buckboard with a small escort of 49th Rangers, he had made good time, and by about August 4 he had established a sort of base camp deep in the foothills somewhere near the site of the Rocky Mountain depot. From there he had been forced to abandon his wagon and continue on horseback, with a two-man escort and pack horses in tow. When Anderson, heading west toward his own attempt to reach the Divide, came upon the camp on about the 9th, he was informed that Cameron had been gone for five days and had been expected back for a day or two. Anderson, with no small amount of pleasure, told the rest of the story in yet another lengthy letter to his mother:

> He turned up at last at my camp late at night and early in the morning in the hope of avoiding an unpleasant scene, I had arranged to move westward, but he sent for me before I started and fortunately there was no disturbance… It turned out that Capt. C. in his journey into the mountains had put himself & his two native attendants to great hardship and they never got to the end of the Line after all, which was rather humiliating.[11]

Dr. Millman, who arrived at the Rocky Mountain depot on August 10, reported that he met Cameron there, "… having just returned from the West. He failed to find the terminal line of the old commission. He reports seeing a grizzly bear."[12] According to Cameron, it was the bear's terrifying effect on his pack animals that prevented him from carrying on to the summit.

On the morning of the 10th, Anderson left the Rocky Mountain depot for his own attempt at the summit, and Cameron prepared for his long ride back to Pembina. Their second encounter of the season had gone no better than the first. Anderson was still smarting from his treatment back at the West Butte, and Cameron was surely more than a little annoyed to have failed in his attempt to reach the Divide. According to Anderson, writing in another long letter home at the very end of the season:

> I told him I expected to finish on 31 Aug. and to be ready to commence our march homewards and that the wintering establishment at Pembina might be broken up. This as you may imagine

was rather a startling proposition, seeing that Capt. Cameron has spent a great deal in a house and farm at Pembina and has moved his wife and family there. It is impossible to say what will be the final arrangements, as Captain Cameron never acts straightforwardly or like a reasonable being.[13]

While Anderson could write that "It is an immense relief that Capt. C. is gone, and no further mischief done,"[14] he was soon to discover that Cameron had, indeed, managed at least one more mean-spirited gesture while on his way back to Dufferin. The chief astronomer goes on to describe what was, for him, yet another outrage:

I got away from him as soon as possible, but two days afterwards a letter from him was sent after me full of complaints and rude language, which I cared very little about, but he was determined to do something practically distasteful to us, so he cut down the ration of meat daily for each man from 1½ lbs to 1 lb. If anything could be calculated to cause mutiny and trouble among our working parties it is a vexatious reduction of their allowance of food. The reduction now ordered is the work of a madman, as our cattle having made a journey of 800 miles are not fat and the principal portion of the ration of beef is bone. After fulminating this order, Capt. C. posts back to Pembina as hard as he can go, so as to be out or reach of remonstrance.[15]

Anderson may have been too quick to criticize his commanding officer for past wrongs, real or imagined, but it is impossible to see any motivation behind Cameron's reduction of the meat allowance other than simple meanness. Not even Cameron was suggesting that the scrawny, worn-out remnants of the cattle herd were to be driven back to Dufferin. Announcing the reduction by letter rather than facing the men himself was also indefensible behaviour in a commanding officer.

Since his terrible fall in mid-June, Valentine Rowe had spent weeks in his tent on the prairie west of the Wood End depot. Under the watchful eyes of Chief Surgeon Burgess and Lieutenant Ward, Rowe had drifted in and out of consciousness, seeming to recover his senses one day and then slipping back into a near-coma the next. It was Burgess's opinion that, if and when Rowe's condition improved significantly, he should be taken back to Dufferin and, from there sent either to New York or home to Liverpool for treatment by a specialist. Feeling he could ill afford to lose yet another officer to accompany Rowe, Anderson had dispatched his sergeant major from Wood Mountain to remain at Rowe's camp until he was ready to travel, and then escort him back to Dufferin.

By the end of July Anderson was receiving encouraging reports from Ward and the doctor, and even received a letter from Rowe himself:

> ... tho' he has certainly improved greatly and is able to reason, it is impossible to say to what extent his brain will ultimately be affected. He wrote me a perfectly rational letter signing his name with the postscript—"at least I believe that it's me." He feels his brain is in great confusion and is able to reason and talk about the symptoms, and he is undoubtedly gaining strength, so all immediate danger is I think at an end...[16]

Finally, just as Anderson came down from his trek to the Divide, Arthur Ward arrived in camp with good news. Rowe had recovered to the point where it had been possible to move him out of his tent on the prairie. Rather than taking him back east immediately, he was well enough to have been brought forward as far as the Wood Mountain depot, ready to be taken east at the beginning of September with the first retreating parties.

Sadly, as Anderson reported, not all of Ward's news was so good:

> Our doctor [Burgess] after seeing Rowe out of danger, was coming on to join us in the front but he unfortunately encountered Capt. Cameron on the way, who turned him back and thus deprived him of the chance of seeing the Rocky Mtns.[17]

Like the cut in the beef allowance, it is hard to see Cameron's treatment of Burgess as anything other than simple meanness.

ON AUGUST 13, when Cameron drove his buckboard into Campbell's camp on the North Branch of the Milk River, it had been almost a year since the two men had set eyes on each other. They had last met at the Wood End depot on September 11, 1873, and that meeting had, as usual, left Campbell in a terrible mood and everyone around him walking on eggshells for several days thereafter.

During the current season, there had been so little contact between the senior officers of the British and American parties, it is probably safe to assume that commissioner Campbell was unaware of what had transpired between Dufferin, Ottawa and London throughout the previous winter and spring. Cameron's easy capitulation on the matter of the Northwest Angle, therefore, may have come as a bit of a surprise. Campbell's account of the meeting in his final report is typically brief and straightforward. It is not, however, entirely accurate. About the Northwest Angle, he writes:

> Captain Cameron stated that he was now prepared to agree to the northwesternmost point of the Lake of the Woods, as determined by the chief astronomers of the United States and British Commissions, his government having directed him to acknowledge the reference-monument pointed out to the chief astronomers by Indians residing in the vicinity.[18]

Campbell then goes on to deal with the other outstanding matter: the disagreement about whether the boundary should be an astronomical or a mean parallel. In this, he suggests that Cameron again capitulated:

> He also agreed to adopt the astronomical parallel as the true boundary instead of the mean parallel, which he had hitherto strongly urged, and which would have been a great additional expense without any corresponding benefit.[19]

In fact, Cameron did no such thing. In a letter he presented at the meeting (whether he had been carrying it around in anticipation of seeing the American commissioner or wrote it on the spot is not clear), the British commissioner made it clear that he still believed in a mean parallel. The letter indicates his willingness to agree both to the authenticity and position of the northwest reference monument and to the positioning of the monuments west from Lake of the Woods, "Provided it be understood that... the line between these astronomically determined points shall follow a course having the uniform curvature of a parallel of 49° of north latitude."[20] In other words, that the line follow a mean parallel between the monuments.

How Campbell could have accepted the letter and, subsequently, allowed the phrase to appear in the final, signed documents is not clear. Perhaps the commissioner, who understood perfectly well what he was agreeing to, was simply willing to do almost anything to get Cameron out of his camp and on his way back to Dufferin. The actual difference between a mean and an astronomical parallel, when the monuments are only a mile or two apart, is so insignificant as to be virtually unmeasurable. In order to get rid of Cameron, Campbell would certainly have been prepared to agree to something that had almost no real effect on the validity of the work and, if necessary, could be countermanded at a later stage by agreement between the two governments, or overturned by a subsequent treaty (as, in fact, it eventually was).

At first light the next morning, Cameron was on his way east. Later that day, Campbell, Twining and their party packed up and headed west toward their own attempt to crest the Great Divide.

FROM THE ROCKY Mountain depot, just west of the St. Mary River, it was less than thirty straight-line miles to the terminal monument up on the Great Divide. In that thirty miles, however, lay an overall ascent of more than 4,000 feet, covered by dense timber, riddled with fast-flowing creeks and cut by precipitous canyons. It was by far the most difficult and unforgiving terrain they had faced since tangling with the bogs and deadfall of the great Roseau swamp.

The rangers' reconnaissances had shown that the 49th Parallel, after crossing the St. Mary, passed about six miles north of the massive Chief Mountain and then struck the Belly River at a point that would probably be inaccessible for even the lightest wagons. Immediately west of the Belly, the line would run hard up against the massive slope of Mount Wilson, pass directly over the mountain crest and then drop precipitously into Waterton Lake. The rangers could not make any determination about the likely position of the line between the lake and the terminal monument beyond and above it but, through their telescopes, the deep ravines and heavily wooded slopes of the lake's western shore did not look the least bit inviting.

In order to keep the work moving as quickly as possible, the commissions had already agreed to a change in procedure. The British would observe at two consecutive stations—38 and 39—at the St. Mary and Belly rivers. When the Americans had finished their observations on the North Branch of the Milk River (station 37), they would swing north and west around Mount Wilson to arrive at the north end of Waterton Lake. From there, they would move south toward the line and establish the final astronomical station, number 40, on the lake's western shore.

With Galwey and his party taking their observations at Rocky Mountain depot, Featherstonhaugh pushed on to the Belly River. Thomas Millman recorded the day in his diary on August 13:

> Clear and mild day—mosquitoes very bad. In the forenoon we shifted camp two miles further up stream—going to observe here with zenith telescope. We are about five miles north of the line, camped on a piece of prairie with [the] river east of us, up against a very high hill and another to west of us, with the mountains about four miles away... Could not get south further with the waggons without a great deal of trouble.[21]

What Millman described in his diary was the major problem faced by any astronomical survey party when working in mountainous or heavily wooded country. The site selected for the observations required clear lines of sight, not only of the sky, but—to enable the zenith telescope to do its work—on the ground for nearly a mile to the north and south.

Finally, according to Featherstonhaugh: "... after about ten days spent in cutting through the dense woods on the foot hills of the mountains, and triangulating up the difficult valley of the Belly River, [we] had made good the boundary up to the sides of Mount Wilson."[22]

Escaping from Commissioner Cameron on August 10, Anderson had taken George Dawson and half a dozen axemen and headed west toward the Divide. From the site of the Belly River station he had gone north and west around the base of Mount Wilson and camped at the north end of Waterton Lake. Unable to take his wagons, or even his pack animals, farther south along the west side of the lake, and with only about seven miles between him and the 1861 terminal monument, Anderson set out on foot:

> I spent one day travelling in the direction required on foot, but made very little progress, as the bottoms of the mountain ravines were rocky and choked up with drift wood, and the only possibility of making any progress at all was by clambering up the mountain sides beyond the limit of the growth of trees, and then picking one's way along the rocky but bare sides of the ravines. This was all very well for a time, tho' walking continuously on a rocky slope is very tiring, and destructive to one's boots, but our progress would not have been stopped except by the side ravines which continually obstructed ones course, and obliged one to descend to a depth of 2 or 300 feet, thro' dense timber and up again on the other side, making very little distance practicable in a the course of a days travel.[23]

Giving up on any hope of hiking up to the monument along the line of the 49th Parallel (something Cameron had also attempted, with much the same result), Anderson was:

> ... glad to take advantage of an Indian trail crossing the summit of the Rocky Mountains at an elevation of about 6,400 feet above

the sea, or 2,000 feet above the plain at the base of the mountains, and joining a track cut out by the former Commission leading from the western country direct to the terminal point.[24]

What Anderson had come upon was the eastern gateway to the old South Kootenay Pass, a trail he had travelled some thirteen years before with the Pacific boundary survey. The pass had first been identified and mapped by Thomas Blakiston, a member of the Palliser expedition who had used the pass in the late summer of 1858 to return across the Divide from his explorations in the Kootenay country of southern British Columbia. He had called it the Boundary Pass, and a copy of his map was in the hands of both the American and British Pacific boundary commissions as they had approached the Divide in 1860–61.

Like most of the other long-used passes that traversed the front range of the Rocky Mountains and led across the Continental Divide, the South Kootenay was badly overgrown and blocked by deadfall. With the collapse of the fur trade several decades earlier, east–west traffic across the west had dropped drastically. Even the old trade routes between the tribes of the plains and those of the inter-mountain valleys had largely been abandoned, and the exact location—even the very existence—of many passes had been lost to memory. It was not until the intensive explorations of the transcontinental railway surveyors that many of them would be rediscovered, only to be abandoned again when the surveyors found some other, more appealing route.

No matter how rough the passage, Anderson would not be denied his return to the Divide monument. Moving slowly through the overgrown pass, he crossed the Divide and, once on the other side, pitched camp at the place where the Pacific boundary surveyors had left the main trail and headed up toward the summit:

> This old track was terribly choked up by fallen timber, and we were 10 hours going 10 miles with four axemen hard at work all the time cutting all the fallen trees that were too high for the animals to stride over... It was necessary to lead each horse, or they would run off the track and roll and break everything... The track

we cut out 13 years ago showed no signs of having been travelled since the time we left it... The axemarks on the trees made 13 years ago were still very distinct... We found the old monument... in perfect preservation and not a stone had rolled out of its place... From the summit, in all directions, a mass of sharp pointed and in many cases snow-clad peaks were seen, and between the mountain ranges lakes fed by the melting snow supplied the springs which found their way westward to the Pacific and on the eastward side to Hudson's Bay.[25]

For Dawson, the climb to the monument and the sights it had afforded had been well worth the effort. It was his first serious attempt at mountaineering, but it would be far from his last. Despite his delicate condition, he would go on to spend many years exploring and mapping the Canadian northwest, happily clambering up countless impossibly rugged peaks (many of which were acknowledged as first ascents) and then sliding back down to camp before dinner, weighted down by great bags of geological samples.

No doubt thoroughly pleased with himself (as he had every right to be), Anderson made good time coming down from the monument. Just as he was emerging from the pass, he met Campbell and Twining, accompanied by Greene and a dozen of his men, on their way up to the Divide. The American chief commissioner and his chief astronomer had arrived at the Waterton Lake camp on August 17, to be followed in the next day by Greene. The lieutenant had already completed all of his tangent work up to the British station at the Rocky Mountain depot and his mound-building and topographical parties were only a short distance behind him.

Dawson's diary entry for the day conveys something of his delight in the work, and his overall good sense of humour:

On this trip food has consisted of bread & boiled beef cold, well enough as long as it lasts but now grub of all kinds becoming scarce. Reduced to bread & tea & barely enough of that. Expect to meet beef tomorrow at noon on arriving at camp No.1.

Found Liet. Greene camped...had lunch with him. Found him luxuriating in fresh butter, ham, various sorts of bread & cakes.[26]

When the Americans had left their Waterton Lake camp on August 20, Campbell was probably not entertaining any serious thoughts of reaching the terminal monument himself. It was thirteen years since he had last been in the Rocky Mountains and he would well remember just how rugged the going could be. As it was, both the commissioner and Twining turned back when they reached the summit of Boundary Pass. If they had not reached the monument, they had at least reached the Divide. Greene and his men, however, pressed on and, on the morning of August 23 they reached the Akamina station. According to Greene, he had travelled forty miles by trail in order to cover just seven straight-line miles.

Akamina had been the final observation station for the Pacific boundary commissions, occupied by the Americans in 1860 and by the British in 1861, and from it, on the 24th, Greene took time to write a letter home:

Leaving camp this morning, it was a hard scramble up on to the divide and from that with our hands and knees we hauled ourselves up over the rocks, where my dog could not follow, to the top. A quarter of a mile to the Southeast in a saddle of the divide at an altitude of 6,700 feet stands a well shapen pyramid of unhewn limestone... It is in an admirable position; from its base you can push a stone loose with your foot and it will go thundering down the mountainside near half a mile into a lake [it would be named Cameron Lake] the water of which eventually reaches Hudson's Bay. Looking west you can fire a pistol shot down into another lake [Upper Kintla Lake] which discharges to the Pacific Ocean.[27]

The party passed three pleasant days at Camp Akamina, where they spent their time exploring the mountains, triangulating the exact height and location for several of the major peaks in the area and, of course, carving their names on the terminal monument.

Featherstonhaugh caught the gentle mood surrounding the commissions' last campsite:

It was now the end of summer, but the weather was still clear and warm, and the beautiful scenery, amidst which the parties suddenly found themselves, contrasted strongly with the monotonous plains on which they had been working for so long. Instead of short and scanty herbage, the grass was now luxuriant and rich; clear and impetuous streams took the place of muddy and stagnant pools, and the eye once more rejoiced with the sight of trees and foliage. Wild fowl and dusky grouse abounded, and the rivers were full of salmon trout of from 3 to 5 lbs in weight.[28]

Of Waterton Lake itself he wrote:

This beautiful piece of water which is 9 miles long and about 1 mile wide, lies between mountains whose sides rise precipitously for 3,000 or 4,000 feet from the water's edge, and resembles somewhat the Lake of Lucerne, in Switzerland... On one side nothing is seen but a crowd of mountain peaks filling the whole perspective; on the other a level plain stretches to the horizon, and seems to differ only in colour from the sea. The lake, lying immediately below the feet of the spectator, lends its beauty to the scene, and a unique grandeur is derived from the reflection that the mountains extend in unbroken series to the Pacific Ocean, 400 miles away, while the plains, bare and treeless, stretch for twice that distance in the opposite direction.[29]

With little in the way of official business to occupy their time, the men of both commissions loafed around the camp, reading or napping in the afternoon sun, or went exploring along the many creeks and valleys that surrounded the lake. For many of the men, however, their time in the Rockies became a grand fishing trip.

Anderson noted: "It was no uncommon thing for a man, during an afternoon's fishing with a rod and line and grasshopper bait, to bring home a sackful of 3lb trout by the evening.["]30 For several days, Mill-man seems to have done little else: "Cap't F. and I went fishing for the day. Got quite a haul. The heaviest weighed 3lbs. Found them very delicious when cooked. They have the taste of soles."31

Elliott Coues thought he could identify four distinct species of trout and "salmon trout" in the mountain lakes and streams and he, too, was impressed by the fishing:

> The main stem of a stout willow bush, or trunk of a young spruce tree, furnished the rod; any stout cord the line; grasshoppers the bait. The men who were the most successful in taking large salmon used a hook that would do for halibut, extemporized out of the iron handle of an army mess-kettle and baited with a chunk of salt pork.32

JAMES GREGORY and his astronomical party completed their work on the North Branch of the Milk River and moved west along the boundary line to the St. Mary River crossing. From there, they fol-lowed the river north for a few miles before turning west again toward Waterton Lake:

> Hemmed in on all sides by ranges of towering, precipitous moun-tains, whose peaks rise from two thousand to six thousand four hundred feet above it, the lake is unapproachable by any route save by the valley of its outlet, the Waterton River.
>
>   By turning northward, therefore, from a point on the bound-ary-line about twenty miles east of the lake, we headed off the outlying mountain-range, and following up the valley of the Waterton River, reached the foot of the lake, with our wagons, on the 18th of August. Camp was pitched the same evening on a fine shingle-beach at the foot of the lake, a position which, besides the practical desideratum of proximity to an abundant supply of pure, cold water, afforded us also a comprehensive view of the lake and mountain scenery, which, for picturesque beauty and grandeur, is probably not excelled, if equalled, by any on the continent.33

It was a beautiful sight, to be sure, but eventually Gregory would have to face a problem that had been patently obvious to anyone who visited the camp. Although the 49th Parallel lay just three and a half miles to the south, it was utterly inaccessible. On the eastern shore, the slopes of Mount Wilson dropped precipitously into the lake, while across the water the western shore looked even less inviting. Anderson had spent a hard day looking for a way to reach the line from the north and given it up for a lost cause. It was also far too late in the season for Gregory to entertain any thoughts of retracing his steps and trying to come at the line from the south. So with more than seven miles of ground that they needed to survey between the western shore and the Divide, there was only one solution: if Gregory could not go around the lake, he would simply have to go across it.

Despite the matter-of-fact reporting of his decision—"I was obliged to cast about for means of water-transportation"—Gregory must at least have sensed the serious risks inherent in such a decision. Although during his years with the geodetic survey of the Great Lakes he would have spent as much time on water as on land, neither he nor his men had any experience with the dangerously unpredictable nature of western mountain lakes. The only water they had so far encountered during their two seasons in the field had either been shallow enough to ford or narrow enough to throw a temporary bridge across. Waterton Lake was something very different at seven miles long and up to a mile wide. Gregory reported, "...the lake is, of course, clear and cold, and of great depth. I regret that I had at hand no means of taking soundings. A piece of twine over three hundred feet long, with a heavy weight attached, did not reach bottom when let out at a point about two hundred yards from the shore."[34]

Had they not been so close to the end of their odyssey, it is unlikely that Gregory would have risked his men and the invaluable instruments on such a harebrained scheme. Were it not the very last piece of the boundary line, the plan would certainly never have been approved by either Campbell or Twining. As it was, they must have learned of it before they left for the Divide, and must therefore have given it at least some sort of official sanction.

Once the decision had been taken, the work proceeded apace:

After some experiments with improvised boats composed of wagon-boxes with covers of tent-canvas, which failed on account of the permeability to water of the thin canvas, I finally achieved success in two boats which were modifications of the above. One of these was a wagon-box with the ends and all cracks covered with pieces of raw-hide closely tacked on, and the whole covered with canvas. The other, as the supply of hide was exhausted, was a wagon-box fastened on top of a raft composed of seven logs, to which additional buoyancy was given by securing empty water-casks between the outside logs on each side of the raft.[35]

Not surprisingly, both craft proved terribly unstable. Their centres of gravity were so high that, as Gregory put it: "Paddles were used for propulsion, the paddlers being squatted in the bottom, as the crankiness of the boats would not permit the use of elevated seats such as are necessary for oarsmen."[36] Lewis Boss, the intrepid assistant astronomer, was the first to take Boat No.1 (as the canvas-covered wagon box had been unromantically christened) out for a shakedown cruise. While waiting for the second craft to be finished, Boss and a small number of men paddled around the northern end of the lake tidying up the last few details of the geodetic and topographical work.

If the leaking and dangerous instability of his new craft did not dissuade Gregory from his plan, the events of the next forty-eight hours perhaps should have. As his makeshift fleet lay on the shore, being loaded with supplies and the precious instruments, one of Waterton Lake's terrible storms blew up out of nowhere, pinning the men in their tents for two days. Fully exposed on the shore, the boats were nearly battered to pieces by the wind and the waves.

With his confidence no doubt shaken, but still in better condition than his boats, Gregory ordered repairs and, two days later, they were ready to depart. Determined to make as short a job of it as possible, he once again tempted fate:

On the evening of the 22nd, the night, though dark, was still, and I determined to take advantage of the lull to make, at least, part of the distance to the boundary-line before daylight... I embarked, about 8 pm, with my assistants, Mr. Boss and Mr. Edgerton, and five men, the necessary instruments, seven days' rations, and as much camp-equipage as was absolutely necessary. Once fairly out upon the lake the darkness appeared thicker than before, and land positions were totally unrecognizable. The labour of forcing the unwieldy and heavily-loaded crafts through the water, and our constrained positions in the bottom of the boats, which we were unable to relieve by change, as the slightest motion produced unpleasant tips, suggestive of capsize and the certain loss of all our instruments, made us all very tired, and we were glad to find a convenient little beach where we landed about 11 pm, and bivouacked for the night. We had made, in the three hours of toilsome paddling, about one and a half miles.

In the early morning we were again under way, and arrived about 9 am at a good landing-place on the western shore, which was opposite a point on the eastern shore previously determined... to be, approximately, in latitude 49°. There we landed our effects, and near by, on a convenient bottom-land, set up the observatory, where the astronomical work was begun the same evening.[37]

With the station established, Gregory began to search for some way to establish a link with the stone cairn perched on the Continental Divide just seven miles to the west. Clambering his way up the steep ravines in search of a suitable place "by means of which a trigonometrical connection could be effected, [after] several hours of toilsome climbing,"[38] he reluctantly abandoned the project. Without finding a spot from which both marker and station were visible, he could not plot a triangle with which to complete the topographical survey. With time running out, that was a task that would have to be left to a future expedition.

While Gregory looked for a way up from the lake, Lewis Boss paddled out in No.1 and worked on his shoreline surveys. "Though the boat was more manageable when not loaded down with freight," wrote Gregory, "it was yet very unwieldy, and could be propelled but slowly with great expenditure of power, and as the lake was subject to sudden flaws and squalls, crossing it in such a craft, was not only difficult but a matter of considerable concern as to safety."[39]

At about noon on August 26, with the final boundary monument built and the lakeshore surveys complete, Gregory and Boss were finished with station 40, and—lacking the time and resources to complete a topographic survey of such mountainous terrain—they had done as much as they could. While their geodetic work may have been completed, however, their nautical adventures were far from over. They were still on the west side of the lake and the afternoon winds were freshening. Realizing that the longer he delayed his departure the more perilous the trip would become, Gregory ordered the camp struck:

> The instruments, &c., were repacked in the boats the same afternoon, and, although the wind was blowing almost a gale from the south, making the lake very rough, it was a fair wind for us, and all hands preferred taking the chances of disaster in the day-time, to risking the possibilities of another night-trip. We therefore started about 3 pm, and by means of square sails extemporized from tent-flies, sped along in quite gallant style. Our unceasing efforts were, however, required to keep the crafts before the wind, and tolerably free from water. The surf was running very high upon the beach near camp, and I greatly feared the danger of capsize in the attempt to land there, for which there was no alternative; but this calamity was averted by several of my men, who from the shore were anxiously watching our progress. They appreciated the situation, and making into the breakers, at exactly the proper moment, seized each boat, as she arrived in shoal water, and bore her upon the wave-crests, high and dry upon the beach.[40]

· 12 ·

THE END
OF THE LINE

I can only say I heartily wish I had more of it to
look forward to. I don't know that I ever enjoyed myself more.

FRANCIS GREENE

O N AUGUST 26, 1874, Captain
Gregory and his nautical party
sailed triumphantly back into
their Waterton Lake camp just in time for dinner. Except for a few
loose ends, the demarcation of the international boundary between
Canada and the United States of America was complete. If there were
great celebrations, no one saw fit to record them in a diary or letter
home. Gregory's only mention of the end of the two-year adventure
was cool and matter-of-fact: "Immediate preparations were made for
the march eastwards, which was begun next morning."[1]

Pulling out with Gregory and his men on August 27 were Commissioner Campbell, Secretary Bangs, Twining, Coues and all the rest of
the Americans save Greene and his parties. They did not come down
from the summit until the 28th, and then spent another day at the
Waterton Lake camp completing his triangulations. On the morning
of August 30, Greene, too, left the lake and headed east.

The British and the Canadians had also begun their final retreat on the 27th. Featherstonhaugh and his men, all of whom had been relaxing at the Waterton Lake camp after completing their astronomical and tangent work, led the way out in the early afternoon, making their way to the Rocky Mountain depot on the St. Mary River. There they found Galwey and his party, happy to be finished with running tangents and building mounds west to station 39 on the Belly River. Secretary Ward and Boswell, the veterinarian, joined them later that evening. Anderson stayed at the lake until the next morning, no doubt making sure nothing had been left behind.

That same morning, Featherstonhaugh and Galwey began to tie up those few loose ends. The British gamble to delay building the boundary markers until after the astronomical work was finished was about to pay off handsomely. With the weather still holding, the two parties started east, building mounds as they went. Millman and Ward went out with them while Anderson and the rest remained at the depot, making sure the animals and equipment were ready for the strain of a 750-mile quick march back to Dufferin.

The stone boundary markers were described by Millman: "They are conical, ten feet in diameter at base and six feet high. They also put a small iron plate in a hole two feet deep and ten feet east of centre of mound. The plate is eight inches in diameter, shaped like a soup plate. It has around the edge 'British and United States Boundary Line.' In the centre is 'North 49th Latitude.'"[2] The iron plate was designed to ensure that the boundary marker could be relocated and rebuilt in the event of being lost.

Ashe and East kept their topographical party at work around Waterton Lake until the morning of August 29. Dawson stayed with them, happy to continue his sketching and painting, and clambering into the rocks in search of interesting strata. He took note of both sandhill and whooping cranes (the first he had seen since crossing the Coteau back in June) and continued to build his collections of rocks and plants—and, when he could, animals. It seems, however, that for a nineteenth-century naturalist, Dawson remained a rather poor hand with a gun. His diary is filled with accounts of shots taken and missed, whether at huge bison on the open prairie or the tiny pika (or, as he called them, "rock rabbits") in the scree beside the campsite.

Though the nights were growing colder, daytime temperatures still pushed up into the mid-70s and, despite the occasional after-noon thundershower, the men finished their work under a brilliant late summer sun. It was an idyllic end to a perfect week in the moun-tains, with the broad, clear lake, in Dawson's words, "... under the influence of the strong and continuous south wind, making a noise like the sea."[3]

Featherstonhaugh, too, was sad to leave, though he had never for-gotten the early storms that had hammered the commission the past two Septembers:

> Nothing more remained to be done in the mountains, and after a day or two spent in visiting the Lake and the Kootenay Pass, the parties struck their camps and commenced their homeward march. It was not without reluctance that the beautiful and lux-uriant scenery of the mountain valleys was left behind and the dreary plains once more entered upon; but all knew how long a journey lay before them, and how suddenly and unmistakeably the winter might commence, so that, once started, the hope of getting back in good time was an efficient stimulus to travelling; the horses and ponies were also in remarkably good condition from their fortnight's repose and good living.[4]

The main body of the American commission had headed back toward the Sweetgrass Hills, from where they would turn south to Fort Benton and the Missouri River. Lieutenant Greene, still two or three days behind, paused at the Rocky Mountain depot where he met with his assistant astronomer, Charles Doolittle. Transferring a num-ber of his own mound builders to Doolittle's party, Greene sent them off to reconnoitre the Riplinger Road, one of the principal whiskey trade trails, which skirted the base of the mountains from Fort Shaw to the Blackfeet Agency on the Teton River and then north across the 49th Parallel to the Oldman River. Doolittle was to follow the road down to Fort Shaw and then track the Missouri east to meet up with the rest of the American commission at Fort Benton. With Doolittle sent on his way, Greene headed for the Sweetgrass Hills, arriving at the depot on September 2.

Whiskey trails like the Riplinger Road and the more famous Whoop-Up Trail, which ran from Fort Benton north to the site of present-day Lethbridge, Alberta, were among the scourges that had brought the need to mark the 49th Parallel to the fore. Suppressing the trade in illicit whiskey would be the first priority for the new Canadian mounted police force when, and if, it finally arrived. Curiously, in all the reports, journals, diaries and letters written by the men of both commissions, there are few mentions of the whiskey traders. Millman reported a small band of Peigan he met just west of the North Milk had urged the commission to wipe out the traders and, as he was leaving the Rocky Mountain depot for the long march home, he wrote that "Many of the men bought Indian ponies from the whiskey traders. The prices ranged from $15.00 to $50.00."[5] Dawson paid $25 for his raw mount: "It *may* be a very nice beast when it learns a thing or two," he wrote to Anna, "but any way will answer my purpose in enabling me to ride or drive as I may please on the way in."[6]

Several histories of the area have included stories of drinking binges involving the traders and the men of the British boundary commission, but most of the tales are either insubstantial or seem unlikely. One encounter is said to have taken place in late September 1874, but the men of the boundary commission were long gone by then. It is not likely that any of the Royal Engineers or American soldiers would have been free to go off drinking with the traders, and since the Americans did not use civilian teamsters anywhere west of the Sweetgrass Hills, that leaves only the British commission's hired men as potential buyers of the illicit whiskey. While the teamsters might well have made good customers, by the time the British commission reached the Whoop-Up Trail, most of the heavy freight wagons had already turned back toward Dufferin for the last time. As for the officers, they had their own special sources of supply. When the

British parties settled in at the Sweetgrass depot, Dr. Millman noted that his medical supplies of brandy and wine had been "freely used."[7]

Dawson certainly met the traders as he wandered the trails along the St. Mary River and, on August 30, he wrote of a meeting between his party and one group that was on its way north to "Fort Hoop-up":

> One of them told me that they had got over 8,000 robes last season. They have plenty good horses and lend them to "young fancy bucks" among the indians who for the mere pleasure of riding a good horse and excitement of the chase hunt buffalo and bring the robes back to the traders. One of the traders said that the other winter he made up his mind to get a "clean thousand" robes himself and did so... Last year when the indians came into trade he mentioned as a very clever business that they had managed to "clean them out" of all they had in a day.[8]

Curiously, no one mentions the rotgut whiskey which was at the very heart of the northwestern robe trade. It beggars belief that those "young fancy bucks" would deliver prime robes simply to say thanks for the loan of a decent horse. More likely, the only reason to have brought in robes (or even to have returned the horses) was the promise of liquor.

AFTER SPENDING LESS than 48 hours relaxing at the Sweetgrass depot, Greene was on the move again. As soon as the last topographical party came into camp, it was reprovisioned and, together with Greene and his tangent party—a total of some 40 men—started south toward Fort Shaw.

It was at the Sweetgrass depot that Greene (in a long letter to his parents written nearly a month later) reported the first real signs of trouble between the commissions and the local Native populations:

> I arrived there on the 2nd of Sept. and found quite a small city of tents, all our own and the English parties being there and 3 Cos. of our escort. While we had been away, ourselves & the English had

each a supply depot there, ours guarded by 25 men & the English by 2 men with red ribbons on their hats, & the English flag flying over the tent! – the two depots were about 1,500 feet apart. One morning a party of about 200 Piegan (Blackfeet) Indians came to make a friendly call, and thinking that English hospitality was not quite equal to its world wide reputation, quietly helped themselves to whatever they wanted. They came over to our depot but the Sergt. of the detachment turned out his men and summarily ordered them off. They did not care to fight and left.[9]

It is not clear whether the raid played out as Greene reported it, or whether he was having some fun at the expense of the British. There had certainly been a genuine threat to the depot. When Millman arrived at the Sweetgrass on September 1, he reported that Canadian sub-assistant astronomer George Burpee was already there: "He left the mountains a few days ago in charge of a small party to help defend the depot as Fish [the depot keeper] thought he was going to 'be gone through' by the Indians."[10]

The account that probably comes closest to describing exactly what happened at the West Butte is contained in George Dawson's letter to his sister. Written from the Sweetgrass depot on September 3, Dawson saw the incident as something less than an outright raid, but more than a simple trading session:

We, that is to say self, Capt A. & party, Ashe & party & East with the scouts constitute the rear guard & are lying over here for a day to get some repairs &c. effected & pack up the remains of the Depot. I say the remains for the indians have got most of what was left here. Only 3 men were left to guard the place & when some 400 Peagins came & camped down beside them they did not feel particularly strong. The indians did not actually take anything by force but came in & examined the things & said they must have so & so & they got it. In this way the whole of the tea & sugar was disposed of & most of the matches & a good many other things besides. The chief presented the depotman with various whips, lariats, &c. & the whole thing was perfectly amicable but much to the disadvantage of the commission. Fortunately we are ahead of our time & consequently have plenty & if the depots at East Fork & Woody Mt are safe will be all right.[11]

Greene's grinning poke at Cameron and his red ribbons belies the real difference in the attitude with which each party had approached the Native populations from the very start. The British and the Canadians simply did not believe there was any real risk to the safety of their men. While they recognized that the theft of supplies and horses from the isolated depots could present them with serious logistical problems, they believed such raids could be minimized by an open friendliness and a few modest gifts, backed up with as small a show of arms as possible. They were also convinced that the plains nations had a fundamentally different attitude toward the British and Canadians than they did toward the Americans.

When he was at the West Butte depot at the beginning of August, Dawson reported hearing of another incident between the Sioux and the boundary parties—this one involving the American chief commissioner himself. A returning scout had reported that Campbell:

... had been met 3 days E. of here by a party of Sioux numbering about 800 lodges. He refused to give them anything and his escort being small (15 men) the indians quietly cut the traces of his mules and took all the provisions they could find, leaving him scarcely enough to get into Camp on.[12]

Dawson concludes his note with the opinion that "the report may be exaggerated," which is probably correct, since neither Campbell nor Reno mention anything like it happening, and Greene would certainly have enjoyed the opportunity to report any incident of American bravado in the face of overwhelming odds.

As far as the Americans were concerned, the only thing that had kept their astronomical and surveying parties safe through two seasons in the field had been the presence of a large military escort. Further, they were convinced it was that same U.S. Army escort, rather than the Natives' attitude, which had kept the British parties from harm as well. Looking at the record of the relationship between the commissions and the various Native populations, it is hard not to agree with the American position.

The United States Cavalry certainly engendered a mixture of fear and respect in the peoples of the northern plains. The small bands of Wahpeton Sioux that had lived in southern Manitoba since the Minnesota troubles of a decade before were genuinely distressed by the idea that once the 49th Parallel had been marked, they would be pushed south across it and back into the United States. While the British officers were careful to assure the Sioux that such a thing was not being contemplated, the Sioux must have believed that any act of aggression toward the British parties—even a minor raid on a depot or a couple of stolen horses—could be enough to change the attitude of the new Canadian government and see themselves driven back across the border into the unwelcome grasp of the American cavalry and, especially, the still-angry settlers of southwestern Minnesota.

Farther west, during the first summer season, it was the British who were always most vulnerable to raiding by the peoples—mostly Sioux—still inhabiting the once-rich bison grounds of the Souris River country. By supplying their parties directly from the Missouri cavalry forts, the Americans avoided the necessity of building, maintaining and guarding a series of supply depots along the line of march. Nevertheless, while the British certainly believed that any missing cattle or horses had been stolen by the locals, they did not suffer a single serious raid on one of their depots, no matter how isolated it might have seemed. When George Dawson was heading west in September 1873 he arrived at a small sub-depot and was pleased (if not more than a little surprised) by what he saw. "Got in to Souris Depot at dusk," he wrote, "Found merely a tent pitched & stores covered with tarpaulins, which speaks well for the honesty & good temper of the indians of whom a large camp have been for some days near the depot..."[13]

It is nice for Dawson to acknowledge such honesty in the Sioux considering the generally low opinion that he and most of the other

commission officers held of the various bands they had encountered east of the Red River. But he may not have been aware at the
time that camped in the valley of the second Souris crossing barely
30 miles to the west were more than 150 troopers of the 7th Cavalry,
whose sole purpose was to punish any act of aggression, no matter
how minor and no matter whether it involved the Americans or the
British. But while Dawson may not have known the cavalry was there,
every Sioux, Assiniboine, Gros Ventre or Plains Cree within 200 miles
most certainly did.

The 1873 season had passed without any serious threat to either
commission and, for the greater part of the 1874 season, nothing of
any consequence was reported, until after the cavalry pulled out. The
incident at the British Sweetgrass depot, and a similar event at Battle
Creek, came after the commissions had moved far to the west and,
more important, after Major Reno had taken his cavalry back to Fort
Buford. The British may have been right in their belief that their men
were in no physical danger, but to think that their supplies and livestock were safe from predation simply because they were not American was pure naïveté.

Anderson may actually have believed that the Blackfeet were "the
gentlemen of the plains," but Greene had a more prosaic (and probably more typical) opinion of the once-feared high plains nation. Of
his march from the Three Buttes down to Fort Shaw, he wrote:

> I was without military escort, having 40 of my own men and half
> armed. We were passing through Blackfeet country, that part of
> it occupied by the Piegan band; it seems we passed quite close
> to their camp on the Marias river, for the next day some of them
> met the men at work on the meridian line. They asked for food of
> course, but made no demonstrations. Five years ago this was as
> bad a tribe of Indians as could be found west of the Mississippi.
> You may perhaps remember that in the spring of 1870 the Peace
> Commissioners called loudly for the blood & head of Maj. E.M.
> Baker, the author of the "Atrocious Piegan Massacre." With three
> Companies of his Reg't—the 2nd Cav'y—this Maj. Baker, one

morning before daylight, surprised a large camp of these Piegans
in the Marias bottom (about where my trail crossed it) and totally
wiped them out—extinguished them, forever for this world. A few
women and children were brought in prisoners—the rest of the
camp were decently buried I think. Perhaps he was a little cruel,
but from that day to this no one has ever heard of Piegan depreda-
tions,—and for my part I owe my cordial thanks to Maj. Baker for
being able to travel through that country as safely as in N.Y.[14]

GREENE ARRIVED at Fort Shaw on September 8, having drawn his
meridian line down from the boundary through "a rather forlorn flat
alkaline country."[15] The Sun River valley was a huge contrast: "It was
a pleasing sight… as I rode forward to the edge of the bluff which I
saw before me, and saw a broad green valley and on the river bank
the buildings and flag of Fort Shaw—the first buildings I had seen in a
trail of a little less than a thousand miles since leaving Fort Buford."[16]

Fort Shaw was under the command of 7th Infantry Colonel John
Gibbon (known to the local Native bands as "The One Who Limps,"
the consequence of serious wounds he received during the Civil War),
the senior officer in the district and a man widely respected by anyone
who knew him. As his long and distinguished career wound toward
its end over the next four years, he would find himself playing a significant role in two of the great events that marked the end of the old
west: the Battle of the Little Bighorn and the final fight with the Nez
Perce in the shadow of the Bear Paw Mountains

After a brief rest, Greene and his party, together with Gibbon,
rode out of Fort Shaw on September 10, headed east toward Fort
Benton:

I reached Fort Benton on the morning of the 11th, and found
there the rest of our people, except the escort who had gone back
to Buford overland.

Fort Benton is a row of whiskey shanties along the river front
and a few adobe buildings in the background—by all odds the
lowest of all the low places I have seen on the frontier. At the other

end of the "town" is a stockade of adobe garrisoned by a Company of the 7th Inf'y—the quarters propped up with sticks and so shaky and full of vermin that the men sleep outdoors and the officers seek refuge with one of the two respectable traders in town. The Great Falls of the Missouri are about 20 miles higher up and this is the first flat or bottom along the river below them—which naturally determined its location as a trading post 30 or 40 years ago, and it grew a little when steamboats began to run on the river and it figured as the head of navigation. The boats run… however only in the early season; this year 6 or 7 reached it.

There are two legitimate licensed traders in the place; but the main commerce is in whiskey, this being the grand depot for the whiskey which is carried over the line near the mountains & traded to the Indians there.[17]

Fort Benton had been one of the first outposts along the upper Missouri, surviving the initial threats of the Blackfeet and thriving as the centre of the trade first in furs and then in bison robes. Although the northernmost areas of the high plains were only just opening to settlement in the mid-1870s, Fort Benton's time had already passed. It had been in steady decline for several years when Greene and the rest of the American commission first saw it, and that decline would steepen over the next few years. As the railways drove west, pushing the riverboats and the whiskey traders into extinction as they came, they signalled the end of the old west, and of places like Fort Benton.

The other members of the American commission had made a somewhat parched but otherwise uneventful trip down from the Sweetgrass Hills, following the valley of the Maria's River most of the way. At Benton, they waited only a day or two for Greene to arrive (which, given the state of the place, they probably felt was probably a day or two too many) and then wasted no time in packing for their last great adventure.

Knowing that, at this time of year, the Missouri was not deep enough for steamboats to come upstream as far as Fort Benton, and no doubt remembering the two consecutive equinoctial blizzards,

Campbell and Twining had anticipated the difficulties inherent in moving large numbers of men and their equipment across the northern plains so late in the season. Their imaginative solution had been to build their own transportation in the form of what they called "Mackinac boats."

At the beginning of the 1874 season, the commission had contracted for the construction of seven such boats at Fort Benton. To universal surprise, they had actually been completed to Twining's exacting specifications by the time the commission came down from the boundary. According to Greene, the boats were misnamed, but were nevertheless a most effective way of travelling the low water of a late summer western river:

> The "Mackinaw" of the north western river is not a mackinaw at all—it is simply a huge flat-bottomed New England skiff. Ours are 35 feet long, 10 feet beam and 2½ feet depth of hold—all open without any decking—made of unplaned pine boards caulked with oakum—loaded each with about 4,000 lbs. We draw 10 inches of water.[18]

The only member of the boundary commission who would not be availing himself of the opportunity for a late-season cruise down the Missouri was Archibald Campbell. He would be returning home by a less direct (though probably less hazardous) route.

Campbell left the Missouri in the company of Colonel Gibbon, who had been assigned the task of providing military protection for the commission as it moved west of the Sweetgrass Hills (allowing Reno to take his precious cavalry home). There had been no reason for him to dispatch his 7th Infantry north to the border, and he had no doubt come to Benton to discharge the last of his official responsibilities. Side by side in a light spring wagon, the two men covered the 63 miles back to Fort Shaw in about eight hours. There, Campbell spent two quiet days as Gibbon proudly toured him around his gardens and showed off the irrigated delights of the Sun River valley. On September 16, Campbell drove himself the 80 miles south to

Helena, where he spent a day at the agricultural fair before board-ing a stagecoach for the four-day trip to Ogden, Utah, on the shore of the Great Salt Lake. There, he climbed aboard an eastbound Union Pacific train and headed home to Washington D.C.

BY THE TIME the Americans began loading their Mackinac boats at Fort Benton, the British and Canadians were already well on their way back to Dufferin.

No one had stayed long at the West Butte depot. Millman arrived in mid-afternoon on September 1 and barely had time to climb a lit-tle way up the shoulder of the hill to take a farewell look at the Rock-ies before he was back on the trail at six o'clock the next morning. He was still moving with the Featherstonhaugh and Galwey parties as they leapfrogged each other across the Milk River plateau, stopping every three miles or so to replace the temporary stakes with the more permanent conical boundary markers of sod or stone.

East of the Sweetgrass Hills, across the 60 miles of parched land between the East Butte and the Milk River, the country was once again alive with bison, and the men took the time to replenish their larder and enjoy a fine roast for their evening dinner. By September 4 the parties were well past the Milk River crossing and the country put on one final, spectacular show:

> Buffalos today were as thick as bees. It was a splendid sight. The prairie was black with them. I believe you could see half a million at once. A large herd came rushing over a hill and almost went through our train. The men opened fire and killed several. For fear they might make a rush on us during the night and stampede the horses, we corralled the wagons, put the tents close together and kept the horses inside. The howling of the wolves at night was almost deafening.[19]

By the end of the next day, it was over:

> Reached the half-breeds' camp lake end of Mr. Galwey's line, and camped there. Half-breeds and Assinaboine Indians were there.

The same ones we saw at our station at Lac des Marons. Went to
the west fork, built mounds on the way. Two or three buffalos seen.
The last I saw.[20]

Since leaving the Sweetgrass Hills, the British commission had
fallen into a steady, mile-devouring pattern of march and rest. Dawson wrote:

We have a regular marching routine now, & the waggons & carts
go off in a certain order & at night draw up in a semi-circular
Kraal on the border of some coulé or stream. The tents are then
pitched outside & the animals all ties up to the waggons at dark.
The camp is called by the watchman at 4 AM when it is barely
light, & always remarkably chilly. Breakfast before 5 & all packed
up and punctually off at 6. March till about 10 or 11 according to
the distance necessary to make for water and feed. Halt for two
hours & then travel on again for two or three hours. Making every
day something over 20 miles.[21]

On the morning of the 17th, Dawson and his travelling compan-
ions were on the trail by 5:30. It was a calm, clear day with the temperature in the low 40s, even though there had been what Dawson
called "a sharp frost" overnight. By noon, they were settled in at
Wood Mountain depot.

On September 18, Albany Featherstonhaugh and his party built
the last of the boundary mounds on the line west of Little Rocky
Creek. The next day, the men rode into the depot where they found all
the other parties waiting for them. After two days of intensive equipment repair, horseshoeing and packing of specimens, the entire cara-
van moved down off Wood Mountain for the last time:

Camps rousted at about 4 AM. Teams taken down to Depot when
tents struck & the remaining goods there apportioned for transport amidst much bustle & some confusion. A lot of indians from
the camp, principally squaws, hovering round & pick up what they
could. Much amusement caused by their eagerness & struggles

for leavings of sugar &c. Three women had almost a fight over an empty sugar barrel. Some surplus remaining at the last, made up of a barrel of flour, [ditto] of beans, some sugar & tea; the chief was sent for & presently arrived puffing & panting from haste, but with the best external appearance of dignity & repose in his power, & arrived with his Red Stone pipe... Capt. A[nderson] spoke to him through an interpreter. Saying that from our friendship to the Indians & for a parting gift we left them these things, enumerating them & pointing them out. Between the words the assembled indians uttered guttural "haryhs" of satisfaction, & having shaken hands all around & replied that we had "great hearts," proceeded to a business like examination of the spoils previous to their distribution.[22]

On this, his first trip into the Canadian west, Dawson was proving a careful and detailed chronicler of the peoples he encountered. This fascination would only grow stronger during his stellar career, but for all his attempts to be an objective recorder of appearance and custom, he simply could not shed all of his high-Victorian condescension:

All the Indians were more or less painted in various designs. Some had only a general appearance of rubbed in vermillion about the face and a streak of same down the parting of the hair. One had his face decorated in horizontal stripes of yellow & red, one a single yellow horizontal line on a red background &c.

The men are not very good specimens of indians being inferior in physique to those seen at Turtle Mt. & the Souris. Some of them are tall however & have not bad profiles. The women are all undersized & generally very ugly & decorated with a rouge patch on each cheek & some vermillion in the hair. Two or three of the younger squaws not worse than plain & one even was rather good looking.[23]

AS THE BRITISH rode cheerfully east and the Americans marched south toward the Missouri, the Mounted Police's "Long March" careened from one near-fatal disaster to another.

Since leaving Dufferin on July 8, Colonel French had followed the boundary commissions' trail along the 49th Parallel all the way to Roche Percée. By staying on the trail, they had been able to limit the consequences of the bad planning and the inaccurate maps (mostly produced fifteen years earlier by the Palliser expedition). Just west of Roche Percée, however, they lost touch with the trail and what little fit water, forage and firewood they had been able to find were about to give out almost entirely.

Hoping to spare his ruined horses and find passable trails for the heavy wagons, French took his troop northwest, trying to skirt the worst of the Coteau badlands, but no matter how far north he went, the country continued to prove utterly inhospitable and he was forced to call a halt to save his animals from certain death. From his camp at Old Wives Lake, French dispatched Major James Macleod with ten men and a short wagon train to try and find the boundary commission depot at Wood Mountain. There, he hoped, they could purchase enough rations to stave off starvation, mutiny or wholesale desertion.

After three days of thrashing about on the Coteau, Macleod found the depot and Lawrence Herchmer was pleased to part with 4,700 pounds of pemmican (emergency rations that the men of the boundary commission had never considered proper food) and 60,000 pounds of oats, priceless forage for their ruined horses. Any philanthropic thoughts aside, Herchmer knew that by selling it to the Mounties he would avoid the trouble of carting it all back to Dufferin.

The Mounted Police continued to stagger west at a snail's pace. Passing to the north of the Cypress Hills and realizing the country ahead looked every bit as inhospitable as what they had been fighting through for over a month, French turned his troop south and made for the Three Buttes. By September 20, they were camped at the abandoned boundary commission depot in the shadow of the West Butte. They had spent six horrific weeks wandering around the Great American Desert in order to cover a straight-line distance of only 400 miles along the 49th Parallel. By comparison, the men of the boundary commission, travelling through the same country at exactly the same time of the year, made the march from the Sweetgrass Hills back to Wood Mountain in 18 easy days, building boundary markers all the way.

Nothing more perfectly sums up the difference between the two grand expeditions than this: On August 15, as the Mounted Police stumbled across the high plains in a desperate search for food and water for both themselves and their animals, Assistant Surgeon Thomas Millman was sitting in front of his tent in the cool, green splendour of the Rocky Mountains. He had passed a pleasant day fishing for trout and was catching up on the news before dinner with a copy of the *Globe*. That newspaper had been printed in Toronto, Ontario, on July 16, more than a week after the Mounties had begun their march into Canadian history.

WHEN GREENE and his men arrived at Fort Benton on September 11, they found everything nearly ready to go. Twining, Gregory, Coues and the rest had arrived on the 8th, and no one, it seemed, wanted to spend any longer at Benton than was absolutely necessary. The commission's "navy" was tied up at the steamboat docks, and unlike Gregory's ad hoc constructions at Waterton Lake, each of the six vessels bore an appropriate name. Four honoured U.S. Army generals Sheridan, Sherman, Terry and Humphreys, and two others had been christened the *Campbell* and the *Twining*. A seventh boat—the *U.S. Grant*—had been built, but was not needed after 30 of the hired men decided to draw their pay and stay in Montana.

Even at 35 feet long and 10 feet wide, the Mackinac boats were a tight squeeze. Each carried an officer, one or two assistants, a cook and perhaps a dozen men to ensure two full shifts at the oars and rudder. Greene's extensive journal entries describe preparing for the voyage:

> In packing the boats the bow is given up to the light baggage and bedding; then come four seats for rowing, and under and over them are packed boxes of rations, tents, &c., in the waist of the boats is the cook stove and its accompaniments, and just back of this the "bridge"—a board with cleats running across from rail to rail on which stands the steersman. The steering oar is like that of a flat boat or raft of logs... The space 6x6 back of the bridge is

pretty well filled up with instruments, desks, boxes of records and the officer of the boat.[24]

At noon on September 12, the fleet sailed, with all the appropriate pomp and circumstance: "Several of the officers from Fort Shaw had come up to see us off and they and the officers of the fort gave us a salute as we passed, with an old mountain howitzer, and we answered with our carbines."[25] For Greene, the scene brought on an attack of rather mawkish sentimentality (leavened with a little of his wry sense of humour):

> There is something rather appalling to me in the idea of a river stretching before you continuously for such an immense distance. We were starting on a three weeks' voyage of 1,256 miles and at the end were to be where? At Bismarck which probably seems to you the very last place in creation. Beyond that the river goes on and on in its endless course, scoring 3,000 miles at St. Louis and still on and on indefinitely its thousands more to the Gulf of Mexico.[26]

Even though they were travelling with the current, their progress was more steady than quick. On the first day, they sailed about 30 miles to the mouth of the Maria's River. It was a trip they could have covered in 12 miles overland.

Downstream from the Judith River, the raw clay badlands along the banks held large herds of bighorn sheep and, although the men only saw two small bands of elk, the whistling of the rutting bulls could be heard "all day and every day" from every patch of brush. There were bison, too, with numerous small herds migrating south across the river in front of the boats. Coues scribbled down one of his typically dramatic portraits of one such crossing:

> A herd of several hundred took the alarm at our approach, and rushed headlong up the bank. They got on very well for some distance—for the buffalo can climb steeper places than one would suppose from their ungainly and unwieldy form; but as they

proceeded the way grew worse. Still those that were in the rear pressed so hard on the leaders of this climb that the latter could neither turn nor even stop; several of them lost their footing, rolled down, end over end, in a cloud of dust, and then tumbled off the cliff to be dashed to pieces on the rocks below.[27]

When the boats were near the same longitude at which Millman recorded his final sight of the bison along the 49th Parallel, a pair of old bulls swimming the river directly in front of their boats provided the Americans with their last look at the great beasts, too.

As the days closed toward the end of summer, the men did not question that they would face another equinoctial blizzard, but only wondered how severe it would be. After two consecutive years of shivering in their tents on September 22, men on both sides of the line began to look up at the sky each morning with a growing sense of foreboding. After a long run of warm days and cool, clear nights (perfect for taking astronomical fixes), the morning of September 16 gave them something to worry about:

> . . . as we emerged from our robes the sky was very black & cloudy, and half an hour after we were under way it began to rain & soon wet us through. After that, the best thing to do was to keep on rowing, which we did all day. You can imagine the misery of being in an open boat, crowded with men, baggage, rations & a little of everything, and staying there for 10 hours quietly absorbing a pelting rain. We officers in the stern sheets managed to get a little shelter from tents & spare canvas but the men stuck to their oars all day; & eagerly counted the minutes to the time of their relief to pull and get warmed up. It held up somewhat just before dark and as we went into camp opposite the Musselshell, the stars were shining brightly; and we partially forgot our troubles before a blazing cottonwood fire.[28]

The 17th gave them more of the same—"our little moist misery" Greene called it—and although the wind continued to blow the next day, at least it had stopped raining.

The big wind marked the end of the spell of bad weather, and when the fall equinox finally arrived it did so on a quiet, warm and sunny day.

By September 21, the country had taken on a familiar look. On that day, the boats sailed past the mouth of Poplar Creek where, just three months before, Greene's parties had detached from the main body and headed north toward the border to begin their season's work. The next day, the flotilla passed Big Muddy Creek and stopped long enough for Greene to visit "his bridge":

> The river now had only a few inches of water in it but the soft mud was several feet deep. The bridge *was there* and the 200 wagons which have now crossed it have sunk the sills so deep into the mud that like snags in the river, I don't think the spring freshets can dislodge them at all.[29]

After turning the great bend in the Missouri where the Yellowstone comes pouring in from the southwest, "Fort Buford loomed up in front like a large city and precisely at noon of the 23rd [they] landed; 11 days exactly from Fort Benton, 800 miles by water and 400 by land."[30]

The desire to get home as soon as possible was now the sole force driving the officers and men of the boundary commission and they did not stay to enjoy the hospitality at Fort Buford. The next morning, they were back on the river before breakfast.

ALTHOUGH THE BISON and the pronghorn were gone, Featherston-haugh, Millman and the other officers supplemented their limited stores with the prairie chickens, ducks and geese that were plentiful everywhere across the plains. With no blizzard or grass fires to deal with, the British retreat toward Dufferin was turning out to be what Anderson described as "a most delightful march."[31] Millman's daily diary of their progress east from Wood Mountain certainly confirmed Anderson's optimism:

> September 20th. Rose at 3:30. We all left at seven going by the trader's road one hundred and eighty three miles to Wood End.

The country we went over is rolling and hilly. Went about twenty-four miles, plenty of water at the five, ten, fifteen-mile points and a spring where we camp. Also found a hay stack and wood. There is hay put up day's marches apart all the way to Dufferin. After camping I was reading the papers. Two of the scouts had a free fight. Their fists and arms were flying about pretty well for five minutes, occasionally their heels would be keeling up in the air.[32]

All the field parties—a total of 157 men—left Wood Mountain together and travelled in a single body. A supposedly reliable report of a possible confrontation with some resident Native bands saw overnight watches doubled and every man told to sleep with his carbine.

Nothing out of the ordinary was reported until the commission camped near the second Souris crossing on the evening of September 24. Just after dusk, W.G. Boswell reported seeing a bright light out on the prairie to the west. It was moving about, he said, as if an Indian were signalling. The camp went to full alert, but nothing more was seen or heard that night.

The next night, the light was seen again, but this time cooler heads prevailed. The light was just Venus, the "evening star," shining particularly brightly as it set in the west. The relief in the camp must have been palpable, and it was the last thought anyone gave to "Indian trouble." The whole incident, however, raises the very large question of how a camp of more than 150 men, including a number of highly trained astronomers and surveyors, ever managed to confuse a setting Venus with an Indian signal light in the first place. It seems a curiously incompetent conclusion to an otherwise impeccable two-year exercise in applied science.

At the beginning of October, the pace of the march began to pick up. Although the country was still "much parched," they had left the Coteau badlands and the Souris valley far behind and were closing in on Turtle Mountain. Most of the men, the last of the oxen and the freight wagons would be following the trail around the north face of the mountain while Featherstonhaugh, Millman and half a dozen sappers rode along the line, checking the clear-cut and making sure the boundary markers were firmly and prominently in place.

On the evening of October 4, Featherstonhaugh and his party finished with the Turtle Mountain line and joined the rest of the men at
the depot. According to Millman, they sat by the camp fire "listening
to some good stories told by Capt. Anderson and Lieut. Galwey."[33]

Almost home and relaxing in camp east of Turtle Mountain,
Anderson wrote to his mother:

> Our horses and ponies are standing this very long march won-
> derfully... and all the animals have had plenty of good food. They
> suffered a little from the effects of the alkaline water which we all
> had to drink for nearly 300 miles of the journey, but the men took
> it as sparingly as possible and then only in the shape of tea infu-
> sion, making it drinkable and not injurious. We had water carts
> which we were often able to fill from a pool of rain water, and by
> economy such a welcome supply would last us for two or three
> days when marching over the very arid plain where nothing grew
> but cactus.[34]

The next morning, and every morning after that, they were on the
trail early, passing Badger Creek and Pembina Mountain and rolling
out onto the broad silt flats of the Red River valley.

Finally, on October 11, at 9:30 in the morning, Anderson, Featherstonhaugh, Galwey and the rest of Her Majesty's North American
Boundary Commission rode quietly back into Dufferin.

BY SEPTEMBER 30, the grand flotilla of Mackinaw boats had swept
the men of the United States Northern Boundary Survey down the
Missouri from Fort Benton almost to Bismarck. Francis Greene took
the time to write to his family and reflect on his first field appointment and what it had all meant to him:

> We are nearing Bismarck and "now my tale is ended." As we sat
> around our last campfire last night, my mind ran back over these
> last two years, eighteen months of which I have spent "on the prai-
> rie," and I can only say I heartily wish I had more of it to look for-
> ward to. I don't know that I ever enjoyed myself more.

Rough and wild you can call the life—and so it is externally, but it need not have any hardening effect on one's mind. The hardships of it become mere pastime to a young man of health and energy—an outlet for his superfluous activity. And the freedom of it is dear indeed; to escape from the trammels of society, to feel perfectly independent of the thousand little requirements which are not points of fine breeding but mere superficial conventionalities, to get out of the narrow rut into which most young people drift in city life, to feel occasionally that your safety depends on your judgement and endurance; and finally the independence and self-reliance which come from being thrown so much on your own resources; the exhilaration of breathing such pure health-giving air—all this, as accessory to scientific work which goes on record with your name and which at any time you can refer to with pride, forms an experience which has exceeded the most sanguine anticipations.[35]

· 13 ·

THE MEDICINE
LINE

They started in one of the ambulances,
took their luggage in a water waggon. They were all in high
spirits at getting away from this solitary place.

THOMAS MILLMAN

A S HE RODE BACK into Dufferin after his long summer in the field, Millman thought the place "in about the same state as when I left it last spring,"[1] but in fact there had been dramatic changes. A group of houses had sprung up around Dufferin. Named West Lynne, it was a community built on the expectation that there would soon be a railway and a thriving border-crossing business. Directly east across the Red River, where there had been only silt and willow scrub the previous spring, another new town had appeared. Its original settlers (all from the state of Wisconsin) named it Emerson, in honour of the eminent American poet and transcendentalist, Ralph Waldo Emerson. West Lynne and Emerson would eventually merge under the latter name, but in the fall of 1874 unbridled boosterism and cutthroat competition were the order of the day.

Back in February, Anderson had written to his mother about the country's prospects for immigration, and referred to the expected arrival of some four hundred Russian Mennonites. By the time he rode back into Dufferin in mid-October, the Mennonites had arrived and were building feverishly ahead of the coming winter on their land reserve east of the river on the Dawson Route. By the end of 1875, another large contingent arrived and moved out to occupy another reserve, this time to the west near Pembina Mountain. Off to the northwest, toward Lake Winnipeg, the first of what would become a substantial settlement of Icelanders were also rushing to beat the coming cold.

While the dismantling of the commission had begun almost the day the parties arrived back at Dufferin, the growing pressure from the new settlements meant that a few loose ends needed to be tied up as soon as possible.

On October 16, George Crompton was sent back out with a party of hired men to replace the original boundary markers from the Red River to the Manitoba boundary at 99° West, about eighty miles from Dufferin. With the markers to be spaced at one-mile intervals, Crompton was to replace every other mound, leaving the balance to be done by the Americans. The original earth or stone cairns were replaced by tall, cast-iron columns.

According to Gregory—who drew the assignment to replace the American share of the original mounds in 1875—the pillars were:

> ...hollow iron castings, three-eighths of an inch in thickness, in the form of a truncated pyramid, eight feet high, eight inches square at bottom, four inches square at top, with solid pyramidal cap, and an octagonal flange, one inch in thickness, at bottom. Upon opposite faces [were] cast, in letters two inches high, the inscriptions "Convention of London," and "October 20, 1818." The inscriptions [began] about four and a half feet above the base and read upward. The interiors [were] filled with well-seasoned cedar posts, sawed to fit, and securely spiked, through spike holes cast in the pillars for the purpose. The average weight of the pillars, when completed and painted, was two hundred and eighty-five pounds.[2]

Immediately, a small but significant inconsistency came to light. The Principal Meridian, the longitudinal line established in 1871 from which all future surveys of western Canada would be drawn, met the 49th Parallel about ten miles west of the Red River station. More important, the nearest commission marker was 385 feet east of the Meridian. Since all the original boundary markers were to be replaced anyway, it was decided to locate the new iron posts between the river and the Manitoba boundary at 385 feet west of their original location, so that each marker was an exact multiple of a mile from the Principal Meridian, greatly simplifying future surveying work. This adjustment would have been greatly appreciated by the army of land surveyors that was soon to descend on the new province.

Under continuing fair skies, Crompton made short work of installing the new posts, even staking out the places in between for the Americans. East of the Red, however, was a different matter. The Roseau swamp demanded some flexibility in the placement of the markers and the border was eventually delineated by a varied combination of stone cairns, earth mounds, timber poles and cast-iron pillars, depending largely on the nature of the surface on which each one had to be erected. As was the case to the west, every other marker was left for the Americans.

As Burpee and Crompton worked the line out from the Red River, D'Arcy East went back yet again to Lake of the Woods and, with a small party of hired men, installed the permanent markers along the north–south line from the Northwest Angle to the 49th Parallel. In the winter of 1874–75, after the ground had frozen, he also installed the iron pillars wherever practicable between the shore of Lake of the Woods and Point D'Orme.

Long after the last of the Royal Engineers had returned to England, Captain James Gregory was ordered back to Pembina to finish the American portion of the work. Between September 2 and October 7, 1875, with a party of four hired men and an escort of twelve soldiers from the 20th Infantry, Gregory set forty-three cast-iron posts west of the Red River and seventeen to the east, filling in the spaces left for him by Burpee and Crompton. He also went back to the Northwest Angle to make a final check of East's work on the north–south line, finding everything to his satisfaction. By early November he was back in Washington, and Cameron could finally write to Canadian Prime Minister Alexander Mackenzie:

> I have the honour to inform you that... a party from the United States Commission under Cap't Gregory completed the demarcation and there is now nothing more to be done on the ground.[3]

Between the Lake of the Woods and the Rockies the two teams had left, as lasting monuments to their toil and dedication, not only a detailed topographical survey of some 9,000 square miles, but also a total of 388 markers delineating both the north–south line along the Northwest Angle and the 853 miles of the 49th Parallel from the lake to the Divide. There were 135 iron pillars, 129 stone cairns, 113 earth mounds and 3 of stone and earth. Finally, in the deepest heart of the Roseau swamps, there were 8 timber poles, each 40 feet long and driven 20 feet down into the bottomless muck.

WHILE CROMPTON, East and Burpee were finishing the last of the work along the line, the commission was quickly being broken up. On October 12, as the Minnesota teamsters and their ox carts were preparing to start south for Moorhead, twenty-five hired men were paid off. The next day, the 49th Rangers were disbanded and the Metis scouts discharged.

On the 17th, Valentine Rowe left Pembina by steamboat, bound home to England. He had held up remarkably well during the long march back from Wood Mountain and, according to Millman, "he is a great deal better."[4]

October 24 saw the departure of the first of the senior field officers. Featherstonhaugh and Galwey, in command of most of the sappers, took the steamer south. Featherstonhaugh was taking the men to Halifax, from where they would be reassigned. Galwey was to stop off in Ottawa to arrange winter living quarters for himself, Anderson and Featherstonhaugh. There they would begin work on their maps and final reports.

Veterinarian W.G. Boswell left on November 10, taking forty-three of the best horses with him to be sold off in Toronto. Finally, on the 15th, Ward (newly promoted to captain) and Doctor Burgess, together with the last of the Canadians—King, Ashe and Coster—left for the railway station at Moorhead to catch their train to Ontario. With the river already frozen and navigation over for the season, according to Millman, "They started in one of the ambulances, took their luggage in a water waggon. They were all in high spirits at getting away from this solitary place."⁵ Their departure left only Cameron and Millman at the headquarters.

Chief Astronomer Samuel Anderson had already left Dufferin, taking one of the last steamers of the season on October 27. With him had gone all the instruments, the "office baggage," Sergeant Kay, four of the Canadian topographers (including George Burpee) and the last few sappers.

Back at Dufferin, Millman was pleased to receive a raise in pay as he went about attending to the sick of Emerson and West Lynne and helping to break up the commission's assets. He reassembled the library and arranged it for sale. Nearly every volume found a ready buyer, returned a total of $72 to the commission's accounts. He and Burgess finished writing their final medical report and, when the senior surgeon and the others left, he collected a carpet, some curtains and a good stove and moved into Anderson's old front room at the headquarters. He was more than ready when winter finally blew in.

Captain Cameron's family had returned from Ottawa for the winter, and the commissioner moved them back into Emmadale, leaving Millman all but alone at the headquarters. As the winter deepened— it was –29° F on the last day of November—his only outside company were the Mounted Police supply officers, who regularly dropped by to purchase stores and equipment. The new police force was by far the commission's best customer. Wagon master Hugh O'Donnell had been hawking livestock in Winnipeg, and the Mounties had purchased twenty of the commission's horses, paying the fine sum of $170 each for them. This was in addition to the forty teams of wagon horses and sixty yoke of oxen they had already acquired. The force's quartermasters were proving quick learners and, unlike the handsomely matched but terribly ill-suited horses that had carried the first troopers out along the boundary trail, the commission's experienced, western-raised remounts would at least be willing to drink the water. Millman was especially pleased to greet one particular visitor: "Another batch of mounted police arrived under the command of Mr. Dickens, son of the famous novelist. I spent the evening talking with him..."[6] Given Inspector Francis J. Dickens's reputation, this was a visit that would have severely taxed the commission's remaining supply of spirits.

Finally, on December 26, after what must have been a rather lonely Christmas, Millman wrote in his diary, "The commission is to be broken. Cap't Cameron told me to-day my services would not longer be required."[7] It was a curious time to tell the one remaining member of the commission that he was dismissed. One might be forgiven for seeing in it another manifestation of the chief commissioner's perverse nature. Given how little work really remained for Millman to do, Cameron could perhaps more thoughtfully have sent the young surgeon back to his family before the holidays.

When he was finally released, Millman wasted no time in getting out. With the thermometer hovering near –30° F, he said his goodbyes, made one last visit to his patients and left for Pembina to wait for the stage. On December 30 he took the freezing coach down to Moorhead and by January 5 he was home with his family in Toronto. "Thus ended my trip to the Great North-west," he wrote, "which I am not sorry I undertook. I spent many a useful and pleasant hour during that time."[8]

As he huddled down for a long, cold winter at Dufferin, Cameron sent a brisk, concise report to the Earl of Derby at the Foreign Office. Dated November 3, 1874, the report briefly outlined the state of the boundary commission's work. As far as the commission's properties and supplies were concerned, Cameron's recommendations spoke to his own uncertain future:

Provision having necessarily been made for the possibility of the field work being continued beyond the present season, there remains on hand a larger stock of supplies than can be disposed of immediately without incurring a loss which may be avoided by a more gradual sale. The real property—land and buildings— here, belonging to the Commission, is too valuable to be disposed of hastily. The prospect—from the opening of railway communi- cations with the United States next year—of a considerable rise in the value of all real estate in this Province is very good, and especially so in the case of such as has the advantages of location offered by the site of the expedition winter quarters.

Under the circumstances I have concluded that the interests entrusted to my charge may be best served by my remaining here during the winter.[9]

In reality, he had nowhere else to go.

ANDERSON, FEATHERSTONHAUGH and Galwey settled easily into life in Ottawa, sharing a rented house close to their offices in the Par- liament buildings, and the work on the maps and final reports pro- ceeded smoothly. Although he was far away in Dufferin, the spectre of Captain Cameron still haunted Anderson, filling his letters home with disdain and recrimination. Early in December, he wrote to his mother:

Capt. Ward the last of our officers, has arrived at Ottawa today, having cleverly broken loose from Capt. Cameron who now reigns at Pembina alone. This is a most happy state of things for all, which I hope will continue all winter. I should think Capt. C. must now realize that there must be some reason for our all run- ning away from him, as soon as our work permits.[10]

The letter also contained the self-serving suggestion that Ander- son was far from alone in his dislike for Cameron:

Some of the officials here have mentioned in a guarded sort of way their penitence in having primarily been the cause of so much annoyance and anxiety to us all, adding at the same time that they will take care that such a thing should not be repeated. This is poor consolation to us, whose only desire & object is now to finish up the whole thing as rapidly and decently as possible and get out of it.[11]

Anderson's vitriol even extended to Canada's former prime minister:

I met at a dinner party the other night Sir John Macdonald... & I sat next to him. He asked me to come and see him as he wished to speak to me about the Boundary Commission, and he added "I saw afterwards I had made a mistake," this with reference to Major Cameron's appointment I suppose... It matters very little however, as he is out of office and can do nothing, but I should not mind having the opportunity of telling him how his mistake affected the happiness & almost imperilled the lives of our party.[12]

It is a rather mean-spirited performance by Anderson, and the fact that Cameron had recently been promoted to major cannot have helped to temper his opinion.

In mid-January 1875, Anderson took the opportunity to travel to Washington, D.C., passing through New York and Philadelphia on the way. Officially, he was meeting with the members of the American commission, but it was also a chance to do some sightseeing (although not at the best time of the year.) "Since my arrival..." he wrote,

I have made a good many friends and received a good many invitations. I dined with Sir Edwd. Thornton the Minister, whose acquaintance I had made some years ago, and the dinner was given principally as a farewell to Mr. Charlton (of the English Legation)... who had lately married the daughter of Mr. Campbell, the American Boundary Commissioner, and going to England next month for good.[13]

This was the same daughter whose marriage had so distracted Campbell (and so frustrated Anderson) in the spring of 1873.

During his trip to Washington, Anderson was pressured by the

Americans to finish what he could in Ottawa and then return home as soon as possible. Campbell and Twining had decided that England would be the perfect place to hold the final meetings (the chief commissioner would have been delighted with any opportunity to visit his daughter) and sign the official copies of their reports. Anderson was in compete agreement and began to make ready to leave Ottawa. "I cannot tell what Capt. Cameron's (Major Cameron now) views are," he wrote, "and I have not broached the subject to him till I see my way a little more clearly."[14]

As Cameron went about his solitary business in Dufferin and Anderson simmered in Ottawa, discussions about the dreaded Northwest Angle continued to bubble up throughout the winter. As early as July 1874 the Canadian Privy Council had sought to end the constant bickering by suggesting a dramatic new approach to the problem. Canada would be prepared to pay the United States to abandon the Northwest Angle and agree to a boundary line running along the south shore of Lake of the Woods. It was a sensible thought, and one that would have cost the Americans almost nothing. The $25,000 Canada was prepared to pay was no more than a token, but the government hoped the Americans would be swayed by the argument that the Angle, cut off as it was from the rest of the United States, would become a haven for crooks and smugglers that would make it a troublesome place for both countries.

While Sir Edward Thornton was willing to put the matter to his long-time Washington colleague, Secretary of State Hamilton Fish, he did so with little expectation that it would be accepted. His expectation was proved right. Fish, realizing how contentious the issue would be, probably never discussed it with anyone else in Washington. His reply to Thornton came in the form of a joke with an old friend:

> I tell him [Thornton] that I do not think it worth while to make the proposal as I do not consider that it would be under any circumstances entertained. But then I add (jocosely) that if they will accompany the proposition with an offer to exchange New Brunswick, Nova Scotia and the Islands together with the territory south of the St. Lawrence, we might possibly consider it.[15]

Once the Canadian Pacific Railway ended the Dawson Route's brief, unpleasant history as Canada's gateway to the west, the Northwest Angle could never become anything more than it had always been: an anomaly, and an unremarkable, almost-forgotten piece of the state of Minnesota. Its sole claim to fame—being the northernmost point in the United States—lasted only until Alaska was admitted to the Union.

Cameron continued to hold on at Dufferin, although there was less and less for him to do. In the early summer of 1875 he managed to negotiate the sale of the headquarters buildings there to the Canadian government for a mutually agreeable price. It would become an immigration station for the expected flood of settlers.

Ward left Ottawa in April 1875, headed to London and the War Office, to make the final settlement of the commission's accounts.

Finally, on June 21, with little or no fanfare, Anderson, Featherstonhaugh and Galwey took the train to Quebec City, marched up the gangplank onto the deck of the steamer *Nova Scotian* and sailed for home.

EARLY IN 1876, commissioners Campbell and Cameron exchanged notes to the effect that each was ready to sign the final documents, and Twining and Campbell sailed for London in late April. At a series of meetings between the Americans and the three senior British officers—Cameron, Anderson and Ward—maps and reports were compared and both sets were found to be in order. On May 29, 1876, Cameron, Campbell, Twining and Anderson affixed their signatures.

Almost as soon as the final documents had been signed and sealed, Sir Charles Tupper began to agitate for some significant recognition for his son-in-law's accomplishments along the 49th Parallel.

In July 1876, Canada's governor general, Lord Dufferin, wrote a private letter to Lord Carnarvon at the Foreign Office suggesting he had come under serious pressure from Tupper to offer some form of promotion or other recognition to Cameron. Tupper had apparently averred that approaching the matter through official Canadian government channels would be a waste of time since the Liberal government of the day was anything but kindly disposed toward him.

Dufferin was blunt in his assessment of Cameron: "We have had reason to doubt whether his action as Commissioner did not tend rather to retard and impede than to expedite the work."[16] He went on to point out, in no uncertain terms, where his true allegiance lay:

> ... I believe myself, though as an R.E. I must expect my advocacy to be somewhat mistrusted, that the success of this difficult work was due to the science and perseverance of Captain Anderson, the chief astronomer, and the officers and men of R.E. under him, and was achieved in the face of much opposition from the Commissioner: but this is of course only my private opinion.[17]

The exact nature of Carnarvon's response is not known, but in August 1876 the Foreign Office recommended that Captain Anderson be awarded a companionship in the Order of St. Michael and St. George (known familiarly as the CMG). Although no such support was apparently forthcoming from the Foreign Office or from Lord Dufferin, Captain Cameron, too, was recommended for the CMG. Of all the Orders, the CMG was the one most often conferred to recognize singular contributions to the security and development of Britain's current and former colonies. In the final analysis, it is obvious that any honour for Anderson that did not also go to his commanding officer would have been completely unacceptable to the Canadians, who had insisted on appointing the chief commissioner. The price for Anderson's CMG was one for Cameron, too.

The Order was bestowed on the two officers by Queen Victoria in a ceremony at Buckingham Palace on May 30, 1877. Coincidentally, another man stood with them to accept a long-overdue CMG for his singular contribution to the exploration and understanding of the Canadian west. He was Captain John Palliser.

DESPITE NEITHER of the parties having been commissioned to do anything more than make a quick and efficient job of marking the 49th Parallel and create a narrow topographical survey of the lands through which it ran, it was impossible for a group of well-educated, highly trained observers to resist forming a wide range of personal opinions on the nature of the country through which they had passed.

In addition to the official minutes, documents and maps signed on May 29, 1876, Commissioner Cameron also submitted a personal final report to the Foreign Office. A broad, rambling document, with over thirty appendices, the report largely reiterates much of what had already been sent to London over the previous four years in the form of regular letters and dispatches from Dufferin. While Cameron's report adds a good deal of detail to the previously transmitted information, it was not widely circulated by the Foreign Office. In the opinion of several senior staff, Cameron's wandering, long-winded style made the document "very bulky and scarcely readable in its present form,"[18] and there were no plans to edit it for eventual publication. In addition to its generalized problems, one of Cameron's many appendices was a long, rambling essay "... upon the past, present and future of the North West Canadian Indians."[19]

Why Cameron would have appended such a document to a report on the drawing of the 49th Parallel (especially when he and the commission had been specifically instructed to avoid anything but minimal contact with the Native populations) is open to debate. In the document, Cameron takes aim at the treatment of the Native populations by (among others) the Hudson's Bay Company, missionaries and the United States government. His solution to the corruption and decline of the western tribes is a call for education of the children and their eventual assimilation into mainstream society. It was not a particularly original nor (for the time) controversial position, but the Foreign Office could hardly have been expected to forward it to the new Canadian government with anything like official sanction. Since 1867, such things were really no longer any of the Foreign Office's business.

While Cameron's report languished in the Foreign Office files, Lord Derby did give his blessing to the publication of two other accounts of the work along the 49th Parallel.

Albany Featherstonhaugh's "Narrative of the Operations of the British North American Boundary Commission, 1872–76" was published in the Royal Engineers' *Professional Papers.* The 45-page report is a lively and readable account not only of the commission's accomplishments but also of Featherstonhaugh's personal impressions of the west.

Samuel Anderson read his paper—"The North-American Boundary from the Lake of the Woods to the Rocky Mountains"—at a meeting of the Royal Geographical Society in March 1876. Later that year it appeared in the Society's journal as a 30-page article with a detailed map and an appendix on the survey's astronomical methodology.

Published in 1878 with funds remaining from the commission's 1874 appropriation, the American commission's final report to Congress is a grand, almost majestic, piece of work that runs to more than six hundred pages of text with fourteen engraved illustrations, any number of figures and charts and eight large fold-out maps. It includes not only pages of exacting detail concerning the exact location of every pillar and post along the boundary line, but a great deal of informed opinion about the true nature of the northern plains and the chances for its successful occupation by the coming flood of ranchers and homesteaders. Greene's detailed manual on wilderness living and surveying at -40° would have been required reading for any army personnel heading north to the new territory of Alaska.

In its oversize, leather-bound format, the expensive production may have been a response to the fact that the official papers and reports of the earlier Pacific survey had languished for many years, unpublished, in a Washington file room—from which they later disappeared without a trace. It is easy to see Campbell's hand at work in ensuring that his second great commission did not suffer the same fate.

For Canadians, new owners of the vast western lands north of the Medicine Line, the single greatest benefit to come from the work of the boundary commission was surely George Dawson's huge final report. *Report on the Geology and Resources of the Region in the Vicinity of the 49th Parallel from the Lake of the Woods to the Rocky Mountains with Lists of Plants and Animals Collected, and Notes on the Fossils* was published in 1875 at a cost of $1,600 in an edition of just 1,000 copies. Addressed to Major Cameron, its nearly four hundred pages cover in great detail everything that Dawson saw and much of what he thought. Profusely illustrated with the author's own detailed sketches of everything from fossilized Pembina River fish scales to vast badlands panoramas, the report is the first honest appraisal of what Canadians could look forward to discovering as they pressed out across the country. Just a quick glance through its seven pages of small-print index is enough to convey the broad range of Dawson's interests, from the obvious—the availability and quality of wood, water and especially of coal—to the esoteric, such as the evidence for glaciation, the evolution of molluscs and various methods of Native burial. It is serious applied science that is easy and thoroughly charming to read. Today, it remains a rare and much-coveted piece of Canadian publishing history.

Of those collections that Dawson lists in the appendices to his report, the geological samples remained in Canada at the offices of the Geological Survey in Ottawa. The zoological collections of 19 mammals and 328 birds were sent to the British Museum, while the plants were deposited at Kew Gardens.

The Royal Engineers' two teams of photographers took photographs from the very beginnings of the survey at Lake of the Woods to its conclusion on the shores of Waterton Lake. Many of the photographs were the first ever taken in parts of the Canadian west. Two hundred and fifty glass negatives were eventually deposited at the School of Military Engineering at Chatham, England. Personal copy prints of the photographs were collected and reproduced by Dawson, Millman and Featherstonhaugh—and by the U.S. commission, which took no photographs of its own but used several of the Royal Engineers' images in its final report. Sadly, there is no sign of the original negatives today; it is generally accepted that they were destroyed during a bombing raid in World War II. Luckily, several complete sets of copy prints still survive in various Canadian archives and libraries.

THE OUTRAGE THAT followed the massacre in the Cypress Hills not only brought the North West Mounted Police out along the boundary commission trail but eventually led to a series of attempts by the

Canadian government to bring the perpetrators to justice. In the summer of 1875 representatives of the new police force rode south into Montana to begin the process of extraditing the Fort Benton wolfers to Canada to stand trial for murder. Warrants were duly issued and, despite a marked reluctance on the part of Montana officials to make any arrests, seven men were eventually taken into custody and shipped off to Helena for an extradition hearing.

That hearing, on July 7, 1875, quickly deteriorated into a grand political circus. Publicly denouncing the defendants as "Belly River wolfers, outlaws, smugglers, cut-throats, horse-thieves and Squaw-men," the Canadian government's hired solicitors turned out to be hard-core Republicans, only too eager to make political hay against the equally rabid Irish Democrats who constituted the team of lawyers for the defence. Unfortunately for the prosecution, their chief witness was trader Abel Farwell, and his confused and contradictory evidence gave the judge all the latitude he needed to deny the extradition and set the men free.

Later that same year, three more wolfers were arrested in Canada and sent to Winnipeg to await trial for "the wanton and atrocious slaughter of peaceable and inoffensive people." When that trial finally opened nearly a year later, Abel Farwell was once again the star witness and, once again, his garbled testimony ensured there would be no convictions.

The whole matter was finally laid to rest in 1882 when the Canadian government dismissed the last of the outstanding indictments against the Montana wolfers. After so much time had passed no one seemed to care about justice denied or even about the truth of what had actually happened on that May day. It was enough, many felt, that the bloody incident had played its part in bringing "Peace, Order and Good Government" to the Canadian west.

Not long after the commissions finished marking the Medicine Line, it faced its first real test. Seeking protection from American retribution in the aftermath of the Battle of the Little Bighorn in June 1876, Sioux chief Sitting Bull led his people north through Montana and across the 49th Parallel. There they joined several other bands that had been drifting up across the line since just after the battle. By the time Sitting Bull settled his people near Wood Mountain, there were perhaps 4,000 Sioux ranged along the Canadian side of the border.

Despite American promises of amnesty for everyone who returned, few of the Sioux were willing to risk recrossing the border. By late 1879, however, the final collapse of the bison herds and the Canadian government's refusal to take responsibility for feeding those it had always considered "American Indians" had pushed many of the remaining Sioux south towards their reserves. Sitting Bull, with the last of his band, followed them back across the Medicine Line in July 1881.

Another of the end-games for the northern plains cultures was played out in Montana's Bear Paw Mountains, just 40 miles south of the international boundary. There, in October 1877, a force of U.S. cavalry finally caught up to Nez Perce chief Joseph and the last of his followers as they rushed desperately toward what they believed would be sanctuary with Sitting Bull in Canada. Trapped and utterly worn out, Joseph and the main body of Nez Perce surrendered, but a few men, women and children (perhaps 200 in all) did manage to slip away and, led by a chief named White Bird, crossed the line into Canada. Like the Sioux, most of the Nez Perce eventually returned to the United States, but some of their descendants still live today along the Canadian side of the Medicine Line.

By the mid-1880s, the buffalo and the Metis' summer hunting camps, which had so impressed the survey parties, were a fading memory, and those families who had settled onto farmlands in the fertile valleys of the Saskatchewan River basin were again under threat, this time from the railway and the new settlers it would bring. In a desperate attempt to protect what they saw as their traditional rights to the land, a second armed rebellion broke out, this time centred on the town of Batoche, in 1885. Louis Riel again emerged as the leading figure at Batoche, as he had during the 1870 rebellion along the Red River, but in terms of the government's response to the crisis, the intervening fifteen years had changed everything. The combination of the railway and the new mounted police force meant that this time government authority could be quickly and decisively deployed. It was over in barely two months, and the Metis had lost another round in their fight to maintain their traditional life.

ALTHOUGH THERE HAD already been some significant damage to the original boundary markers within a year or so of their construction (the bison apparently liked to rub against them), more than thirty years would pass before a new treaty called for a complete re-examination of the boundary line. The need for a re-examination grew from ongoing problems with the Pacific survey. New and often overlapping mineral claims were being registered all along the border between Washington and British Columbia, and over five years, beginning in 1901, the entire line from the Pacific to the Continental Divide was re-examined and all but a handful of the original markers recovered and replaced. The addition of intermediate markers also reduced the greatest distance between them from over twenty-five miles to less than two. The chief Canadian official in this process was none other than former subassistant astronomer, William F. King.

Under the terms of a new treaty, adopted in 1908, the line from the Divide to Lake of the Woods was also to be re-examined and, between 1909 and 1913, Canadian and American parties (each accompanied by a representative of the other) once again leapfrogged each other across the plains. All but one of the nearly 400 original markers were recovered (the missing one was re-established using the previous and following markers, just as had been intended in the original working agreements). The parties also added more than 600 new intermediate points, reducing the greatest distance between the markers along this section to something less than a mile and a half. Finally, all the new points and the sites of the original cairns and mounds between the Manitoba border and the North Milk River crossing were marked with cast-iron posts that matched those used along the line from Red River to the Manitoba boundary. From the North Milk to the Divide, the original mounds and new intermediate points were marked with the same monuments used from the Divide to the Pacific.

It almost goes without saying that all the reconstruction and rediscovery triggered yet another discussion of a mean parallel. This time, however, the decision would stick. In Article 11 of yet another new treaty, adopted in 1925, the boundary would comprise "... a series of right or straight lines joining adjacent monuments as now established."[20] With the new intermediate markers connected by a series of short straight lines, the greatest difference between the actual boundary line on the ground and the perfection of a mean parallel amounted to something less than four inches. The new commissioners felt that was close enough. The 1925 treaty also established the first permanent international commission and charged it with maintaining a programme of continuous maintenance, ensuring all 5,525 miles of the boundary line between Canada and the United States remains in "an effective state of demarcation."

One thing the international commission has never had cause to do is correct that segment of the line that stretches for more than 800 miles across the high plains of the North American west. To this day, the great Medicine Line remains exactly where Campbell and Cameron and Twining and Anderson first drew it. All the latest in high-tech surveying technology has served only to confirm how good their work really was.

EPILOGUE

THE BRITISH AND THE CANADIANS

DONALD RODERICK CAMERON, CMG: With the formal signing of the boundary documents in May 1876, Cameron's tenure as chief commissioner came to an end. While there were no appropriately senior postings available immediately, Sir Charles Tupper continued to look out for his interests.

After some peripheral involvement in the question of the Alaska Panhandle boundary, Cameron and his wife remained close to his father-in-law and, in 1888, Tupper managed to secure his appointment as Commandant of the Royal Military College (RMC) at Kingston, Ontario.

As many had predicted, Cameron's tenure at RMC was marked by controversy over perceived political interference, inconsistent standards for admission and declining enrolments. With the Liberal Party's election victory of 1896, Cameron lost what remained of his political support and was forced to resign.

Cameron returned to his native Scotland in 1901, settling back in Dingwall, where he had been born and where he died on December 23, 1921, at the age of 87.

Survived by the dedicated but long-suffering Emma, a son and four daughters, Cameron's obituary makes it clear that age had done little to mellow the man:

> Those who knew him best were struck with the almost military method and order which ruled the common actions of his daily life. His particularity entered into everything: exactness and precision were his constant care and loose statement of fact unsupported by evidence had no place in his conversation.[1]

SAMUEL ANDERSON, CMG: Sadly, Anderson did not live nearly long enough to fulfill the great promise he had shown in his appointments up to and including the boundary commission. Soon after returning to Britain, he married Louisa Brown, a second cousin, and settled back into the life of a Royal Engineers officer. He was appointed assistant inspector of submarine defences in 1876 and, following the publication of his paper on the boundary commission, elected a fellow of the Royal Geographical Society. With his CMG in hand, he was promoted to major in 1879, served as British Commissioner of a new survey of the Serbian frontier, and appeared as a significant witness before Lord Morley's 1880 committee on the pay and conditions of service for officers of the Royal Artillery and Royal Engineers.

In 1881, Anderson rose from assistant to chief inspector of submarine defences at the War Office and, in August that year, he took leave for a month of salmon fishing in his native Scotland. On the last day of his holiday, he contracted a severe chill and died within a week, three months shy of his forty-second birthday.

ALBANY FEATHERSTONHAUGH, WILLIAM GALWEY and ARTHUR WARD were all promoted to colonel and remained with the Royal Engineers until their retirements in the 1890s. Featherstonhaugh never married; he commanded the Engineers' detachment at Newcastle-on-Tyne. Galwey went on to head the Royal Engineers' detachment on the island of Mauritius, while Ward married the daughter of the Bishop of Bath and Wells, and served as commandant at Woolwich.

VALENTINE ROWE recovered from his ordeal on the prairies but was never strong enough to resume active field work with the Royal Engineers. He remained with the regiment, however, and taught surveying at Woolwich until he retired in 1884. Following his retirement, he returned briefly to Canada as a missionary, but failing health forced him home again. He died at Torquay in 1920 at the fine old age of 79.

LAWRENCE HERCHMER chose to remain in the west. In 1876, he was appointed Indian agent at Birtle, Manitoba, and in 1885 was promoted to inspector of Indian agencies for the North-West Territories.

In April, 1886, Sir John A. Macdonald chose Herchmer to succeed A.G. Irvine as commissioner of the North-West Mounted Police. Under his direction, selection and training were greatly improved and, while Herchmer's reforms made the police a more professional organization, he remained remarkably unpopular with his fellow officers, facing several attempts to have him dismissed.

In 1899 he took a leave to serve in South Africa, where he was soon in trouble with his commanding officers. On his return to Canada, he publicly demanded a full inquiry into his complaints, but Prime Minister Wilfrid Laurier, believing that his police commissioner was no longer fit to serve, ordered Herchmer's retirement from the force in August 1900.

Though he is remembered as something of a tyrant, Herchmer left the Mounted Police a much stronger force than he had found it. Most memorably, perhaps, he was responsible for the introduction of two of the Mounties' most enduring symbols: the flat-brimmed Stetson hat and the musical ride.

THOMAS BURGESS: After leaving Dufferin in mid-November 1874, Burgess returned to his chosen area of medicine, holding a series of senior positions in a number of asylums in Ontario and Quebec until his retirement in 1916.

Burgess retained the passionate interest in plants that he had developed through his association with George Dawson and Thomas Millman. He wrote and published extensively on Canadian botany (including a monograph entitled "Notes on the Flora of the 49th Parallel") and was made a fellow of the Royal Society of Canada in 1885, rising to the presidency of the Geological and Botanical Section in 1889. He was also elected a Fellow of the American Association for the Advancement of Science. He died in 1925.

THOMAS MILLMAN: Almost as soon as his work with the boundary commission was finished Millman left for Britain where he spent two years studying in London and Edinburgh. He then returned to his home town of Woodstock, Ontario, and established his medical practice. He is remembered as a founding member of Canada's Children's Aid Society, a charity to which he remained committed for the rest of his life. Professionally, Millman joined Burgess in working for a series of asylums before returning to private practice with the Independent Order of Foresters, a fraternal association, where he remained until his death in 1921 at the age of 71.

Like Burgess, Millman maintained his passion for botany. When he died, his collection of 3,000 specimens of Canadian flora was given to the University of Toronto.

W.G. BOSWELL: From the moment he left Dufferin with his string of horses, the details of Boswell's life become largely a matter of speculation. One W.G. Boswell graduated from London's Royal College of Veterinary Surgeons (RCVS) in July 1876, and the 1881 UK census lists a Canadian-born veterinarian of that name practising in Lewisham, Kent (now in southeast London).

Early in 1911, the RCVS received a communication from a Miss Annie Looms reporting that her uncle, Walter George Boswell, had died of cardiac failure on February 4. It is likely (though far from certain) that this English veterinarian was the same man who had served with the boundary commission.

GEORGE MERCER DAWSON: On his return to Montreal, Dawson went to work turning his voluminous notes and diaries into a final report. That magnificent book, published simultaneously in Montreal, London and New York, represents the first serious study of Canada's new western lands. *Report on the Geology and Resources of the Region in the Vicinity of the Forty-Ninth Parallel* is a model of its kind, and it is hard to remember that Dawson was just twenty-six years old when it was published.

As he had been promised when he agreed to join the boundary commission, Dawson was hired by the Geological Survey of Canada in 1875 and returned almost immediately to the west. He explored and mapped huge tracts of hitherto largely unknown lands, offering his expert analysis not only on their geology (and, therefore, on their mineral resource potential), but on their flora and fauna too. In his understanding of Canada's Native peoples he had few peers, and his published studies of west coast native culture and language were standard works for many years. In 1895, he succeeded Alfred Selwyn as director of the Geological Survey of Canada, a post he held until his early death. The Canadian towns Dawson City (in the Yukon— epicentre of the Klondike Gold Rush) and Dawson Creek (in British Columbia) are named after him, as are dozens of other geographical features and places in northwestern Canada.

George Dawson never married. He died on March 2, 1901, at the age of just fifty-one. It is hard to imagine what he might have accomplished had the long-term damage inflicted by childhood disease not cut his life so short.

WILLIAM FREDERICK KING: Of all the young men whom the Canadian government appointed to the boundary commission, only W.F. King proved Dawson's equal. Immediately following his release from the commission in November 1874, he returned to the University of Toronto and finished his degree, graduating in 1875 with the highest honours and the gold medal in mathematics. He then rose quickly through a series of increasingly important positions to become director of the Dominion Observatory and superintendent of the Geodetic Survey. Among his many awards and accolades were honorary president of the Astronomical Society of Canada and president of the Royal Society of Canada. King died in Ottawa on April 23, 1916.

THE AMERICANS

ARCHIBALD CAMPBELL: On July 3, 1876, Campbell's term as chief commissioner expired and he went into retirement. He continued to live in Washington, D.C. until his death on July 27, 1887, at the age of 74.

JAMES BANGS: Bangs returned to Washington, D.C. and a series of jobs with the federal government, including stints at the pensions office, the geological survey and the tenth U.S. census. He was, it was said, "popular in literary and social circles, and... an entertainer of high order."[2]

In 1883, he returned to the west, working as an accountant and newspaper writer in Portland, Oregon and Denver, Colorado. In 1899, failing health took him back to Washington and a position in the office of the adjutant general. James Bangs died, probably of heart failure, in May 1901. Like Dawson, who died the same year, he was just fifty-one.

FRANCIS U. FARQUHAR: Following his resignation from the boundary commission in the spring of 1873, Farquhar was appointed to a series of marine engineering projects, culminating with command of the river works and harbour improvements from Lake Erie to Lake Superior. For some months before this last appointment Farquhar's health had been failing, and he died on July 3, 1883, at the age of only forty-five.

WILLIAM J. TWINING: Like his British opposite number, Samuel Anderson, the American chief astronomer did not have the opportunity to fulfill his great potential. After returning from Europe and the signing of the final documents, Twining was assigned to a series of engineering and surveying projects until, in 1878, Congress passed an act to create a permanent form of government for the District of Columbia. The district would be headed by a three-man commission, one of whom was to be an officer from the Corps of Engineers. Twining was appointed to fill the position and effectively took charge of all public works in the nation's capital. From that desk, he planned and executed a bold series of improvements to the district's water and sewage systems, and paved several miles of its streets. His final great plan sought to reclaim the malarial flats of the Potomac River, long a source of chronic health problems in the city.

Twining did not live to see all of his plans come to fruition. In the spring of 1882 he suffered an attack of what was described as pleurisy, and it soon developed into pneumonia. He died on May 5, at only forty-two years of age. His friend and colleague from the boundary commission, Francis Greene, was sitting with him at the end. Before his burial at West Point, a memorial service in Washington was attended by the president, several members of the cabinet and a number of senators and representatives. The head of the Corps of Engineers wrote of him:

> To this office [of district commissioner] he brought unsullied integrity, steady good sense, and executive ability of the highest order... [He] was distinguished for the strength and gentleness of his character, and his intelligent devotion to duty.[3]

JAMES F. GREGORY: With the disbanding of the boundary commission in July 1876, Gregory took a brief leave of absence and then reported for reassignment. A series of increasingly senior appointments (during which time he was promoted to major) led to his posting as head of various engineering works along the Ohio River near Cincinnati. It was there, on July 31, 1897, that Gregory died at the age of 54.

FRANCIS VINTON GREENE: Of all the officers who drew the 49th Parallel across the west, none went on to enjoy as long and varied a career as Francis Greene. With the dissolution of the boundary commission, Greene found himself attached to the office of the Secretary of War, and by June 1877 he was serving as the State Department's military attaché in St. Petersburg during the Russian-Turkish War. Attached to Russian Army headquarters, he earned several honours for bravery, including the Order of St. Anne and the Order of St. Vladimir.

While preparing his detailed report on the Russian campaign, Greene was appointed as Twining's assistant in Washington, a post he held until 1885. His promotion to captain finally came through in 1883.

After his stint under Twining, Greene spent the last eighteen months of his military career teaching at West Point, until he resigned his commission at the end of 1886. In civilian life, he held a number of senior positions with several private corporations. He remained active in the militia, however, serving as colonel of the 71st Regiment of the New York National Guard. In the Spanish-American War he commanded the second U.S. expedition to Manila and saw special duty in Havana, where President McKinley offered him an appointment as military and civil governor. However, Greene seems to have had enough of the militia as he had of the regular army, and he resigned his commission at the end of February 1899.

After serving as Police Commissioner of New York City in 1903–04, and then president of the Niagara, Lockport and Ontario Power Company, he retired in 1915. Greene authored several significant works of history, including a biography of his ancestor General Nathaneal Greene, books on the Russian military and a number of papers and articles on the American military during World War I. He died on May 15, 1921.

ELLIOTT COUES: After returning to Washington from the 49th Parallel, Coues retained his commission and continued his relentless schedule of writing and publishing. Between 1876 and 1880, he edited all the publications of the U.S. geological and geographical surveys. When the army tried to assign him to yet another frontier post—in Arizona—in 1881, he resigned and devoted himself full-time to his scientific work.

He held the chair of anatomy at the National Medical College in Washington and lectured there from 1882 to 1887. Through the 1870s and 1880s, he developed a strong interest in the then-popular theosophical movement, becoming a founder of the American Society for Psychical Research and serving as president of the esoteric Theosophical Society of America. Eventually, he began to question the movement and his role in it, leading to an article in which he attacked Madame Blavatsky, the movement's leading light. The resulting lawsuits ended only with Blavatsky's death in 1891.

A founder of the American Ornithologists' Union in 1883, Coues wrote often for its journal, *The Auk,* and, in addition to his landmark publications, *A Key to North American Birds* and *A Checklist of North American Birds,* he edited the exploration journals of Lewis and Clark (1893), Zebulon Pike (1895), Alexander Henry and David Thompson (both 1897).

Elliott Coues died on Christmas Day, 1899, and is buried in Washington's Arlington National Cemetery.

Captain A.A. HARBACH of the 20th Infantry was eventually promoted to colonel of the 1st Infantry in 1899 and later retired with the rank of brigadier general. Captain EDWIN AMES of the 6th Infantry resigned his commission in 1876 and died just six years later. His fellow officer, Captain MONTGOMERY BRYANT, was promoted to colonel of the 13th Infantry in 1888 and retired in 1894.

In June 1876, General JOHN GIBBON, who took so much pride in his gardens at Fort Shaw, arrived at the Little Bighorn too late to do anything but relieve Reno's beleaguered troops and begin to bury the dead. A year later, he was in the Bear Paw Mountains, in the thick of the last firefight with Chief Joseph and the shattered remnants of his Nez Perce nation. Gibbon finally took his retirement in 1891 and died just five years later.

Among those whom Gibbon found lying on the hill above the Little Bighorn were 7th Cavalry Captain MYLES KEOGH, Lieutenant JAMES E. PORTER and the sixty or so men of Company I, every one of whom fell with Custer. THOMAS B. WEIR and his Company D had been assigned to Captain Frederick Benteen and survived the battle with few casualties only for Weir to die of unrelated causes the following December.

By far the saddest story of the boundary commission's escort was that of its commander, Major MARCUS RENO. Never a popular figure among his officers and men, it was Reno's misfortune to survive the Little Bighorn. As the second ranking officer after Custer, he was generally (though never officially) held responsible for failing to come to Custer's aid. So great was the contempt for Reno that on the fiftieth anniversary of the battle, Custer's widow was still campaigning against any official recognition for him. Years later, a grand-nephew managed to have Reno's case reopened, and finally, in September 1967, Major Marcus Reno's remains were taken to the Little Bighorn and buried with full military honours in the Custer National Cemetery.

TODAY, MANY (but certainly not all) of the senior men of the boundary commissions are remembered in the names of mountains, peaks, creeks and lakes, mostly to be found in Canada's Waterton Lakes National Park. In Montana's Glacier National Park, 8,300-foot Campbell Mountain, just south of the international boundary, is the only major feature named for a member of the American commission. Francis Farquhar's fellow officers tried to commemorate his brief tenure by naming a lake after him. That lake, near Turtle Mountain in North Dakota, has since been renamed Lake Metigoshe.

The British and Canadians are far better memorialized in the landscape, though not all of the commission's attempts have stood the test of time. If Lake Farquhar did not survive, neither did Lake Anderson, also on Turtle Mountain. In Waterton Park, however, one can find Cameron Falls on Cameron Creek, which flows into Cameron Lake. Also featured on maps of the park and its surrounding area are Anderson Peak, Mount Galwey, Mount Ward and Mount Boswell. For a man who never saw the Rocky Mountains, the injured Valentine Rowe was well commemorated by his colleagues, with Mount Rowe, Rowe Creek and the Rowe Lakes.

Unfortunately, no one thought to name anything for Albany Featherstonhaugh, the most senior of the officers after Anderson and a man well respected and genuinely liked by everyone on the commission. Doctor Burgess and his assistant, Thomas Millman, have also been ignored, as have been the leaders of the 49th Rangers.

NOTES
ON SOURCES

———

WHILE RESEARCHING a book on the Montana–Alberta borderlands of western North America, I happened across the story of the international boundary commissions in the form of John E. Parsons's West on the 49th Parallel: Red River to the Rockies, 1872–1876 (New York: Morrow, 1963). Still the only previous book-length study of drawing the international boundary across the high plains, it proved a brisk and thoroughly reliable guide to the fundamentals of the story and was of immense help in locating both primary and secondary sources.

The official records of the two boundary commissions rest in their respective national archives and are fully open to research. At the National Archives in London, the British commission's extensive files of correspondence, accounts and maps are held with the Foreign Office records in FO302. The records of the American commission reside at the National Archives in Washington, D.C., within State Department record group 76.2.

While the British records exist only in their original form and order, the records of the American commission were published soon after the conclusion of the work. *Reports upon the Survey of the*

Boundary between the Territory of the United States and the Posses-sions of Great Britain from Lake of the Woods to Summit of the Rocky Mountains. Authorized by an Act of Congress Approved March 19, 1872 (Washington, D.C.: Government Printing Office, 1878) is a large, elegant volume containing over 600 pages of narrative history and scientific findings, profusely illustrated and supported by a series of large-format maps. Original copies of the report are rare, but it is freely available online through the University of Alberta's *Peel's Prairie Provinces* database (the full details of which can be found below).

Samuel Anderson's voluminous correspondence with his mother and sister are by far the richest source of detailed information about the day-to-day business of drawing of the boundary. They are central to any telling of this story. Through the efforts of John Parsons, Anderson's family gave the original letters to Yale University, where they remain in the Beinecke Library (WA MSS S-1292) and are available on microfilm. In 2000, C. Ian Jackson edited and published Anderson's correspondence as *Letters from the 49th Parallel, 1857–1873: Selected Correspondence of Joseph Harris and Samuel Anderson* (Toronto: Champlain Society, 2000). The volume also contains a good deal of Anderson's correspondence from his time with the Pacific Boundary survey, and only the most dedicated reader need look beyond Jackson's generous and judicious selection.

Unfortunately, Parsons did not manage to have William Galwey's letters deposited in a suitable repository. They remained with his family and have subsequently disappeared. Francis Vinton Greene's papers, including a number of letters from the boundary, are held in the Manuscript Division of the New York Public Library.

George Dawson's diary for 1873 has been transcribed and edited by W.J. Ross and privately published as *The Travels of George M. Dawson with the British North America Boundary Commission in the Year 1873* (Lethbridge, AB: Historic Trails West, [1993]). Southern Alberta historian Bruce Haig coordinated the transcription of Dawson's diary for 1874 and has made it freely available online at www.ourheritage.net/index_page_stuff/Following_Trails/Dawson/Dawson_74/Dawson_1874_Intro.html

Dawson's diaries also form the core of his majestic *Report on the Geology and Resources of the Region in the Vicinity of the Forty-Ninth Parallel, From the Lake of the Woods to the Rocky Mountains: With Lists of Plants and Animals Collected, and Notes on the Fossils* (Montreal: Dawson Brothers, and New York: B. Westermann, 1875). Addressed to Chief Commissioner Cameron, it remains one of the seminal works of Canadian science and natural history.

Dr. Thomas Millman's diaries were edited and published by his wife as "Impressions of the West in the Early Seventies from the Diary of the Assistant-Surgeon of the British North American Boundary Survey, 1872–1875" in the *Annual Report and Transactions of the Women's Canadian Historical Society of Toronto, 1927–1928*.

The brief diaries of American commission secretary James Bangs for the years 1873 and 1874 are held by the North Dakota State Archives. The 1873 diary was published in *Collections* (North Dakota State Historical Society, vol. 4, 1913).

Subassistant astronomer W.F. King was barely eighteen when he joined the boundary commission. His letters home are full of youthful enthusiasm and remain, to this day, a source of a great pride and pleasure for his family, who generously shared them with me.

Both Anderson and Featherstonhaugh published lively accounts of their time with the British boundary commission. Anderson's "The North American Boundary from Lake of the Woods to the Rocky Mountains" appears in the *Journal of the Royal Geographical Society*, vol. 46 (1876) while Featherstonhaugh's "Narrative of the Operations of the British North American Boundary Commission, 1872–1876" can be found in *Professional Papers of the Corps of Royal Engineers*, vol. 23 (1876).

The historical background and context for the work of the boundary commissions can be found in a number of excellent works. Francis M. Carroll's *A Good and Wise Measure: The Search for the Canadian-American Boundary, 1783–1842* (Toronto: University of Toronto Press, 2001) meticulously sets out the political and geographical problems in drawing the boundary from the Atlantic coast to the Great Lakes. Morris Zaslow's *Reading the Rocks: The Story of the Geological*

Survey of Canada , 1842–1972 (Ottawa: Macmillan, 1975) deals with Canada's steps to understand its new western lands, as do the three volumes of Donald W. Thomson's *Men and Meridians: The History of Surveying and Mapping in Canada* (Ottawa: Queen's Printer, 1966–69). For the American context, Richard A. Bartlett's *Great Surveys of the American West* (Norman: University of Oklahoma Press, 1980) and Wallace Stegner's seminal *Beyond the Hundredth Meridian: John Wesley Powell and the Second Opening of the American West* (New York: Penguin, 1992) are invaluable. The story of the trouble in the Cypress Hills has been told and retold a hundred times but never better nor more accurately than by Hugh Dempsey in *Montana Magazine of History* (Fall 1953) and Paul F. Sharpe in the same magazine (Winter 1954).

George Dawson is long overdue for a major biography, but until that appears, *No Ordinary Man: George Dawson, 1849–1901* (Toronto: Natural Heritage, 1993) by his niece, Lois Winslow-Spragge, provides a selection of his letters from the west. Elliott Coues has been more fortunate. *Elliott Coues: Naturalist and Frontier Historian* (Champaign: University of Illinois Press, 1981; reprinted, 2001) by Paul Cutright and Michael Brodhead is a comprehensive and eminently readable life of one of America's premier naturalists. Sadly, most of Coues's own works, including his 1874 volume *Birds of the Northwest: A Hand-book of the Ornithology of the Region Drained by the Missouri River and its Tributaries* (Washington, D.C.: Government Printing Office, 1874) are long out of print.

The University of Alberta's *Peel's Prairie Provinces* database contains a bibliography of over 7,000 published works important to the history of the Canadian west. About 4,000 of these works are freely available in fully searchable facsimile form, including several that are central to the story of the boundary commissions. The complete texts of the US official report (Peel #859), Dawson's report (#731), both Anderson and Featherstonhaugh's accounts (#687 and #777) and Millman's diary (#751) can all be accessed at http://peel.library.ualberta.ca

ENDNOTES

PROLOGUE

1 Obituary, *Evening Star* (Washington, D.C., May 7, 1901).

2 *Letters from the 49th Parallel, 1857–1873: Selected Correspondence of Joseph Harris and Samuel Anderson,* ed. C. Ian Jackson (Toronto: Champlain Society, 2000), 328.

CHAPTER I

1 Ibid.

2 Letter, FO302/I/I.

3 *Letters* (2000), 324–25.

4 Ibid., 325.

5 Ibid., 324.

6 Ibid.

7 Ibid., 326.

8 Albany Featherstonhaugh, "Narrative of the Operations of the British North American Boundary Commission, 1872–1876," *Professional Papers of the Corps of Royal Engineers,* 23 (1876), 25.

9 Ibid., 26.

10 *Letters* (2000), 327.

11 Ibid., 328.

12 Ibid., 329.

13 Ibid.

14 Donald W. Thomson, Men and Meridians, vol. I (Ottawa: Queen's Printer, 1966), 163.

15 *Reports upon the Survey of the Boundary between the Territory of the United States and the Possessions of Great Britain from Lake of the Woods to Summit of the Rocky Mountains. Authorized by an Act of Congress Approved March 19, 1872* (Washington, D.C.: Government Printing Office, 1878), 18.

16 Ibid., 19.

17 Ibid., 22.

18 Ibid., 21.

19 Featherstonhaugh (1876), 27.

20 *Reports upon the Survey* (1878), 265.

21 Featherstonhaugh (1876), 27.

22 Ibid.

CHAPTER 2

1 *Letters from the 49th Parallel, 1857–1873: Selected Correspondence of Joseph Harris and Samuel Anderson,* ed. C. Ian Jackson (Toronto: Champlain Society, 2000), 334.

2 Ibid., 336.

3   Ibid., 334.
4   Ibid.
5   Ibid., 335.
6   *Reports upon the Survey of the Boundary between the Territory of the United States and the Possessions of Great Britain from Lake of the Woods to Summit of the Rocky Mountains. Authorized by an Act of Congress Approved March 19, 1872* (Washington, D.C.: Government Printing Office, 1878), 23.
7   Ibid., 55.
8   *Letters* (2000), 335–6.
9   Ibid., 337.
10 Ibid., 343.
11 Samuel Anderson, "The North American Boundary from Lake of the Woods to the Rocky Mountains," *Journal of the Royal Geographical Society,* 46 (1876), 232.
12 Albany Featherstonhaugh, "Narrative of the Operations of the British North American Boundary Commission, 1872–1876," *Professional Papers of the Corps of Royal Engineers,* 23 (1876), 29–30.
13 Anderson (1876), 232–33.
14 Ibid., 233.
15 Ibid.
16 *Letters* (2000), 344.
17 Ibid., 345–46.
18 Ibid., 347.

CHAPTER 3
1   L.F. Hewgill, "In the Days of Pioneering," [clipping, unknown periodical, probably from Winnipeg or Regina] c. 1894 (Archives of Manitoba, MG1 B23–5).
2   FO302/6.
3   *Letters from the 49th Parallel,*

1857–1873: Selected Correspondence of Joseph Harris and Samuel Anderson, ed. C. Ian Jackson (Toronto: Champlain Society, 2000), 348.
4   Albany Featherstonhaugh, "Narrative of the Operations of the British North American Boundary Commission, 1872–1876," *Professional Papers of the Corps of Royal Engineers,* 23 (1876), 30.
5   Ibid., 31.
6   *Letters* (2000), 349.
7   Ibid., 350–51.
8   Ibid., 351.
9   Ibid., 351–2.
10 Featherstonhaugh (1876), 31.
11 *Letters* (2000), 353.
12 Ibid.
13 Ibid., 354.
14 Ibid., 366n.
15 Ibid., 355–56.
16 Ibid., 357–58.
17 Samuel Anderson, "The North American Boundary from Lake of the Woods to the Rocky Mountains," *Journal of the Royal Geographical Society,* 46 (1876), 237.
18 *Letters* (2000), 367.
19 Ibid., 359–60.
20 Featherstonhaugh (1876), 34.
21 *Letters* (2000), 367.
22 Ibid., 369.
23 *Letters* (2000), 378.
24 Ibid., 379.

CHAPTER 4
1   *Letters from the 49th Parallel, 1857–1873: Selected Correspondence of Joseph Harris and Samuel Anderson,* ed. C. Ian Jackson (Toronto: Champlain Society, 2000), 383.

2 Ibid., 390.
3 Ibid., 383.
4 Ibid., 390.
5 Ibid., 389.
6 Ibid.
7 *Letters* (2000), 387.
8 Ibid.
9 *Letters* (2000), 391.
10 Ibid.
11 Ibid.
12 Thomas Millman, "Impressions of the West in the Early Seventies from the Diary of the Assistant-Surgeon of the British North American Boundary Survey, 1872–1875," *Annual Report and Transactions of the Women's Canadian Historical Society of Toronto* (1927–28), 24.
13 Albany Featherstonhaugh, "Narrative of the Operations of the British North American Boundary Commission, 1872–1876," *Professional Papers of the Corps of Royal Engineers*, 23 (1876), 59.
14 Millman (1927–28), 26.
15 Ibid., 24.
16 *Letters* (2000), 385.
17 Ibid., 384–5.
18 Ibid., 388.
19 Ibid., 393.
20 Millman (1927–28), 26–27.

CHAPTER 5

1 Albany Featherstonhaugh, "Narrative of the Operations of the British North American Boundary Commission, 1872–1876," *Professional Papers of the Corps of Royal Engineers*, 23 (1876), 53.
2 *Reports upon the Survey of the Boundary between the Territory of the United States and the Possessions of Great Britain from Lake of the Woods to Summit of the Rocky Mountains. Authorized by an Act of Congress Approved March 19, 1872* (Washington, D.C.: Government Printing Office, 1878), 293.
3 Featherstonhaugh (1876), 49.
4 Ibid., 52.
5 Ibid.
6 Ibid., 55.
7 Ibid.
8 Ibid., 50.
9 Ibid.
10 Ibid.
11 *Reports upon the Survey* (1878), 260.
12 Ibid., 261.
13 John E. Parsons, *West on the 49th Parallel: Red River to the Rockies, 1872–1876* (New York: Morrow, 1963), 63.
14 Ibid.
15 *Letters from the 49th Parallel, 1857–1873: Selected Correspondence of Joseph Harris and Samuel Anderson*, ed. C. Ian Jackson (Toronto: Champlain Society, 2000), 362.
16 Although Pembina was the headquarters, the astronomical stations were numbered from Lake of the Woods, making Pembina number 4. The Americans numbered their stations (including those jointly observed) independently, with Pembina as their number 1 (for instance, U.S. number 8 was the fifteenth west of Lake of the Woods. For consistency, the stations are referred to by their "cumulative" number from Lake of Woods. Distances to various points on the western line, however, are given in miles from Pembina.
17 *Letters* (2000), 394.

18 Ibid.

19 Paul Cutright and Michael Brodhead, *Elliott Coues: Naturalist and
Frontier Historian* (Champaign:
University of Illinois Press, 1981;
reprinted, 2001), 160.

20 Parsons (1963), 62.

21 Cutright and Brodhead (1981,
2001), 155.

22 Ibid.

23 Ibid., 161.

24 C.C. Marble, "The Late Dr. Elliott
Coues," *Birds and All Nature* 7/2
(February 1900).

25 Morris Zaslow, Reading the Rocks:
*The Story of the Geological Survey
of Canada, 1842–1972* (Ottawa:
Macmillan, 1975), 112.

26 Letter, FO302/16.

27 *The Travels of George M. Dawson
With the British North America
Boundary Commission in the Year
1873*, ed. W.J. Ross (Lethbridge, AB:
Historic Trails West, [1993]), 1.

28 Lois Winslow-Spragge, *No
Ordinary Man: George Daw-
son, 1849–1901*, ed. Anne V. Byers
(Toronto: Natural Heritage,
1993), 101.

29 Ibid.

30 *Letters* (2000), 394.

31 Ibid., 395.

32 Ibid.

33 Letter from W.F. King, August 1873
(private collection).

34 *Reports upon the Survey* (1878),
275. A "computer" was a clerk
who specialized in mathematical
calculations.

35 Parsons (1963), 66.

36 Ibid.

37 Ibid.

38 Thomas Millman, "Impressions of
the West in the Early Seventies from
the Diary of the Assistant-Surgeon
of the British North American
Boundary Survey, 1872–1875,"
*Annual Report and Transactions of
the Women's Canadian Historical
Society of Toronto* (1927–28), 30.

39 Parsons (1963), 66.

40 Ibid.

41 Ibid., 48..

42 Ibid.

43 *Reports upon the Survey* (1878), 49.

44 Cutright and Brodhead (1981,
2001), 161.

45 Ibid.

46 Ibid.

47 *Letters* (2000), 395.

48 Ibid.

49 Ibid., 396.

50 Ibid.

51 Ibid.

52 Parsons (1963), 72.

53 Featherstonhaugh (1876), 38.

54 *Travels of George M. Dawson*
[1993], 19.

55 Ibid., 21.

56 Ibid., 22.

57 Ibid., 40.

58 Ibid., 49.

59 Ibid., 49–50.

60 Millman (1927–28), 32.

61 Ibid.

62 Ibid., 33.

63 Ibid., 30.

64 Ibid., 32.

65 Ibid.

66 Ibid., 33.

67 Bangs diary (1873), *Collections*
(North Dakota State Historical
Society, Vol. 4, 1913), 226.

68 Elliott Coues, "The Bivouac of
Death," *Forest and Stream* (May
1879).

69 *Letters* (2000), 397.

70 Ibid.

CHAPTER 6

1 *Letters from the 49th Parallel,
   1857–1873: Selected Correspondence
   of Joseph Harris and Samuel
   Anderson,* ed. C. Ian Jackson
   (Toronto: Champlain Society,
   2000), 400.

2 Thomas Millman, "Impressions of
   the West in the Early Seventies from
   the Diary of the Assistant-Surgeon
   of the British North American
   Boundary Survey, 1872–1875,"
   *Annual Report and Transactions of
   the Women's Canadian Historical
   Society of Toronto* (1927–28), 33.

3 John E. Parsons, *West on the 49th
   Parallel: Red River to the Rockies,
   1872–1876* (New York: Morrow,
   1963), 75.

4 *Reports upon the Survey of the
   Boundary between the Territory of
   the United States and the Posses-
   sions of Great Britain from Lake of
   the Woods to Summit of the Rocky
   Mountains. Authorized by an Act of
   Congress Approved March 19, 1872*
   (Washington, D.C.: Government
   Printing Office, 1878), 338.

5 *Letters* (2000), 401.

6 Millman (1927–28), 41.

7 Letters (2000), 403.

8 Samuel Anderson, "The North
   American Boundary from Lake of
   the Woods to the Rocky Mountains,"
   *Journal of the Royal Geographical
   Society,* 46 (1876), 245.

9 Ibid., 245–46.

10 Ibid., 246.

11 Emphasis original.

12 Bangs diary (1873), *Collections*
   (North Dakota State Historical
   Society, Vol. 4, 1913), 228.

13 Paul Cutright and Michael Brodhead, Elliott Coues: *Naturalist and
   Frontier Historian* (Champaign:
   University of Illinois Press, 1981;
   reprinted, 2001), 163.

14 *The Travels of George M. Dawson
   With the British North America
   Boundary Commission in the Year
   1873,* ed. W.J. Ross (Lethbridge, AB:
   Historic Trails West, [1993]), 73.

15 George Dawson, *Report on the
   Geology and Resources of the Region
   in the Vicinity of the Forty-Ninth
   Parallel, From the Lake of the Woods
   to the Rocky Mountains: With Lists
   of Plants and Animals Collected,
   and Notes on the Fossils* (Montreal:
   Dawson Brothers, and New York: B.
   Westermann, 1875), iv.

16 Ibid., 20.

17 Ibid.

18 Ibid., 20–21.

19 Morris Zaslow, *Reading the Rocks:
   The Story of the Geological Survey
   of Canada, 1842–1972* (Ottawa:
   Macmillan, 1975), 112.

20 Dawson (1875), 82.

21 *Travels of George M. Dawson*
   [1993], 79.

22 *Birds of the Northwest: A Hand-
   book of the Ornithology of the
   Region Drained by the Missouri
   River and its Tributaries* (Wash-
   ington, D.C.: Government Printing
   Office, 1874), 531.

23 *Travels of George M. Dawson*
   [1993], 74.

24 Ibid., 78–79.

25 Ibid., 79.

26 Cutright and Brodhead
   (1981, 2001), 163.

27 Ibid.

28 Cutright and Brodhead
   (1981, 2001), 164.

29 *Travels of George M. Dawson*
   [1993], 87.

30 Bangs (1873), 229.

31 Millman (1927–28), 34–35.

32 Ibid., 35.

33 Ibid.

34 *Letters* (2000), 404.

35 Ibid.

36 Ibid., 405.

37 Ibid., 404.

38 Ibid., 407.

39 Ibid.

40 *Travels of George M. Dawson* [1993], 88–89.

41 Anderson (1876), 246.

42 Ibid., 247.

43 *Report upon the Survey* (1878), 71.

44 *Travels of George M. Dawson* [1993], 91.

45 Ibid., 94.

46 Ibid., 92.

47 Albany Featherstonhaugh, "Narrative of the Operations of the British North American Boundary Commission, 1872–1876," *Professional Papers of the Corps of Royal Engineers*, 23 (1876), 40.

48 *Travels of George M. Dawson* [1993], 97.

49 Ibid., 97.

50 Ibid., 107.

51 Dawson (1875), 87.

52 Parsons (1963), 76.

53 *Reports upon the Survey* (1878), 60–61.

54 *Travels of George M. Dawson* [1993], 102.

55 Ibid., 108.

56 Ibid., 108–19.

57 Ibid., 110.

58 Ibid.

59 *Letters* (2000), 408.

60 Personal communication from Michael Brodhead.

61 Ibid.

62 *Reports upon the Survey* (1878), 72.

63 Ibid.

64 Ibid., 72–73.

65 Ibid., 334.

CHAPTER 7

1 Thomas Millman, "Impressions of the West in the Early Seventies from the Diary of the Assistant-Surgeon of the British North American Boundary Survey, 1872–1875," *Annual Report and Transactions of the Women's Canadian Historical Society of Toronto* (1927–28), 37.

2 Ibid.

3 *Letters from the 49th Parallel, 1857–1873: Selected Correspondence of Joseph Harris and Samuel Anderson,* ed. C. Ian Jackson (Toronto: Champlain Society, 2000), 409.

4 *Reports upon the Survey of the Boundary between the Territory of the United States and the Possessions of Great Britain from Lake of the Woods to Summit of the Rocky Mountains. Authorized by an Act of Congress Approved March 19, 1872* (Washington, D.C.: Government Printing Office, 1878), 371.

5 Ibid.

6 Ibid.

7 Ibid., 378.

8 Ibid., 377–78.

9 Ibid., 377.

10 Ibid., 378.

11 Ibid., 372.

12 Ibid., 373.

13 Ibid.

14 Ibid., 374.

15 Ibid.

16 Ibid.

17 *Letters* (2000), 409.

18 George Monro Grant, *Ocean to Ocean: Sandford Fleming's*

Expedition through Canada in 1872 (Toronto: J. Campbell, and London: Sampson Low, Marston, Low & Searle, 1873), 57.

19 Lois Winslow-Spragge, *No Ordinary Man: George Dawson, 1849–1901*, ed. Anne V. Byers (Toronto: Natural Heritage, 1993), 103–04.

20 *Reports upon the Survey* (1878), 380.

21 Ibid., 381.

22 Ibid., 382.

23 Millman (1927–28), 38.

24 *Reports upon the Survey* (1878), 384.

25 Ibid., 379.

26 Ibid., 385.

27 Ibid., 393–94.

28 Ibid., 386.

29 Ibid., 387–88.

CHAPTER 8

1 *Letters from the 49th Parallel, 1857–1873: Selected Correspondence of Joseph Harris and Samuel Anderson*, ed. C. Ian Jackson (Toronto: Champlain Society, 2000), 414.

2 Ibid., 414–15.

3 John E. Parsons, *West on the 49th Parallel: Red River to the Rockies, 1872–1876* (New York: Morrow, 1963), 86.

4 Ibid.

5 Ibid., 86–87.

6 Ibid., 88.

7 *Letters* (2000), 414.

8 Ibid.

9 Ibid., 418.

10 Ibid.

11 Ibid., 420.

12 Ibid., 423.

13 Ibid., 424.

14 Ibid.

15 Ibid.

16 Thomas Millman, "Impressions of the West in the Early Seventies from the Diary of the Assistant-Surgeon of the British North American Boundary Survey, 1872–1875," *Annual Report and Transactions of the Women's Canadian Historical Society of Toronto* (1927–28), 39.

17 *Letters* (2000), 425–26.

18 Lois Winslow-Spragge, *No Ordinary Man: George Dawson, 1849–1901*, ed. Anne V. Byers (Toronto: Natural Heritage, 1993), 107.

19 *Letters* (2000), 428.

20 Ibid., 426.

CHAPTER 9

1 Thomas Millman, "Impressions of the West in the Early Seventies from the Diary of the Assistant-Surgeon of the British North American Boundary Survey, 1872–1875," *Annual Report and Transactions of the Women's Canadian Historical Society of Toronto* (1927–28), 39.

2 *Letters from the 49th Parallel, 1857–1873: Selected Correspondence of Joseph Harris and Samuel Anderson*, ed. C. Ian Jackson (Toronto: Champlain Society, 2000), 430.

3 John E. Parsons, *West on the 49th Parallel: Red River to the Rockies, 1872–1876* (New York: Morrow, 1963), 96.

4 *Reports upon the Survey of the Boundary between the Territory of the United States and the Possessions of Great Britain from Lake of the Woods to Summit of the Rocky Mountains. Authorized by an Act of Congress Approved March 19, 1872* (Washington, D.C.: Government Printing Office, 1878), 74.

5 Parsons (1963), 83.

6 *Reports upon the Survey* (1878), 74–75.

7 Parsons (1963), 98.

8 *Reports upon the Survey* (1878), 75.

9 Paul Cutright and Michael Brod-head, *Elliott Coues: Naturalist and Frontier Historian* (Champaign: University of Illinois Press, 1981; reprinted, 2001), 166.

10 Parsons (1963), 99.

11 Ibid., 100.

12 Millman (1927–28), 42.

13 George Dawson, *Report on the Geology and Resources of the Region in the Vicinity of the Forty-Ninth Parallel, From the Lake of the Woods to the Rocky Mountains: With Lists of Plants and Animals Collected, and Notes on the Fossils* (Montreal: Dawson Brothers, and New York: B. Westermann, 1875), 303.

14 Ibid., 25.

15 Samuel Anderson, "The North American Boundary from Lake of the Woods to the Rocky Mountains," *Journal of the Royal Geographical Society*, 46 (1876), 249.

16 Ibid., 249.

17 *Letters* (2000), 433.

18 *Reports upon the Survey* (1878), 278–79.

19 Ibid., 280–81.

20 Ibid., 281.

21 Ibid., 62.

22 Albany Featherstonhaugh, "Narrative of the Operations of the British North American Boundary Commission, 1872–1876," *Professional Papers of the Corps of Royal Engineers*, 23 (1876), 42.

23 Millman (1927–28), 44.

24 Dawson (1875), 23.

25 Ibid., 45.

26 Ibid., 48.

27 Elliott Coues, *Birds of the Northwest: A Hand-book of the Ornithology of the Region Drained by the Missouri River and its Tributaries* (Washington, D.C.: Government Printing Office, 1874), 359.

28 Dawson (1875), 49.

29 Millman (1927–28), 45.

CHAPTER 10

1 *Letters from the 49th Parallel, 1857–1873: Selected Correspondence of Joseph Harris and Samuel Anderson*, ed. C. Ian Jackson (Toronto: Champlain Society, 2000), 435–36.

2 *Reports upon the Survey of the Boundary between the Territory of the United States and the Possessions of Great Britain from Lake of the Woods to Summit of the Rocky Mountains. Authorized by an Act of Congress Approved March 19, 1872* (Washington, D.C.: Government Printing Office, 1878), 282.

3 Ibid., 282.

4 *Letters* (2000), 437.

5 John E. Parsons, *West on the 49th Parallel: Red River to the Rockies, 1872–1876* (New York: Morrow, 1963), 105.

6 Ibid., 106.

7 Ibid.

8 *Reports upon the Survey* (1878), 282.

9 *Letters* (2000), 436.

10 Albany Featherstonhaugh, "Narrative of the Operations of the British North American Boundary Commission, 1872–1876," *Professional Papers of the Corps of Royal Engineers*, 23 (1876), 44.

11 Thomas Millman, "Impressions of the West in the Early Seventies from the Diary of the Assistant-Surgeon of the British North American Boundary Survey, 1872–1875," *Annual Report and Transactions of the Women's Canadian Historical Society of Toronto* (1927–28), 45.

12 Ibid.

13 Featherstonhaugh (1876), 43.

14 Dawson diary (1874), www.our heritage.net/index_page_stuff/ Following_Trails/Dawson/ Dawson_74/Dawson_1874_Intro. html, 168.

15 Ibid., 169.

16 Samuel Anderson, "The North American Boundary from Lake of the Woods to the Rocky Mountains," *Journal of the Royal Geographical Society,* 46 (1876), 251–52.

17 Ibid., 43.

18 George Dawson, *Report on the Geology and Resources of the Region in the Vicinity of the Forty-Ninth Parallel, From the Lake of the Woods to the Rocky Mountains: With Lists of Plants and Animals Collected, and Notes on the Fossils* (Montreal: Dawson Brothers, and New York: B. Westermann, 1875), 295–96.

19 *Reports upon the Survey* (1878), 47.

20 Ibid., 63.

21 Dawson (1875), 296.

22 Anderson (1876), 252.

23 Parsons (1963), 110.

24 Anderson (1876), 253.

25 *Letters* (2000), 438.

26 Ibid., 438–39.

27 Ibid., 439.

28 Ibid., 442.

29 Ibid.

30 Anderson (1876), 253.

31 Featherstonhaugh (1876), 44.

32 *Letters* (2000), 440–41.

33 Ibid., 442.

34 Ibid., 439.

35 Ibid., 442–43.

36 Dawson diary (1874), 86–87.

37 Parsons (1963), 114.

38 *Reports upon the Survey* (1878), 26.

39 Ibid., 26.

40 Ibid., 27.

41 Paul Cutright and Michael Brodhead, *Elliott Coues: Naturalist and Frontier Historian* (Champaign: University of Illinois Press, 1981; reprinted, 2001), 167.

42 Parsons (1963), 111.

43 Cutright and Brodhead (1981, 2001), 168.

44 Ibid., 167.

45 Ibid.

46 Parsons (1963), 111.

CHAPTER 11

1 Thomas Millman, "Impressions of the West in the Early Seventies from the Diary of the Assistant-Surgeon of the British North American Boundary Survey, 1872–1875," *Annual Report and Transactions of the Women's Canadian Historical Society of Toronto* (1927–28), 47.

2 Ibid.

3 Ibid., 48.

4 Ibid., 47.

5 *Reports upon the Survey of the Boundary between the Territory of the United States and the Possessions of Great Britain from Lake of the Woods to Summit of the Rocky Mountains. Authorized by an Act of Congress Approved March 19, 1872* (Washington, D.C.: Government Printing Office, 1878), 338.

[6] Ibid., 339.

[7] Ibid.

[8] Paul Cutright and Michael Brodhead, *Elliott Coues: Naturalist and Frontier Historian* (Champaign: University of Illinois Press, 1981; reprinted, 2001), 168.

[9] Ibid.

[10] *Reports upon the Survey* (1878), 27.

[11] *Letters from the 49th Parallel, 1857–1873: Selected Correspondence of Joseph Harris and Samuel Anderson*, ed. C. Ian Jackson (Toronto: Champlain Society, 2000), 443.

[12] Millman (1927–28), 48.

[13] *Letters* (2000), 443.

[14] Ibid., 444.

[15] Ibid.

[16] Ibid., 442.

[17] Ibid., 444.

[18] *Reports upon the Survey* (1878), 27.

[19] Ibid., 27–28.

[20] John E. Parsons, *West on the 49th Parallel: Red River to the Rockies, 1872–1876* (New York: Morrow, 1963), 117.

[21] Millman (1927–28), 48–49.

[22] Albany Featherstonhaugh, "Narrative of the Operations of the British North American Boundary Commission, 1872–1876," *Professional Papers of the Corps of Royal Engineers*, 23 (1876), 46.

[23] *Letters* (2000), 445.

[24] Ibid., 445–46.

[25] Ibid., 446.

[26] Dawson diary (1874), www.our heritage.net/index_page_stuff/ Following_Trails/Dawson/ Dawson_74/Dawson_1874_Intro. html, 144.

[27] Parsons (1963), 119.

[28] Featherstonhaugh (1876), 45.

[29] Ibid.

[30] *Letters* (2000), 254.

[31] Millman (1927–28), 49.

[32] Parsons (1963), 120.

[33] *Reports upon the Survey* (1878), 313.

[34] Ibid.

[35] Ibid.

[36] Ibid., 314.

[37] Ibid., 314–15.

[38] Ibid., 315.

[39] Ibid., 316.

[40] Ibid., 315.

CHAPTER 12

[1] *Reports upon the Survey of the Boundary between the Territory of the United States and the Possessions of Great Britain from Lake of the Woods to Summit of the Rocky Mountains. Authorized by an Act of Congress Approved March 19, 1872* (Washington, D.C.: Government Printing Office, 1878), 315.

[2] Thomas Millman, "Impressions of the West in the Early Seventies from the Diary of the Assistant-Surgeon of the British North American Boundary Survey, 1872–1875," *Annual Report and Transactions of the Women's Canadian Historical Society of Toronto* (1927–28), 50.

[3] Dawson diary (1874), www.our heritage.net/index_page_stuff/ Following_Trails/Dawson/ Dawson_74/Dawson_1874_Intro. html, 156.

[4] Albany Featherstonhaugh, "Narrative of the Operations of the British North American Boundary Commission, 1872–1876," *Professional*

Papers of the Corps of Royal Engineers, 23 (1876), 46.

5 Millman (1927–28), 50.

6 Lois Winslow-Spragge, *No Ordinary Man: George Dawson, 1849–1901*, ed. Anne V. Byers (Toronto: Natural Heritage, 1993), 111.

7 Millman (1927–28), 50.

8 Dawson diary (1874), 159–60.

9 Parsons (1963), 169.

10 Millman (1927–28), 50.

11 Winslow-Spragge (1993), 110.

12 Dawson diary (1874), 86.

13 Ibid., 82.

14 John E. Parsons, *West on the 49th Parallel: Red River to the Rockies, 1872–1876* (New York: Morrow, 1963), 173.

15 Ibid., 170.

16 Ibid., 172.

17 Ibid., 174–75.

18 Ibid.,175.

19 Millman (1927–28), 50.

20 Ibid.

21 Winslow-Spragge (1993), 110.

22 Dawson diary (1874), 197–98.

23 Ibid., 194.

24 Parsons (1963), 175.

25 Ibid.

26 Ibid., 177.

27 Paul Cutright and Michael Brodhead, *Elliott Coues: Naturalist and Frontier Historian* (Champaign: University of Illinois Press, 1981; reprinted, 2001), 170.

28 Parsons (1963), 182–83.

29 Ibid., 188.

30 Ibid., 189.

31 *Letters from the 49th Parallel, 1857–1873: Selected Correspondence of Joseph Harris and Samuel Anderson*, ed. C. Ian Jackson (Toronto: Champlain Society, 2000), 448.

32 Millman (1927–28), 51.

33 Ibid., 52.

34 *Letters* (2000), 448.

35 Parsons (1963), 197.

CHAPTER 13

1 Thomas Millman, "Impressions of the West in the Early Seventies from the Diary of the Assistant-Surgeon of the British North American Boundary Survey, 1872–1875," *Annual Report and Transactions of the Women's Canadian Historical Society of Toronto* (1927–28), 52.

2 *Reports upon the Survey of the Boundary between the Territory of the United States and the Possessions of Great Britain from Lake of the Woods to Summit of the Rocky Mountains. Authorized by an Act of Congress Approved March 19, 1872* (Washington, D.C.: Government Printing Office, 1878), 285.

3 FO302/15, 88.

4 Millman (1927–28), 52.

5 Ibid., 54.

6 Ibid.

7 Ibid., 55.

8 Ibid.

9 Foreign Office, "Correspondence Respecting the Determination of the North-West Boundary... Presented to Both Houses of Parliament by Command of Her Majesty" (London: 1875), 2.

10 Ibid., 452.

11 Ibid.

12 Ibid., 456.

13 Ibid., 454.

14 *Letters from the 49th Parallel,*
    1857–1873: Selected Correspondence
    of Joseph Harris and Samuel Ander-
    son, ed. C. Ian Jackson (Toronto:
    Champlain Society, 2000), 456.
15 John E. Parsons, *West on the 49th*
    Parallel: Red River to the Rockies,
    1872–1876 (New York: Morrow,
    1963), 133.
16 Ibid., 143.
17 Ibid.
18 Ibid., 136.
19 Ibid., 137.
20 Ibid., 147.

EPILOGUE

1 Obituary, *Ross-Shire Journal* (Dingwall, U.K., December 30, 1921).
2 Obituary, *Evening Star*
   (Washington, D.C., May 7, 1901).
3 Memorial by U.S. Army Corps of
   Engineers (personal communication from Michael Brodhead).

INDEX

Airey, George, 232–33
Alabama Claims, 28–29, 31
Ames, E.R., 259, 277, 300, 367
Anderson, Samuel D., 7–8, 368; attitude toward American counterparts, 78–79, 238–39; budget estimates, 31–32, 85; Cameron and, 13, 86, 105, 111, 130, 229–30, 240, 241–42, 288–90, 302–3, 347–49; Campbell and, 13, 91; eastern line resurvey, 80, 90–92, 206; on Farquhar's resignation, 110; field work (1872), 17–25, 54–59, 67–68, 69; field work (winter 1872–73), 71, 73–76, 92–95; field work (1873), 80–84, 111, 122, 130–31, 141–42, 146, 151–54, 163, 164–65, 169–72, 182–85, 188–90, 196; field work (1874), 245–46, 257–58, 272, 273–74, 287–88, 292–94, 298, 302–3, 308–10, 319, 339; field work logistics, 80, 85, 154, 230, 272; leadership style, 81, 87, 111, 130; longitude determination, 67–68, 69; mean parallel issue, 153, 207, 231–32; on Northwest Angle and North West Point, 48–49, 51–52; postcommission activities, 345, 347–51, 353, 360; professionalism, 52, 58;

winter (1872–73), 60–62, 71, 73–76, 77–79, 84–86, 92–95; winter (1873–74), 203, 204–5, 228–30, 237–38. *See also* 49th Rangers
Archibald, Adams, 66, 103–4
Ashe, William, 75, 239, 298, 319–20, 323, 345
Assiniboine, 4, 114–15, 193–94, 234, 252, 263, 273, 277–80, 284, 292
astronomical observations: challenges, 122–23, 219–20, 307–8; equipment and record-keeping, 22–23, 60–61, 68–69, 122, 123–25, 219–20; latitude determination, 38–40, 122–29; logistics, 144; longitude determination, 60–61, 67–68, 343; surprises, 267–68, 338
astronomical stations, *x–xi*, 120–21, 166–67; Belly River, 301, 307, 319; Big Muddy, 184, 185, 337; Buffalo Point, 46, 54, 85; Bully Spring, 184; Chief Mountain Lake, 307, 313–17; Cottonwood Coulee, 256; Frenchman's Creek, 255; Goose Lake, 274, 277; Grand Couteau, 164, 166; Little Rocky Creek, 189, 256; Long River, 141; Mid-Couteau, 171, 182–83; Milk River, 271, 290, 293, 297–98;

ACKNOWLEDGEMENTS

I AM MOST GRATEFUL for the support of the Canada Council, whose generous assistance, in the form of a writer's grant, could not have come at a better time.

Sincere thanks must go to Michael J. Brodhead. Co-author of the definitive biography of Elliott Coues, he was expansive (and wonderfully prompt) in his responses to my questions about the American naturalist's activities with the boundary commission. And later, from his desk at the U.S. Army Corps of Engineers' Office of History, he was generous with his time in tracking down information about other commission officers.

I was excited to learn that a sheaf of a young W.F. King's letters home from the boundary were still in the possession of his descendants. Thank you to Jeff Motherwell and his family of Lethbridge, Alberta, for allowing me to borrow those letters and make them a part of this narrative.

Scott Steedman of Douglas & McIntyre decided to take on this project at a time when I was close to putting the manuscript on the shelf and then convinced Jonathan Dore to be its editor. This is a much, much better book than it would have been without them.

Thanks as well to my old friend and colleague Victor Russell, who turned up valuable biographical information about some of the more obscure Canadian members of the commission, and to Jennifer Bobrovitz, then of the Calgary Public Library, for her invaluable technical assistance in accessing the Peel Bibliography. Professor Don Smith of the University of Calgary read several sections of the manuscript in its early form and offered his usual mix of careful criticism and contagious enthusiasm.

Special thanks to my sister, Carole Baird, for her unflagging support and inspiration.

I'm truly sorry that my friend and mentor Duncan Cameron will not be around to celebrate this story finally appearing between covers. His encouragement and tough-minded guidance are behind every page.

Last and most important, "thank you" is utterly inadequate in acknowledging the part that Donna Kynaston has played. Both this book, and its author, almost literally owe her their lives.